Rural-Urban Fringe

About the Editors

Professor S.S.A. Jafri was awarded his Ph.D. degree in 1979 from Jawaharlal Nehru University, New Delhi, He is presently working in the Giri Institute of Development Studies, Lucknow since 1985. During his last 38 years of academic career he worked/taught in various places like Census of India. North Eastern Hill University. Lucknow University, Egerton University (Kenya, E. Africa) and Giri Institute of Development Studies. He has more than 70 papers published in Indian and international journals. He has two books published by World Library. He has supervised two Ph.D. thesis and about two dozens of M.Phil. Dissertations. He has completed 23 sponsored research projects in the Institute, some of them became the basis of Government's development policies. He has established the Centre for Rural Development under NEHU in Nagaland., which is now under Nagaland Central University. For research and teaching he has visited several countries of the world. He is member of Board of Governors of many Institutions. He is also teaching since 2002 in the Department of Geography, University of Lucknow as a Guest Professor. His main focus of teaching and research is environment, socio-economic development and urbanization.

Dr. B.K. Bajpai (b. 1956) working as Senior Fellow at Giri Institute of Development Studies, Lucknow, Uttar Pradesh. Having Masters Degree in Economics and Business Administration and Ph.D. in Economics. He has over three decades of research experience in social sciences and has been working in the field of agricultural economics, Industrial economics, environmental economics and issues relating to the health, education and poverty. Along with this, conducted over 50 research projects for different National and International Organizations including studies on poverty and social monitoring, community participation, Panchayati Raj System, Decentralized Planning and Studies on Land use Pattern, Natural Resource Management, Rural Diversification and National Flagship Programme sponsored by Planning Commission. He has visited many European countries; presented research papers, and delivered lectures in Aston University, Birmingham, U.K. Many research scholars have submitted their Ph.D. dissertations under his supervision. There are about three dozens of research papers in different journals and edited books, working papers along with five books to his credit. Apart from this, he has presented many research papers in national and international seminar and conferences on contemporary policy issues relating to his research fields. He has also held the position of the Director at Jhujhunwala Business School, Faizabad, U.P. for 2 years during 2004 and 2006.

Rural-Urban Fringe

Problems and Management

Edited by

S.S.A. Jafri

and

B.K. Bajpai

Jointly Published for

Giri Institute of Development Studies

Lucknow-226024

by

CONCEPT PUBLISHING COMPANY Pvt. Ltd.,

NEW DELHI-110059

ISBN-13: 978-81-8069-905-4

First Published 2012

Published and Printed by

Concept Publishing Company Pvt. Ltd.
A/15-16, Commercial Block, Mohan Garden
New Delhi-110059 (India)
T: 25351460, 25351794, *F*: 091-11-25357109
E: publishing@conceptpub.com, W: www.conceptpub.com
Editorial Office: H-13, Bali Nagar, New Delhi-110 015, India.

Cataloging in Publication Data--*Courtesy:* D.K. Agencies (P) Ltd. <docinfo@dkagencies.com>

Rural-urban fringe : problems and management / edited by S.S.A. Jafri and B.K. Bajpai.
p. cm.
Includes bibliographical references and index.
ISBN 9788180699054

1. Wildland-urban interface—India—Uttar Pradesh—Congresses. 2. Urbanization—India—Uttar Pradesh—Congresses. 3. City and town life—India—Uttar Pradesh Congresses. I. Jafri, S. S. A. II. Bajpai, Brijesh K. III. Giri Institute of Development Studies.

DDC 307.7609542 23

Foreword

The rapid expansion of urban area in the metropolitan cities has given rise to the phenomenon of rural-urban fringe, a transition zone between urban and rural settlement sharing the features of both. The contact of urban area with the rural area affects the lifestyle and economy of the rural area on the outskirts of big cities bringing about phenomenal socio-economic transformation. As a result of the influence of the sprawling city, the rural character of the fringe is gradually and sometimes very abruptly replaced by a more urban profile in terms of land use, employment, income and culture. More recently, the issue of displacement and livelihood due to transfer of agricultural land to non-agricultural uses has emerged as a political explosive issue. Development projects have brought prosperity for very few but acute miseries for many. Compensation amount in most of the cases has been very low. Corruption and delayed disbursement of cash compensation has added misery to the poor. In other cases, compensation amount has caused a sudden change in the lifestyle of the people and created serious social and economic problems for the families affected as well as the local community. Another dimension of the rural-urban fringe is the poor health care and educational facilities in the areas located in the fringe areas of the city.

The rural-urban fringe remains an ill-defined and grossly mismanaged area, with little policy initiatives in this direction. There is an urgent need to adopt a broader approach while studying and planning for the rural-urban fringe. With a view to discuss the problems of rural-urban fringe and its management the Giri Institute of Development Studies, Lucknow organised a national seminar on 17-18 November 2009. The seminar was sponsored by the Land Use Board, U.P. It was attended by over 50 social scientists, geographers, town and country planners, administrators and policy planners from U.P. and other states. The present volume includes the papers presented at the seminar.

I take this opportunity to thank the various persons who have made special contribution in organising the seminar and compiling the seminar papers. First and foremost thanks are due to the Land Use Board, Department of Planning, U.P. Government for sponsoring the seminar. Special mention may be made of Ms. Neeta Choudhary, Principal Secretary Planning and Smt. Mridula Singh, Additional Director, Land Use Board U.P. for their variable suggestions and support in organising the seminar.

I am especially thankful to my colleagues Prof. S.S.A. Jafri and Dr. B.K. Bajpai for taking the onerous responsibility of organising and coordinating the seminar and editing the papers included in the volume. I am also thankful to the administrative staff of the Institute, who worked hard in organising the seminar and providing secretarial support for preparation of this book.

Finally, I express my gratitude to all the paper writers, who responded warmly to our invitation and took the trouble of writing their papers and presenting them in the seminar and revising them for publication.

It is hoped that the present volume will help focus attention of scholars and policy planners to an important but hitherto neglected dimension of urban development in the country.

Ajit Kumar Singh
Director
Giri Institute of Development Studies

18th March, 2012
Lucknow

About the Institute

Founded in 1973 the Giri Institute of Development Studies has established itself as an internationally reputed centre of social science research on development studies. An autonomous and independent think tank on development issues, the institute is financially supported by the Indian Council of Social Science Research and Government of Uttar Pradesh. The institute has carried out a large number of empirical studies on different aspects of social and economic development sponsored by various government departments on the Central and State Governments and reputed bodies like the Planning Commission, ILO, UNDP and the World Bank. The institute faculty has served on various committees and working groups of the Central and State Governments and has been providing guidance and consultancy on various policy issues. The institute is managed by an autonomous Board of Governors currently consisting of eminent social scientists headed by eminent labour economist Professor T.S. Papola as Chairman of its Board of Governors. Professor Ajit Kumar Singh, a reputed economist of the country is the present Director of the institute.

Contents

PART II

DELIMITATION OF THE RURAL-URBAN FRINGE

PART III

URBAN SPRAWL AND CHANGING SCENARIO OF RURAL-URBAN FRINGE

PART VII
PLANNING FOR RURAL-URBAN FRINGE

List of Contributors

Abdul Munir (Prof.), Department of Geography, Aligarh Muslim University, Aligarh.

Ali Mohammad (Prof.), Department of Geography, Aligarh Muslim University, Aligarh.

Alpana Chandra Scott (Dr.), Reader, Department of Geography, I.T. College, Lucknow.

Amit Sinha (Dr.), Remote Sensing Applications Centre, Lucknow. E-mail: amitsinharsac@rediffmail.com

Anisur Rehman (Mr.), Project Fellow, Department of Geography, Aligarh Muslim University, Aligarh.

Archana Gupta (Dr.), Guest Faculty, Department of Geography, University of Lucknow, Lucknow.

Arshi Azmi (Ms.), Research Scholar, Department of Geography, Aligarh Muslim University, Aligarh.

Ashwani K. Srivastava (Dr.), Remote Sensing Applications Centre, Lucknow. E-mail:ashwani_sriv@rediffmail.com

B.K Bajpai (Dr.), Senior Fellow, Giri Institute of Development Studies, Lucknow.

Deepika Varshney (Ms.), Research Scholar, Department of Geography, Aligarh Muslim University, Aligarh.

Gaurav Bisaria (Dr.), Assistant Professor, Department of Business Management, Integral University, Lucknow.

Ghazal Salahuddin (Ms.), Research Scholar, Department of Geography, Aligarh Muslim University, Aligarh.

Halima Sadia Rizvi (Prof.), Department of Economics, Jamia Millia Islamia, New Delhi.

Hifzur Rahman (Prof.), Department of Geography, Aligarh Muslim University, Aligarh.

J.B. Kshirsagar (Mr.), Chief Planner, Town and Country Planning Organization (Ministry of Urban Development, Government of India) E- Block, Vikas Bhawan, I.P. Estate, New Delhi.

J.S. Simlai (Dr.), Reader and Head, Department of Geography, I.T. College, Lucknow.

Krishanu Sarkar (Mr.), Research Scholar, Department of Economics, Burdwan University, Burdwan.

M.S. Khan (Dr.), Head and Dean, Faculty of Business Management, Integral University, Lucknow.

Milita Haldar (Ms.), Lecturer, Shri Ramswaroop Memorial Engineering and Management College, Lucknow and Doctoral Fellow, Giri Institute of Development Studies, Lucknow. E-mail: haldar.milita@gmail.com Mob. : 9889440389

Mohd. Sadiq Salman (Mr.), Research Scholar, Department of Geography, Aligarh Muslim University, Aligarh.

Mushir Ali (Dr.), Assistant Professor, Department of Geography, Bahirdar University, Bahirdar, Ethiopia. E–mail: mushirspn@rediffmail.com

Nadia Anis (Ms.), Research Scholar, Department of Geography, Aligarh Muslim University, Aligarh.

Nawaz Malik (Mr.), Research Scholar, Department of Geography, Aligarh Muslim University, Aligarh.

Neelam Pal (Ms.), Research Scholar, Deptt. of Geography, Banaras Hindu University, Varanasi. E-mail: neelampalresearch@yahoo.com

Nizamuddin Khan (Dr.), Reader, Department of Geography, Aligarh Muslim University, Aligarh.

N.M.P. Verma (Prof.), Department of Economics, Babasaheb Bhimrao Ambedkar University, Lucknow.

Pankaj P. Singh (Mr.), Research Scholar, Department of Geography, Banaras Hindu University, Varanasi. E-mail: p.pankaj10@gmail.com

Pawan Kumar (Mr.), Asstt. Town and Country Planner, Town and Country Planning Organization (Ministry of Urban Development, Government of India) E-Block, Vikas Bhawan, I.P. Estate, New Delhi.

Pratima Ghosh (Ms.), Research Scholar, Giri Institute of Development Studies, Lucknow.

Priyanka (Dr.), Remote Sensing Applications Centre, Lucknow.

Rakesh Singh Kushwaha (Dr.), Remote Sensing Applications Centre, Lucknow.

Ram Kumar Chaturvedi (Mr.), Department of Geography, Banaras Hindu University, Varanasi. E-mail: ramkumar_bhu@yahoo.com

Rana P.B. Singh (Prof.), Department of Geography, Banaras Hindu University, Varanasi. E-mail: ranapbs@gmail.com

Ravi S. Singh (Dr.), Associate Professor, Department of Geography, Banaras Hindu University, Varanasi. E-mail: ravisingh.geog@gmail.com, ravi_geog_bhu@yahoo.com

Ravindra Kumar (Mr.), Senior Staff Officer, State Water Resources Agency, Lucknow, E-mail: ravindra53@ahoo.co.in, Mobile: 91-9415021334, Fax: 0522 2440863.

Rewa Singh (Dr.), MBA–RD Faculty, G.B. Pant Social Science Institute, Allahabad.

Rupinder Kaur (Ms.), Research Scholar, Centre for the Study of Regional Development, Jawaharlal Nehru University, New Delhi.

S.A.M. Rizvi (Dr.), Associate Professor, Department of Computer Sciences, Jamia Millia Islamia, New Delhi.

S.B. Singh (Dr.), Department of Geography, Banaras Hindu University, Varanasi.

S.S.A. Jafri (Prof.), Giri Institute of Development Studies, Sector O, Aliganj Housing Scheme, Lucknow. E-mail: jafri_ssa@rediffmail.com, Mob: 9335806198.

Sahila Salahuddin (Ms.), Research Scholar, Department of Geography, Aligarh Muslim University, Aligarh.

Salahuddin Qureshi (Prof), Department of Geography, Aligarh Muslim University, Aligarh.

Sana (Ms.), Research Scholar, Department of Geography, Aligarh Muslim University, Aligarh.

Sarika Shukla (Dr.), Guest Faculty, I.T. College, Lucknow. E-mail: sarikashukla11@yahoo.co.in

Satyendra Narayan Singh (Mr.), Research Scholar, Department of Geography, Banaras Hindu University, Varanasi.

Shahab Fazal (Dr.), Associate Professor, Department of Geography, Aligarh Muslim University, Aligarh.

Sister Marion Mathew C.J. (Prof.), Head and Dean, College of Education AAI-DU, Allahabad.

Soumyendra Kishore Datta (Prof.), Department of Economics, Burdwan University, Burdwan. E-mail: soumyendra_d@rediffmail.com

Sudhakar Shukla (Dr.), Remote Sensing Applications Centre, Lucknow. E-mail: sudhakarshukla1@rediffmail.com

Sunit Singh (Dr.), Associate Professor, G.B. Pant Social Science Institute, Allahabad.

Vinit Kumar (Mr.), Research Scholar, Department of Economics, Babasaheb Bhimrao Ambedkar University, Lucknow.

Virendra Kumar (Dr.), Remote Sensing Applications Centre, Lucknow.

Introduction

Urban sprawl is a natural phenomenon accompanying rapid urban growth. The rapidly growing urban population in the large cities and high rate of migration spills into the rural areas surrounding the city boundaries. The settlement of the urban people into the surrounding areas and location of economic activities like factories, amusement parks, commercial complexes etc. gradually brings about a change in the land use pattern in the rural areas. This gives rise to the problem of rural-urban fringe, which is a transition zone between urban and rural settlement sharing the features of both.

The emergence of rural-urban fringe brings about significant changes in the land use as well as in the occupational pattern, cultural behaviour, environment and quality of life of the people in the rural areas adjoining the cities. While creating new job opportunities for the local residents, this process also brings about significant changes in the quality of life of the rural people both negative and positive. The phenomenon of rural-urban fringe which happens to be unplanned and haphazard leads to the problems of rise in land values, dispossession of farmers from land, increasing congestion, deterioration in physical environment, pressure on infrastructural facilities, cultural shock, social tensions and proliferation of criminal activities. The changes in the land use from agricultural to non-agricultural activities have larger implications for food security at the family and the country level. The problems of rural-urban fringe thus pose a major challenge to urban policy-planners.

The present book takes up the issues relating to the problems of rural- urban fringe and its management based on the papers discussed in a seminar on the same theme held at Giri Institute of Development Studies, Lucknow. In this book all the papers on the related theme, are classified into following sub-themes:

1. Rural-Urban Fringe: Conceptual Issues and Challenges.
2. Delimitation of the Rural-Urban Fringe.
3. Urban Sprawl and Changing Scenario of Rural-Urban Fringe.
4. Dynamics of Land Use in Rural-Urban Fringe.
5. Land Acquisition and Livelihood Issues.
6. Civic Amenities and Quality of Life.
7. Planning for Rural-Urban Fringe.

On the conceptual issues and challenges of Rural-Urban Fringe, S.B. Singh found that the newly developed fringe areas are seldom provided with adequate facilities. Rural-urban fringe areas of Indian cities present change in land use and expansion of residential areas. This phenomenon is nothing but the reflection of poor urban fringe management. Whereas in the west they have planned development in such areas as well. More vertical rather than horizontal expansion has to be encouraged so as to prohibit and control the continuing invasion of the countryside. A new term "peri-urban interface", a "zone where the urban and rural areas meet", has come into popular usage according to Ravi S. Singh and Satyendra Singh. While endeavouring to understand spatial dynamics of cities, especially the highly dynamic mega-cities, according to them, it is pertinent to focus on the peri-urban interface and issues emerging thereof which are not the same across the world.

Rapid changes in *urban* tastes and preferences for specific accommodation and infrastructure facilities as well as spread of the culture of consumerism have given rise to a worldwide trend for industrial expansion and real estate development along the urban fringes. It has been found that the owners of industries or real estate developers generally prefer fringe area of cities/towns to take advantage of easy transport of necessary inputs and delivery of finished products through the network of transport connection as well as some open and spacious area that these places are blessed with. The dynamics of trade off between the use of urban fringes for industrial/real estate development and protecting it for agricultural growth is critically analysed by employing a dynamic optimization model presented by Soumyendra Kishore and Krishanu Sarkar. Policy focus is made on a finding of some sort of compatibility between developmental urgencies and preserving agricultural productivity at the urban fringe areas on the basis of well guided principles. Halima Rizvi and Sam Rizvi in their study noted the details of the nature of characteristic features and conditions of rural-urban fringes, land use patterns and policies in India and the world over with special reference to the State of Uttar Pradesh. Their study revealed that there exist a great scope for planners and developers to work on promoting and providing the State with decent adoptable land use policy and creation of an environmentally healthy fringes. The need of the hour, in this context, it is found to be the strong political will to pronounce and promote legislative measure to undertake land reforms, land management and better utilization techniques so that sustainable rural-urban fringes may be a part of the future generations to come. According to Sister Marion Mathew though the urbanization brings about development in the social, economical and cultural spheres of life, it disturbs ecological systems. The increase in urban population results in asymmetric patterns in resource utilization, land use and transportation. Rapid and uncontrolled growth of urban agglomeration generates a series of negative environmental and social effects. These include : lack of infrastructure and basic services, housing problems, congestion, health problems, etc. While interpreting the transformation of rural space, she argued that much attention has to be given to the macro scale processes shaping capitalist society, particularly those of accumulation and uneven development. She concluded that India is heading towards a dismal future, in terms of population, food and space. Alpna Chandra Scott in her study put forth the concept that faces of urban geography and rural-urban spatial system on the urban fringes never reflect anything abstract. There is a legacy of the past. It is profound to find out the rural-urban spatial system in the light of urban fortune and urban performances to trace the aspects of development and disparity on the urban fringes. This will also be helpful in identifying the problems on the fringes and making suggestions.

In the second section of the book the issues relating to delimitation of the rural-urban fringe are discussed in two studies. In the first study by Sudhakar Shukla and others the importance of advance remote sensing and GIS has been highlighted for identifying the encroachment of urban areas into rural areas. In this study Lucknow City has been chosen as study area, which is one of the fastest growing Metropolitan regions. The results of the study indicated that due to increasing urban sprawl in Lucknow city, drastic land use change is taking in its 'RUF' (Rural-Urban Fringe) which is leading to inadequacy of public amenities and services. It is further suggested that the authorities and planners should adopt holistic approach for 'Greenfield Site' in order to have integrated functional as well as social segregation of land use. Role of Space-Borne Technology in Monitoring the Urban-Rural Fringe Areas is analysed by Ashwani Kumar Srivastava, Amita Sinha and others in another paper of this section. The study suggests that rapid urbanization and population growth causes the complexity of urban patterns, as such a high degree of detailed classification is often needed in mapping the urban areas. Study found out that during the recent years, the rate of urbanization was so fast that there was very little planned expansion thereby leading to poor management practices, which have created many urban.problems like slums, traffic congestion, overspill of sewage and transport network etc. Therefore, it is found important to monitor the growth of urban settlements periodically in a systematic way.

The third section of this book takes up the issues relating to the urban sprawl and changing scenario of rural-urban fringe. Urban sprawl and changing Peri-urban scene around Varanasi City: A case study of Chamaon Gram Sabha by Rana P.B. Singh shows that Peri-urban interface represents areas of dynamic institutional and environmental change. The increasing impact of the urban sprawl introduced a new look to intensive agriculture to supply the demand of the city turning to commercialisation of agriculture. Focus is also thrown by the study as to how the urban and peri-urban impacts and encroachments can transform the land, life and agricultural heritage in the rural India. Ali Mohammad and Nawaz Malik in their study argued that usually sprawl takes on the fringe, at the edge of an urban area, or along the highways. At the urban-rural fringe, the agricultural land becomes fragmented with farmers unable to take advantage of economies of scale, and land prices have become inflated due to non-agricultural values, so farmers are unable to realize reasonable returns to land. Some of the causes of the sprawl include—population growth, economy and proximity to resources and basic amenities. Study suggests that one of the first tasks of the land use planning should be to strike a balance between various interests. The multi-purpose use of land, wherever possible should be taken into consideration and no piece of land should be allowed as far as possible, to remain vacant or wasteland. The impacts of the development at the rural fringe on agriculture and rural land is presented by Shahab Fazal highlighting that city's fringe has been placed under pressure increasingly with increased demand due to rapidly changing values associated with land and its resources. The rapid sprawl of cities, outside their administrative boundaries and beyond their real physical-cultural domain possesses several attendant conflicts and stresses and has also stimulated various adaptations of human activities. The study tries to assess the influence of urbanization on the agricultural and rural land resource in the urban fringe of Aligarh city, based entirely on primary data. The attempt is made to draw out main factors instigating the changes in land use under agriculture sector and also on other urban land. Paper on Changing Environs and its Impact on Peri-urban Zone of Varanasi by Neelam Pal and Rana P. B. Singh argues that cities are the living organism and expanding rapidly in the whole world, particularly in the developing world. In the process of expansion, they are covering a large area surrounding its municipal corporation boundary which is called Peri-urban zone. The Peri-urban zones are the extension of the city rather than entirely separate area. The paper highlights the impact, problems, and suggestions for the improvement of Peri-urban zone with respect to the city. The results are presented through various maps and tables generated in ArcGIS.

The study on Rapid Urban Sprawl in Large Cities and its Swift Encroachment on Agriculture Fringe Land by S.S.A. Jafri and Milita Haldar has put forth the argument that the decadal growth rate of urban population in U.P. has been reported to be 33 per cent during 1991–2001, which is ahead than the all-India average urban growth, i.e. 31.5 per cent. This rapid growth of urban area has transformed to a great extent the land use pattern of various cities of the State of Uttar Pradesh. As is often observed due to market forces a large chunk of fertile lands on the fringes of mainly large cities are acquired hurriedly but they are urbanized at slow pace. In this process not only the encroached agricultural land of fringe are affected, but the entire neighbourhood of agri-system is adversely influenced. Urban sprawl or urbanization is an unstoppable process, but the need of the present hour is to have a development with a pinch of sustainability in it, so that all-round development could be achieved of the rich as well as the poor. Spatial Behaviour of Daily Commuters of Aligarh City and its Impact on Fringe has been analysed by Abdul Munir, Deepika Varshney and Arshi Azmi. It is revealed in their study that there were large variations in commuting behaviour from the city to varying distances. It is further found that there were variations in commuters' frequency and number of settlements within each demarcated zone. It is evident that centres having large number of facilities induce pulling effect and become centres with greater chances of further growth by attracting and accommodating more people from surrounding areas. The paper suggests that a comprehensive planning policy should be taken to promote urban growth to such an extent that each and every small and medium urban centre can serve its population and those living in surrounding rural areas. The paper presented by Ram Kumar Chaturvedi and Rana P.B. Singh envisages a case study of Peri-urban areas around the Ballia city, lying in eastern Uttar Pradesh, while presenting the changing scenarios of peri-urban areas and giving some suggestions for managing these problems in better way. In Ballia city, peri-urban areas have been developed in patches, and keep a sufficient distance between the two types of habitat. Consequently, this results to loss of agricultural fields and further encourages different land uses that was earlier not practiced and in many cases not suited too. The agricultural production has been largely to fulfil the demand of urban centres. Archana Gupta in her study Glimpses of the Rural-Urban Fringe of Lucknow Metropolis analysed that with the expansion of population and increase in number of migrants, the city is unable to accommodate all people and hence there is physical expansion of the city in two steps. The first step involves the occupancy of the vacant city areas and the second step includes the encroachment on land areas lying outside the city limits. The study conducted by Pankaj P. singh analysed that the utilization of land depends upon physical factors like topography, soil and climate as well as upon human factor such as density of population, duration of occupation in the area, land tenure and technical level of the people. There are spatial and temporal differences in land utilization due to the continued interplay of physical and human factors. The last paper of the third section of this book is written by Ghazal Salahuddin on Dynamics of the City Periphery in Aligarh and its Rural-Urban Fringe. The paper highlights the urban problems and the levels of urbanism in a city periphery of Aligarh which is largely inhabited by the Muslim community in the south-western part of the city. The spatial variation in the socio-economic conditions of the city periphery has been enquired in terms of social structure, built-up environment and the quality of life.

The fourth section of the book comprises of seven research papers dealing with the issues related to the Dynamics of Land Use in rural-urban fringe. According to the study presented by Salahuddin Qureshi urban gravity is the function of urban hierarchy. The impact of city gravity shows that there is often a linear relationship between the rural land use intensity and the city size in urban hierarchy. The city size also influences the rural land use pattern and the land use diversity. Hence, the law of urban hierarchy can be complementary to the widely acknowledged spatial law of distance-decay in geography. In this context, the paper raises a question, whether geographers can develop a working methodology to demarcate a functional and mathematically precise boundary of rural-urban fringe or the gradient of the inner and the outer fringe. Kamal Asif and S. Hifzur Rahman in their study found Agro-processing as an employment intensive sector which is gainful to the people living in urban catchment areas rather than the areas marked with low level of entrepreneurial urge, which hinders the activities due to the constraints of finance, assured market and proper training on technology. The study highlights the prospects of developing agro-processing centres for sustainable development and saving the livelihoods in the rural-urban fringe areas. It is a better tool for propelling prosperity in rural areas because such activities are fruitful as they ensure the availability of raw material and labour. Another study conducted by Nizamuddin Khan revealed that the vegetable cultivation is mainly practiced due to its remunerative value, fast returns and regular demand. It has become a major source of income and employment to urban poor. The beneficiaries are not only the producer and traders but all the people involved from production to marketing of the produce. The major problems regarding the vegetable cultivation is negligible incentive to the producer, improper marketing facilities and inadequate place for transaction of vegetables. Thus, there are many issues to be addressed for the sustainable development of vegetable cultivation in the rural-urban fringe of the Aligarh city. Rural-urban Fringe and Socio-Economic Structural Analysis of Vegetable Traders in Uttar Pradesh presented by Mushir Ali found that non-producer vegetable traders are common in the fringe areas and their share is nearly 77 per cent. The proportion of producer-cum-traders is at least 23 per cent in which more than 84 per cent producers belong to marginal and small farmer categories. It is due to prevailing unemployment and underemployment conditions. The study further suggests that agro-based industries should be established in rural-urban fringe areas. It will increase the price of commodities and provide job for the population of surrounding areas directly and indirectly to promote the well-being and socio-economic development among the people of the rural-urban fringe. Pratima Ghosh in her paper analysed the impact of the urban sprawl on some blocks in Kanpur city. The study looks upon the position of nine-fold classification of land. Trend analysis of the cropping pattern is made to analyze food security. The study also throws light upon the increased amenities; housing facilities availed in these areas. It involves studying the current stage of city's development, setting out the direction for change, identifying the thrust areas and suggesting the alternative strategies and interventions for bringing in the required change. Another study falling in this section of book presented by Sahila Salahuddin found out that the large farmers often have ownership landholdings bigger than the operational landholdings. Hence, the surplus land is rendered unused in the form of old fallow and culturable wastes. This renders a lower per unit area productivity of large landholdings. The lands left uncultivated for more than 5–7 years may be transferred to the landless people in the village. There should be atleast 1 efficient tube well of the Gram Panchayat for every 20 hectares of the agricultural lands in the villages. Farm produce exploitation by the middleman should be minimized. The rural marketing system should evolve a mandatory "Protection Prices" particularly for the perishable produce.

The last study of the fourth section of book by Mohammad Sadiq Salman and Abdul Munir is undertaken to analyze the role of common land resource in the socio-economic development of the landless and small farmers in the fringe areas of Allahabad. The study is based upon primary and secondary data. The study revealed that the Common Land Resources are mostly utilized by the landless and small farmers. The major modes of utilizing the Common Land Resources are agro-forestry, crop cultivation, grazing and other purposes and more than half of the total income of landless and small farmers is obtained from these resources. Thus, the proper utilization of the CLR can only lead to sustainable socio-economic development of the people in the fringe areas.

The fifth section of this book is devoted to land acquisition and livelihood issues. There are three studies grouped in this section in which different aspects of land acquisition and displacements are analysed. The study undertaken by N.M.P.Verma and Vinit Kumar argues that for developing economy like India SEZs may be regarded as vehicle of growth, employment generation and income augmentation on a sustainable basis. In order to fulfil these objectives various state governments have allotted hundreds of acres of land to each SEZs. The government acquired first the land from farmers who were hesitated to sell land. The most contentious issue relating to SEZs is land acquisition. Study finds that though industry-led growth is very much possible through SEZs and EPZs but shifting of land from agricultural sector to industrial sector may be judiciously done. The shifting must take care of the interest of landowners, poor labourers, displaced villagers and a mechanism be developed for involving them as a shareholder in SEZs. There is hardly any reason to shift the ownership of land, in many such cases. This may also reduce legal battle and bring faster development of private industries. The problem of development induced displacement is analysed by B. K. Bajpai in his study entitled Rural-Urban Fringe in Uttar Pradesh: Issues of Development Induced Displacement. The study analyses the problems of development projects related displacement of rural population owing to increasing urban fringes in rural areas. Displacement of rural population, falling in the catchment area of six development projects, located in four geo-economic regions of Uttar Pradesh and one in Uttarakhand (earlier Hill region of UP), shows a widespread mismanagement of the resettlement and rehabilitation programme. The impact of the development projects on displaced population has been assessed taking into consideration the existing rehabilitation policies of the government. The impact of displacement on affected families has been assessed and attempt has also been made to evaluate the existing rehabilitation policies and the compliance of Government orders in this connection. The analysis indicates that the development projects may be a boon for some, but they are a curse for the rest. The psyche of the affected population is to be understood properly. The government agencies involved in the rehabilitation programmes are hardly capable of such understanding. In the absence of a proper resettlement and rehabilitation plan for the displaced households under the development projects, there were negative impacts on the lives and livelihood of these affected households. The research findings arrived manifestly indicates that in certain cases the Government Orders were observed in breach rather than in compliance. The last study of this section by Sunit Singh and Reva Singh undertakes a debate on spatial planning of urban fringe. The study makes an endeavour to study the areas of institutional conflicts between the State Governments and the local bodies in urban fringes, its impact on the lives of local communities as well as residents of the expanded cities and the subsequent consequences on the effectiveness of local body institutions in terms of decentralized planning and participatory management of local resources. The study intends to bring forth the larger debate on the conflicts between the state and the people latter representing the crumbling people's voice while the former as vanguard of grand projects in the name of development.

The sixth section of the book comprises four studies relating to the problems of civic amenities and quality of life. M.S. Khan and Gaurav Bisaria have observed the social impact of rural-urban fringe in their study. This study contains research work which focuses on the process of urban expansion in Lucknow with special reference to the process and patterns of land acquisition for urban expansion. The geographical area of research was based in Lucknow, the capital of U.P. The study later on throws light on the issues like urban pattern, features of urban society, advantages and disadvantages of urbanization and concludes that despite changes due to urbanization but the essence of rural environment should be maintained. Though the people are moving to cities, still the real and the majority of India lives in the villages having their own importance and the lifestyle. The second study of this section is conducted by Nadia Anis and Hafizur Rahman on health care facilities in fringe area of Aligarh city. An attempt in this study has been made to take into account the health care facilities in wards located in fringe areas of the Aligarh city. The study further explores the extent and efforts involved by the concerned departments in providing these facilities and finally concluded that health and health care can bring a substantial improvement in social well-being of the society, if they are equally made available in all wards, more especially the wards located in peripheral areas. Educational facilities in fringe areas of Azamgarh district have been explored by Sana. The empirical evidence of the study indicated that there exist central and fringe areas inequalities in educational development. Education is highly concentrated in urban location and at places with better connection. Study further suggests that in order to remove the regional inequalities, considering the socio-economic and geographical features of the region appropriate regional planning for education at grass roots level is required. People's awareness need to be developed through motivation programmes. The last study of this section by Ravindra Kumar deals with the threat to inland water bodies emanating from rural-urban fringe due to land use transaction. The study found out that land degradation in some form or other is in half area of the state. Half of the problematic areas have been treated so far. Land zoning based on ecological aspect concept often evaluated on parameters–average depth to water table, land damage index, water quality (pH, salinity, alkalinity index and salt balance). It is suggested that framing of suitable legislation and its sincere enforcement is the key of success by imposing penalties, on violations thereof. Thus, the problem of land management of rural-urban fringe is the issue of governance and requires support of all in its implementation.

The last section of the book contains the studies related to the planning for rural-urban fringe. According to the study 'Spatial Planning for Rural-Urban Fringe Areas' presented by J.B. Kshirsagar and Pawan Kumar, the growth of rural-urban fringe is dynamic in character, interactive and transformative because it is directly related to land use, socio-cultural transformation, demographic characteristics and propagation of urban values. These areas are also affected by the process of migration, poverty, provision of basic services, infrastructure, transport, disposal of waste, atmospheric contamination, pollution of surface and groundwater, etc. Environmental degradation in such areas threatens the sustainability of cities in respect of health and essential life support systems. In view of these, spatial planning approach is required to ensure healthy spatial growth of rural-urban fringe as well as reduce vulnerability of stakeholders such as farmers, landless labourers, etc. to prevent slumming. According to the study on rapid urbanisation in India and governance challenges by J.S. Simlai urbanization is not a side effect of economic growth but an integral part of the process. The urban regions of the north make major contributions to the country's economy. Given the paucity of resources, it would be more feasible and desirable to promote strategic development initiatives in the selected secondary cities, growth centres and their hinterlands. In the growth centres, the location of infrastructural and environmental services could form the 'core' of the development plan. Simlai emphasized that the zoning regulations need to be simplified. The land use package should not be altered by any authority except as part of the review of the development plan at the city/town level.

The last study of this section entitled, 'Post Reform Restructuring of Employment in Urban Peripheries–A Case Study of National Capital Region of India' by Rupinder Kaur argued that the existing metropolitan central business districts are very congested and therefore unmanageable and inefficient, so the growth has to be accommodated elsewhere within the metropolitan area. In this connection, it is expected that these structural changes would alter the pattern of urbanization as well as employment structure in metropolitan areas which combine an agglomeration and peripheral zones not themselves necessarily urban in character but closely bound to the centre by employment or commerce. Author concludes that the economic reforms adopted in early 1990s and decentralisation oriented policy has a significant impact on employment structure of NCR. As a result, there is emergence of a new polycentric spatial structure of employment and urbanization in this region with rise of new industrial districts around Delhi. The evolution of NCR from monocentric to polycentric metropolis suggests a restructuring of employment as well as reordering of urban space which manifests on space as concentrated decentralisation. To end the studies presented in seven sections, the book contains the recommendations based on the discussion on these studies.

It is a pleasure for us to acknowledge the contribution of each one in the completion of this book. At the outset we express our deep sense of gratitude to Prof.A.K.Singh, Director of Giri Institute of Development Studies who has taken initiative to hold this seminar, on which this book is based, and encouraged us to take up this task. We received full support from Land Use Board, Department of Planning, Govt. of U.P., the sponsoring agency of this event, and Additional Director Mrs. Mridula

Singh. We are thankful to them. We extend our sincere appreciation and thanks to all the paper writers, too numerous to be mentioned by name, who took interest in writing their papers and came to Lucknow from different parts of the country to attend the seminar. We are also thankful to all of them who were behind the scene in supporting us in the accomplishment of this task.

We will consider it enough rewarding if our study, with all its limitations and shortcomings, leads to greater awareness about the subject and related issues among researchers and scholars.

S.S.A. Jafri
B.K. Bajpai

Part I

Rural-Urban Fringe
Conceptual Issues and Challenges

1

Rural-Urban Fringe: Problems and Management

S.B. Singh

The 'rural-urban fringe: problems and management' topic is of urgent and critical relevance. Any scheme that existed in the first decade of planned development were relegated to oblivion in the subsequent years. For example there used to be a Development of Town and Country Planning endowed with statutory authority. There were master plans for major urban centres, improvement trusts, and developmental authorities, all have their own story of success.

Cities are dynamic human artifacts and they constantly undergo structural change, redevelopment and growth. Such processes also involve changes in urban relationships with the surrounding territory, most conspicuously on their outskirts. According to 1951 census, about 45 per cent of the countries urban population lived in Class I cities which have increased to 69 per cent in 2001. Over the years there has been continuous concentration of population in class I towns. On the contrary, the concentration of population in medium and small town either fluctuated or declined (Kundu, 1994). Indeed basic reason for increasing dominance of class I cities is graduation of lower order towns into class I categories. It may be observed that in 1901 there were only 24 class I cities that has gone up to 393 in 2001 which explains largely the increase in the share of population in this size categories to class I has resulted top heavy structure of urban population in India. The gain in population of Indian cities, to a greater extent, is due to immigration of rural labour, artisans and educated youth from rural areas in search of better livelihood.

Urbanisation in developing countries is marked by large increases in population and as a physical phenomenon, it takes two paths: firstly through the independent transformation of rural areas into urban areas and secondly expansion of existing urban bodies by engulfing adjoining

Table 1.1 Percentage Distribution of Urban Population by Size-Class of towns/Urban Agglomerations in India, 1901-2001

Census Year	Cities	Large Towns	Medium Towns	Small Towns		
	Class-I	Class-II	Class-III	Class-IV	Class-V	Class-VI
1901	26	11.29	15.64	20.83	20.17	6.10
1911	27.48	10.51	16.40	19.73	19.13	6.57
1921	29.70	10.39	15.92	18.29	18.67	7.03
1931	31.2	11.65	16.80	18.00	17.14	5.21
1941	38.23	11.42	16.35	15.78	15.08	3.14
1951	44.63	9.96	15.72	13.63	15.97	3.09
1961	51.42	11.23	16.94	13.77	6.87	0.77
1971	57.24	10.92	16.01	10.94	4.45	0.44
1981	60.42	11.63	14.33	9.54	3.58	0.50
1991	65.20	10.95	13.19	7.77	2.60	0.29
2001	68.62	9.73	12.29	6.80	2.33	0.23

Source: Census of India, 1901-2001.

villages into their territory. The latter process is predominated in India; the trend has been more towards concentration. During process of transformation adjoining areas acquire new character which are neither totally urban nor rural in nature, rather combination of both, which is often called as 'urban fringe'. The study of available literature reveals that the term urban fringe was first introduced by Smith in 1937 to describe built-up area just outside the corporate limit of the city. Later the concept of the 'rural-urban fringe' was formulated by Wehrwein in 1942 as the area of transition, between well recognized urban land uses and the area devoted to agriculture, followed by studies of Rodehever (1947), Berg (1948), Cozen (1960), Pryor (1968), Dickinson (1970), Gopi (1978), Patel (1980) Berg and Ijkelenstam (1989), Oort (1996), Singh and Gupta (1997) and Dube (2001) which broadly point out the loss of valuable agricultural land to non-agricultural uses, showing variation in demography, morphology and infrastructural facilities.

Thus, the term Rural-Urban Fringe is comprised of two groups of words—Rural Fringe—Urban Fringe. These two terms denote overlapping boundaries with respect to area, which is distinct in matters of form and function and is often referred as Rurban Fringe. It is a bridge between the rural area on the one side and urban centre on the other. All the characteristics of urbanity and ruralism are medium in the fringe area. These characteristics vary from town to town on the basis of their physical and cultural status.

Urban fringe development is not only a process of transition of land from its rural use to urban use, rather, it is a complex process that involves many concerns such as change in landownership pattern, land transfer process, types of development, regulatory measures and their enforcement. The process of fringe development is not monolithic and may take place either by rural actors or by urban actors, in formal or informal way. In the process of urban development the adjoining villages are gradually changing their rural character into urban landscape and are further sub-divided into primary and secondary fringes based on their proximity to the city and present typical characteristics with regards to the socio-economic set-up, and conversion of land uses with rapid increase in population.

Several villages of the fringe, having been deprived of their agricultural land are in the state of flux and remains waiting for their amalgamation within the city limit. In addition urban fringes as the proliferation of various forms of a part-time farming seek additional income from the jobs in the town and develop residential or agricultural specialization and intensification, all the urban fringes contain specialized non-agricultural land uses such as vehicle and garbage dumping yards, quarries, water supply areas and sewage and farms. Thus rural-urban fringe areas of Indian cities present change in land use, increase in commuting population, fast expansion of residential areas, slum development with low public utility services etc. whereas in the west they have planned development in such areas as well.

Hence, land use in the fringe will be looked at from a dynamic point of view, for instance, rural land which is taken over by various urban and rural uses. The agricultural holdings in the fringe tend to be smaller than in the surrounding rural areas as a result of sub-divisions and land shortages caused by urban growth. Parts of the remaining agricultural land are insufficiently and inefficiently used as 'social fallow'. Elsewhere in the fringe, farmland may be used more intensively than in the surrounding rural area as market gardening, horticulture, poultry and piggeries.

Gottman's statement that 'the problem of land use changes caused by urban explosion become chronic' is quite valid in case of rural-urban fringes of Indian cities, where part of the cultivable land is sold for houses and factories and much of the farmland lies derelict and abused as a consequence of urban interference into the farming system, enhanced land values through competition between colonizers and industrialists (Gottman, 1963; Dicknson, 1964). Most of the developing countries experience spontaneous development pattern rather than planned growth. The built-up area of Indian cities have swelled even more than ten times during a span of hundred years. For instance, the four largest cities of the country have registered growth in their built-up area measuring even more than 100 km^2 showing a huge concentration of industrial and commercial population. For example, Kanpur, the largest metro city of UP has enlarged its built-up area from 5 km^2 (1965) to 50 km^2 (2001). More and more of our fringe villages are likely to fall of urban invasion in the years to come.

Therefore, the problem associated with urban fringe in most developing countries is development of land in informal way where associated land development activities take place without conforming State rules and regulations. Due to high demand of land low lying areas are also being filled up for various development purposes without considering any environmental impact. The emphasis is only on accommodating the increasing population, not to ensure better living standard. Therefore, the newly developed fringe areas are seldom provided with adequate facilities. All the phenomena are nothing but the reflection of poor urban fringe management. It is ironical that our planning processes still give rise to complexities and contradictions that are integral parts of the urban environment: non-conforming and unsustainable land uses, relocation of polluting industries, regularisation of illegal settlements and slums. There remain many such rural 'pockets' in the city fabric that are not well integrated and are subjected to the vagaries of market forces, manipulations and speculations.

Due to lack of proper administration and taxation, homogeneous development of the fringe zone is out of question. As a matter of fact, this zone paradoxically lies at a time under the influence of the three administrative agencies—Municipal Board, District Board and Block, among which there is hardly any coordination and integration. It is inevitable to explore the ways and means to stop and restrict such encroachment. In general, more vertical rather than horizontal expansion has to be encouraged so as to prohibit and control the continuing invasion of the countryside.

2
The Peri-Urban Interface: Some Conceptual and Future Research Issues

Ravi S. Singh and *Satyendra N. Singh*

Introduction

Urban growth moves on at unprecedented rate. Even the countries in the developing world of the global South, including India, apparently march ahead with a soaring urban population (cf. Tables 2.1, 2.2, 2.3 and 2.4) and even in percentage terms, sizeable chunk of their huge population is going to live in the urban areas before the mid-21st century. This trend is an indicator of strong urbanisation. However, urbanisation should not be treated only as the process which has to do with the demographic dimension that is the growth in urban population and attendant changes. Scholars unanimously recognise at least four forms of urbanisation, *viz.* urbanization as a socio-cultural process, urbanization as a political-administrative process, urbanization as an economic process, and urbanization as a geographical process (Ramachandran, 1989: 75-95). We will have to accept here that no matter how are we looking at this process, it has clear and direct implication for ecology and human habitat. Geographers, especially in India, have largely been interested in analysing the urban demographic dynamics, land use, urban landscape(s) of poverty, infrastructure, environment, and the role of urban centres in the broader regional frame, particularly in the context of regional planning. We have fairly long list of studies dealing with the "macro-urbanization" and "metropolization", to use the labels used by Ramachandran (1989: 90-94); but, rather weaker and feeble tradition of "suburbanization" studies. With the spreading out of existing cities, many spatial consequences have emerged; specifically, such new areas which exhibit neither the characteristics of urban nor the rural areas. Similarly, a variety of emergent features strongly suggest a situation of fluidity instead of any type of fixedity.

The present exercise aims at discussing the emergence of Peri-Urban Interface (PUI) in the developing countries with special reference to India and diagnoses the future research challenges (with special reference to Geography). The following discussion is organised into four sections: definition and classification of the PUI, nature of PUI in the developing global South (with special reference to India), the future research issues, and the conclusion.

Definition and Classification

Definition

Cities have a natural tendency to spread out and sprawl; nevertheless,

Table 2.1: Growth of urban population in India, 1901-2001

Year	Population (million)	%age (of Total Population)
1901	25.87	10.84
1911	25.96	10.42
1921	28.09	11.32
1931	33.47	12.12
1941	44.17	14.02
1951	62.44	17.29
1961	78.93	19.97
1971	109.11	19.91
1981	159.72	23.34
1991	217.18	25.72
2001	285.30	27.75

Source: Based on reports of the Census of India.

Table 2.2: Class-wise growth of towns in India, 1951-2001

Class of Towns	Census Years					
	1951	1961	1971	1981	1991	2001
I.	76	102	148	218	300	393
II.	91	129	173	270	345	401
III.	327	437	558	743	947	1151
IV.	608	719	827	1059	1167	1344
V.	1124	711	623	758	740	888
VI.	569	172	147	253	197	191
Total	**2795**	**2470**	**2426**	**3696**	**3768**	**4368**

Source: Based on Census of India 1951, 1961, 1971, 1981, 1991, 2001.

Table 2.3: Distribution of population by class of towns in India, 1951-2001 (%)

Class of Towns	*1951*	*1961*	*1971*	*1981*	*1991*	*2001*
I.	44.6	51.4	57.0	60.4	65.2	68.5
II.	10.0	11.2	11.0	11.6	11.4	9.6
III.	15.7	16.9	17.0	14.4	13.2	12.4
IV.	13.6	12.8	10.0	9.5	7.8	7.0
V.	13.0	6.9	4.5	3.6	2.1	2.3
VI.	3.1	0.8	0.5	0.5	0.3	0.2
Total	**100**	**100**	**100**	**100**	**100**	**100**

Source: Based on Census of India 1951, 1961, 1971, 1981, 1991, 2001.

Table 2.4: Growth of million-plus cities in India

Year	*Cities*	
	Number	*Name*
1901	01	Calcutta
1911	02	Calcutta, Bombay
1921	02	Calcutta, Bombay
1931	02	Calcutta, Bombay
1941	02	Calcutta, Bombay
1951	05	Calcutta, Bombay, Delhi, Madras, Hyderabad
1961	07	Calcutta, Bombay, Delhi, Madras, Hyderabad, Bangalore, Ahmedabad
1971	09	Calcutta, Bombay, Delhi, Madras, Hyderabad, Bangalore, Ahmedabad, Pune, Kanpur
1981	12	Calcutta, Bombay, Delhi, Madras, Hyderabad, Bangalore, Ahmedabad, Pune, Kanpur, Lucknow, Nagpur, Jaipur
1991	23	Calcutta, Bombay, Delhi, Madras, Hyderabad, Bangalore, Ahmedabad, Pune, Kanpur, Lucknow, Nagpur, Jaipur, Surat, Kochi, Vadodara, Indore, Coimbatore, Patna, Madurai, Bhopal, Visakhapatnam, Ludhiana, Varanasi
2001	35	Calcutta, Bombay, Delhi, Madras, Hyderabad, Bangalore, Ahmedabad, Pune, Kanpur, Lucknow, Nagpur, Jaipur, Surat, Kochi, Vadodara, Indore, Coimbatore, Patna, Madurai, Bhopal, Visakhapatnam, Ludhiana, Varanasi, Agra, Meerut, Nashik, Jabalpur, Jamshedpur, Asansol, Dhanbad, Faridabad, Allahabad, Amritsar, Vijayawada, Rajkot.

Source: Based on Census of India 1951, 1961, 1971, 1981, 1991, 2001.

this pattern is not uniform owing to one or a combination of the following demographic, socio-cultural, economic, infrastructural, and politico-economic factors (cf. McGregor, Simon and Thompson, 2006: 4):

- Size and structure

- Composition of the urban and migrant population (age and sex; family and household structure; ethnic, cultural and religious diversity; education and income levels; etc.)
- Extensive oscillating/circular migration
- Physical terrain and environmental barriers
- Transport networks (orientation, accessibility and affordability)
- Land (tenure system, values, and uses)
- Intense differences between administrative/political and *de facto* urban boundaries.

Peri-urbanization can be understood as a specific phase of urban expansion (Oliveau, 2005). This spreading out creates altogether a different zone/area characterised by hybridity, "chaos", complexity and in a way it is the melting zone where the urban and rural characteristic features tend to mix with each other. They are "transitional spaces subject to and also characterized by rapid and multiple transformations: physical, morphological, socio-demographic, cultural, economic and functional". As the natural consequence, heterogeneity appears rather prominent over any homogeneity. However, the basic nature of such a zone varies depending upon the period of its existence. The most striking feature of this zòne is its dynamism manifested in a variety of ways especially through the landscape change.

The peripheral areas of the cities have been termed as 'Peri-Urban Interface' (PUI), "basically as an area with a mix of urban as well as rural development processes, situated on the periphery of cities". A few other terms like "metropolitan fringe"/"urban fringe", "rural-urban fringe", "metropolitan peripheries", and "semi-urbanised"/"urban transition zone" too have been used to denote the same. However, it was the Office of Rural and Institutional Development (ORID) which used the term 'peri-urban' in the late 1980s in the process of explaining schemes of development assistance aid to priority areas (cf. Rohilla, 2005a: 103). These zones are called differently: *Halfstedig* (semi-urban) in Dutch, *Urban—ländlichen Zone* (Urban-rural zones) in German, *Buitestedelik* (outer city/beyond the city) in Afrikaans, and *Desakota* (city village) in East Asia and parts of South-East Asia (cf. McGee, 1991). It need to be underlined here that PUI, in realistic terms, is *not* exactly the same rather a little different from its 'synonymous' terms used interchangeably. The other terms connote a contiguous geographical area at the fringe of the urban limit whereas in the PUI case one may or may not find such a characteristic as several types of the PUI, as discussed below, including even discontinuous one are known. In such a context, the PUI is a term that better captures and covers the nuances of peri-urbanization.

Types

Though the consequence of the same basic process, the PUIs acquire different characteristics in terms of their distance from the city concerned, nature of migration experienced and also the Institutional Context (IC). Iaquinta and Drescher (2000) identify the following peri-urban types (cf. Fig. 2.1):

2.2.1. Village Peri-Urban (VPU)

It is non-proximate to the city either geographically or in travel time and derives from sojourning, circulation and migration. This peri-urban type embodies a 'network induced IC' wherein change is effected through diffusion or induction while institutions remain traditional in orientation and stable.

2.2.2. Diffuse Peri-Urban (DPU)

Geographically speaking, the DPU is the urban fringe deriving from multiple-source point in migration. It represents an 'amalgamated IC' where there is a high demand for negotiating novel institutional forms tc address conflicting traditions and worldviews.

2.2.3. Chain Peri-Urban (CPU)

The CPU too is an urban fringe geographically which develops primarily from chain migration. It includes a 'reconstituted IC' wherein links to the donor area remain strong and traditions and institutions are transplanted with some modification from the donor area and take on a slightly defensive character.

2.2.4. In-place Peri-Urban (IPU)

Geographically, the IPU is close to the city located in the urban fringe. Its development owes to in-place urbanization, natural increase and some degree of migration as well. It embodies a 'traditional IC' with long-term stable institutions evidencing strong defensive insulation.

2.2.5. Absorbed Peri-Urban (APU)

The APU is different from all the above types in the sense that geographically speaking, it is within the city after having been absorbed by the expanding city limits. Its development is attributed to 'succession/ displacement and traditionalism (ritualism)'. It incorporates a 'residual IC' wherein the roots of social arrangements lie in the traditions of a previously resident culture group and are now maintained through ritualism (cf. Iaquinta and Drescher, 2000).

Factors of Peri-urbanization

The factors of the peri-urbanization though may vary from one PUI to

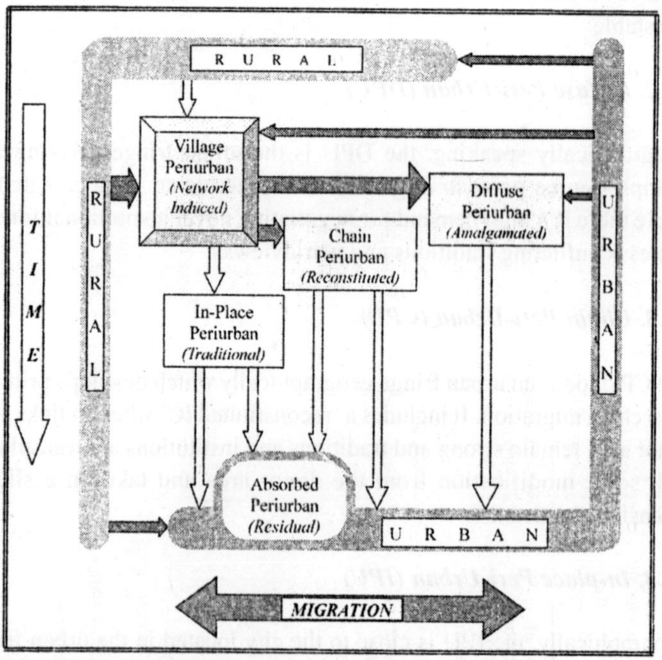

Fig. 2.1: Peri-urban typology with institutional contexts (after Iaquinta and Drescher, 2000).

Table 2.5: Characteristics of institutional contexts by peri-urban type (*Source*: Iaquinta and Drescher, 2000)

Institutional-Context Characteristic	*Peri-Urban Type*				
	Linked Across Space		*Linked Across Space And/or Over Time*[1]	*Linked Over Time*	
	Village PU	*Diffuse PU*	*Chain PU*	*In-Place PU*	*Absorbed PU*
Name of Institutional-Context "Type"	Network Induced (tradition oriented)	Amalgamated	Reconstituted	Traditional	Residual (Traditionalism)
Creation Process	Out-migration with networking; Circulation	Diffuse migration	Chain (point source) migration	Annexation; In-migration	Succession-displacement
Proximity to Urban Centre	Non-proximate	Proximate	Proximate	Proximate	Absorbed[2]
Organizing Principle	Integrative maintenance of traditional links	Survival and collective formation	Defensive reconstruction of cultural identity	Defensive maintenance of tradition	Maladaptive adherence to tradition
Primary stimulus for change	Emigrant influences (remittances, circulation, participation)	Compositional heterogeneity; Interface with urban formal structures;	Interface with urban formal institutions	Urban in-migrants; Interface with urban formal institutions	Interface with urban formal institutions; Loss of traditionalist legitimacy
Primary mechanism limiting or effecting change	Traditional (i.e., existing) structures	Negotiation among residents; Emergent/novel structures	Reconstituted structures organized along traditional lines	Traditional (i.e., existing) structures	Ritualized structures
Need for Change	Low	High	High	Moderate	High
Resistance to Change	High	Low	Moderate	High	High
Pace of Adaptation	Slow	Fast	Moderate	Slow	Very slow

(Contd.)

Institutional-Context Characteristic	*Peri-Urban Type*				
	Linked Across Space		*Linked Across Space And/or Over Time*[1]	*Linked Over Time*	
	Village PU	*Diffuse PU*	*Chain PU*	*In-Place PU*	*Absorbed PU*
Likelihood for Disruptive Conflict	Low	Moderate	Moderate	High	High
Characteristics of Change	Existential and tradition oriented (maintenance of ideal culture *via* redefinition of adaptation)	Experimental; democratic or consensus based; function oriented	Tradition oriented incorporating some urban components	Polarized between traditional and modern sectors	At best external compliance only
Most Likely Types of Adaptations	Novel solutions which maintain the appearance of tradition and meet modern sector needs	Novel solutions which meet modern sector needs and create a new basis for legitimacy	Solutions which make inefficient use of the formal sector	Solutions which make inefficient use of the formal sector due to slow pace of change in high need situation	Solutions imposed from the outside formal sector
Impact on Stratification Systems	Greater individual access with formal maintenance of system	More opportunity for egalitarianism; Erosion of system	Maintenance of system, possibly in new forms	Heightened conflict over system; Increased oppression	Strong support for maintenance of system

Notes: 1. *Chain peri-urban* is linked across space as a receiving area for migrants coming from rural and *village peri-urban* areas. It is linked through time to *absorbed peri-urban* areas insofar as succession/displacement produces ritualism in institutional maintenance.

2. Formally speaking, *absorbed peri-urban* types lie within the city. Its roots lie in the peri-urban zone with *in-place peri-urban* and *village peri-urban*. Thus, we include it as a form of peri-urban to underscore this temporal linkage.

another, a few of them could be common, however, not affecting in similar way and same degree. They are as under:

- The role of transport and the sociological factors in urban sprawl (there is a growing tendency of dissociation between areas for living, work and leisure)
- The influence of single family housing [problems with multi-storey flat system, owning property (*kothi* or a "farm-house"), relatively cheaper, status-symbol]
- New urban population (desire to simultaneously live in both city and village: quite surroundings and life, comparatively cheaper living, healthier environment, aesthetic rural setting, etc.)
- Security and "Fenced and Gated Communities"

Nature of Peri-urban Interface in the Developing Global South

General Nature of the Peri-Urban Interface

No matter how we conceptualise and define "peri-urban interface", the basic fact remains that it is a dependent process on urbanisation and it provides a direct linkage between what we term 'urban' and 'rural' environments and their respective activities. Perhaps it will not be incorrect to argue that the process of peri-urbanization in its basic form is an urban settlement oriented process. That is the reason why the first most important factor affecting the formation of PUI is the size of the urban settlement and also its structure as mentioned above. Hence, it may be stated that there exists a direct, strong and positive correlation between size of urban settlement and pace of peri-urbanization, i.e. larger is the size of an urban settlement greater/intense is the peri-urbanization. That is the reason why lower order urban settlements which are either sluggish or stagnant, in India, do not show existence of any PUI; whereas, on contrary, the larger urban centres have vast area of PUI. Similarly, it may be noted that the city concerned also act as the driver of change(s) in its peri-urban zone. The PUIs are marked by various changes—functional, organizational and institutional which are multi-layered as shown in Fig. 2.2 and are characterized by their highly dynamic nature because they move outward with the expansion of the city in the geographic space. That is to say the peri-urban inertia depends on the force generated within the city concerned. We can say that PUI always remains in the changing or transitory state—with the becoming of a PUI

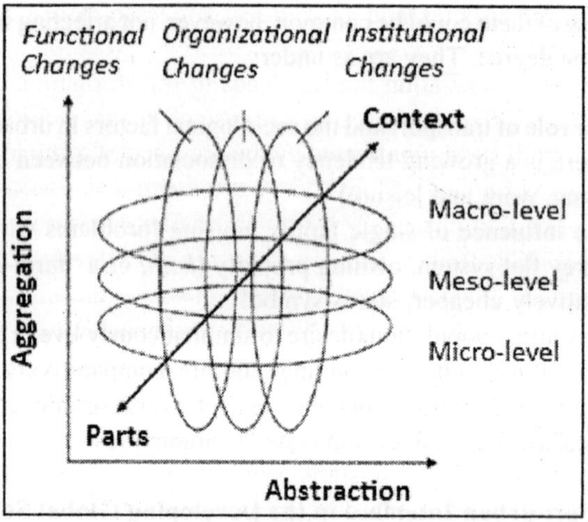

Fig. 2.2: Multi-layered peri-urban transition processes.

Source: Adapted from http://www.plurel.net/images/, accessed on 17.5.10.

'urban', the peri-urban in geographical sense pushed further out. It also suggests that the peri-urban population experiences "continuous shifts in lives and livelihoods" as well.

The Peri-Urban Interface in the Developing Global South

Now, the question is whether the nature of PUI is uniform across or does it varies? Though in general terms, every PUI is induced by the urban expansion, as noted above; the nature of evolution is bound to be different. That is how the experience of the PUI in the global South is different from other parts of the world in terms of two basic features. Firstly, migration from the rural and lower order urban settlements is playing important role in intensifying the urban population pressure and also pushing out of the urban limits; and on the other hand, it is also occupied by the migrant workers. Secondly, the consequences on the land and the 'original' inhabitants are deeper and dark. The stress on land and environment as a whole is quite a grave issue in the PUIs in this part of the world due to prevalent poverty situation and also a negligent attitude of administrators. The environmental stress in one hand is on account of local level mis-/mal-treatment and on top of that the international and national level policies and consequent processes too often produce negative effects.

The peri-urbanization process leads to transformation of the rural areas through different phases. In the case of the developing countries, the typical rural stage, unaffected by the presence of a city in the region, in due course of time develops some basic functional relationship as the supplier of certain products for the city market chiefly in the form of vegetables, milk, flowers and fruits. In the next phase, villagers start availing the employment opportunities available in the city which marks a new form of village-city interaction. It results into a new relationship with profound effect on rural areas through the initial change in occupational pattern which acts as a catalyst to a host of other economic and socio-cultural changes. With the growing interaction between city and villages, urban land use starts penetrating rural landscape generally through the real-estate agents developing residential "colonies". The state-owned urban development authorities too can play similar role as has been experienced since the recent past. With the intensification of interaction, urban uses take over the past non-urban agricultural uses and the villages become the part of the city concerned. However, all the signs of rural past do not vanish entirely. Their retention does not allow full assimilation of the rural settlements concerned in the city and they maintain their identity as the "urban villages" (cf. Ramachandran, 1989: 310-316). Such transformations, with many desirable effects like creation of employment opportunities in the PUIs and also the future job potential, necessarily create a variety of problems too for the PUIs. Some problems like land use problems are direct and others might be indirect. As far as the employment opportunities are concerned, the larger issue here is most of such opportunities are availed by migrant labour and that is how 'original' inhabitants, having already lost the traditional livelihood(s), become more vulnerable. It becomes crucial to underline that an average PUI dweller's vulnerability is an issue more pertinent in the global South than elsewhere.

Scholars believe that if peri-urbanization is the direct consequence of the urban expansion and growing interaction between the city and villages around, the expansion should be planned (cf. *ibid.*, 319-320). The question is can we do that? If yes, how to do that? Which body will regulate? The existing system is insufficient to address and deliver the desirable results. We will have to shed our vision which looks at the rural and urban settlements as in binary opposition and accordingly correct the current practises. It appears difficult and much easier would be to create a separate regulatory body for the PUIs.

Looking critically at this problem, one may doubt the outcomes. Often the ideas like planning are ultimately treated as a *sarkari* kind of venture in spite of all good intensions of policy-makers. Moreover, the sufficiency and efficiency of skill and expertise of the general administrators to handle such problems and deliver the desirable is also doubtful, as per the general experience. Hence, planning must be supplemented strongly with monitoring to avoid negative consequences. Some scholars have attached priority and weightage to the use of Modern Information Technology (MIT), e.g. the Geographical Information System (GIS). They argue that the 'traditional database and land use measures give a vague picture of the land use dynamics' and the 'current urban based definitions are poorly suited to delineate these areas and low density, ex-urban land use is difficult to measure using existing land cover databases. Relying solely on urban based land cover classification will likely underestimate large areas of low density human settlement beyond the urban fringe' (Theobald, 2000). However, even those not averse to such MITs will agree that these tools should be over expected to give magic wand like results. Therefore, ground level monitoring should be taken as the base supplemented by GIS like tools.

Future Research Issues

Scenario

It is not that the cities have started expanding only during the last few years. As a Natural response to it, one finds multitude of studies addressing the issues of rural-urban fringe. The published literature reflects gross negligence of peri-urban interface studies even in the developing countries of the global South where a typical nature of peri-urbanization has given rise to vast peri-urban zones and multiplicity of complex emergent issues. Most of the studies are focused on the distribution of towns/cities as settlements and urban population growth and distribution. For a brief period extending between the late fifties and sixties, the umland study had become a fashion which soon faded out without getting re-vigourated with the emerging dimensions of interaction between a city and its region. In all such studies, attempts were made to describe the nature of interaction between a city and its surrounding region. The scale considered was by and large meso; and, that is how, the micro level interactions of the city with its immediate surroundings and associated issues did not get desirable academic attention, especially from geographers. It needs no elaboration that the PUI, basically the outcome of interaction between the city and its hinterland, by and large corresponds to the primary umland.

We chose to replicate the same model of Prof. R.L. Singh (1955) without critically assessing the criteria and methodology employed by him and examining in different contexts.[1] It was enough to end a strong beginning due to the lack of life supporting oxygen in the form of fresh and innovative ideas. Geographers have an edge over the fellow workers in studying the spatial interactions and their consequences. But, alas! By treading on the path of others, we forgot our destination and lost own privileged bastion.

A random survey of the *Economic and Political Weekly (EPW)*[2], doctoral works at Banaras Hindu University[3] and two successive reports of (*Progress in Indian Geography*[4]) 2004 and 2008 too lend clear evidence to the fact that little attention has paid towards such zones, as observed by McGregor, Simon and Thompson (2006: 313-325). The following sub-section identifies and emphasises the need of taking up a few issues for the future studies of the PUIs.

Research Issues

Seeing the tempo of metropolitan growth in the developing countries of the Global South, the PUIs will expand by leaps and bounds. They should be taken as an emerging spectacular and special settlements in which the landscape elements as well as the nature of issues are so unique that they cannot be captured and dealt with full justice with the conventional academic view of taking the settlements and their problems simply as the binary opposites of rural-urban. The issues are multiple and often interlinked than not; thus, creating a complex web—quite challenging to disentangle and address adequately. An apt response needs a realistic (academic) understanding of the processes of change, scale of their impacts, and also their basic nuances as shown through a simplistic diagram in Fig. 2.1. The recent shifts and turns in Social Sciences in general, and Geography in particular, under the wider umbrella of post-modernism now present far more alternative approaches and methodologies than ever. However, the issues for future research could be broadly put into following non-exhaustive and suggestive heads:

1. Demographic Implication

Migration to the PUIs have got direct bearing on the composition of population and have several demographic implications expressed in terms of skewed age-sex structure, fertility and population growth, etc. So far, majority of the studies have largely dwelt upon demographic dimensions from the city-centric perspective. It is time to analyse the PUIs, demographics and their repercussions.

2. Land Use Changes

Of the important consequences of peri-urbanization, land use changes in the PUIs are most pertinent. Most visible change is from rural to urban, precisely speaking, from agricultural to non-agricultural. Fortunately, good many available studies on the PUIs, especially from the geographical perspective, deal with it. The scope for future studies lies in the process and implication dimensions which remain neglected due to obsession of geographic works with descriptive approach based on simple quantitative (secondary) information rather than analytical one. Similarly, lop-sided quantification needs to be replaced by a judicious blend of qualitative-quantitative methods complimented with modern techniques of GIS and remote sensing.

3. Economic Changes

In the process of peri-urbanization, the economic changes are inevitable but they are not formidable in all cases. To begin with, the changes in land use indicate change in the PUI economy which has to do with all the people there—may they be the original inhabitants or the new migrant settlers. The emergent research issues are sectoral shifts (agriculture→manufacturing→services—trade and transport); production system (and their changes); livelihoods: pattern, change, diversity, insecurity, risk and coping up issues; peri-urbanization *vis-à-vis* poor and poverty; impact of external (international and national) forces on the PUI economies, etc. These could be considered at various scales and wait to be attended by researchers.

4. Environmental Implications

Environmental issues in the PUIs range from biodiversity impacts, i.e.

loss of biodiversity due to expanding PUIs, to eco-environmental pressure. The land use and economic changes have severe environmental consequences for the PUIs. Often, the PUI space is used as dumping ground of urban municipal solid waste without caring for the stipulated safety measures. Resultantly, the PUI ecology becomes vulnerable and there is heavy pollution and environmental stress. That's why the PUIs have termed "environmentally choked" areas. Interestingly, there are ample indications, in (urban/municipal) solid waste management studies, of the poor-handling of such wastes; but, there is dearth of environmental studies from the PUIs' perspectives. Of course, a few studies like that of Agrawal, *et al.*, (2001) and Singh and Sen (2001) have tried to assess environmental impact in the PUIs. Still, there is a vast scope to understand this dimension from various perspectives.

5. Social and Cultural Consequences

The peri-urbanization exposes rural societies and their culture to several sudden transformations for which they are often not prepared. Sometimes, the land use changes bring in unexpected high income which gives rise to a variety of social consequences, both positive and negative. As a matter of fact, the socio-cultural impacts are least addressed by the academic geographers. Issues like contrast between original inhabitants in the traditional caste based occupations and new settlers with higher paid urban and modern occupations; relative deprivation, envy, conflict; contestation of the (original) social entity; household level consequences in the form of property sharing/division, intra-household conflict; crime and delinquency; gender consequences (disproportionate sex ratio, vulnerabilities like crime against women, etc.) could be profitably undertaken for deep and serious research works.

6. Resource Management

Changes in the land use, economy, environment and ecology are bound to take their toll on natural resources. Actually, they together directly affect natural resource quality and use, availability, and accessibility too. There are studies which have tried to analyse the impact of peri-urban resources impact on urban development (cf. Rohilla, 2005b) but the impacts of peri-urbanization on Common Property Resources (CPRs), e.g. village grazing land, forests and water bodies need to be analysed seriously. And, geographers' contribution is still awaited here.

7. Policy Implications: Administrative, Governance and Management

The PUIs are generally found lurching in doldrums. They are actually nobody's child. Experiences tell that there is no effective mechanism for their desirable administration and governance in the existing system. Since, they fall out of urban boundary; the municipal authorities technically cannot exercise their power, if they at all are willing. On the other hand, rural administration's instruments are inadequate and ineffective in handling "alien" emergent issues. It gives abundant scope to research into civic amenities and infrastructure requirement and available provision; prioritisation of peri-urban issues of governance and public policies; and, also the sustainability issues in PUIs by various disciplines including Geography.

Conclusion

Urbanisation in its complete sense leads to variety of consequences and hence manifested in more than one way. Urban expansion is one among them. Peri-urbanization is one of the specific phases of such urban expansion resulting into the emergence of the PUI. The PUI is different from other such zones found in the urban fringe or periphery precisely for the fact that it is not strictly a zone/area (immediately) at the city-edge and continuous. Unprecedented "urban explosion" in the developing world of the global South has rendered the PUIs there a typical character, dynamics and problems posing research challenges. Still, the PUIs impacts on people, places and environments are not the same, which gives a fertile ground for geographic harvests. Unfortunately, Geography like discipline having edge over such interdisciplinary issues has not been able to respond sufficiently. With the postmodern turn offering far more alternative approaches and methodologies, there is greater possibility of undertaking PUI studies in emerging directions—they may or may not mapable in the geographic sense. At the end, it is also relevant to think on whether we can develop a new specialisation as "Peri-Urban Interface Studies" for a holistic treatment and addressing the PUI issues in a focused manner?

Notes:

1. Perhaps it is only Ramachandran (1989, 272) who has questioned the criteria

used by R.L. Singh and observed that "....of the six criteria used, four do not constitute central place functions".

2. *EPW* is one of the highly circulated and active research magazines considered as the mirror of contemporary academic engagements, especially in social sciences and humanities.
3. BHU's department of Geography is perhaps the pioneer centre for urban studies.
4. *Progress in Indian Geography* is a country report brought out on behalf of the Indian National Science Academy (INSA) New Delhi and presented at the International Geographical Congress held every four years.

References

Agrawal, Madhoolika *et al*., (2001): Evaluation of air pollution impact on peri-urban agriculture around Varanasi city. *National Geographical Journal of India (NGJI)*, 47 (1-4): 73-80.

Dupont, Véronique (ed.) (2005): Peri-urban dynamics—population, habitat and environment on the peripheries of large Indian metropolises: A review of concepts and general issues. *CSH Occasional Paper* No. 14, CSH, New Delhi.

Dupont, Véronique and N. Sridharan, (2006): Peri-urban dynamics: Case studies in Chennai, Hyderabad and Mumbai. *CSH Occasional Paper* No. 17, CSH, New Delhi.

Fazal, Shahab, (2000): Urban expansion and loss of agricultural land—a GIS based study of Saharanpur City, India. *Environment and Urbanization*, 12(2): 133-149 (DOI: 10.1177/095624780001200211.

Gupta, Rahul and Sumita Gupta, Gangopadhyay, 2006. Peri-urban agriculture and aquaculture. *Economic and Political Weekly*, 41(18), May 06-May 12, 2006.

HUDCO-HSMI., (2001): *The State of Indian Cities 2001*. New Delhi: HUDCO-HSMI.

Iaquinta, David L. and Axel W. Drescher, (2000): Defining Peri-urban: Understanding Rural-Urban Linkages and their Connection to Institutional Contexts. Paper presented at the *Tenth World Congress*, IRSA, Rio, August 1, 2000.

Kaba, Oumar Salim Mohamed, (2007): Pilot project for the installation of domestic biogas in peri-urban zones of the city of Bamako. *International NGO Journal*, 2(3): 057-059.

Kaushik, S.P., 2006a. Impact of the development of farmhouses on the land aspects: A case study of peri-urban space of National Capital Territory of Delhi. *Transactions of the Institute of Indian Geographers*, 28(1): 67-75.

Kaushik, S.P., (2006b): Dynamics of the growth of farmhouses on Delhi's urban fringe. *NGJI*, 52 (1-2): 91-102.

Khairkar, Vijaya P., (2009): Recent trends and future directions in Urban Geography. In, Ravi S. Singh (ed.) *Indian Geography in the 21st Century: The Young Geographers Agenda*, Cambridge Scholars Publishing, New Castle upon Tynne, pp. 297-312.

Kumar, Sant, P.K. Joshi and Suresh Pal, 2003. Growing vegetables. *Economic and Political Weekly*, 38(08), February 16-February 22, 2003.

Mahadev, P.D. (ed.) (1986): *Contributions to Indian Geography: Urban Geography* (General Series Editor: R.P. Misra). Heritage Publishers, New Delhi.

McGee, T.G., (1991): The emergence of 'Desakota' Regions in Asia: Expanding a hypothesis. In N. Ginsberg (ed.) *The Extended Metropolis: Settlement Transition in Asia*. University of Hawaii Press, Honolulu, pp. 3-26.

Misra, H.N., (2004): Urban Geography. In H.N. Sharma (ed.) *Progress in Indian Geography 2000-2004*, Indian National Science Academy, New Delhi, pp. 54-61.

Misra, H.N., (2008): Urbanisation. In, Debendra Kumar Nayak (ed.) *Progress in Indian Geography 2004-2008*, Indian National Science Academy, New Delhi, pp. 46-50.

Moench, Marcus and Dipak Gyawali, 2008. Desakota: Reinterpreting the urban-rural continuum (available at *http://www.nerc.ac.uk/*, accessed on 15.5.2010).

Murgante, Beniamino Giuseppe Las Casas, Maria Danese, (2007): *The use of spatial statistics to analyze the peri-urban belt.* 10th AGILE International Conference on Geographic Information Science, Aalborg University, Denmark.

Nelson, Sara, (2007): *Farming on the fringes: Changes in agriculture, land use and livelihoods in peri-urban Dar es Salaam, Tanzania.* Honors Project, Department of Geography, Macalester College, Minnesota (USA).

Oliveau, Sébastien, (2005): Peri-urbanization in Tamil Nadu: A quantitative approach. *CSH Occasional Paper* No. 15, CSH, New Delhi.

Ramachandran, R., (1989): *Urbanization and Urban Systems in India.* Oxford University Press, New Delhi.

Ranganathan, Malini, Lalitha Kamath and Vinay Baindur, 2009. Piped water supply to Greater Bangalore: Putting the cart before the horse? *Economic and Political Weekly*, 44(33), August 15-August 21, 2009.

Reddy, V. Ratna and B. Suresh Reddy, (2007): Land alienation and local communities. *Economic and Political Weekly*, 42(31), August 04-August 10, 2007.

Rohilla, Suresh, (2005a): Defining 'Peri-urban'—A review. In, Véronique Dupont (ed.) Peri-urban dynamics: population, habitat and environment on the peripheries of large Indian metropolises: A review of concepts and general issues. *CSH Occasional Paper* No. 14, CSH, New Delhi, pp. 103-120.

Rohilla, Suresh K., (2005b): *Role of Ground Water in Urban Development: Case of Delhi and its peri-urban region*. Ph.D. dissertation in Geography, Queen's University, Belfast.

Sharpe, L.J., (1994): *The Government of World Cities—The Future of the Metro Model.* John Wiley and Sons, Chichester.

Shaw, Annapurna, (2005): Peri-urban interface of Indian cities. *Economic and Political Weekly*, 40(02), January 08-January 14, 2005, pp. 129-136.

Shekhar Shashi *et al.*, (2000): Changing face of the rural hinterland of a fast growing town. Case study: Gurgaon and its hinterland. *Indian Journal of Regional Science*, 32(1): 106-117.

Singh, R.B. and Singh, B.N., (2003): Land use transformation and crop substitution in peri-urban fringe of Varanasi. *NGJI*, 49(4): 17-30.

Singh, Arun K., (2009): Urbanisation, urban growth and urban management in India: Shifting paradigms. In, Ravi S. Singh (ed.) *Indian Geography in the 21st Century: The Young Geographers Agenda*, Cambridge Scholars Publishing, New Castle upon Tynne, pp. 313-332.

Singh, Nina, (2004): Settlement Geography. In, H.N. Sharma (ed.) *Progress in Indian Geography 2000-2004*, Indian National Science Academy, New Delhi, pp. 47-53.

Singh, R.L., 1955. *Banaras: A Study in Urban Geography*. Nand Kishore and Brothers, Banaras.

Singh, Rana P.B. and Chandra Sen, (2001): *The structure of peri-urban agricultural environment in Varanasi Development Region*, *NGJI*. (1-4): 61-72.

Singh, Surendra, (2008): Settlement. In, Debendra Kumar Nayak (ed.) *Progress in Indian Geography 2004-2008*, Indian National Science Academy, New Delhi, pp. 44-45.

Somda, Jacques, Mulumba Kamuanga and Éric Tollens, (2006): Resources endowment, income distribution and needs for technologies among peri-urban smallholders in the Gambia. *Biotechnol. Agron. Soc. Environ.* 10 (3), 229-236.

United Nations, (2004): *World Urbanization Prospects: The 2003 Revision*, United Nations (Department of Economic and Social Affairs: Population Division), New York.

Yasmeen, Gisele, (2001): Urban Agriculture in India: A Survey of Expertise, Capacities and Recent Experience. *CFP Report 32*, International Development Research Centre, South Asia Regional Office, New Delhi, India.

3

Trade-off between Development and Agriculture Related Land Use of Rural-Urban Fringes: A Quest for Compatibility

Soumyendra Kishore Datta and *Krishanu Sarkar*

Introduction

In view of rapid changes in urban tastes and preferences for specific accommodation and infrastructure facilities as well as spread of the culture of consumerism there has been a recent trend worldwide for industrial expansion and real estate development along the urban fringes (lands located around developed areas of the city but still within municipal limits). It has been found that the owners of industries or real estate developers generally prefer fringe area of cities/towns to take advantage of easy transport of necessary inputs and delivery of finished products through the network of transport connection as well as some open and spacious area that these places are blessed with. The fringe areas usually border with a rural ambience which may or may not be inhabited by a rather sizeable population depending on the texture, quality and productivity of the soil and adjacent terrain.

Urban development focusing on residential, commercial and industrial development and agricultural expansion create competing demands on a limited land base in the urban fringe. Apart from competing land requirements, the different user groups often get locked into conflict unless their hopes and desires are not properly addressed to in planned negotiation. For instance, urban and country-residential dwellers often cherish the desire to have access to cosy and comfortable residential structures, availability of multiple services and amenities, efficient transport and communication infrastructure, open space to have recreational breath and have limited experience and forbearance of inhabiting in an agricultural neighbourhood. Development of agriculture on the other hand require relatively unhindered access on the part of the farmers, to fertile lands, water for irrigation, supplies of necessary inputs and implements, roads convenient for conveying cartloads of harvest and heavy machinery, as well as protection from undesirable intrusion by people not associated with agricultural activities. Agricultural activities carried on in urban fringes may often involve some untoward experience in the midst of conflicting forces of urban expansion and maintaining a rural ambience. There may arise different types of problems that may have to be faced by farmers operating at urban fringes, some of which may be of the following types.

Right-to-Farm Issues—Farmers at the urban fringe often feel that their representation in municipal governance is relegated backside as they are overpowered both politically and socially by a number of other interest groups of land users who have neither the will nor the motivation to accommodate the interest of the farming population. They are hardly aware of the importance and potential of complementary and competitive existence of farm and non-farm sector in the fringe areas.

Expanding Urban Populations and Land Speculation—Burgeoning growth in urban population creates pressure on increased housing and infrastructure needs as well as diversification and proliferation of industrial base in order to cater to the culture of urban consumerism. Expansion of urbanization always takes place at the cost an irretrievable impact on the converted agricultural land. This in turn, affects surrounding agricultural land values by raising the speculative value of land based on an assumption that this growth trend will continue into the future. The spiralling impact of the lure of a speculative profit earning motive often leads to receding of farming lines with the penetrative impact of industrial/real estate development activities.

Preference for Outskirts Living and Land-Fragmentation—With the increasing choice and preference of people to live outside cities and then commute to into urban centres as a lifestyle preference, the phenomenon of sub-division of agricultural lands for country-residential development, sometimes referred to as 'rurbanization,' is becoming more common now-a-days. The relatively lower land prices at the outskirts and availability of relatively more open space have caught the attention of new settlers with the consequential stress on agricultutal lands. The limit to this tempo is likely to be set by the prohibitive commuting cost from peripheral residential areas to urban centres.

Demand for Tourism and Recreation Activities—Increasing demand for more of outdoor recreational amenities for city dwellers has an untoward impact on the agricultural lands located around the municipalities and suburban areas. Inroads by tourist parties from nearby towns/cities often leave a lasting scar on the serenity and freshness of the farming environment.

Dumping Sites at Fringe Areas—Specified urban fringe areas are often marked and used as dumping sites of urban municipal and industrial solid wastes which often contain biodegradable as well as non-biodegradable wastes. While the former part does not cause a great concern, the latter form may sometimes get littered in agricultural land through winds, storms and rains. This throws a great problem in terms of reducing farm productivity as well as soil-fertility loss.

Interest and importance in protecting farmland arises in part from desires to maintain crop production and food security together with the manifold rural amenity values perceived by the citizens who want to protect farmland to preserve non-market benefits as listed below:

Environmental Amenities

- Open space
- Soil conservation
- Biodiversity
- Wildlife habitat
- Recreational opportunities
- Scenic views
- Isolation from congestion
- Watershed protection
- Flood control
- Groundwater recharge

Rural Development Amenities

- Rural income and employment
- Viable rural communities
- Preservation of local traditional knowledge
- Diversified local economy

These rural amenities are often a by-product of the agricultural production process. Ensuring the continued availability of these rural amenities may be the most important reason for farmland protection, especially for farmland protection near urban areas.

The dynamics of trade-off between use of urban fringes for industrial/ real estate development and protecting it for agricultural growth may be well focused on the basis of the following model.

Analysis of Alternative Use of Urban Fringes: A Dynamic Optimization Model

Here we consider a very simple model similar to the type used by Parks (1995) in explaining alternative uses of urban fringe areas. We assume that the socio-economic planner can take the policy decision regarding converting a defined stock of agricultural land resources (in urban fringe areas) T_t at time t, which may be put to industrial or real estate or infrastructure development operation. For the sake of simplicity of analytical presentation, henceforth these operations are classified under industrial head. The benefit at time t from maintaining aforesaid landstock T_t for agricultural purposes is given by $\pi_A(T_t)$. Benefits from land used for industrial/developmental activities at time t is given by $\pi_I(R_t)$ where R_t stands for the land stock used for industrial purposes. Environmental benefits that may be derived from maintaining agricultural land is indicated by $\pi_E(T_t)$. Clearance of marginal agricultural land for industrial use is assumed to involve certain cost of C_t per unit of agricultural land while the amount of converted agricultural land at time t is indicated by a_t.

Now the economic planner is assumed to maximise the present value of net benefits from extraction of both agriculture and industrial activities (in urban-rural fringes) by choosing the optimum level of agricultural land to be converted to industrial purposes. So he maximises

$$\int_0^{\infty}[\pi_A(T_t)+\pi_1(R_t)+\pi_E(T_t)-C_t a_t]e^{-rt}\,dt \text{ by choosing } a_t \qquad \dots(1)$$

subject to the following agricultural and industrial land resource dynamics

$$dT_t / dt = -a_t \qquad \dots(2)$$

$$dR_t / dt = a_t \qquad \dots(3)$$

The current value Hamiltonian of the aforesaid problem stated in linear control variable a_t stands as

$$H=\pi_A(T_t)+\pi_1(R_t)+\pi_E(T_t)-C_t a_t-\lambda_{Tt} a_t+\lambda_{It} a_t \qquad ...(4)$$

where $\lambda_{Tt}, \lambda_{It}$ indicate shadow prices of agricultural land and industrial land respectively at year t. Applying the maximum principle we have

$$a_t = a_{\max}, if\, \partial H' \partial a_t = -C_t - l_{Tt} + l_{It} > 0, \qquad ...(5)$$

$$a_t = 0, if\, \partial H / \partial a_t = -C_t - \lambda_{Tt} + \lambda_{1t} < 0, \qquad ...(6)$$

$$and\; a_t = a_t{}^*\; if\, \partial H / \partial a_t = -C_t - \lambda_{Tt} = 0, \qquad ...(7)$$

Implication is that if the net shadow value of a unit of land $-C_t + \lambda_{It}$, after conversion for industrial purposes, exceeds the opportunity cost of agricultural land λ_{Tt}, then all the agricultural land at the margin tends to be cleared for industrial purpose. There is no basis for the re-conversion to industrial purpose if the reverse inequality holds. There is often found a tendency among planners to consider the multiple spread effect benefits from land for industrial use at a premium value compared to the low value benefits that may be available from heterogeneous qualities of agricultural land. And if the available tangible benefits from agriculture are perceived to be of little value compared to that in industrial use, all the agricultural land (in the defined area) tend to be cleared very quickly despite its function as carbon sequestrator, maintenance of bio-diversity, amenity value, psychological/attachment value etc. This involves a bang-bang solution due to the linearity of the Hamiltonian on a_t.

The last case i.e. $a_t = a_t{}^*$ becomes relevant when conversion of agricultural lands (considered as an aggregate entity) to industrial use takes place only up to a certain level where the net shadow value of an additional unit in industrial use equals the marginal opportunity cost for some unit of agricultural land at time t. In order to understand the steady state condition for agricultural land conversion we consider the adjoint equation in the form

$$d\lambda_{Tt} / dt = r\lambda_{Tt} - \partial H / \partial T_t = r\lambda_{Tt} - [\partial\pi_A / \partial T_t + \partial\pi_E / \partial_{Tt}] \qquad ...(8)$$

$$\text{Or}\, r(\lambda_{It} - C_t = [\partial\pi_A / \partial_{Tt} + \partial\pi_E / \partial_{Tt}] + d\lambda_{Tt} / dt \qquad ...(9)$$

as $\lambda_{Tt} = \lambda_{It} - C_t$ when $\partial H / \partial a_t = 0$.

and $d\lambda_{It} / dt = r\lambda_{It} - \partial H / \partial R_t = r\lambda_{It} - \partial\pi_1 / \partial R_t$

At the steady state shadow value of industrial land does not change so that we have $d\lambda_{It} / dt = 0$ implying

$$r\lambda_{It} = \partial\pi_1 / \partial R_t$$

Putting this value in equation (9) we get

$$\partial\pi_1 / \partial R_t - rC_t = [\partial\pi_A / \partial_{Tt} + \partial\pi_E / \partial_{Tt}] + d\lambda_{Tt} / dt \qquad ...(10)$$

In the steady state however, opportunity cost of agricultural land does not change (i.e. $d\lambda_{Tt} / dt = 0$) so that optimal condition for agricultural land conversion at steady state appears as

$$\partial\pi_1 / \partial R_t - rC_t = [\partial\pi_A / \partial_{Tt} + \partial\pi_E / \partial_{Tt}] \qquad ...(11)$$

The implication is that net marginal benefit from land in industrial use should be equal to the foregone marginal benefit from agricultural land.

Following the basic logic of this argument, we can say that so long as the net marginal benefits from industrial land use exceed the combined marginal benefits from agricultural uses and environmental benefit, conversion of agricultural land would continue to occur and the socially efficient rate of conversion to industrial use at any time t occurs when the aforesaid marginal benefits from land converted to industry is equated to of foregone marginal benefit from agricultural land, as expressed in the last equation.

It might reasonably be expected that the marginal agricultural benefits and environmental benefits would go up as the remaining agricultural land resources becomes smaller and smaller because of urban proliferation to rural areas. This is likely to lessen the rate of conversion of agricultural land to industry. But this effect might be countered by a rise in the value of marginal net benefit from land converted to industrial use resulting from higher pressure on industry associated with an increasing population and higher incomes. If the process is repeated period after period, this might eventually result in all the agricultural land being converted to industry. Moreover, given the fact that environmental benefits (being non-marketable in nature) are often not perceived and hence tend to be neglected, the likelihood of all the specified stock of agricultural land being converted to industry is all the more strengthened. This view comes closer to the bang-bang solution implied in $a_t = a_{max.}$ Empirically, considering the case of U.S.A. metropolitan cities, it has been observed that conversion of farmland and open space on the rural-urban fringe has been growing faster than population growth in the suburban areas. There is little question that if present high rates of conversion continue, entire regions in some parts of the East, South, and far West will be empty of the farms and agricultural industries once located at those places. This finding accords well with the theoretical nicety of bang-bang solution.

The fact that non-consideration of environmental benefit of agricultural land leads to speedy and larger scale conversion of these land resources to industrial uses, can be demonstrated by the following diagram. We may reasonably assume that as conversion of agricultural to industrial land rises, the marginal benefit of remaining agricultural land rises and *vice versa*. Symmetrically with rises in converted industrial land its net marginal benefit falls and *vice versa*. In the following diagram converted industrial land is measured along the horizontal axis while available agricultural land resources are measured along the reverse direction of the horizontal axis. The more agricultural land is converted to industry, the less is the available agricultural land.

Accordingly the net marginal benefit schedule of land converted to industry (MB^I) is downward sloping one while the marginal benefit schedule of available agricultural land in rural fringes is MB^{A+E} (composed of both agricultural output benefit and environmental benefit) and

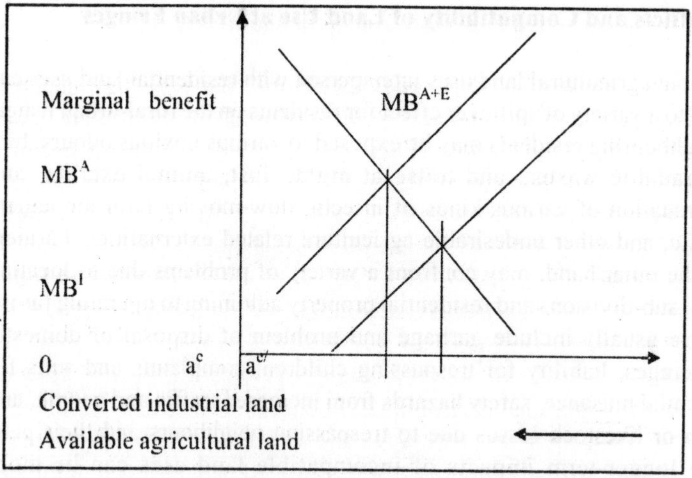

presented as an upward one as the axis has been defined. For simplicity the marginal benefit schedules are represented by straight lines.

The socially optimal allocation of agricultural land at any time period *t* requires that marginal benefit from agricultural land and associated environmental benefit taken together coincides with the marginal net benefit of land converted to industrial production. In the diagram this occurs at point a^e on the horizontal axis. However, if the component of opportunity cost associated with allocating land to industrial use in terms of foregone environmental benefit of agricultural land is not taken into account, then the MB^{A+E} curve shifts down to MB^A (without the environmental benefit component). As a result, the new equilibrium through intersection of MB^A and MB^I occurs to the right of the old equilibrium, at a point (say)$a^{e/}$, indicating that more of agricultural land is converted to industrial use. The underlying reason is that exclusion of environmental benefit from agricultural land lowers the marginal benefit from agricultural use. In order to establish the optimum condition, marginal net benefit of agricultural land needs to be lowered which requires conversion of more agricultural land for industrial purposes (because of the assumption of diminishing marginal benefits). The greater the degree of marginal environmental benefit and its non-consideration, the greater will be the rate of conversion of rural agricultural fringes into industrial use. Besides this if the MB^I curve be relatively flatter (resulting from a slower rate of decrease of marginal net benefit of land converted to industry), then also use of rural agricultural fringes for industrial use is likely to occur at a higher rate.

Conflicts and Compatibility of Land Use at Urban Fringes

Certain agricultural land uses interspersed with residential land uses can lead to a variety of spillover effect for residents on the rural-urban fringe. Neighbouring residents may be exposed to various noxious odours, biodegradable wastes, and noise at night, dust, animal excreta, and depredation of various kinds of insects, slow-moving farm implement traffic, and other undesirable agriculture related externalities. Farmers on the other hand, may confront a variety of problems due to locating rural sub-divisions and residential property adjoining to operating farms. These usually include garbage and problem of disposal of domestic sewerages, liability for trespassing children, complaints and suits for potential nuisance, safety hazards from increased traffic and people, and crop or livestock losses due to trespassing neighbours and their pets. The longer-term impacts of incompatible land uses can be more substantial for agriculture on the rural-urban interface than for agriculture in the hinterland. As the demand for urban development land rises on the fringe, some farmers become land speculators who sell out to the highest bidder. Their unexpected fabulous earnings can be used to maintain them on the basis of simply the returns from invested assets in banks or to establish farming operations at a new, more distant location leaving their traditional land exposed to uncertain uses. In the process, traditional markets for the agricultural supply and marketing industries become less profitable and competitive on the fringe. The remaining farmers are likely to face increasing financial squeezes between output prices and input costs. Farmers located in the path of development are less likely to make large investments to expand operations. These farmers are also less likely to incur depreciation expenses for replacing out-of-date or worn out farm structures and equipments. Some studies throw light on aspects of underutilized and idled land developed near and between larger urban areas, due to the impermanence of agriculture on the rural-urban fringe. At the same time, not all agricultural activity is incompatible with urban development, while some small size industrial activities requiring less of land areas compared to large ones may be integrated with agricultural development in the web of backward and forward linkages. Increasing demand for processed and semi-processed agro-products generates wide opportunities and new markets for horticultural products, orchards, and farmer markets for fresh produce. The processing industries may be of a wide variety like soybean processing, honey and floriculture, herbal processing, fishery processing, dairy processing, fruit and vegetable processing industries etc. The rural-urban fringe areas seem eminently suitable for converting raw agricultural products into final marketable form with the rural hinterlands providing raw materials while urban areas providing the easily reachable outlets of market for such processed items. However, supplying these markets requires a subtle shift in the farmer's focus. In contrast to traditional farm commodity marketing systems, diversification through improved form of packaging, labelling and other value added techniques for retailing through discount stores, super-markets, convenience stores etc. as well as direct marketing skills become extremely important as farmers begin to interact in a market with a sophisticated customer base and niche markets. Again locating some small scale agro/forest based industries, food processing units, oil pressing, cotton ginning, flour milling with not a great intervention in agriculture and environmental amenities, can serve to promote agricultural productivity in adjoining region in an integrated network.

Concluding Observation and Policy Recommendation

Town and Village Enterprises (TVE) for Rural Industrialisation based on Chinese model can have a great impact in forging the hiatus between developmental efforts and agricultural activities in urban fringes. TVE model focuses on two-way nexus: Focus on agricultural output together with farm machinery tools, maintenance service, and fertilizer, industrial inputs, agro-processing units and locally needed consumer goods. The establishment of a community-based initiative that promotes locally grown agricultural items linked with a chain of processing industries, and which is concerned with social justice, economic equity and environmental sustainability seems to be a compatible solution at the urban fringes. Changes in tastes and preference in favour of processed food items throw open the possibility of connecting the consumers directly with local farmers, value-added processors and retailers thus enabling the system to challenge corporate consolidation of the food industry while protecting the interest of both the agriculturists and small firm producers. Growing health consciousness among people have been the driving force behind the emergence of niche markets especially for "green products" and thus linking them to farmers operating at their doorsteps in the fringe areas.

In recent times emergent focal priority amongst municipal officials, regional planners and socio-economic groups across the globe has been to promote and design communities that meet a variety of needs by incorporating a mixture of land uses within neighbourhoods and by using land resources more efficiently at the regional scale. Farmland constitutes one of the significant components of green infrastructure resources that provide economic and environmental benefits within cities by contributing to reduce emission of green-house gases and preventing toxic pollutants damaging to the environment. Again concepts of eco-municipality extended to fringe areas utilizing local resources and interfacing with imported substances in an eco-friendly and self-sustaining manner holds great prospect towards attaining sustainability. This is also largely conditioned by the involvement of local youth as well as women in decision-making, planning, implementation, monitoring and adaptation.

Apart from this any step for undertaking industrial programme in fringe areas of towns/cities should focus on—

(a) Proper land mapping followed by analysis of soil quality.
(b) Decentralization in management.
(c) Liaison and interaction at grass roots level with agriculturists.
(d) Direct bargaining with the farmers and owners of agricultural land.
(e) Generation of adequate alternative employment for people thrown out of agriculture.
(f) Provision of adequate compensation for agricultural land based on the opportunity cost of foregone perennial source of income.
(g) Pressurizing for donation from industrial owners for social sector development.

Again imprudent and unplanned intervention in rural-urban fringes may have irreversible and irretrievable impact on rural amenities that often appear to be associated with agricultural production process. The imperative to ensure sustained availability of these rural amenities may be the most important reason for farmland protection, especially near urban areas.

The effects of farmland protection on the provision of rural amenities has received little attention. Despite the numerous programmes nationwide to protect rural open space and to preserve farmland, very little is definitively known about which individual rural amenities taxpayers really care about when they support farmland protection programmes. Given the non-market existence, option and bequest values of rural amenities attendant to farmland protection programmes, conducting contingent valuation exercises can be most pragmatic in assessing the preservation priorities and ranking of rural amenities on the part of the public.

This strategy holds implications for the set of amenities that are likely to be preserved in these programmes. For example, emphasizing protection of cropland *versus* pastureland yields different scenic views, and has different implications for water quality, wildlife habitat, and other environmental amenities. It also implies a trade-off between long-term survival of some form of agriculture, at the possible cost of providing a mix of rural amenities that is less than optimal today.

Prospect of profitable use of land for production of traditional commodities is often not perceived by farmers especially when significant pressures from urban developers or other industries raise land values. The highest-and-best-use, in terms of economic profitability, may often be not to use the land for agricultural purposes but to sell it for urban or industrial development. This is likely to be relevant in low productive mono-cropped areas.

There is often a tendency among planners to consider agricultural land values from the perspective of its short-term economic benefits only compared to the multifaceted benefits of industrial or other developmental programmes. Urban development and industrial uses almost always command much higher returns than agricultural uses, meaning that the preservation issue of lands for agricultural production is relegated backside. Hence it seems imperative to consider the agricultural land character and map it according to its different graded values, instead of reducing analyses to short-term economic considerations alone. This is crucial for comparing its potential with a contemplated developmental project for fostering a socially and economically beneficial and compatible solution of land uses at urban fringes.

References

Adelman, M.A., Jon Roe and D.B. Patton (1999). *Land Use Conflict: When City and Country Clash*, A Project of National Public Policy Education Committee in Cooperation with Farm Foundation.

Clouser, R.L. and Stephen Gran (2009). Issues at the Rural-Urban Fringe: Hillsborough County Agriculture Stewardship Programme, part of *a* series titled *Issues at the Rural-Urban Fringe*.

http://edis.ifas.ufl.edu/TOPIC_SERIES_Issues_at_the_Rural_Urban_Fringe.

Datta, S.K., (2005). "Sustainable Development: Context, Concept and Related Issues" in *Environment: Science and Thought edited* by Arabindo Das, ACB Publication, Kolkata.

Hite, Jim. (1998). *Land Use Conflicts on the Urban Fringe: Causes and Potential Resolution.* Prepared by the Strom Thurmond Institute. http://www.strom.clemson.edu/publications/hite/landuse-hite.pdf

Iqbal, B.A., (2006). Agro-Industries: Key to Economic Progress, *Kurukshetra*, Vol. 54, No. 4.

4

Sustainable Rural-Urban Fringe: Nature, Causes and Solutions

Halima Sadia Rizvi and *S.A.M. Rizvi*

Introduction

The concept of sustainability emphasizes that the process of consumption patterns should be such that it not only fulfils the needs of the present, but preserves the resources for the future generations to use. Sustainable rural-urban fringe is one such important element in the process of utilization of the most prominent, fixed and essential resource-land. Almost all human activities depend on land—agricultural land, residential land, industrial land, waterways, common lands, etc.

Land use is the ability of human beings to manage their eco-system in order to satisfy some of their needs. Ecology *versus* economy has attained a plethora of debate and discussion in the academic circles. While the significance of economic development cannot be undermined, the cost of degradation of ecology is extremely high and it destroys the very concept of sustainability. Ecology or protection of environment even at any cost for the present must be undertaken as otherwise it might as well destroy the survival of the present leave apart the protection of the future.

The history of environment studies of the present times reveals that never before in the earlier centuries has ecology been so very much abused or misused and it is one of the most important reasons why at world forums the debate on environmental protection issues has attained so much of significance.

The rural-urban fringe is one such important issue of environmental degradation where there is a forward movement [backward movement] of land encroachment. The rural-urban land fringe in India has both the directions and while it is very clear that the urban expansion into the rural areas is referred to as land fringe, the movement from rural to urban is often termed as creation of hinterlands.

The history of rural-urban fringe in India has its evolution with the industrialization in India since independence after the Second Five Year Plan.

When India attained Independence in 1947, nearly 70 per cent of its then population was predominantly living in the rural areas; agriculture being the most predominant occupation. The villages of India were basically self-sufficient in the sense that the demands of the indigenous rural population were very few and were satisfied through supply of goods and services produced within the villages themselves.

The village culture was independent, artisans used their indigenous skills in the production of crafts and products through generations, utilized mostly within the village and their fewer exchanges *via* barter were also satisfied within peripheral limits. This led Pandit Jawaharlal Nehru to state that 'India lives in its villages'.

The attainment of independence and with it the formation of socialistic pattern of society meant that India provide magnitude of opportunities to its teaming millions. With planning and emphasis on agriculture-led growth strategy during the First Five Year Plan agriculture, land use, irrigation, land classification, land management and peripheral issues assumed significance. However, our predominant village culture, the strong and powerful prevalence of the centuries old *zamindari* system was unprepared for this immediate socio-institutional and economic transformation. While India was able to attain food self-sufficiency, it is overall rural areas were gradual to attain development.

The geographical extent of land in our country is finite and its optimal utilization is warranted. The total geographical area is 328.73 m. ha. and 305.8 m. ha. is the reporting area for land utilization purpose. In the last forty years, net area sown is constant around 140 m. ha. The net sown area, however, increased from 118.75 m. ha. in 1950-51 to 140.27 m. ha. in 1970-71. The area under non-agricultural use also increased to 8.0 per cent from 3.3 per cent and the area under barren and uncultivated land has been decreased to 5.8 per cent from 13.4 per cent during 1950-51 to 2007-08. However, forest area has increased to 22.8 per cent from 14.2 per cent during the same period. The area under the non-agricultural use such as common land, hinterland, forests and unsown and uncultivated barren land and deserts form the rest of the area of our land.

The net irrigated land and gross irrigated areas have increased nearly two and three folds, from 20.85 m. ha. to 55.10 m. ha. and 22.56 m. ha. to 76.82 m. ha. respectively in the years 1950-51 to 2007-08. Due to increase in irrigation, introduction of new crops and early maturing varieties cropping density increased from 111 per cent in 1950-51 to 137 per cent at the moment. Consequently, gross cropped area also increased from 131.89 per cent in 1950-51 to over 190 per cent at present. The conversion of good quality of land from non-agriculture to agriculture purposes have compensated for increasing cultivation and agricultural production has marginally increased.

The conversion of good quality of agriculture to other non-agriculture purpose has been compensated by increasing cultivation in forest areas and other inhospitable terrain which were unused till now. It is a fact that a large area under very poor quality marginal land is being cultivated in large parts of central and north-east India. As a matter of fact, if the net sown area has not shown, much decrease, it is possibly because of the marginal lands are being brought under the plough.

Presently, the research focus is on the dynamics of land use. Land represents an important resource for the economic life of a majority of people in the world. The way people handle and use land resource is decisive for their social and economic well-being as well as for the sustained quality of land resources. Land use, however, is not only a realm of those directly using it; it is exposed to a part of the wider reality of social and economic development and change. Land use, therefore, is a highly dynamic process. This implies that policy discussion and development planning need to be based on a sound understanding of these dynamics.

If, in the future, human requirements are to be met in a sustainable manner, it is essential to resolve these conflicts now and move towards more effective and efficient use of land and natural resources. Integrated physical land use planning and management are an eminent method of achieving this. By examining all uses of land in an integrated manner, it makes it possible to minimize conflicts, to make the most efficient trade-offs and to link social and economic development with environmental protection and enhancement, thus helping to achieve the objectives of sustainable development. The essence of the integrated approach finds expression in the coordination of the sectoral planning and management activities concerned with the various aspects of land use and land resources. Land resources are used for a variety of purposes which interact and may compete with one another, therefore, it is desirable to plan and manage all uses in an integrated manner. Integration should take place at two levels, considering, on the one hand, all environmental, social and economic factors and on the other, all environmental and resource components together (i.e., air, water, biota, land geological and natural resources). Integrated consideration facilitates appropriate choices and trade-offs, thus maximizing sustainable productivity and use.

Case for Land Use Policy

It is well established fact that 80 per cent of the world's population lives in countries where agriculture and land are primary sources of earning and livelihood. In these countries the rising trend of land degradation is a distinct feature. Deforestation, inadequate land use, unsuitable farming and grazing practices, demographic pressure, lack of appropriate and improved technologies, poor markets and other legal institutional faults are the main cause of this. And this is, indeed, a concern for all in terms of food security and sustainable development.

Conflict over land use has become inevitable. The rise in population has put more pressure on arable land, grazing, forestry, wildlife, tourism and urban development. It is estimated that the population dependent on land for food, fuel and employment will double within next 50 years. Most of the land available to meet current and future food requirements is already in production, any further expansion must necessarily involve fragile and marginal lands. This is particularly so in developing countries where population growth is high, poverty is endemic and existing institutional capacity for land management is weak. In spite of this knowledge the question is why land use planning is not a reality even now.

The World economy which is presently dictated by urbanization, industrialization and other development activities, is outstripping the land capability. As a result, serious concerns of land and environmental degradation and declining productivity growth rate have come into prominence the world over, in recent years. Approximately 5-7 million hectares of usable lands are lost every year through land degradation, and 2 billion ha of land are already degraded due to various causes. The relative influence of soil degradation is estimated at 39 per cent in Asia, 25 per cent in Africa, 12 per cent in South America, 11 per cent in Europe and 5 per cent in Oceania. India plagued with high population and poverty, rank very high among the developing countries. Half a billion people in developing countries live in arid regions with no access to irrigation systems. Another 400 million are living on land with soils unsuitable for agriculture, 200 million in slope-dominated regions, and more than 130 million in fragile forest ecosystems. These areas covering an estimated 73 per cent of Earth's land surface face significant problems for agriculture investment and have limited ability to sustain growing populations. Sensitive to land use patterns, they are particularly vulnerable to degradation, erosion, floods, and landslides.

One-quarter of the people in developing countries, 1.3 billion in all survive on fragile lands, area that present significant constraints for intensive agriculture and where the people's links to the land are critical for the sustainability of communities, pastures, forest and other natural resources. The least productive area should have been abandoned first, as people migrate out to better opportunities. While some people have left, many remain behind and others are migrating in (the estimated population on fragile lands has doubled since 1950) improving their livelihoods is essential for meeting many of the Millennium Development Goals for the coming decades.

People living on fragile lands are vulnerable but have a modest portfolio of assets that can help bring them out of poverty: the land, traditional social capital, human capital, and indigenous knowledge and know-how. However, the potential productivity of even these assets has not been fully developed by either local or national institution. Living in disperse settlement and working in the informal or subsistence economy, people on the rural periphery are largely invisible to decision-makers. As a result, institutions have not been picking up social and environmental distress signals from the periphery—nor have these institutions been able to balance interests in setting their development agendas. For the past 50 years, the governments and private sector have focused the bulk of their attention and agricultural spending on the development of lands with commercial potential even though much of the rural population remains on marginal land.

Population pressure on arable land in Asia is considerable and growing. Severe land degradation affects some 35 per cent of productive land. The result has been to put more population pressure on the Inner Asian dry lands. Most affected are Afghanistan, China, India, and Pakistan and Inner Asia's high steppe, the largest remaining pastureland in the world, which includes Mongolia, north-western China, and parts of Siberia. Over thousands of years, these grasslands have been home to nomadic herders of horses, camels, goats, sheep, and cattle, practicing elaborate systems of seasonal pasture rotation across wide stretches of land in response to climate fluctuation.

Then there is a larger issue which humanity is confronting today. It is a self-generated environmental crisis. The patterns and ever accelerating pace of economic development has been in conflict with the environment for quite some time now, and if this trend continues, the cumulative effects of population increase, resource depletion and degradation of the environment will take a heavy toll. Statistics accumulated over the years show clearly deterioration in global resources. Our air, soil and water are getting polluted; there is ozone depletion in the upper part of the atmosphere while accumulation in the lower part is leading to global warming. Something must be done urgently and on a large enough scale to arrest this deterioration. There is need for an agreed agenda of action promoting an all-encompassing concept of sustained development in order to ensure that the needs of the present generation are met without compromising the ability of the future generations to meet their own needs. This implies a commitment not to damage or destroy the basic life support system of our planet 'Earth', namely, the air, water, the soil and the biological system. Development must be economically sustainable to ensure a continuous flow of goods and services derived from the earth's natural resources to all generations.

Water is also one of the most critical of natural resources. This precious gift of nature is the essence of the life and the cradle of life on our planet. Throughout the wide spectrum of historical experience, we find that civilization were born and flourished around water sources. Water crisis have precipitated social and political turmoil throughout human history; and for good reason. Life cannot be sustained without water. Moreover, it is a crucial input for development.

There is a growing water crisis today. One can understand the scarcity of water where nature has withheld its bounties, but there should be none as a result of mismanagement of the available. Water engineers and scientists are confronted with challenges of sustainable development and have the responsibility to meet these challenges both at the macro-level of overall demand and supply and at the micro-level by designing, operating and maintaining water resources and water projects in a manner consistent with the objective of sustainability.

Indian Perspective on Land Use and Rural-Urban Land Fringes

Indian economy is predominantly an agricultural economy, even in

2009. Nearly two-thirds of its population is directly or indirectly associated with agriculture. Following the successful completion of the First Five Year Plan, planners in India diverted their attention towards industrialization of the economy. This had important reasons from generating higher growth rates to creating employment opportunities for its masses to producing goods and services in large scale and more than most to prove the emergence of India in the world arena as an important industrially developing nation.

The process of industrialization with great emphasis on basic heavy and capital goods public sector enterprises in certain parts of the country due to reasons more political and institutional rather than economic and viable resource availability options created regional disparities, besides creation of haphazard industrial clusters. This in-turn led to huge migration of rural population into unplanned and unorganized industrial areas. The culmination of which has been creation of many crowd and unmanageable industrial, residential settlements with unlimited peripheral problems.

India during the Second Five Year Plan (1956-1961) generated output and created employment opportunities to a number of people which led to movement of labour force towards the new towns and emerging urban areas. There was substantial migration of population to some of the prominent cities such as Bombay, Calcutta, Delhi and Madras and over the decades, this migration and movement hassled to creation of hundreds of towns and cities.

India, with only 2.3 per cent of world's total land area is supporting 18 per cent and 15 per cent of world's human and livestock population, respectively. The per capita arable land in the country is only 0.15 ha and it is expected to come down to 0.08 ha. by 2025. The increasing pressure on the scarce soil resource and unscientific practices adopted for short-term gains to meet the mounting multiple demands has led to overexploitation and degradation of these resources. Long-term sustained productivity is being ignored for short-term gains.

It is a paradoxical situation that on the one hand, more production is required from the scarce soil resources for meeting the demand of ever expanding population, on the other hand vast areas are either going out of cultivation or showing alarming reduction in productivity due to land degradation at an alarming rate. Therefore, reclamation of the degraded lands and prevention of any further degradation of land, are among the serious national challenges.

As per the recent estimates of National Bureau of Soil Survey and Land Use Planning, out of a total of 146.5 million ha of degraded land, water erosion affects 103.9 million ha, wind erosion 13.1 million ha physical deterioration 12.23 million ha, chemical deterioration 10.3 million ha and deterioration due to other complex problems is 7.2 million ha.

On the other hand, the water resources in the country are unevenly distributed, spatially and temporarily. Rainfall is erratic and most of the rainfalls in four months of the monsoon season. The problem is compounded by the unnecessary/inefficient use of water, both surface and groundwater. This has led to waterlogging and soil salinity: the groundwater table has fallen in many areas and the numbers of dark blocks/areas have increased. The challenge before us is how to conserve and relocate rainwater, so that four months rainwater can be utilized for twelve months for multiple uses. Rainwater harvesting is what will push agricultural productivity, create employment and hence eradicate poverty.

Since land is a state subject, the Centrally Sponsored scheme on Strengthening of State Land Use Board (SLUB) was launched in 1983. From November 2000, onwards, this scheme is being implemented in the states through the Macro Management of Agriculture.

All the states have constituted SLUB under the chairmanship of Chief Ministers. However, any serious discussion on land use is avoided because of the conflicting interests and decisive action are difficult to arrive at which has to a very great extent hampered the utilization of land for productive purposes.

India, still does not have good National Land Use Policy. Even though some policy guidelines prepared way back in 1983 under the chairmanship of the Prime Minister has taken up certain issues there exists substantial scope for better utilization of land for productive purposes.

Main Objectives of Land Use Policy

- Resource use efficiency to meet the growing consumption needs.
- To restore productivity of degraded lands.
- Suitable institutional mechanism for scientific management, conservation and development of land resources.
- Plan and resource linkages for land related programme.
- Expansion of effective forest cover to restore ecological balance.
- Conjunctive use of surface and groundwater resources.
- Preservation of prime agricultural land.
- Translate policies through plan efforts into action.
- Greater awareness through education, training, extension programmes.

Land Use Planning as a tool for sectoral allotment/utilization of land has been attempted in India only in urban areas through a Master Plan document. The National Bureau of Soil Survey and Land Use Planning have attempted the soil based land use planning at watershed, farm and village levels. Attempts have been made to highlight the soil properties at district level through a suggestive soil based crop alternatives popularly called suggested land use maps.

The time has come to take a hard look in an integrated perspective land use planning exercises at district levels to fulfil the aspirations of the stakeholders. The problem is that any suggested land use plan will have no sanctity in the absence of a policy and legislative framework.

The methodology for each of these is different but the ultimate aim is to evaluate the land and present land use and select those combinations that best achieve the desired goals in a diverse country like India, the land use systems for multifunctional agriculture shall be varied, best suited to local agro-ecological conditions but ultimately aiming for over all rural development. Integrated Farming Systems that contribute to poverty alleviation and providing a stronger local economy would also be the part of the plan.

In addition to the goal of rural development, multifunctional agriculture can also be used as a strategy to increase agriculture production through cultivation in the productive soils of the urban fringes. A system of multifunctional land use would thus also provide an opportunity for promoting agriculture in and around the city. The integration of agriculture in the process of urban planning linked through green belt requirement of the city can also provide the much needed solution to the problems of loss of good quality agricultural land through urban encroachment.

All our Five Year Plans emphasized the need for efficient use of land water and other natural resources for accelerated as well as sustainable economic development. Nevertheless, the problems of land degradation groundwater depletion and environmental pollution have assumed alarming proportion since many areas.

Hence, it is felt the need for serious National Debate on how to address various issues related to land use planning in a country where pressure on land is 4-6 times more as compared to world average. Here, it is worth mentioning that we have 17 per cent population and 11 per cent livestock on only 2.3 per cent land of the world.

We need to keep in mind that land use patterns will be largely governed by market forces. However, keeping in view the need for conservation of land, water and other natural resources for sustainable development, food and livelihood security, suitable policy, direction and planned intervention from time to time would be necessary.

Uttar Pradesh and Rural-Urban Fringes

Uttar Pradesh is a state located in the northern part of India. With a population of over 190 million people, it is India's most populous State, as well as the world's most populous sub-national entity.

With an area of 93,933 sq. mi. (243,286 km²), Uttar Pradesh covers a large part of the highly fertile and densely populated upper Gangetic plain. It shares an international border with Nepal to the north along with the Indian State of Uttarakhand, Himachal Pradesh to the north-west, Haryana, Delhi and Rajasthan on the west, Madhya Pradesh on the south, Chhattisgarh and Jharkhand on the south-east and Bihar on the east.

The State can be divided into two distinct hypsographical regions:

The larger *Gangetic Plain* region is in the north: it includes the Ganga-Yamuna Doab, the Ghaghra plains, the Ganga plains and the Terai. It has highly fertile alluvial soils and flat topography—(slope 2 m/km)—broken by numerous ponds, lakes and rivers.

The smaller *Vindhya Hills and Plateau* region is in the south: it is characterized by hard rock strata and varied topography of hills, plains, valleys and plateau; limited availability of water makes the region relatively arid.

Constituent regions: The State comprises several distinct regions:

- The Doab region which runs along UP's western border from north to south; this region is further divided into *three* zones:
  - The Upper Doab in the north-west,
  - The Middle Doab in the west, including the Brajbhumi in the trans-Yamuna area,
  - The Lower Doab in the south-centre,
- The Rohilkhand region in the north;
- The Awadh (or Oudh), the historic country of Kosalas in the centre;
- The northern parts of Bundelkhand in the south;
- The northern parts of Baghelkhand in the south-east; and

- The south-western part of the Bhojpur country in the east, commonly called Purvanchal ("Eastern Province").

The State of Uttar Pradesh is a true representation of India's Unity in Diversity in all aspects. Historically and culturally, it is an enriched State with the pomp, glory and splendour of the prominent rulers such as Mughals, Rohillas, Bundellas and the Awadh. It has distinct demographic dividend with 40 per cent of its present population is in the age group of 15 to 45 years. The State is house to a number of educational and research centres of national repute. Political vulnerability over the years has not allowed the State to develop and flourish as an industrial State and hence has witnessed a large migration of its productive, hardworking and efficient manpower.

The administrative and legislative capital of Uttar Pradesh is Lucknow and the financial and industrial capital is Kanpur. The State's High Court is based at Allahabad. It is home to many historical cities like Varanasi and Agra. Kanpur is its largest city; other big cities are Meerut, Bareilly, Allahabad, Ghaziabad and Noida.

Administrative divisions and districts (as in 2007): The State of Uttar Pradesh consists of seventy districts, which are grouped into eighteen divisions:

Agra Division, Aligarh Division, Allahabad Division, Azamgarh Division, Bareilly Division, Basti Division, Chitrakoot Division, Devipatan Division, Faizabad Division, Gorakhpur Division, Jhansi Division, Kanpur Division, Lucknow Division, Meerut Division, Mirzapur Division, Moradabad Division, Saharanpur Division and Varanasi Division.

The largest district in terms of area is Lakhimpur Khiri. The largest district in terms of population is Allahabad, followed by Kanpur Nagar (Census 2001).

Demographics: Uttar Pradesh is the most populous State in India with a population of over 190 million people as on July 1, 2008. If it were a separate country, Uttar Pradesh would be the world's fifth most populous nation, next only to China, India, the United States of America and Indonesia. As of the 2001 Census of India, slightly over 80 per cent of Uttar Pradesh population is Hindu, while Muslims make up 18 per cent of the population. The remaining population consists of Sikhs, Buddhists, Christians and Jains.

Economy: Uttar Pradesh is the second largest State economy in India after Maharashtra, contributing 8.17 per cent to India's total GDP.

Between 1999 and 2008, the economy grew only 4.4 per cent per year, one of the lowest rates in India.

The major economic activity in the State is agriculture, in 1991, 73 per cent of the population in the State was engaged in agriculture and 46 per cent of the State income was accounted for by agriculture. UP has retained its prominent position in the country as a food-surplus state.

Uttar Pradesh is home to largest number of Small Scale industrial units in the country, with 12 per cent of over 2.3 million Units. But industrial output has been adversely affected by erratic power supply from the UP State Electricity Board and remains far below its full production capacity. Unavailability of adequate raw materials at competitive prices is another negative factor. Also, like in most parts of India, traders and middlemen make most of the profits while the labour class lives at subsistence level.

In spite of these, labour efficiency is higher in UP at (26) than the National Average of (25). Following are some of the important industrial hubs in the state:

- Kanpur is the largest shoe-manufacturing centre in the country.
- NOIDA and Lucknow are among the top IT (Information Technology) destinations of the country.
- Meerut, a manufacturing centre of sports goods, sharp tools like scissors and also of gold ornaments, is regularly listed among the top tax-paying cities in the country.

Globalization as well as the Western influence through the media is impacting the Uttar Predesh's lifestyle, and economy is gearing itself to cater to new tastes and consumerism. A visible sign of this is seen in the elegant shopping Malls coming up in up beat localites in big cities.

In the vast fields of urban-rural relationship, fringes of the cities i.e., zones where cities are transforming tracts of rural territory within their fold has been emerging. In India, city growth is synonymous with demographic growth besides technical and social innovations. Urban fringes are becoming important characterizing unplanned squatter settlements, traffic problems, congestions, unplanned infrastructure and overutilized existing land.

In the developing countries the rural-urban fringes are a major problem unlike in the western developing nations where rural-urban fringes have been created by reasons less of demographic growth than of vast official programme of slum clearance, industrial relocation and traffic management and these pressures have been further strengthened by extensive sub-urban building by individuals and speculators.

Rural-urban fringe is a zone of land on the periphery of urban area which is experiencing a process of transformation from characteristically rural modes of production, social interaction and land use to characteristically urban one. It is a zone of transition in both space and time and as parallel and complementary manifestations of the same land.

There are clear differences between rural-urban fringes and the hinterland of the city. This reflects the lack of a clear boundary between these zones as well as conceptualized inconsistencies in the literature. There are, however, fundamentally different both as a phenomenon and as a concept.

Due to both population growth and urbanization there will be growing demand for conversion of agricultural land to non-agricultural uses. It is, therefore, important to develop a long-term perspective plan on type of land to be allocated for urbanization/industrialization in various regions. Besides proper urban planning would reduce the extent of conversion of prime agricultural lands to non-agricultural uses.

The existing database on land use is highly inadequate. Therefore, strengthening of the database, using traditional cadastral surveys, modern remote sensing techniques, GPS, GIS and computerization of land records would be necessary. In fact, the available techniques for data collection should be complementary to each other. There is a need for a strong monitoring mechanism to document the on-going land use changes either driven by market or policy or both.

Issues for Consideration for Land Use and Rural-Urban Land Fringes

- Achievement of desirable land use pattern through sectoral approach/Plan linkages.
- Formulation of economical viable projects for each sector i.e. forests, agriculture, horticulture to translate land care into people's movement.
- Application of modern science and technology to enhance productivity.
- Preparation of Land Use Atlas.
- Generation of strong political/administrative will.
- Computerized and updated Land Records.

- Strict laws/rules for land use conversion.
- Maintaining and improving soil fertility and unit area land productivity.
- Surveys of land resources—climate, water, soils, landforms, forests, and rangelands to improve efficiency of investment.
- Need to generate systematic database on land utilization and land management practices at national, state and local levels in the country.
- Training/orientation programmes for land use practitioners.
- Publicity of success stories in case of soil conservation and better land management.
- Effective reclamation of degraded lands.
- Measures to check further degradation of land.
- Effective watershed management and reduction in disparities and regional imbalances prevalent in the State through policy interventions.
- Diversification of land use.
- Awareness generation based on local needs/environment.
- Preventive measures on adverse effects from industrial waste and effluents on good forest and cultivable land.
- Development of rural agro-based industries.
- Treating water as an economic good and not as a free commodity.
- The State Land Use Boards should be suitably strengthened with statutory powers to integrate and monitor activities of Land User Department.

Conclusion

Having noted the details of the nature of characteristic features and conditions of rural-urban fringes, land use patterns and policies in India and the world over with special reference to the State of Uttar Pradesh, the present study reveals that there exist great scope for planners and developers to work on promoting and providing the State with decent adoptable land use policy and creation of an environmentally healthy fringes. The need of the hour is of strong political will to pronounce and promote legislative measures to undertake land reforms, land management and better utilization techniques so that sustainable rural-urban fringes may be a part of the future generations to come.

References

Abaza, H., editor. 1992. The present state of environmental and resource accounting and its potential application in developing countries. *UN Environmental Economics Series Number 1*. United Nations, New York, USA.

Costanza, R., J. Cumberland, H. Daly, R. Goodland, and R. Norgaard. 1997. *An introduction to ecological economics.* St. Lucie Press, Boca Raton, Florida, USA.

Peskin, H.M., and E. Lutz. 1993. A survey of resource and environmental accounting approaches in industrialized countries. Pages 144-176 in E. Lutz, editor. *Toward improved accounting for the environment.* A UN Stat-World Bank Symposium, IBRD—World Bank, New York, USA.

Prudham, W.S., and S. Lonergan. 1993. Natural resource accounting (I): A review of existing frameworks. *Canadian Journal of Regional Science* 16(3):363-386.

Prugh, T. 1995. Natural capital and human survival. *International Society of Ecological Economics Press*, Solomons, New York, USA.

Ritu Ahlawat, (2008), "E-Learning in Land Records Information System", Sharing Good Practices: E-Learning in Surveying, *Geo-information Sciences and Land Administration, FIG International Workshop* 2008 Enschede, The Netherlands.

Sinha, M.M.P. (1980) *"The impact of urbanization on land use in the rural-urban fringe"*, Concept Publishing Co., Delhi, India.

5

Socio-Spatial Impact of Rural-Urban Fringe

Sister Marion Mathew

Introduction

To a very large number of people, the dullest landscape may have a story back of it packed with events and human interest out of all proportion to its apparently ordinary appearance. Anywhere in the world, the face of the land faithfully reflects the culture of the people who live upon it. Where the land is poor and worn, so are the people who strive to maintain themselves on its inhospitable surface, and where the land is rich and bountiful, the people who inhabit it have an opportunity to live a rich and bountiful life. This reality fits very well within the Indian context of urban-rural fringe.

The social and political categorization of an area reflects the need of a changing society. The growth of population puts great pressure on agriculture for more food and industries for further development. In the early industrial era, the area was an enclave of industrial ground in a completely rural setting. In the post-industrial era this scenario is totally changed, all the same the city sprawled closer, with the semi-urban populations' need.

Urban Sprawl and Slum Expansion

To understand the socio-spatial impacts of property-led redevelopment, we ought to be aware of the wide changes taking place in the life and living standard of the present day population. On the one hand, an extensive residential displacement occurs during redevelopment even though a process of gentrification emerges. It is indeed an undeniable fact that the re-imaged inner city often promotes economic growth at the cost of an extensive residential displacement. Urban sprawl and slum expansion are major problems which create many social and environmental problems. The highly productive agricultural land is encroached on urban houses, roads and industries.

The Role: Individual *Vs.* Local Community

The role of the individual and particularly the local community in shaping development processes has received more and more attention. Proactive roles have been recognized increasingly for communities and individuals in relatively certain regions as being an integral part of the emerging 'new economy', but the urban fringe has received little attention from this perspective. Glimpses of the role of local agency came partly from varied research into urban fringe agriculture over the past 20 years which has profiled the role of the individual farmer and farm family, but little progress has been made in the appreciation of locality, or socially constructed localized action space, in the urban fringe, particularly in its manifestation through the actions of local groups, organizations and communities. A conceptual framework is proposed to advance our understanding of local agency in the processes of differentiation within the urban fringe. Local agency acts upon the transformation of the local environment to become one of the driving forces behind the process of uneven development and, more generally, differentiation of urban fringe space.

Urbanization, a Global Phenomenon

In contrast to the above scenario, urbanization is a global phenomenon experienced by economically-advanced as well as developing countries. As countries place emphasis on industrial development, there is a movement of people from villages to towns and cities and an impetus to the growth of metropolitan areas. In general, cities provide large economies of agglomerations. They also provide a variety of choices—such as educational facilities, health-care services, entertainment options and even friends to people—that are not available in small towns. People migrate to cities for economic opportunities and urban lifestyles.

Although urbanization brings about development in the social, economical and cultural spheres of life, it disturbs ecological systems. The increase in urban population results in asymmetric patterns in resource utilization, land use and transportation. Rapid and uncontrolled growth of urban agglomerations generates a series of negative environmental and social effects. These include: lack of infrastructure and basic services, housing problems, congestion, health problems, etc.

In terms of urbanization levels, India is one of the least urbanized countries in the world. Between1951 and 2001, the level of urbanization increased by only 13 per cent. However, if the size of the population is considered, India has the second largest urban population in the world **(307 million).** The significance of urbanization for India is in terms of population rather than the level of urbanization which is to be taken note of.

In India, natural growth rates and rural to urban migration are expected to raise the country's urban population from 30 per cent of the total in 2001 to as high as about 45 per cent in 2021 spread over about 4,000 urban agglomerates and towns. There were only 25.8 million urban populations in 1901 and it shot up to over 230 million, as per the 2001 census. The share of economic activity in urban areas would increase from 56 per cent of GDP in1990 to about 75 per cent in 2020. Most of this growth is expected to take place in the major cities of Mumbai **(12 million),** Kolkata **(4.6 million)** and Delhi **(9.8 million)** not to speak of the other six mega cities viz. Chennai, Hyderabad, Bangalore, Ahmedabad, Pune and Kanpur together containing 21 million population.

The Current Crisis in Urban Development

Sixty years since Independence, India is yet to have a comprehensive and integrated approach to guide and plan for the growth and development of human settlements and the relationship of population distribution between urban and rural areas. The fact of the matter is that in the global context today's rural is tomorrow's urban, and that urbanization is inevitable in the face of the economic growth models adopted by our country. The current crisis in urban development is due to multiple factors, such as stereotype plan formulation, weak and wrong policies, and lack of co-ordination among implementing agencies and lack of all-round communication between various agencies responsible for the implementation of the policies.

Characteristic Features of Indian cities

Most Indian cities are characterized by high densities, intensely mixed land use patterns, short trip distances, and high share of walking and non-motorised transport. The transport and land use patterns found in these cities are so influenced by poverty and high level of complexity that it becomes difficult to analyze their characteristics using the same indices as used for cities in highly motorised countries. There is ample evidence to illustrate the mismatch between urban transportation planning methods and the growing transportation problems. Consequently, these cities continue to face environmental decay, congestion, poor health conditions, etc. Unless we understand the basic nature of problems faced by these cities, the adverse impact of growing mobility on the environment will continue to multiply in the future.

Changing City Profile

The spatial spread of Indian cities has been changing as in other cities all-over the world. The city limit is now indicated by urban sprawl. The cities include the old core area, which is usually congested, has narrow streets, old houses, and the land use mixed and relatively unregulated. Then there are unplanned parts of the city, which have developed spontaneously and are often beyond the municipal limits but also within it often along the arterial road or the main highway going out of the city. These spontaneous developments are of two types: one inhabited by lower and middle classes who, due to mismanagement of the land market, cannot afford to buy land for housing. The other category consists of squatter settlements. These can be spread all-over the city. These are largely inhabited by the poorer sections of the society specially the construction labourers and the informal workers of the city. In a large city the slums and squatter settlements also increase.

In the mega-cities and million plus cities of India, 40-50 per cent of the population lives in these informal housing colonies. The third category of settlements consists of planned residential colonies built by the public, private or co-operative sectors. These are high-income residential houses and multi-storied flats with well-laid out roads, and other urban services. Public transport and private cars give easy access from these locations to the city centre as well as the shopping areas. The fourth category is commercial. It is planned and has multi-storied buildings. These have been located to create multi-centred cities. The fifth and the final category are the urban fringe where the urban and rural divide becomes blurred. Thus the structure that emerges out of complex interplay of physical, social, economic, cultural and behavioural factors does not follow the classical "rich centre and poor periphery" type of model.

There are no clear-cut concentric zones of different activities. Central core areas depict not only commercial but also high housing concentration. The manufacturing activities are spread not only in the peripheral zone but also in intermediate and inner zones. Unlike the Western countries, Indian cities have more than one Central Business District; therefore, commercial activities are spatially dispersed. Manufacturing activities are concentrated not only in the earlier old commercial areas but also newly developed industrial areas at the outskirts of the most Indian cities are characterized by high densities, intensely mixed land use patterns, short trip distances, and high share of walking and non-motorised transport.

Land Use Patterns of the City

The transport and land use patterns found in these cities are so influenced by poverty and high level of complexity that it becomes difficult to analyse their characteristics using the same indices as used for cities in highly motorised countries. There is ample evidence to illustrate the mismatch between urban transportation planning methods and the growing transportation problems. Consequently, these cities continue to face environmental decay, congestion, poor health conditions, etc. Unless we understand the basic nature of problems faced by these cities, the adverse impact of growing mobility on the environment will continue to multiply in the future.

Land Use Planning

Land use planning is the formulation of policies and programmes for guiding public and private land use in areas of any size where different uses compete for land. The word 'land' in this context implies attributes of place and other factors besides soil. Planners must consider place, size of area, relation to markets, social and economic development, skill of the land users and other factors. Local government units such as those of cities, towns do local planning. The planning applies to complexes of farms and ranches, to housing developments, shopping centres, industrial parks and to entire communities or political unit.

Building Sites

Interpretations and instructions are made for the construction of small buildings; for the installation of roads, streets, and utilities and for the establishment of lawns and landscaping of the grounds around the building. Such soil uses involve high capital expenditures in relatively small areas. The preparation of building sites may alter soil properties markedly. Constructions and maintenance of buildings belong primarily to architecture and engineering. Additionally, large multi-storied structures are generally supported by footings placed below the depth of soil. The constructions of buildings, roads, parks, parking lots and other similar structures often disturb and displace the local people from their familiar surroundings.

Rural-Urban Migration and the Changing Urban Landscape

Cities are centres of opportunities, of all types: entertainment, employment, education, healthcare and so on. When it is a matter of development, it is true that everything new comes to the city first. But sometimes it takes ages for a particular technological innovation find its way to the fringes of rural India. By the time they manage to reach the last person in the village, the other side of the world dominated by metros and urban landscapes would have gone nautical miles ahead, and the process keeps repeating. This is not going to be practical anymore. Educated youngsters from around the cities migrate to urban landscapes looking for opportunities.

What happens to the urban landscape when it comes to hold more population than what it is really able to hold? It is growth. Landscapes have to grow both vertically and horizontally. Vertical growth is taking place much faster than horizontal growth. Though slowly, horizontal growth takes place really steadily, and it makes our urban landscapes look unorganized and haphazard.

Slums sprout out in every strip of public place. Makeshift living arrangements surface overnight. Streets get congested with people and vehicles. Those small strips of open spaces in the urban areas disappear. Pollutions of all types increase; consumption multiplies as population gets doubled.

People carry on their lives by doing things both legal and illegal. Pressures of life make many pick up bad habits and asocial professions. Crimes increase, law and order get halted and life gets threatened. Drainages get clogged, wastes accumulate, mosquitoes breed, epidemic break out and the city loses its green belt and green cover. Ultimately, the physical appearance of our urban landscapes takes an ugly look, and ordinary life in the cities becomes near impossible. Can we afford to be so for long? Can our cities be anymore accommodative to this perpetual movement of men and material in its landscapes?

As long as cities remain attractive or rural areas remain aloof, deprived of the benefits of the developments and the eventual opportunities offered by the new world order, we cannot imagine of a city without rural-urban migrants. Modern world is more mobile than it was, and the size of the floating population is increasing everyday. Added to this are the settlements formed by migrants from distant places.

The vertical growth of the cities is mainly dominated by business houses, real estate holdings, and the affluent section of the society. This growth most of the time gives way to a set of entirely different problems. The pressure these problems exert on the urban landscape is more environmental than aesthetic. City planners and corporation authorities may be able to put some check on any growth that is against the rules on lands and their holdings in cities.

The story is different when it is a matter of men and women from a different social landscape transplant their families to an entirely different environment. These people are least bothered of the effects of their presence in a new locale. For them the way ahead is very hard, and making both ends meet is more important than making their places look good. So they live their lives the same way they lived in their native places. The physical appearance of the urban landscape changes without the knowledge of anyone. Only a bird's-eye view can get a clear picture of our cities.

What is the way out? Opportunities should go evenly to semi-urban and rural areas. The attractions that cities hold need to be accessible to all irrespective of whether one belongs to rural or urban or semi-urban area. Inclusive growth paradigm is the only possible way out we have in front of us. It is natural that people move from place to place. It is more so when it comes to improving their lives. But it is not natural that developments and opportunities are concentrated in a particular place, call it city or metro. If we want to keep people where they are, we have to make their places attractive by way of developments, opportunities, facilities and sustainable growth.

Private players in the growing sectors like IT, ITES management streams, insurance and finance may be encouraged to establish their wares in semi-urban and rural areas and they may be asked to give priority to candidates hailing from rural areas. This is to be cautiously executed because, rural landscapes are environment-sensitive, and any development activity aimed at stopping rural-urban migration needs to be thoroughly studied to ensure that its impact on the environment is sustainable.

Health Vulnerability: The Distance between Urban Poor and Others

Urban poor have been categorised as core poor, intermediate poor and transitional poor communities. Core poor households are those whose incomes fall between zero and half the urban poverty line of Rs. 454.11p. (Planning Commission, 2001). Intermediate poor are households whose incomes fall between half the poverty line and poverty line (Rs. 227.05 and Rs. 454.11p.). Transitional poor are households with incomes above the poverty line and half the poverty line (Rs. 454.11p and Rs. 681.16p; NIUA, 2001). The Planning Commission in the recently finalised Tenth Plan on Urban Development, Chapter 6.1, has quoted this classification. Urban poor are worse-off than rural people on almost all counts; mortality, morbidity, literacy, etc. and at all levels; national, state and city. Urban poor living in authorised/settlements recognised by local bodies are better off on all social indicators when compared with poor living in unauthorised/illegitimate settlements.

In interpreting the transformation of rural space, much attention has to be given to the macro scale processes shaping capitalist society, particularly those of accumulation and uneven development. **In conclusion, India is heading towards a dismal future, in terms of population, food and space.**

References

Geetam Tiwari, Urban Transport Priorities: Meeting the Challenge of Socio-Economic Diversity in Cities—Case Study Delhi, India *20th South African Transport Conference South Africa*, 16-20 July, 2001.

'Meeting the Transport Challenges in Southern Africa' Organised by: Conference Planners *Conference Papers* Produced by: Document Transformation Technologies.

G. Tiwari, D. Mohan *et. al.*, *Bicycle Master Plan for Delhi*, Final Report submitted to Transport Department, Delhi.

Government, *TRIPP*, Indian Institute of Technology, Delhi, 1998.

Genesis of White Paper on *Town Planning at Cross Roads*, Dr. Manmohan Singh, Hon'ble Prime Minister, India, 60th Independence Day Address, 15th August 2007.

www.merinews.com/.../rural-urban...urban.../Rural-urban migration and the changing urban landscape.

6
Development and Disparity on the Urban Fringes: A Conceptual Framework

Alpana Chandra Scott

Objectives

1. To Define the "Rural-Urban Spatial System" on the Urban Fringes.
2. To build a concept of "Urban Fortune" in the dimensions of past, present and future for urban fringes.
3. To pry the concept of working with the urban world to draw out the art of living on the fringes which leads to development.
4. To protrude the window to urban vision in future through organizational performances of the past and organizational accomplishments.

Methodology

Intensive literature survey is made to derive the new concept to demarcate the condition and level of development and disparity on the urban fringes. Extensive survey of urban fringes of different cities was made through questionnaires to find out the condition of urban fringes. The data collected was processed and conceptual findings were drawn out.

Findings

- The geographical space is exposed to natural processes and human activities, e.g. the way in which Rural-Urban Fringe around Delhi, Mumbai and Kolkata is used in the last twenty years. It has slowed down the fast speed of cities.

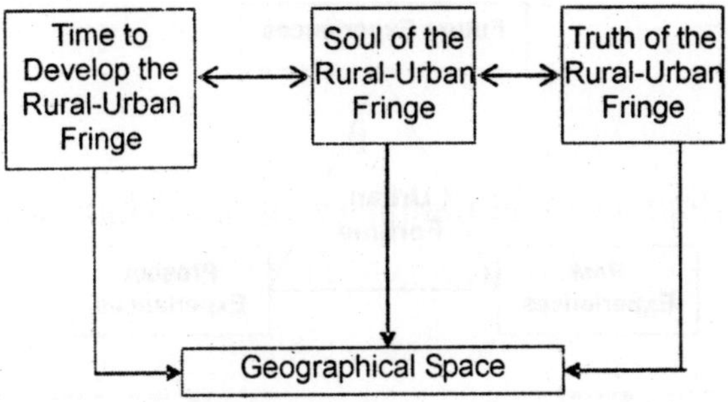

- The face of geographical spatial system has experienced dynamic change over the time. If this model is followed it could lead to absorb the cultural shock, remove social tension and stop the proliferation of criminal activities, e.g. in Lucknow, the urban continuity beyond the ring road needs to be gracefully used which will stop the amount of accidents increased within twenty years.

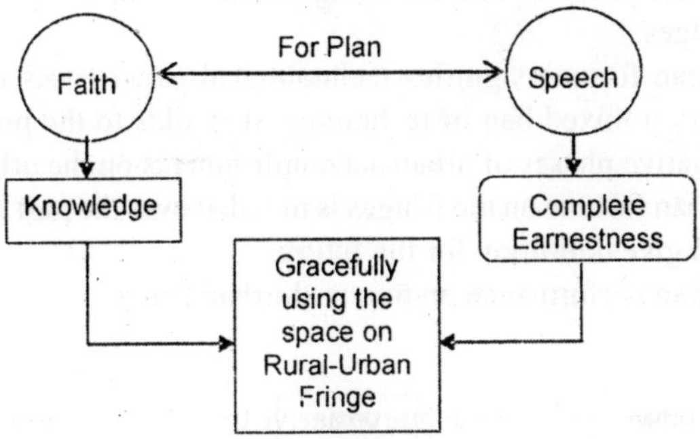

- Natural and human process corresponding to the world situations is multifaceted and accordingly changed also.
- The temporal progress of rural-urban spatial system is defined as past, present and future.
- This temporal progress could be comprehended as present defines the end of past and beginning of the future on the urban fringes.
- Such a temporal progress involves continuity by phases of evolution in past, present and future.
- The past face of geography basically spoke about the Natural face. In other words nature's dominance everywhere. 'Febvert' said that "geographers start from soil not from the society." This

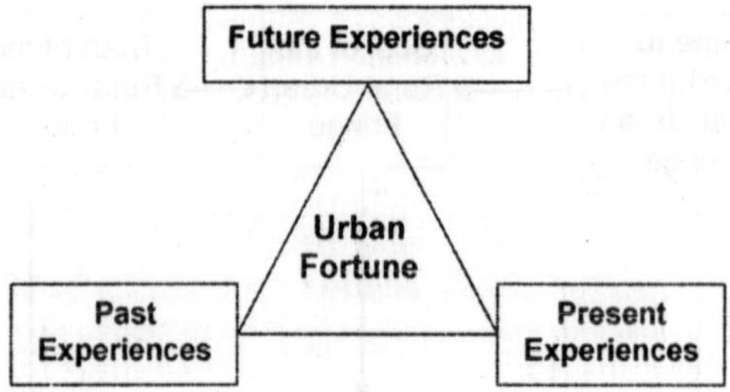

is an important aspect of food security, which is looked through the availability of spece for agriculture on R.-U. Fringe.

- The present face of geography marked the cultural face, which is the outcome of man's creativity out of nature. The cultural face of geography emerged as a prominent aspect and carved the path to the future.
- The urban fortune builds in time, through growing physical framework and accumulating cultural complex on the urban fringes.
- Urban fortune signifies technological experiences too. Cities carry a mixed bag of technology that adds to the positive and negative phases of urban accomplishments on the urban fringe.
- Urban fortune on the fringes is to rediscover the past for present and give definition for the future.
- Urban performance on the rural-urban fringe.

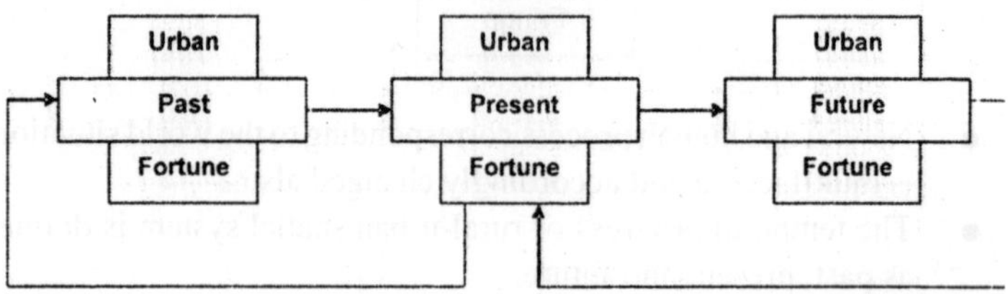

Conclusion

Faces of urban geography and rural-urban spatial system on the urban fringes never reflect anything abstract. There is a legacy of the past. It is profound to find out the rural-urban spatial system in the light of urban fortune and urban performances to trace the aspects of development and

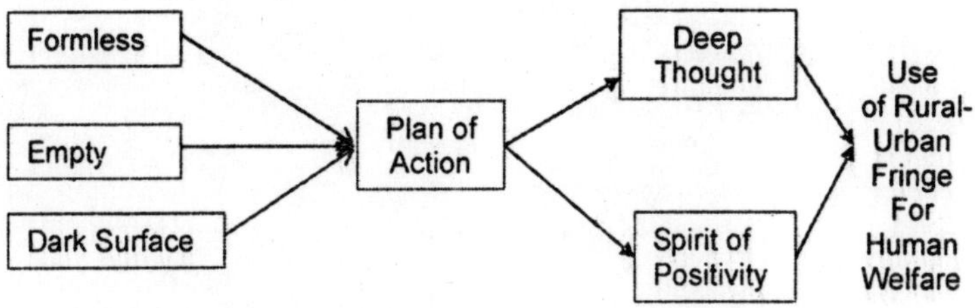

disparity on the urban fringes. This will also be helpful in identifying the problems on the fringes and making suggestions.

In this formless and empty and dark surface of the Rural, Urban fringe of any city; so vulnerable to cultural shock, raising enmity, social tension and wide criminal activities the plan of action should depend upon deep thoughts and spirit of positivity of the commonality and the planners.

References

Adams, R.M. (1966): *The Evolution of Urban Society: Early Mesopotamia and Per-Hispanic. Mexico,* Chicago.

Christaller, W. (1966): *The Central Places of Southern Germany*. Trans. C.W. Baskin. Englewood Cliffs, N.J. Prentice Hall.

Clark, D. (1996): *Urban World/Global City,* London: Routledge.

Gottmann, J. (1961): *Megalopolis: The Urbanized Northeastern Seaboard of the United States*, New York.

Webber, A.F. (1963): *The Growth of Cities in the Nineteenth Century: A Study in Statistics*, New York.

Merlin, P. (1971): *New Towns, Regional Planning and Development*, London.

Mumford, L., (1956): "The Natural History of Urbanization" in Thomas, W.L. (ed). *Man's Role in Changing the Face of the Earth*, Chicago.

Part II
Delimitation of the Rural-Urban Fringe

7

Application and Importance of Advanced Remote Sensing and GIS Technique in Identifying the Encroachment of Urban Areas into Rural Areas—An Attempt in Chinhat Block of Lucknow District, U.P.

Sudhakar Shukla, Sarika Shukla and *Rakesh Singh Kushwaha*

Introduction

Cities are the index of economic development of a region. Initially, urban areas were generated through internal forces rather than through secondary diffusion. Even the largest cities were small and few by modern standards but in present global scenario, many of modern cities are experiencing explosive urban growth. Haphazard settlement is continuously igniting multifaceted environmental problems which are becoming more novel.

Lucknow city, which is one of the fastest growing Metropolitan regions in the State of Uttar Pradesh. Last decade this city of '*Nawabs*' has witnessed growth, dynamism and economic boom which has lead to numerous environmental scenes therefore delimitation of Lucknow city has become more difficult. Due to increasing urban sprawl, drastic land use change is taking in its 'RUF' (rural-urban fringe) which is leading to inadequacy of public amenities and services.

Study Area

Lucknow is a historical city and administrative hub, which still is having some clear impressions of Nawabs of Awadh, the British regime and the post-Independence developments. Nestled on the banks of the Gomti river and covering an area of 2528 sq. km, U.P.'s capital city,

LUCKNOW, encompasses the stretch ranging from 26°31' to 27°10' North latitude and 80°30' East longitude. It is centrally placed district in middle Ganga plain, flanked by Barabanki district on the east, Unnao on the west, Raibarelli on the south and Sitapur and Hardoi districts on the north direction respectively. The boundary of the district is not a natural one but seems to have been fixed in keeping view administration convenience. Although it is the second smallest district in area, it is one of the most important districts because it is a seat of Uttar Pradesh Government. This city of Nawabs is divided into different blocks, out of these different blocks the Chinhat block has been considered for the study as shown in Fig. 7.1.

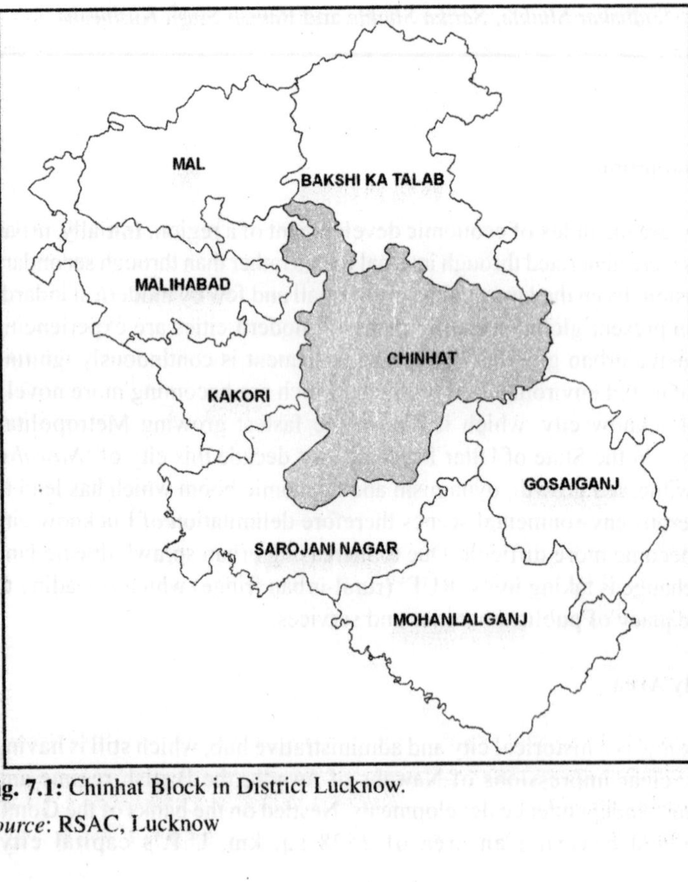

Fig. 7.1: Chinhat Block in District Lucknow.
Source: RSAC, Lucknow

Geology and Soil Type

Lucknow city, falls in the central Ganga alluvial plain chiefly forms a part of Sai-Gomti sub-basin, hydro-geologically the city as a whole is represented by unconsolidated alluvial sediments, comprising sand of varying grades with kanker and clay and their admixtures, wherein fine grained sand mostly constitutes the aquifers, i.e. groundwater bearing strata. Jal Sansthan provides the existing water supply in the city. The city falls in the central Ganga Plain and lies in the interfluvial belt of Gomti and Sai basins. It has conspicuous natural depression in north-eastern part around Janki Puram and Bakshi Ka Talab. The general slope of the area is from north and north-west to south and south-east. The highest elevation is 123.5 msl. above mean sea level in the north-west and the lowest 110 msl. in the east in flood plain of river Gomti. The whole area of Lucknow may be divided into two geologic units, namely, younger and older alluvium of quaternary age. The younger alluvial plain lies all along the river Gomti and forms a wide flood plain. The older alluvial plain occupies higher elevation than the younger alluvial plain. The alluvium consists of a sand clay and kanker of different proportions.

Data Used

To perform the study, high resolution data (QUICK BIRD) as downloaded from Google earth, of different dates, viz. 2003, 2006, 2009, have been used.

Survey of India Topographical sheets on 1:50000 scale, pertaining to Chinhat block have been used for preparation of base layers such as road network, settlements etc. SRTM data has also been used to have the three dimensional picture of the area.

Other ancillary data as taken from Census Department and Land Use Board has also been incorporated in the study to get a meaningful result.

Methodology

The conventional methodology has been adopted in view of assessing the changes in the land use and land cover. The Survey of India topographical sheets surveyed in 1962 on 1:50,000 scale and multi-date, multi-sensor satellite data, pertaining to the study area have been used. Then after the base maps *viz.* transport, drainage and settlement maps were prepared for each of the SOI sheets for further detailed mapping.

After the preparation of base maps, contour maps at 1m. interval was prepared using SOI top sheets, and SRTM data for assessing the terrain characteristics in the form of relief. A GIS based analysis on GRID/TIN module was accomplished in order to derive the desired classes.

After preparation of these terrain characteristics maps, all the base layers when coupled with the already existing land use maps, gives the information of different time periods for the changes occurred. The statistics related to these themes and terrain characteristics were generated, using statistical analysis of the study area.

The Facts Lucknow has witnessed a radial growth—greater along the Faizabad Road and the Trans-Gomti area. In recent years, the city is witnessing a real estate boom with a large number of private developers entering the market. The latter has not been factored into the Master Plan—the formal basis for Government planning. Estimates of infrastructure requirements and population projections are therefore likely to be conservative.

The city has developed mostly towards north and north-east in the Trans-Gomti area; Ravines and waterlogged area in the north-west and

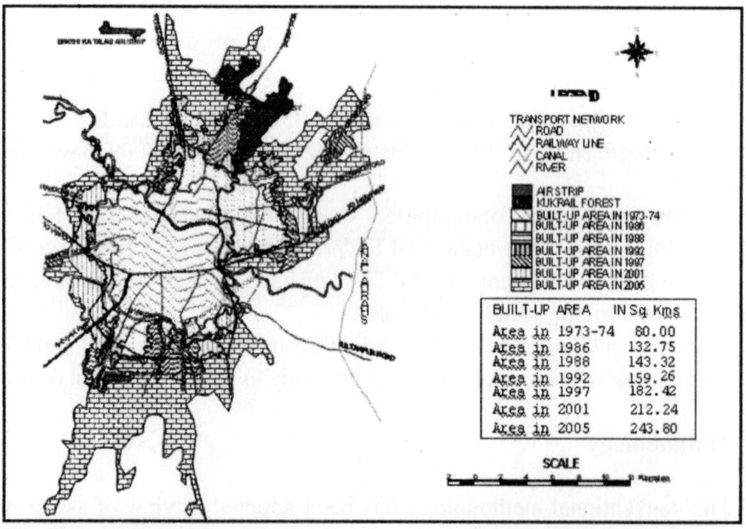

Fig. 7.2: Lucknow city showing Trends of Urban Sprawl between 1973-74 to 2005 as Inerpreted From SoI Toposheet, Landsat-TM IRS-1A,1B,IC, & PG Data

Source: RSAC, Lucknow.

defense land in the south-east have restricted rapid growth of town in these directions. The growth of the town has being along Faizabad Road in the north-east, Kursi Road and Sitapur Road in the north, Kanpur Road in the south and as well as Rae Bareli Road in the south-east. This is because Lucknow is well linked with Kanpur, Faizabad, Sitapur, Hardoi, Unnao and Barabanki by railway (junction of Broad and Metre Gauge railway lines) and roads (4 National Highways, 3 State Highways).

According to Master Plan 2021, total urban area of Lucknow cover an area of 16,270 hectares in 2004-05. Compared to 1987 when the area was estimated at 9170 hectares, there has been a 77.4 per cent increase in the total area in 2004-05. This is expected to increase to 45,544 hectare by 2021. The area under cultivation is reported to be 1,46,544 hectares constituting 58.1 per cent of total geographical area of the district as against 62.5 per cent in 1981 census. Thus 4.4 per cent decrease in the area under cultivation during 1981-91 is probably due to speedy sprawling and urbanization of the district. The highest increase has been in the residential areas from 1981 to 2001 nearly 99.4 per cent. Trends in land uses has been interesting, especially the fact that residential use has grown dramatically in comparison to all other uses, although there has also been notable growth in commercial, industrial and public service land use.

Since 1981-84 villages have been merged fully and 6 villages partly within the municipal limit of Municipal Corporation, Lucknow. The current analysis points to the fact that the growth has happened at a much faster pace than manageable efforts thus degrading the status of infrastructure and services in terms of water supply, sewerage and sanitation, housing drains, storm water drains, solid waste management and transport. Overall service levels are inadequate and the situation is worse for the urban poor. The service sector forms the main economic base of the city. Lucknow is also an important education centre, especially for primary and secondary education and houses a number of research and development institutions. The state of infrastructure is one of several constraints that prevent the city from achieving its economic potential. (CDP:2006). The total Municipal area as per 2001 census is 143 sq. km.

Analysis and Results

From temporal assessment of high resolution satellite data, from 2003 to 2009, an importance of remotely sensed high resolution imageries and GIS techniques in assessing is proven, where one can notice the

Table 7.1: Existing Land use - Lucknow city area (in Hectares) 1987, 2004-05

Land use	*1987*		*2004-05*		*Growth in %*
	Growth	*Percentage*	*Land use*	*Area %*	*Area %*
Residential	4,485.98	48.92	8,945.00	54.98	99.40
Commercial	223.77	2.44	360.00	2.21	60.88
Offices	474.69	5.18	560.00	3.44	17.97
Industrial	596.22	6.50	990.00	6.08	66.05
Parks/ Playgrounds	346.48	3.78	435.00	2.67	25.55
Public Services	902.02	9.84	1,410.00	8.67	56.32
Traffic	952.00	10.38	1,240.00	7.62	30.25
River/water bodies	193.66	2.11	310.00	1.91	60.07
Open Land	996.14	10.86	2,020.00	12.42	102.78
Total	**9,170.96**	**100.00**	**16,270.00**	**100**	**77.43**

Source: Master Plan 2021. Area other than Cantonment.

Fig. 7.3: Temporal assessment of high resolution satellite data.
Source: Google Earth

changes occurring in the surrounding environment near *Rahmanpur, Simra, Utardhana and Shahpur* villages of Chinhat block along Faizabad road.

It is well-known fact that in Lucknow city, a maximum urbanization growth has taken along the Faizabad road only. The settlement of the urban people into the surrounding areas and location of economic activities like factories.

Amusement parks, commercial complexes, educational institutes etc gradually brings about a developmental change in the land use pattern in the rural areas that makes difficult to separate the urban area from rural one and forms a transition zone.

In order to have integrated functional as well as social segregation of landuse, authorities and planners should adopt holistic approach for 'Greenfield Site'. A usage of high resolution satellite data helps a lot in deciphering the intermixed zones between rural and urban parts. On the one hand, this technology gives the real time picture, similarly on the other hand, a cost-effective and unbiased approach increases the value of information.

Acknowledgement: Authors of this paper are thankful to Director Remote Sensing Applications Centre, U.P., Lucknow for giving their kind consent to prepare this manuscript.

References

Ahluwalia, M.S., 2002: State Level Performance under Economic Reforms in *Indian Economy*, Edited by A.O. Krueger, Oxford University Press, New Delhi.

Banerjee, R.K. & Banerjee Bireswar, 2000: *Remote Sensing Techniques for Regional Development*.

Bharucha, Erach, 2005: *Environmental Studies*: University Grant Commission, New Delhi.

Bhat, L.S, *et. al.*, 1976: *Micro Level Planning: A Study of Karnal Area*, Haryana India, K.B. Publications, New Delhi.

Jensen, J.R., *Introductory Digital Image Processing: A Remote Sensing Perspective,* Prentice-Hall, Englewood Cliffs, NJ, 1996 2nd Edition.

Michael N. Demers, John Wiley & Sons, Inc. 2000, *Fundamentals of Geographic Information Systems* (Second Edition).

Sabins, F.F. *Remote Sensing: Principles and Interpretation,* 3rd Edition, Freeman, New York, 1996.

8

Role of Space-Borne Technology in Monitoring the Urban-Rural Fringe Areas

Ashwani K. Srivastava, Amit Sinha, R.S. Kushwaha, Priyanka and *Virendra Kumar*

Introduction

In most of the urban centres of our country, the physical expansion of built-up areas beyond their municipal boundaries has been found very conspicuous. Such type of development has occurred in a spontaneous, haphazard and unplanned manner. Allahabad is one of the fastest growing city of Uttar Pradesh, which is also known as Prayag. It was founded by Mughul emperor Akbar in the year 1575 A.D. by the name of 'ILLAHABAS' and today it is an important city of the State where history, culture and religion create a magical confluence known as 'Sangam'.

City of Allahabad is placed among the other rapidly expanding cities of Uttar Pradesh like Noida, Lucknow and Agra. Besides having many premier educational institutions and organizations, the presence of key government offices gives city an important status.

The record process of urbanization is normally accompanied by spatial expansion. This has an adverse impact on surrounding agriculture land, through the creation of uncovered settlements. Accretion which takes place on peripheries of built-up area generates a zone of transition between rural and urban landscape known as rural-urban fringe. In view of the rapid influence of urban activities beyond the political boundaries and absence of development controls, it becomes difficult to administer these areas, successfully. In this context, the orbital Remote Sensing (RS) data and Geographical Information System (GIS) techniques play a major role by providing reliable, accurate, timely and periodic data and methods of integration of spatial and non-spatial data to create various planning scenario for decision-making.

In the present study, an attempt has been made to monitor the temporal growth of the city using multi-date satellite data which ultimately resulted in assessment of the urban sprawl of the city in a span of last 35 years.

Study Area and Its Location

The city of Allahabad enjoys a strategic location at the confluence of the Ganga, the Yamuna and the invisible Saraswati. The city lies between 25°20' to 25°31' N latitude and 81°45' to 81°56'E longitude.

Earlier Allahabad happens to be the least populated city among the 'KAVAL' towns of the State but it has the third highest growth rate in the State only after Lucknow and Agra.

The population of the city is growing continuously and there has also not been much variation in the growth rates over the past few decades. As per the Census of India, the total population of the city is about 10,81,622.

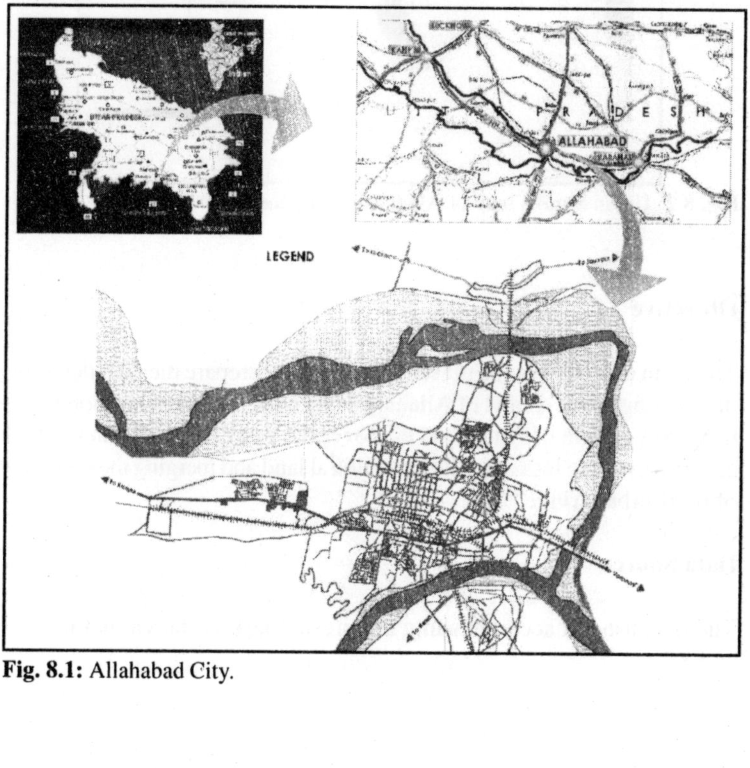

Fig. 8.1: Allahabad City.

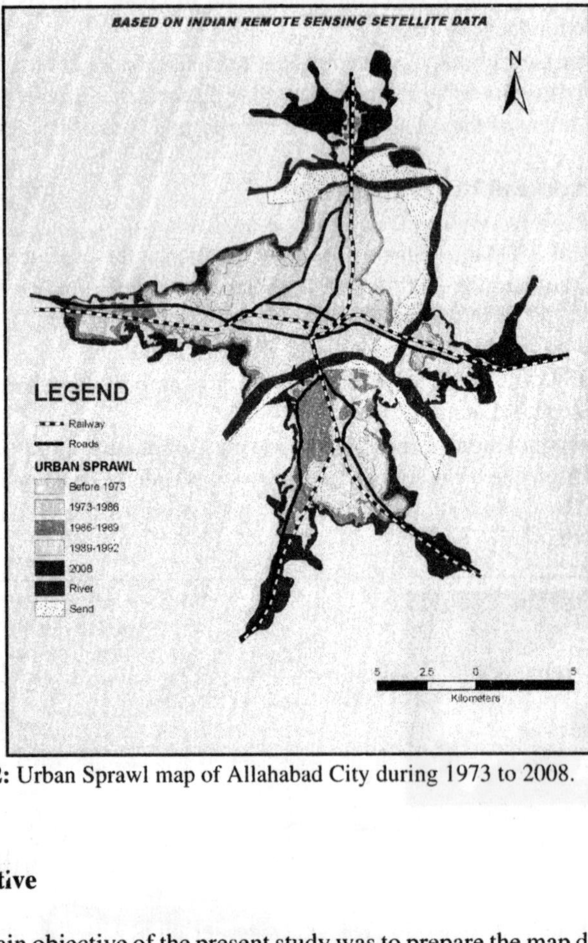

Fig. 8.2: Urban Sprawl map of Allahabad City during 1973 to 2008.

Objective

The main objective of the present study was to prepare the map depicting the existing urban sprawl of Allahabad city area. This enables monitoring the urban growth of Allahabad city over the past 'Four' decades, which clearly shows the loss of fertile agricultural land and merging the boundary of rural-urban fringe.

Data Source

The data used in accomplishing the present task is shown in Table 8.1 and 8.2.

Table 8.1: Decadal Growth of Population

Year	*Uttar Pradesh*	*Growth Rate*	*Allahabad*	*Growth Rate*
1951	6,32,00,000	16.71%	3,32,295	–
1961	7,38,00,000	16.17%	4,30,730	29.62%
1971	8,83,00,000	19.65%	5,13,036	19.11%
1981	11,09,00,000	25.59%	6,50,070	26.71%
1991	13,20,00,000	19.03%	8,44,546	29.92%
2001*	–	–	12,00,000	42.08%
2001**	16,62,00,000	25.91%	10,81,622	28.07%

Source: JICA Report.
* Allahabad Master Plan, 2021.
** Census of India, 2001.

Table 8.2:

Sl. No.	*Description*	*Scale*	*Year*
1.	Topographical Map no. 63G/15	1:50,000	1973
2.	Landsat –TM	1:62,500	1986
3.	IRS-1 A LISS-II	1:1,25,000	1989
4.	IRS-1 B LISS-II	1:50,000	1992
5.	IRS-P6 LISS-III	1:50,000	2008

Methodology

The Survey of India topographical maps on 1:50,000 scale were used for preparation of 'Base Maps' from which the relevant information were extracted for the interpretation of satellite data of different years in demarcating the boundary of the city. The final outcome of the study i. e., urban sprawl map was generated using GIS software ARC-GIS 9.2 version.

Result and Discussions

To monitor the temporal growth of Urban sprawl, the Survey of India topographical map has been used as the database. A comparison of data obtained from the Survey of India topographical map (surveyed in1972-73) and LANDSAT-TM satellite data of 1986 shows an expansion of 6.19 sq. km of fertile agricultural land in the fringe areas of Allahabad city (Table 8.3). The urban sprawl of Allahabad city as computed from IRS-1A data of 1989, when compared to data obtained from Survey of India topographical map of 1973 shows an increase in 18.28 sq. km. It is important to mention here that during the period between 1973-86, the expansion in urban area was only 6.19 sq. km (Table 8.3). Thus in a span of 17 years (1973-89), the total growth in urban area was observed as 26.57 per cent, which accounts for 1.56 per cent of average growth per annum. This also means a loss of 18.28 sq. km of rich agricultural land. The satellite data of IRS-1B of 1992 reveals that the urban area has increased from 87.07 sq. km. to 116.18 sq. km during the period between 1989 to1992 showing a phenomenal growth of 47.39 sq. km between 1973 and 1992. Hence, during the period of 20 years (1973-92), the growth of urban expansion was observed as 68.89 per cent, which accounts for 3.44 per cent of average growth per annum. The study reveals that the Allahabad city has consumed 47.39 sq. km. of agricultural land at the cost of city expansion over the past two decades. The average annual growth rate of the city during the period between 1989-92 was found 33.43 per cent, which accounts for 8.35 per cent of average growth per year and thus record a loss of 29.11 sq. km of agricultural land during this period (Table 8.3). The recent satellite data of IRS-P6-LISS III of 2008 shows that the urban area has increased from 116.18 sq. km to 173.00 sq. km. during the period between 1992 to 2008, showing a record growth of 104.21 sq. km. in a span of last 35 years (1973-2008).

In view of the above, it is very much clear that the spatial growth of the city by increasing the accessibility of sites on the periphery of the city, the road and the rail sectors play very significant role in Allahabad.

Conclusion

The present study of monitoring the urban sprawl and the loss of agricultural land around the fringe areas of Allahabad city using satellite

Table 8.3: Growth of Allahabad City

Sr. No.	*Year*	*Database*	*Urban Area (in sq. km.)*	*Urban Growth (in sq. km.)*	*% of Urban Growth*	*% of Growth per Annum*
1.	1972-73	Topographical map	68.79	–	–	–
2.	1973-86	LANDSAT-TM	74.98	6.19	8.99	0.64
3.	1973-89	IRS-1A,LISS-II	87.07	18.28	26.57	1.56
4.	1973-92	IRS-1B	116.18	47.39	68.89	3.44
5.	1992-08	IRS-P6-LISS-III	173.00	104.21	151.49	8.91

Source : Based on IRS data

image interpretation reveals that satellite based remote sensing technique is the most appropriate technique by which the urban spatial extension can effectively be assessed and could be used as a data base for the physical plan preparation, in order to achieve the goal of planned and regulate growth of the city.

The above study also reflects that there is an urgent need to assess the carrying capacity of all the urban centres of the State and there should be criteria to check the growth of built-up land according to the capacity of the urban centre.

Acknowledgement: The authors are thankful to Director, Remote Sensing Applications Centre, UP, Lucknow for permitting the publication of the present study.

References

Census of India, 2001. Registrar General and Census Commissioner, New Delhi, India.

Shukla, S.K., Moitra Madhusmita and Dhiran N.K. Monitoring Urban Sprawl and loss of agricultural land in Allahabad, using conventional and multidate satellite data, *Proceedings of National Symposium on Remote Sensing for Sustainable Development*—Nov. 1992.

Part III

Urban Sprawl and Changing Scenario of Rural-Urban Fringe

9

Urban Sprawl and Changing Peri-urban Scene Around Varanasi City: A Case Study of Chamaon Gram Sabha

Rana P.B. Singh

Orientation and Background

The area surrounding the city is a subject of constant threat and encroachment by the urban sprawl. This process leads to create a transitional belt between the city and the rural areas, known as peri-urban (suburban). The growing pressure of urbanisation frequently results in sub-standard and transitional lifeways. A pull factor in this respect is that industries often are located in the peri-urban areas, providing employment to nearby inhabitants. Thus peri-urban areas function as a buffer zone for cities absorbing migration on the one hand, and locate industrial types of economic activities on the other. In the process, land use changes rapidly from rural, agricultural to urban types and both urban and rural lifestyles occurring in these areas, in varying degrees. There are a number of specific environmental threats to vegetable yield, quality and safety in peri-urban areas. The peri-urban interface represents areas of dynamic institutional and environmental change. The increasing impact of the urban sprawl introduced a new look to intensive agriculture to supply the demand of the city turning to commercialisation of agriculture. There are examples of young farmers who practice intensive and commercial farming, and also engage themselves in other part-time jobs available in the suburban areas of the city.

Varanasi Master Plan and Perspective of Peri-urban Area of Chamaon GS

The Varanasi Development Region (VDR; 82° 48'E—83° 13'E longitudes and 25° 08'N—25° 30'N latitudes; 477.34 km^2) is defined as the "area to be selected for the expanded Master Plan in future". The present Master Plan of Varanasi (1991-2011) has been prepared on February 26, 1996. Together with urban areas of Varanasi Urban Agglomeration (VUA; 82° 56'E—83° 03'E and 25° 14'N—25° 23.5'N; area 112.26 km^2) and Mughalsarai Municipal Board, the VDR includes 460 villages of Varanasi and 141 villages of adjacent Districts of Chandauli and Mirzapur. The VUA forms the core, while the boundary of VDR marks the periphery.

In 1982, the Varanasi Development Authority (VDA, formed in 1974) made an assessment of the earlier plans of the city. And, under its direction, the Town & County Planning Organisation, TCPO, prepared a comprehensive Varanasi Master Plan (VMP) 1991-2011, during which time the population of Varanasi Agglomeration was expected to double of the 1991. This Plan was submitted to the Government of Uttar Pradesh in February 1996, and after approval it returned back for implementation in August 2000; simply it took 4½ years to get it approved!

The five-tier areal units are defined on the basis of administration and planning strategy, taking Varanasi Development Region, VDR (as in Master Plan projection for 2021), recording 477.34 km^2, defined as the "area to be selected for the expanded Master Plan in future, 2021", constitutes four tiers areal units (cf. Fig. 9.1) in descending order as Varanasi Peri-urban (suburban) area (298.07 km^2), Master Plan Projected Area (179.27 km^2; planned for 2011), Master Plan Operative Area (144.94 km^2; as extended in 1991), Varanasi Urban Agglomeration (115.27 km^2; expanded city limit in 1981), and Varanasi City Municipal Corporation (84.55 km^2; as followed since 1971). The VDR includes 460 villages of Varanasi and 141 villages of adjacent Districts of Chandauli and Mirzapur.

Under the Master Plan 2011, the expanded area proposed for the Greater Varanasi is 179.27 km^2, however, no way the land use categories fit to the standard norm of ecological balance. The most noticeable change during 1991-2011 plan is expansion of the area of the city (+112 per cent). According to the New VMP, the major drastic increase will be under land category of Government and Semi-Government uses (+390.50 per cent) and public and community facilities (+190.63 per cent), while in agriculture and open space only there will be 7.55 per cent of increase (cf. Table 9.1). This catastrophic change spoils the ecological system of the land use; the most crucial group is park and open ground that records decrease of over 60 per cent in comparison to 1999. The increasing pace of population results to increase area under residential uses up to 253.63 per cent over 1988. This indicates that agriculture in the peri-urban areas would lose its areal extent. Nevertheless to get more economic benefits,

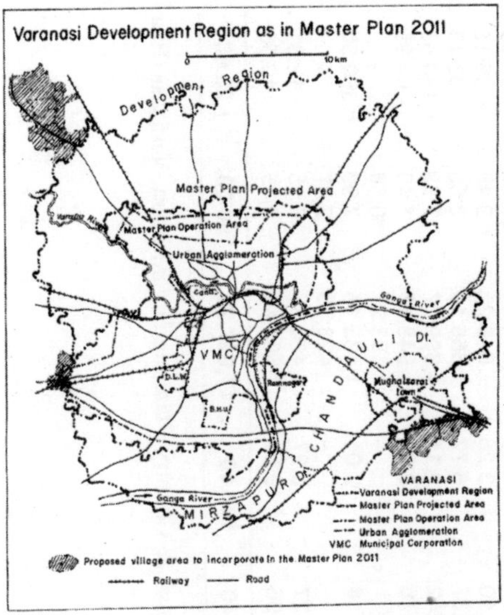

Fig. 9.1: Varanasi Development Region, as in Master Plan 2011.

there will be more intensive, market-oriented and fertiliser-based farming, especially cash crops like vegetables. Considering the increasing pressure of population, the area of open space is expected to decrease at –52.54 per cent. However, at the marginal areas, like Chamaon Gram Sabha, the commercial gardening and vegetable farming have already taken turn in competitive manner to support the increasing demand due to urban growth and sprawl.

Another change is that farmers today practise more intensive and productive agriculture than previously. Production in rice and wheat has doubled since the farmers changed to so-called High Yield Varieties (HYV). Compared to the old varieties HYV crops demand plenty of water, so irrigation has been extended in the area. There is one government owned tube well and 15 privately owned tube wells in the area. Most fields in the area can be irrigated from these tube wells. However, presently farmers suffer by interruption and irregularity of electricity supply.

Since, early 1980s, the expansion of Varanasi city has not only brought about external job opportunities for men in the area but also an increase in demand for farm produce; farmers in Chamaon Gram Sabha have been able to profit from this increased demand. One of the most profound changes in agriculture is that farmers in the area have altered their

Table 9.1: Varanasi Master Plans, MP: Land Use, I: 1961-91, and II: 1991-2011

Sl.	Land Use Category	*1988*		*I: MP, as in 1999*		*II: MP, as in 2011*		*Change, I -II, %*
		Area, ha	*% of area*	*Area, ha*	*% of area*	*Area, ha*	*% area*	
1.	Residential	2,615.64	46.16	5,457.24	37.65	9,254.61	51.62	+ 69.58
2.	Commercial	176.08	3.11	475.10	3.28	618.23	3.45	+ 30.13
3.	Industrial	195.31	3.45	981.37	6.77	656.19	3.66	- 33.13
4.	Public & Community facilities	261.05	4.61	450.42	3.11	1,309.07	7.30	+ 190.63
5.	Recreation (Park/Open ground)	53.04	0.94	2,705.76	18.67	948.47	5.49	- 64.95
6.	Services & Utilities	–	–	–	–	103.97	0.58	–
7.	Govt. & Semi-Government	56.69	1.00	292.18	2.01	1,433.15	7.99	+ 390.50
8.	Tourism (area) & Heritage zone	–	–	–	–	423.73	2.37	–
9.	Transport & Communication	914.30	16.13	1300.27	8.97	1,460.35	8.15	+ 12.31
10.	Other (agriculture & open space)	1,393.79	24.60	2,832.06	19.54	1,683.45	9.39	- 40.56
	Total Area	**5,665.90**	**100.00**	**14,494.40**	**100.00**	**17,927.22**	**100.00**	**+ 23.68**

Source: *Varanasi Master Plan-2011*. Varanasi Development Authority, & Town & Country Planning Organisation, Varanasi Uttar Pradesh. 13 July 2001; 50pp + 1 Map; ref. page 5.

production from subsistence to a more commercialised farming; the demand for farm produce at the markets in Tarna, Shivpur and Varanasi now-a-days determine the farmers' choice of crops. This shift of production is not unique for the farmers in CGS; similar alterations in production are also noticed in the neighbouring villages.

Changes in agriculture have also led to increased expenses for farmers. Today farmers have to purchase seed, fertiliser and pesticide; they also have outlays hiring tractors, getting fields ploughed, and transporting the produce. During 1950s and 1960s farmers used seeds from the previous year's harvest, animal manure as fertiliser, and did the ploughing with the help of oxen. A small farmer claimed that the rising costs were eating up the profits from the rise in yield. However, the intensification of agricultural production has been economically profitable for many, especially for the younger and better educated farmers who use new methods (Lejonhud, 2003: 149). The increased demand for farm produce from Varanasi city is not the only cause behind the changes in farming in Chamaon Gram Sabha. Part of the transformation in agriculture has been facilitated and stimulated by political decisions and State interventions. Other changes in the area could be related to various government programmes aiming to improve living conditions in the rural area.

A Peri-urban Place, Chamaon Gram Sabha: Geographical Personality

Chamaon Gram Sabha (Fig. 9.2) is a viable unit of the "village council" defined by the government programme of village development in line with the old tradition of co-operative development called Panchayat (literally five together), introduced in 1952 under the first land reformation in the Indian Republic. Since 1956, CGS consists from east to west of three village-settlements along the Varana river, which demarcates the southern boundary: Chamaon, Pachhimpur, and Shahabuddinpur, lying at 25°21' north and 82°58' east, located at a distance of about seven kilometres from the main city of Varanasi. The first election to the village council was held in 1958. CGS is a part of the Harahua Development Block, which is part of Varanasi District. It is through the Development Block that the government's village development programmes are canalised to the village level. There are thirteen built/occupancy units in different directions dominated by a particular caste. The total area of CGS is 181.3 hectares.

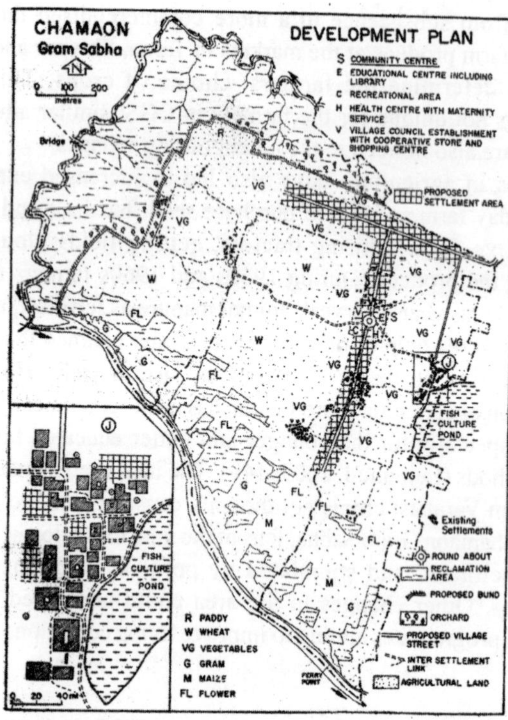

Fig. 9.2: Chamaon Gram Sabha, Varanasi.

In 1977, CGS has already been incorporated in the regulated area of the Greater Varanasi Municipal Corporation, and recently in 2001 given emphasis as part of the future Master Development Plan for Varanasi. Nevertheless, CGS has maintained its village character like that of other Indian villages. The village lies on the alluvial plains of the Ganga valley with little variation in height; the average height is 80m. Based on the texture of loamy soil (i.e. sand, silt, and clay), the village has four types of loamy soils: silty loam in the middle and eastern part, sandy loam in most of the parts, the clayey loam in patches along the Varana river, and some patches of sandy soil. The climate of the area is of the monsoon type, recording three seasons of summer, winter, and rainy (cf. Singh & Singh, 1977: 3-5).

It appears from the historical records that until the late 12th century this area was occupied by a non-Aryan race, known as the Soiris, who after the Kaushik Rajputs had taken control of the region. Some of them

Table 9.2: Population and caste structure in CGS

Caste	*Total Population*		*% of Population*		*Variation, % (+)*	*Caste rank, social hierarchy*
	1977	*2007*	*1977*	*2007*	*1977-07*	
1. Brahmin	29	69	2.3	2.4	137.9	Higher
2. Rajput	121	291	9.7	10.1	140.5	– ,, –
3. Kayastha	79	135	6.3	4.7	70.9	– ,, –
4. Ahir	77	197	6.2	6.9	155.8	Middle
5. Kurmi	362	786	28.9	27.4	117.1	– ,, –
6. Soiri	82	212	6.5	7.4	158.5	– ,, –
7. Lohar	90	209	7.2	7.3	132.2	Servants/ Craftsmen
8. Kumhar	24	40	1.9	1.4	66.7	– ,, –
9. Gareria	26	52	2.1	1.8	100.0	– ,, –
10. Gonr	22	37	1.8	1.3	68.2	– ,, –
11. Chamar	278	685	22.2	23.9	146.4	Low caste
12. Pasi	6	9	0.5	0.3	50.0	– ,, –
13. Musahar	56	146	4.5	5.1	160.7	Semi-tribal
Total	**1,252**	**2,868**	**100.0**	**100.0**	**129.1**	**–**

Source: Singh & Singh 1977 and personal surveys.

Table 9.3: Landownership in Chamaon Gram Sabha

Caste	*Total land ownership (ha)*		*% of land ownership*		*Variation, %*
	1977	*2007*	*1977*	*2007*	*1977-07*
1. Brahmin	6.83	5.23	5.2	4.2	- 23.4
2. Rajput	48.81	43.67	37.0	35.2	- 10.5
3. Kayastha	11.38	8.32	8.6	6.7	- 26.9
4. Ahir	11.64	11.23	8.6	9.1	- 3.5
5. Kurmi	32.63	34.54	24.7	27.8	+ 5.8
6. Soiri	10.05	9.63	7.6	7.8	- 4.2
7. Lohar	3.84	3.56	2.9	2.9	- 7.3
8. Kumhar	0.04	0.05	0.0	0.0	+ 25.0
9. Gareria	2.82	3.36	2.1	2.7	+ 19.1
10. Gonr	–	0.38	–	0.3	–
11. Chamar	2.06	2.94	1.6	2.4	+ 42.7
12. Pasi	–	0.35	–	0.3	–
13. Musahar	2.02	0.79	1.5	0.6	- 60.9
Total	*** 131.87**	**124.05**	**100.0**	**100.0**	**- 5.9**

Source: Singh & Singh 1977 and personal surveys.

* In addition to this, 57 hectares in the area are owned by people from outside, primarily farmers from surrounding villages.

accepted the sovereignty of the Kaushik and later on started calling themselves Rajputs. Close to the Varana river one can still see the ancient mound of original settlers. Until the middle of the nineteenth century most parts of this rural area were woodlands and pastures. Animal husbandry was the main occupation (cf. Singh, 1975: 139). The old people still tell stories of settling in the historical past.

Land ownership

The power and importance of landholding has been well recognized. As Mandelbaum (1970: 208) states, "Local power flows mainly from land. Land is the prime good in this agrarian setting; land is the main source of wealth; land is a main need for a jati (caste) on the rise". Out of a total of 389 households (families), 15.7 per cent are landless, and 71.5 per cent own less than 2 hectares of land. Rajputs record a population of a little less than one-tenth. However, they own a little more than one-third of the land. At the other extreme, it is notable that the Chamar (formerly the leather-worker caste) in 2007 recorded a population of 22.6 per cent of the total, but they own only 2.2 per cent of the land (Tables 9.2 and 9.3). Families belonging to scheduled castes like the Chamar, Musahar, Kumhar, Pasi and Gonr own little or no land at all. About 2/3 of the families in CGS own enough land to be self-sufficient in food. Optimally, a family of five members needs at least 0.25 ha to be self-sufficient in food.

These contrasting and complex patterns at different levels and different contexts make the Indian village an unique unit of habitat. In a mosaic of socio-cultural diversities common life is regulated by an interrelated web of taboos, traditions and religious systems as well as the economic structure, transformation, ways and means of prosperity and development. This system makes the character of the habitat and mental set-up of the people living there.

Changing Land Use and Agricultural Scenario

Agriculture is the base of the village economy, which still dominate the scene, still covering about 72 per cent of total land area (181.3 ha, in 2008). Those land earlier were not suitable for agriculture (i.e. cultivable barren, current fallow, and other fallow), are used for orchard and gardens, and also for seasonal vegetable gardening. The guava orchards grown only since last twenty years, and are flourishing quite well along the Varana river. This area was earlier cultivable barren, but now transformed into

Table 9.4: Chamaon Gram Sabha, Varanasi, 1954 - 2008: Land use Pattern

Area, ha (hectare) (a)	*1954*		*1974*		*1994*		*2004*		*2008*	
	Area	% of a	Area	% of a	Area	% of a	Area	% of a	Area	% of a
Land Use	*1*	*2*	*3*	*4*	*5*	*6*	*7*	*8*	*9*	*10*
1. Area	181.3	100.0	181.3	100.0	181.3	100.0	181.3	100.0	181.3	100.0
2.	35.5	19.6	35.6	19.6	24.2	13.3	16.8	9.3	12.3	6.8
3.	23.4	12.9	18.7	10.3	13.5	7.4	8.3	4.6	5.2	2.8
4.	11.3	6.2	10.7	5.9	6.2	3.4	3.8	2.1	2.1	1.2
5.	4.8	2.6	2.4	1.3	2.4	1.3	2.0	1.1	1.9	1.0
6.	0.8	0.4	0.8	0.4	7.5	4.1	10.2	5.6	11.7	6.5
7.	5.3	2.9	3.2	1.7	3.6	2.0	6.8	3.7	7.3	4.0
8.	4.8	2.6	5.3	2.9	5.7	3.1	7.7	4.2	9.6	5.3
9. Net AS	95.4	52.6	104.6	57.7	118.2	65.2	125.7	69.3	131.2	72.4
(a)	13.9	14.6	22.2	21.2	33.2	28.1	58.4	46.5	65.7	50.1
(b)	35.7	32.7	60.9	48.0	117.9	77.9	155.9	84.7	169.9	86.4
(c)	73.6	67.3	65.9	52.0	33.5	22.1	28.2	15.3	26.8	13.6
(d) Gross A	109.3	100.0	126.8	100.0	151.4	100.0	184.1	100.0	196.7	100.0

1. Total Reported Area. 2. Cultivable barren. 3. Current Fallow. 4. Other Fallow. 5. Land under Water. 6. Non-agricultural uses. 7. Orchards, gardens. 8. Settlement, & paths. 9. **Net Area Sown**: (a) sown > than once, (b) Net Irrigated area, (c) Unirrigated Area, (d) **Gross Cropped Area**.

Source: Revenue Records at Varanasi Tahsil, *khatauni*, & village records; collation by Singh.

commercial gardening. The unirrigated area reduced to half during the last 25 years (cf. Table 9.4). In 1974 half the cropped area was unirrigated, but it reduced to a little over 13 per cent in 2008. Formerly, the CGS was known for eggplant, however, now most of the neighbouring villages are producing and thus the original specie of CGS is now lost. Agriculture is based on three growing seasons, characterised by four main crops. Since last ten years the four prevalent crops, i.e. wheat (39%), paddy/rice (24%), vegetables (10%), and maize (6%) cover most of the gross cropped area (197 ha, in 2008). Among the notable vegetables grown are eggplant, cauliflower, potato and green beans. The land consolidation has introduced a new look to intensive agriculture. Due to the impact of commercialisation of agriculture, different groups of farmers have experienced an economic growth during the 1990s. There are examples of young farmers who practice intensive and commercial farming, and also engage themselves in other jobs.

One of the obvious major changes in agriculture during recent decades is the market orientation. The farmers in the area are very well aware of the market prices and changes in the market prices that affect their choice of produce. The production of eggplant (brinjal) can be taken as an example of commercialisation in agriculture. Formerly, CGS was very famous for its successful production of eggplant. CGS was even called the 'eggplant village' ("bainganwalla gaon"). The soil in Chamaon was very suitable for this kind of vegetable. Today, with the help of chemical fertilisers, other farmers in the surrounding areas are also able to grow eggplant. As a result of the increased output of eggplant, the market price has fallen. In response the farmers in CGS changed their production and are replacing the eggplant with, for instance, green peas, which give higher profit.

Due to the impact of commercialisation of agriculture and increasing demand from the growing urban population, different groups of farmers have experienced an economic growth during the 1990s through change in the selection of crops and expansion of cultivated area. The most successful in economic terms were the medium and small farmers mainly due to their concentration on growing vegetables. Big farmers are producing more grains, which is relatively not so profitable compared to vegetables. The saving from the other jobs supported the poor people to purchase some piece of land and to perform farming as part-time job. In 1954 around 59 per cent household were landless which fell down to around 7 per cent in 2008 (see Table 9.5). The two big landlords (1977) have sold their land lying at good distance from their main houses.

Moreover, many of the rich landlords get tube well installed at their plots and engaged in intensive farming. This practice has encouraged them either to sale their land, which are unmanageable for them, or considered not viable for extensive farming. A huge mass of marginal farmers has grown up since 1974, mostly because of land transaction by the earlier poor farmers and landless labourers (cf. Singh and Sen, 2001).

Another change in recent years has been the scarcity of farm workers. Males who belong to the Scheduled Caste who earlier worked on the farmers' land have recently started working in small towns and in Varanasi city, where they earn more and are paid in cash instead of in kind. However, the women belonging to the Scheduled Caste still work as day labourers in the area. The women are less mobile because of their responsibility for the children and the household.

Land ownership and Consolidation of Fields

The power and importance of landholding has been well recognised, as Mandelbaum (1970: 208) states, "Local power flows mainly from land. Land is the prime good in this agrarian setting; land is the main source of wealth; land is a main need for a jati (caste) on the rise". Of course after passing sixty years of independence and fifty-five years of Land Reforms Act, still landholding plays an important role. The increasing pace of urban sprawl pushed the land prices very high even in the surrounding peri-urban areas. In Chamaon Gram Sabha, at present out of 445 total households (families), about 7 per cent are landless, and 79 per cent own less than one hectare of land. Rajputs record a population of a little less than one-tenth. However, they own a little more than one-third of the land. Taking India as a whole, it is observed that big top 5 per cent of landlords account for about 40 per cent of total holdings. Even today, majority of agricultural labourers have no work for about 100 days per year (cf. Singh, 1999: 63). At the other extreme, it is notable that the Chamar (formerly the leather-worker caste) records one-fifth of total population, but they own only 2.4 per cent of the land (Table 9.5), recording increase of 42.7 per cent over 1977. For those families earlier landless, possession of land is a mark of identity and a sign of upward mobility. Families belonging to Scheduled Castes like the Chamar, Musahar, Kumhar, Pasi and Gonr own little land, and perform their subsistence on the manual labour and rent-basis farming. About 2/3 of the families in CGS own enough land to be self-sufficient in food at the minimum of requirement. For an optimal family of five members at least

Table 9.5: Chamaon Gram Sabha, 1954 – 2008: Households (hh) by landownership

Landownership size		*1954*		*1974*		*1994*		*2004*		*2008*	
Standard Bigha, bh	*hectare ha*	*Total hh*	*% of hh*	*Total hh*	*% of hh*	*Total hh*	*% of hh*	*Total hh*	*% of hh*	*Total hh*	*% of hh*
landless	landless	98	58.7	85	33.7	67	18.0	46	10.8	32	7.2
< 1.6	< 0.4	18	10.7	88	34.9	133	35.8	185	43.3	195	43.8
1.6–4	0.4 – 1	17	10.2	29	11.5	121	32.6	143	33.5	158	35.5
4–8	1 – 2	21	12.6	31	12.3	37	10.0	47	11.0	56	12.6
8–12	2 – 3	6	3.6	13	5.2	11	3.0	6	1.4	4	0.9
12–16	3 – 4	3	1.8	2	0.8	1	0.3	0	–	0	–
16–20	4 – 5	2	1.2	2	0.8	1	0.3	0	–	0	–
20–32	5 – 8	1	0.6	1	0.4	1	–	0	–	0	–
> 32	> 8	1	0.6	1	0.4	0	–	0	–	0	–
Total	**Total**	**167**	**100.0**	**252**	**100.0**	**372**	**100.0**	**427**	**100.0**	**445**	**100.0**

Source: Revenue Records at Varanasi Tahsil, *Khatauni*, & personal surveys; collation by Singh.
Note: 3.95 Standard *Bighas* equal to 1 ha; and 1.60 *Bighas* equal to 1 Acre, i.e. 0.40469 ha.

Table 9.6: Distribution of field plots in Chamaon Gram Sabha by size, 1954 to 2008

Size of plots, in hectares, ha	*Field plots, 1954*		*Field plots, 1974*		*Field plots, 1994*		*Field plots, 2004*		*Field plots, 2008*	
	No.	*%age*	*No.*	*%age*	*No.*	*%age*	*No.*	*%age*	*No.*	*%age*
less 0.10	452	46.9	387	44.7	186	24.3	141	21.0	138	20.2
0.10–0.20	335	34.7	304	35.1	356	47.4	294	43.8	283	41.5
0.20–0.30	109	11.3	107	12.4	127	17.1	132	19.7	144	21.1
0.30–0.40	27	2.8	29	3.3	43	5.3	47	7.0	53	7.7
0.40–0.50	31	3.2	26	3.0	32	4.0	39	5.8	42	6.2
0.50–0.60	6	0.6	5	0.8	5	0.7	7	1.0	9	1.3
0.60–0.70	2	0.2	3	0.3	4	0.5	5	0.7	6	0.8
0.70–0.80	2	0.2	3	0.3	3	0.4	4	0.6	5	0.7
+ 0.80	1	0.1	1	0.1	1	0.3	3	0.4	3	0.5
Total	**965**	**100.0**	**865**	**100.0**	**741**	**100.0**	**672**	**100.0**	**683**	**100.0**

Source: Revenue Records at Varanasi Tahsil, *Khatauni*, & personal surveys; collation by Singh.

0.25 ha. is required to be self-sufficient in food. These contrasting and complex patterns at different levels and different contexts make the Indian village a unique unit of habitat. In a mosaic of socio-cultural diversities common life is regulated by an interrelated web of taboos, traditions and religious systems as well as the economic structure, transformation, ways and means of prosperity and development. This system makes the character of the habitat and mental set-up of the people living there.

The Consolidation Act was passed in 1956 by the Government of India. The plot pattern in the traditional Indian village was widely scattered and each plot size very small. A farmer could have his landholdings of a few hectares divided into more than 20 different plots, scattered in the village he lives, or in other villages. The purpose of the Consolidation Act was to reduce the number of plots each farmer had and make each of the plots larger. The aim was for big farmers to have their plots distributed in at least at three places, medium farmers in two places, whilst small farmers will have their landholdings in just one or two places. In this area farmers are divided into four groups according to the size of landholdings: first grade (big farmer) who holds more than 2 ha. of land, second grade (medium farmer) possessing land between 1ha. to 2 ha., third grade (small farmers) holding below 0.4 ha. to 1ha, and fourth grade (marginal farmers) holding less than 0.4 ha. (Table 9.6). It is not only the size of the landholding that matters but also perception of the family's status that played a strong role during the British period in which big landlords were given status and power of control. The most successful in economic terms were the medium and small farmers mainly due to their concentration on growing vegetables. Many big farmers those earlier producing more grains, during last ten years realised that it was not profitable in comparison to vegetables, resultantly they now shifted to vegetable farming. The saving from the other jobs supported the poor people to purchase some piece of land and to perform farming as part-time job (Singh and Sen, 2001: 68).

The struggle for survival, more individualist perspective and involvement in agriculture as part-time job, supported landless people to purchase land, while this encouraged big farmers to sale their land (Singh and Sen, 2001: 69). This tendency is obviously marked by the comparison of statistical data of 1974, 1994, 2004 and 2007 (cf. Table 9.5). Of course, the land consolidation has introduced a new look to intensive agriculture, the encroaching impact of urban sprawl has encouraged to vegetable farming (green peas, beans, okra, etc.), which is more profitable. This tendency further encouraged young farmers to practice intensive and commercial vegetable farming, and apart from farming engage themselves in other jobs (cf. see the narrative of farmers of various group in Gustafsson, *et al.*, 2000: 211-213). In CGS land consolidation has been carried out in Pachhimpur and Shahabuddinpur but not in Chamaon. As shown in Table 9.6, consolidation has resulted in the number of plots being reduced by 293, from 965 in 1954 to 672 in 2004. However, in the last three years the family disputed promoted further fragmentation of the field plots, resulting to increase of plots-reaching 683 in 2007. The most common size of plot since 1994 has been between 0.10-0.20 ha. compared to earlier years when the most common size of plot was below 0.10 ha. More commonly the size category of 0.20-0.30 ha. has constantly recorded increase in the number of plots and their percentage frequency. This size suits for family level management together with keeping involved in other jobs too.

Towards Conclusion: From Perspective to Prospect

As obvious, the traditional Indian village has been described as a self-sufficient unit where everything was run in its own way, however, today, the situation seems to be different, especially in the peri-urban area. One of the reasons for this change is the new administrative system that the Indian Government implemented at the beginning of 1950s after Independence in 1947, in addition with the catastrophic increase of population of urban places and their sprawl in the environs. Once the area is delineated as part of the future urban expansion, the system of governance and rural development policy change to cope with urban system of land uses and service delivery. The case study of Chamaon Gram Sabha indicates the problems faced after its inclusion in the Master Plan; in fact, transitory location is the more crucial issue that serves as obstacles for the development.

With the common consensus a spatial development plan was prepared in 1977 (Fig. 9.3), but no way it has been followed, mainly due to lack of social integrity and sense of community. In 1999, the CGS village council had several sustainable infrastructural plans for the future; but even after a decade (2008) least completion is noted; of course the project is still in process (cf. Table 9.7).

It has been realised that Indian Village has in many ways maintained its multiplex character of spatiality, cultural integration, social and economic diversity, and traditional continuity, while on the other hand the change is obvious, acceptance and challenges too. Life in the Indian

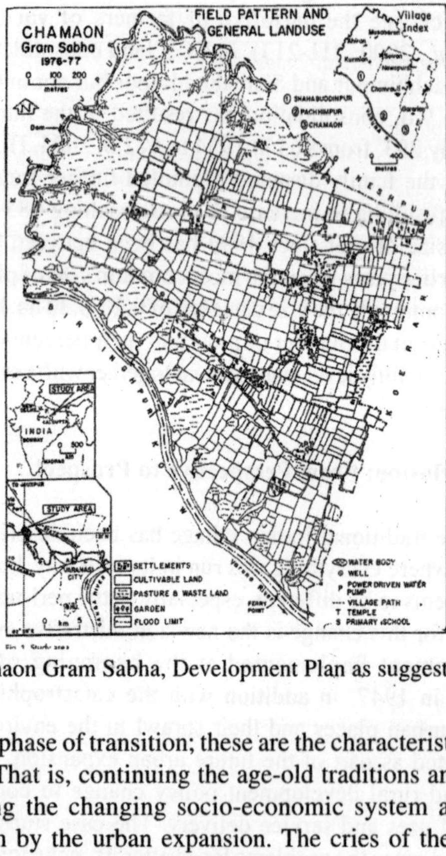

Fig. 9.3: Chamaon Gram Sabha, Development Plan as suggested in 1977.

village is in a phase of transition; these are the characteristics of the peri-urban areas. That is, continuing the age-old traditions and, at the same time, adopting the changing socio-economic system and the values imposed upon by the urban expansion. The cries of the poor masses, distrust of the governmental system and the ideology of gain without work are common expressions of this situation (cf. Gustafsson, *et al.*, 2000: 214). The issue of transition (the peri-urban characteristics) will be more crucial in the near future: trying to achieve a balance with a foot in both camps, i.e. traditional village life and urban life. The ideology and allocation of funds for development are very far-sighted, but the perspective of conservative thought and the lack of work ethics result into crisis.

The impact of the Master Plan for Varanasi will certainly change village life into an urban pattern though the villagers are neither prepared nor willing to fully accept this. The present life pattern and life philosophies are the product of traditionalism together with recently introduced individualism and consumerism.

Table 9.7: Chamaon GS: The Planned and Present Scenario

The planned attributes, 1999	*The present status, April 2009*
– Panchayat building	Completed in 2006
– Electricity to Shahabuddinpur (the western part of CGS)	Partly installed, but not operative
– More link roads within CGS	Some pavements and links added
– Toilets	No progress
– Distribution of settlement land	Not functional
– Promotion of the Ambedkar School up to the 8th grade	Achieved, but lacking infrastructure
– Village–based small factories and village crafts to be established (like soap and carpet making)	No progress at all
– Promotion of basic education	A little progress
– Helping weavers to prevent them being exploited by merchants.	No success, No implementation

Source: Personal survey.

References

Gustafsson, Gerhard; Singh, Rana P.B.; Lejonhud, Kristina & Vålvik, Karl Ivar, 2000. Change and continuity in village India: crisis and prospects in Chamaon, Varanasi. *FENNIA, International Jl. of Geography* (Geogr. Soc. of Finland, Helsinki). Vol. 178 (No. 2): pp. 203-214.

Lejonhud, Kristina, 2003. Indian Villages in Transformation. A Longitudinal Study of Three Villages in Uttar Pradesh. *Karlstad University Studies*, 2003: 11. Karlstad University, Karlstad (Sweden).

Mandelbaum, D.G., 1970. *Society in India*. University of California Press, Berkeley.

Singh, R.B., 1975. Rajput Clan Settlements in Varanasi District. *NGSI* Pub. 12. National Geographical Society of India, Varanasi.

Singh, Rana P.B., 1999. Rethinking development in India. Perspective, crisis and prospects. In, David Simon and Anders Närman (eds.), *Development as Theory and Practice*. DARG Ser. 1. Longman, London: pp. 55-75.

Singh, Rana P.B. and Sen, Chandra 2001. The Structure of Peri-Urban Agricultural Environment in Varanasi Development Region. *National Geographical Journal of India*, Vol. 47: pp. 61-72.

Singh, Rana P.B. and Singh, Ravi S., 2002. Development in India: Scenario and Ideology. In, Anders Närman and K. Karunanayake (eds.), *Towards a New Regional and Local Development Research Agenda*. Deptt. of Geography, Göteborg University (Sweden), Series B, No. 100 and Centre for Development Studies, University of Kelaniya (Sri Lanka), No. 1: pp. 65-78.

Singh, R.L. and Singh, Rana P.B. 1977. Rural Development in Indian Environment: Assessment and Prospect. A Case Study of Chamaon Gram Sabha near Varanasi City, U.P. *NGSI* Pub. 29, for UNO-CHBP. National Geographical Society of India, Varanasi.

Singh, Rana P.B.; Gustafsson, Gerhard and Lejonhud Kristina, 2005. Changing Land and Changing Lifeworld: A study of Chamaon Village, Varanasi. *Eastern Anthropologist*, (EFCS Lucknow, pub. by Serials Publs., New Delhi), Special Number: "Rural Profile: Scenario 2005", Vol. 58 (nos. 3-4), July-December: 593–604.

10

Urban Encroachment on Agricultural Lands

Ali Mohammad and *Nawaz Malik*

Introduction

Towns and cities are blooming with a change in the land use along the highways and in the immediate vicinity of the city. This dispersed development outside of the compact urban and village centres along the highways in rural countryside is defined as sprawl. (Theobald, 2001)

The direct implication of such sprawl is the change in the land use and land cover of the region. It refers to some type of development with inputs such as loss of agricultural land, open spaces and ecologically sensitive habitants. Landscape changes can be distinguished into conversion from one land cover type into another one and transformations within a given land cover type.

Usually sprawl takes on the fringe, at the edge of an urban area, or along the highways. At the urban-rural fringe, the agricultural land becomes fragmented with farmers unable to take advantage of economies of scale, and land prices have become inflated due to non-agricultural values, so farmers are unable to realize reasonable returns to land. Some of the causes of the sprawl include—population growth, economy and proximity to resources and basic amenities. Patterns of infrastructure initiatives like the construction of roads and service facilities (such as hotels etc.) also often encourage the regional development, which eventually leads to urbanization. The direct implication of such urban sprawl is the change in land use and land cover of the region.

Economic growth derives urban expansion in the form of construction of business dwellings, roads and leisure centres etc. and the metropolitan regions face growing of problems of urban sprawl, including decline in natural vegetation, wildlife habitats and agricultural land. Land loss from agriculture has been the focus of considerable research in India. Loss of agricultural land does not necessarily equate to loss of agriculture industry as land productivity is irrelevant in intensive industries such as poultry and mushrooms etc. Concern has been expressed at the loss of prime land in Lucknow to prevent its permanent loss through sub-division and urban development while other states are considering similar action. Residential sub-division and hobby farm development are often blamed for loss of both prime land and agricultural industry, but the true extent of such loss in Lucknow is questionable.

Thus, the amount of rural land lost to sprawl is the key issue from an environmentalist and agricultural perspective but the amount of rural land loss and urban expansion is also significant to the quality of life of urban dwellers.

They may in fact, foster retention of otherwise non-viable agriculture in a region but carry greater risk of land and environmental degradation. Changes to agricultural land use with urban and residential encroachment often result in the intensification of agricultural industry and new, financially viable alternative forms of agriculture.

Limiting sub-division of agricultural land could, thus, inhibit the emergence of new forms of agriculture that might contribute significantly to regional socio-economic development. Intensive industries are less dependent on land quality but often create undesirable impacts and conflict when co-located with rural residencies. Hence, the case for preservation of prime land in peri-urban areas solely for its traditional agricultural value cannot be sustained. Data on the extent of loss of both prime land and agricultural industry in peri-urban areas is limited but both are major issues for local government.

Urban Encroachment on Agricultural Lands in Lucknow

Demographic data for the Lucknow Urban Agglomeration and Lucknow City from Census 2001 and other available documents were analyzed to understand the growth patterns (Table 10.1). The Master Plan 2021 is the basis of information for the projected population and land use in peripheral areas where considerable private development has been taking place. Growth rates have been arrived at through projecting geometric growth, arithmetic growth and incremental growth rate methods and adding an additional population at 1,00,000 every five years for additional areas that might get incorporated within the city. This seems a conservation estimate, however, given the current pace of real estate development and the intention of government to attract new investment in Lucknow.

Urban growth currently is largely on par with other cities of similar size, and is anticipated to be slightly faster in the immediate future. This needs to be considered in city planning.

Although the city has potential positive economic comparators, such as its heritage and educational institutions, lack of infrastructure and business concerns about the regulatory have been limited the economic base, which has meant inadequate employment opportunities and limits on the local government and service agency revenue bases. The percentage of people engaged in the tertiary sector is higher than the other sectors. Although literacy levels among the workforce are high, qualifications in technical areas is limited. City has a significant slum population with slums more or less uniformly distributed across the city and marked below levels of access to basic infrastructure.

The Master Plan 2021 shows a dramatic increase in land for residential use although it does not take into consideration the real estate boom underway by private developers. New development areas have not kept pace with levels of infrastructure development. Pollution—air, noise and that of the river Gomti are areas of critical concern.

Lucknow has a rich heritage that has been compromised by the pressures of urbanization—mainstreaming heritage with modernization is a challenge. Inner city areas are characterized by urban decay. There are several water bodies within the city limits that have been encroached, reclaimed and polluted through the discharge of sewage.

The Master Plan 2021, which is the source of the information, estimates that Lucknow covered an area of 16,270 hectares in 2004-05.

Table 10.1: Population Projection of Lucknow (2006–2021)

Projection Type	*Years*			
Lucknow City	*2006*	*2011**	*2016**	*2021**
1. Geometric Rate	25,82,190	30,21,162	35,34,760	41,35,669
2. Arithmatic Rate	25,01,000	27,95,000	30,89,000	33,83,000
3. Increment Rate	26,07,791	30,81,366	36,40,942	438,32,137
Average Population Growth in Lucknow City	25,63,660	29,65,843	34,21,567	39,40,269
Lucknow Cantonment	60,000	60,000	60,000	60,000
Lucknow District	26,24,000	30,26,000	34,82,000	40,00,000

Source: Master Plan 2021, * Projected Population.

Compared to 1987 when the area was estimated at 9170 hectares, there has been a 77.4 per cent increase in the total area in 2004-05.

Trends in land uses has been interesting, especially the fact that residential use has grown dramatically in comparison to all other uses, although there has also been notable growth in commercial, industrial and public service land use.

The demand of land for residential areas is quite enormous, as seen from Table 10.2 that there is an increase of 99.4 per cent from 1987 to 2004-05. This exerts a great pressure on the surrounding peri-urban land which is very fertile as a result huge amount of land is consumed. This results in the loss of net sown area as can be noted from Table 10.2.

It is clear from Table 10.3, that cropping intensity has increased quite considerably during the period of 1991 to 2005. It was 138.73 in 1991 while it increased to 157.96 in 2005. Grossed cropped area also increased from 2,01,890 hectares in 1980 to 2,18,220 hectares in 2005. But what was more altering is the reduction in the net sown area. Net sown area showed an increase from 1981-1991 and thereafter it reduced considerably during the last decade 1991-2001. Actual net sown area at present is 1,38,148 hectares.

This might be attributed to the fact that Lucknow City has grown tremendously over the period of 3 decades. As stated earlier, large area under fertile land is consumed up by the expansion of the city on its

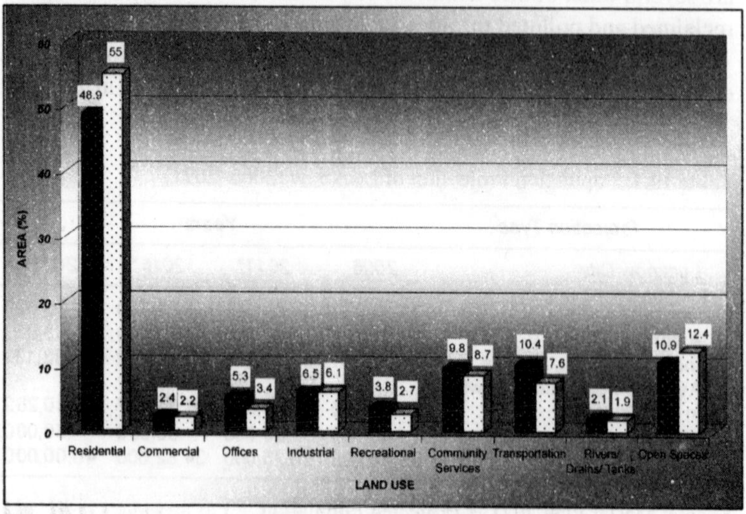

Fig. 10.1: Land Use in Lucknow City (Except Cantonment).

Table 10.2: Land Use in Lucknow City (Except Cantonment) (1987– 2005)

Land Use	Year (1987)		Year (2004–05)		
	Area (Hectares)	Per cent	Area (Hectares)	Per cent	Growth Percentage
Residential	4,485.98	48.9	8,945	55.0	99.4
Commercial	223.77	2.4	360	2.2	60.9
Offices	474.69	5.3	560	3.4	18.0
Industrial	596.22	6.5	990	6.1	66.0
Recreational	346.48	3.8	435	2.7	25.5
Community Services	902.02	9.8	1,410	8.7	56.32
Transportation	952.00	10.4	1,240	7.6	30.25
Rivers/Drains/ Tanks	193.66	2.1	310	1.9	—
Open Spaces	996.14	10.9	2,020	12.4	—
Total	**9170.00**	**100**	**16,270**	**100**	—

Source: Master Plan 2021.

periphery. There has been an increase of 77.4 per cent in the total area in 2004-05. Total area was 9,170 hectares in 1987 while it became 16,270 hectares in 2004-05.

No. of villages in 1981 were 917 in total (inhabited and uninhabited). While it reduced to 835 in 2001 census year.

Table 10.3: Agricultural Land Use in Lucknow District (1981– 2005) (Area in Hectare)

Year	Reported Area	Forest	Net Area Sown	Area Sown More Than Once	Gross Cropped Area	Cropping Intensity
1981	2,50,757	9,472	1,43,270	58,620	2,01,890	141.00
1991	2,52,162	9,472	1,45,933	56,524	2,02,457	138.73
2005	2,51,845	11,726	1,38,148	80,072	2,18,220	157.96

Source: Various Statistical Abstracts, UP.

Table 10.4: Number of Villages and Towns in Lucknow (1981–2001)

Year	Villages			Towns
	Inhabited	Uninhabited	Total	
1981	899	18	917	10
1991	824	10	834	8
2001	822	13	835	8

Source: Statistical Abstracts, UP.

Conclusion

India is one of the world's biggest countries with 328.73 million hectares of geographical area or 32.8 lakh sq. kms. The vastness of India along with substantial cropland gives the general feeling for the abundance of land and the concern for at least preserving the land is totally lacking. The rapid growth of population, changes in social and economic structure and trends of urbanization in the last few decades has made researchers to think over the judicious use of land based on land capability survey and analysis it is now becoming very difficult for the country to afford to engage the fertile crop land in the name of unplanned town development. Especially, the rate at which the crop land is being converted for built up and non-built up development due to expansion of settlement. The crucial fact is that "land is finite" and the converted land cannot be recovered back in future. The present study raises many issues with loss of crop land use to urban expansion:

(1) *Urban Shadow Effect*: The study area has recorded a major loss of agricultural land mainly due to urban shadow impact because it is the capital town, thickly populated state with poverty and high level of urban migration. Especially the conversion of agricultural lands to tree plantation and vacant land for the glaring examples of it. Farmers living in the vicinity of the cities face problems resulting in either lower yields or lands not farmed, even though the land is not actually converted to urban uses. Farmers of fringe areas are subjected to present or short-term future development pressure; begin to devote less capital from farm maintenance and management. The productivity of the land begins to decline which ultimately results in selling these lands to property dealers. They do not maintain it as agriculturally productive land, but allow it to remain idle until such time as advancing suburbs justify transforming it into suburban areas. The net effect of these forces cause a much greater loss of crop land to urban uses than the figure normally given for land transferred to urban uses indicate.

(2) *Quality of Crop Land Converted*: Not all land is equally suitable for farming purposes. In India especially in Indo-Gangetic region, almost the whole land is flat well drained, adequately watered and fertile land, which makes it very suitable for agricultural activities, but these same characteristics also make

it a prime land for the development of the settlement in this region. The study area also recorded conversion of 1/3rd of the prime land with Class I capability class indicative of the disproportionate concentration of development on good quality agricultural land. The significance of this is obvious. The land in Class I yield a much higher return for the same inputs of labour capital. These are the lands which are of primary importance in maintaining the agricultural productivity.

(3) *Cost of Crop Land Conversion*: A more significant factor intensifying the problem of loss of prime crop land is associated with the cost of such land conversion. The cost are two-fold and are related to the actual cost of replacing lost farmland as well as to government programmes that prompt urban expansion and encourage loss of crop land. When the prime crop land is lost, the value of the crop production is immediately foregone. The cost to replace that land is fairly substantial. The government makes effort to bring some additional land for agricultural uses by reclaiming wasteland but the question is how much and at what cost.

Land use is not static, but a dynamic interactive system. Changes are occurring in each of the category of land use for example from Class I land to Class VII land which have an impact on the residents of the nation both at local as well as regional level. Urban sprawl with its attendant destruction of prime crop land seems far severe than popularly supposed. Although the urban expansion cannot be restricted, with proper management and planning, we can restrict and direct this expansion in desired and sustainable ways, and protect the fertile agricultural lands. It needs stricter implementation of agricultural land conversion loss. The farmers should be provided some incentives to remain in farming activities, as this is the only way to control migration of rural population to urban centres. Even they should be encouraged to go back to farming activities and this is the only way to restrict conversion of crop land into vacant land. Land capability maps should be prepared and be considered for developing national land utilization for urban expansion. These maps are more relevant in developing countries like India, where planned and unauthorized urban expansion is very common in smaller towns. The urban and regional planners should make sure that urban expansion would not be in any case on Class I land and it should be diverted towards Class V land.

The basic objective of land use planning is to devote the land of special qualities for special uses. If the land is suitable for cultivation, it should be used for cultivation and it is up to the human efforts and needs that they convert the land either in Class I land or Class IV land. Every effort should be made to find the optimal use of land in the national and people interest. Naturally every claimant puts forth his demand as most important. One of the first tasks of the land use planning is to strike a balance between various interests. The multi-purpose use of land, where-ever possible should be taken into consideration and no piece of land should be allowed as far as possible, to remain vacant or wasteland.

References

Ali, M. (2008) *Land Classification and Land Use Planning, Use of Remote Sensing GPS and Digital Cartography in Resource Management and Planning,* Varanasi.

Ali, M. (2008) *Agro Ecological Zones and Sustainable and Profitable Farming System Model for Small and Marginal Farmers, Sustainable Management of Land Resources through Land Management,* State Land Use Board, Lucknow.

Das Gupta, K. (2000), Is the Joyride Over? *Down to Earth*, Centre for Science and Environment, Vol. 9(6), New Delhi.

Fazal, S. (1998), *Agricultural Production and Price Mechanism,* Chugh Publications, Allahabad.

Fazal, S. (2000), *The Need for Preserving Farm Land: A Case Study from a Predominately Agrarian Economy, Landscape and Land Use Planning Elsewhere.*

Master Plan 2021, Lucknow, Town and Country Planning Department, LDA, Lucknow.

Ranade, A. and Dev, M.S. (1998) Agriculture and Rural Development, *India Development Report,* Oxford University Press, New Delhi.

Shafi, M. (1969) Land Use Planning, Land Classification and Land Capability: Methods and Techniques, *The Geographer*, Aligarh.

Stamp, D. (1962) *The Land of Britain: Its Use and Misuse*, Longmans Green and Company Ltd., London.

11

Development at the Rurban Fringe: Impacts on Agriculture and Rural Land

Shahab Fazal

Study Area

Aligarh is an old city, which grew from an uplifted part (*Kol),* witnessed a long and cherished history including *Mughal's, Maratha's* and *Britisher's rule*. Aligarh city situated in the western part of Uttar Pradesh, between *Ganga* and *Yamuna* rivers at 27°53′ north latitude and 78°35′ east longitude. It is district headquarters and is famous as educational and industrial city. This city has gained importance because of its proximity to the national capital (New Delhi) and industrial cities of Uttar Pradesh (Kanpur and Ghaziabad). Systemic and planned development of Aligarh city would serve dual purpose—it would reduce the pressure on these cities, as it would provide employment opportunities in the city and it can even supply raw materials to these cities. Although the desired level of progress has not been attained, still the city has a well developed hinterland and an important city acting as service centre to its rural hinterland.

Data and Methodology

The unit for analysis for the present study is village as the context of change and household as the unit in which changes can be explained. The data were gathered from a comprehensive, purposeful and well structured survey. The survey was conducted during February, March and April 2008. The sample was based on 'Stratified Random' basis. The sample design adopted was of two stage. In the first stage, selection of villages from the Fringe areas of Aligarh city was made and 12 villages were selected. All the villages were located in the Aligarh city fringe, ranging from 0-10 kilometre from the municipal limits of the city. Significantly, all the villages apparently belonged to the same stage of urbanization of village (Box 11.1) and the selected villages were passing through 2nd and 3rd stage of urbanization. The sampled villages were namely, Barautha, Machua, Cherat, Panjipur, Lekhrajpur, Atalpur, Chanduri, Haibatpur, Shahpur, Gadrana, Alampur and Nanau (Figure 11.1). In the second stage, selection of households were made for in-depth analysis, as it is the lowest level unit within which individuals have collectively organized their activities. From the 12 sampled villages, 134 households were selected and they were categorized on the basis of their landholdings (Table 11.1). Of the 134 households sampled, 82 were engaged in the agricultural activity, while rest of the 52 households has left the agricultural activity, disposing of their land and switched to other occupations.

Discussion

- Farmers in the agricultural occupation, 23 households came under the large category (agricultural landholding of more than

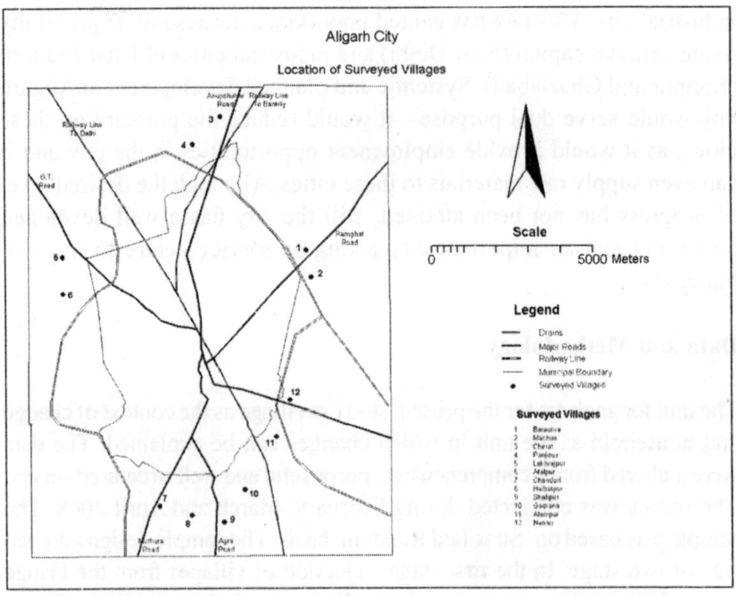

Fig. 11.1: Aligarh City.

10 hectares), the total area operated was 426 hectares and the average size of agricultural landholding was 18.5 hectares.

- Farmers who have left the agricultural occupation, 16 households came under the large category (size of disposed land is more than 2 hectares), the total land disposed was 46.5 hectares.
- 30 households came under the medium category (agricultural landholding of 4 to 10 hectares), the total area operated was 191 hectares and the average size of agricultural landholding was 6.3 hectares.
- Farmers who have left the agricultural occupation, 25 households came under the medium category (size of disposed land is 0.5 to 2 hectares), the total land disposed was 30 hectares.
- 29 households came under the small category (agricultural landholding of less than 4 hectares), the total area operated was 41 hectares and the average size of agricultural landholding was 1.4 hectares.
- Farmers in small category left the agricultural occupation (where the size of disposed land is less than 0.5 hectares), the total land disposed was 5 hectares.

Land Use in the Agricultural Sector

Agriculture in the rurban fringe is in a paradoxical situation. While on the one hand, it derives value from its links with the urban centres, the other side of it is that a variety of different and contradictory values, interests and images associated, creates stress in the system. Here, we

Table 11.1: Size and Number of landholding in different category of sampled households in the fringe areas of Aligarh city (2008)

A: Households in agricultural sector.

Farm category	*Size of holding*	*Number of sampled holding*	*Total sampled area (in hectares)*	*Average area per holding (in hectares)*
Large	More than 10 hectares	23	426	18.5
Medium	4 to 10 hectares	30	191	6.3
Small	Less than 4 hectares	29	41	1.4
Total sampled farms		82	658	

B: Hosueholds outside agricultural sector

Land owner category	*Size of land disposed of*	*Number of sampled holding*	*Total land disposed of (in hectares)*	*Average land disposed of (in hectares)*
Large	(land disposed more than 2 hectares)	16	46.5	2.9
Medium	(land disposed 0.5–2 hectares)	25	30	1.2
Small	(land disposed less than 0.5 hectares	11	5	0.4
Total sampled farms		52	81.5	

Source: Based on Field Survey, 2008.

try to investigate the agricultural land use pattern adopted by the farmers who are practicing agriculture as economic activity in the rurban fringe.

Cropping Pattern Adopted by the Sample Farmers

The entire land is used for agriculture in *rabi* season while in *kharif* season 94 per cent of total land was under agriculture, leaving the remaining land as fallow. There are two main agricultural seasons namely, *rabi* and *kharif*. Rabi season pertains to the winter period, it is the main dry crop season, while *kharif* season pertains to the rainy period. The cropping pattern is found to be greatly influenced by urban proximity and some crops like vegetables, peas, *arhar* and *chara* etc. have substantial acreage, these commodities are basically grown to meet the urban demands. Whereas, a similar study in rural interior areas have shown subsistence orientation in their cropping pattern, dominated by foodgrains (Fazal, S., 1994).

Field surveys revealed that there were vast differences in the cropping pattern adopted by the sample farmers in the study area (Tables 11.2 and 11.3). The farmers whether small or large always try to make best use of their land according to their own judgment.

Large Farmers: During the *rabi* season, every piece of land was under cultivation. They were found to be allocating little over half of their total land to cereals (Wheat-53.2% in *rabi* and rice (35.7%) and

Box 11.1: Stages of Urbanization of Villages in the Rurban Fringe

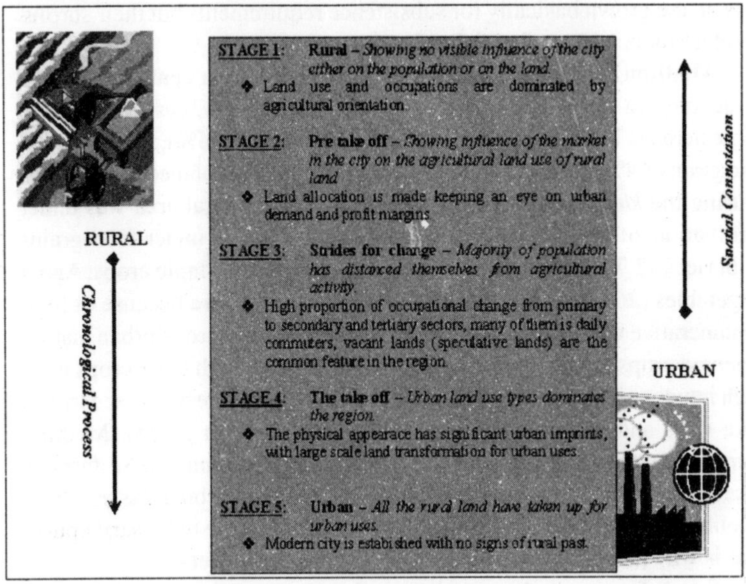

maize (19.6%) in *kharif* season. These are the staple food of the region as well as they are remunerative and have assured market. Rest of the crops grown by large farmers have distinctive urban influence. Vegetables have substantial share in their cropping pattern in both *rabi* and *kharif* season, even other crops such as peas, gram and *arhar* can also be put into vegetable category as they have same demand and use in the region. Another crop—*chara* grown in *kharif* season, its acreage is also influenced by urban proximity. *Chara* is basically a fodder crop, which has significant demand as the region have well developed household dairy activity and farmers supplement their income by domesticating some cattle (buffaloes and cows). Almost 80 per cent of the *chara* grown by the sampled farmers are grown on large farms.

It was observed that the large farmers were devoting substantial area to foodgrains but they also devote a fairly large proportion of their land to the cultivation of cash crops. Most of the large farmers concentrated more on the cultivation of cereals, while some of the large farmers, who were engaged full time with the farming activities, devoted significant proportions of their land to cash crops and were earning high income. Although wheat and gram in *rabi* and rice, maize and *arhar* in *kharif* season are grown basically for subsistence requirements but their surplus production is marketed with handsome returns.

Medium Farmers: During the *rabi* season 43 per cent of their land is devoted to the cultivation of cereals. Significantly, cash crops have large acreage led by vegetables (25.6%), mustard (11.6%), peas (10.4%) and gram (8.4%) dominating the *rabi* cropping pattern of medium farmers. During the *kharif* season about 93 per cent of the total area was under cultivation, of which about 60 per cent of the land was under food-grains with rice (42.7%) and maize (17.1%) were important staple crops. Again vegetables (26.1%) and *arhar* (12.6%) have good share because of their remunerative nature and assured urban market. The share of urban market oriented crops among medium farmers is high, although these crops need high inputs and the chances of crop failure is always there but these farmers take risks and in return they get comparatively high profits. Medium farmers are the most progressive farmers of the region. These farmers take agricultural activity seriously and consider it as a business and their livelihood is based on agriculture. They provide all the necessary inputs, that is why the yield in their farms are higher than others.

Small Farmers: Among the small farmers, entire area was under cultivation during *rabi* season, of which about 48 per cent was under cereals. Significantly, vegetable is devoted 31.7 per cent of *rabi* land. During the *kharif* season the share of vegetable acreage is 38.6 per cent followed by maize 29.3 per cent. It was noticed that small farmers grow largely cereals for their subsistence requirements. Here too, they are growing cereals which need lesser inputs and investments (wheat and maize needs lesser inputs than rice). Small farmers belong to low income strata of the society. They don't have the resources to invest for costly inputs in their farms, they also can't take the risk of crop failure, which is associated with crops like mustard, gram etc. The only crop, which they grow for the market, is vegetable and their survival is greatly dependent on these crops, which fetch them income on daily basis. The cropping pattern of small farmers is largely of subsistence type and is characterized by traditional style of farming in which the main aim is to grow cereals. It was noticed that because of hand to mouth situation of the small farmers, they grow cereals to fulfil their subsistence requirements. These farmers neither have the resources nor can they take risks of a crop failure in growing cash crops. The yield obtained by these farmers were the lowest because their cropping pattern is based on traditional system, they rely

Table 11.2: Cropping pattern adopted by the sampled farmers during *rabi* season in the fringe areas of Aligarh City (2008)

Farm Category	*Total sample areas*	*Area under rabi season*	*Rabi crops*					
			Crops	Wheat	Mustard	Peas	Vegetables	Gram
			Rank	1	2	3	4	5
			Area	227	58	57	54	30
Large	426	408		(53.2%)	(13.6%)	(13.6%)	(12.6%)	(7%)
			Production	5289	383	604	N.A.	258
			Yield	23.3	6.6	10.6	N.A.	8.6
			Crops	Wheat	Vegetables	Mustard	Peas	Gram
			Rank	1	2	3	4	5
			Area	83.5	49	22.5	20	16
Medium	191	178		(43.4%)	(25.6%)	(11.6%)	(.104%)	(8.3%)
			Production	2329	N.A.	146	210	131
			Yield	27.9	N.A.	6.5	105	8.2
			Crops	Wheat	Vegetables	Peas	Gram	Mustard
			Rank	1	2	3	4	5
			Area	20	13	3	2.5	2.5
Small	41	37.5		(48.7%)	(31.7%)	(7.3%)	(6%)	(6)
			Production	472	N.A.	28	17	15
			Yield	23.6	N.A.	9.3	6.9	6.00
			Crops	Wheat	Vegetables	Mustard	Peas	Gram
			Rank	1	2	3	4	5
			Area	330.5	116	83	80	48.5
Total sampled farms	658	623.5		(50.1)	(17.6)	(12.6)	(12.1)	(7.3)
			Production	8090	N.A.	544	842	406
			Yield	24.4	N.A.	6.5	10.5	8.3

Note: Area in hectare, production in metric tons and yield in quitals per hectare.
Figures in brackets are percentages to the total area under cultivation in the respective farm category.

Source: Based on Field Survey (2008).

Table 11.3: Cropping pattern adopted by the sampled farmers during *kharif* season in the fringe areas of Aligarh City (2008)

Farm Category	*Total sample areas*	*Area under Kharif season*		*Rabi crops*				
Large	426	408	Crops	Rice	Vegetables	Maize	Arhar	Chara
			Rank	1	2	3	4	5
			Area	146 (35.7%)	104 (25.5%)	88 (19.6%)	38.5 (9.4%)	31.5 (7.7%)
			Production	2832	N.A.	1276	404	N.A.
			Yield	19.4	N.A.	14.5	10.5	8.6
Medium	191	178	Crops	Rice	Vegetables	Maize	Arhar	Chara
			Rank	1	2	3	4	5
			Area	76 (42.7%)	46.5 (26.1%)	30.5 (17.1%)	22.5 (12.6%)	2.5 (1.4%)
			Production	1497	N.A.	470	227	N.A.
			Yield	19.7	N.A.	15.4	10.1	8.2
Small	41	37.5	Crops	Vegetables	Maize	Rice	Arhar	Chara
			Rank	1	2	3	4	5
			Area	14.5 (38.6%)	11 (29.3%)	5 (13.3%)	3.5 (9.3%)	3 (8%)
			Production	N.A.	153	82	34	N.A.
			Yield	N.A.	13.9	16.4	9.7	N.A.
Total sampled farms	658	623.5	Crops	Rice	Vegetables	Maize	Arhar	Chara
			Rank	1	2	3	4	5
			Area	224.5 (36%)	165 (26.5%)	129.5 (20.7%)	64.5 (10.3%)	39 (6.2%)
			Production	4411	N.A.	1899	665	N.A.
			Yield	19.6	N.A.	14.6	10.3	N.A.

Note: Area in hectare, production in metric tons and yield in quintals per hectare.
Figures in brackets are percentages to the total area under cultivation in the respective farm category.

Source: Based on Field Survey (2008).

on traditional seeds and could not provide much modern inputs in their farms.

Factors Influencing Land Use in the Sample Farms

Several factors influence the decision-making process of the farmers in the selection of crop grown by them. But some factors may be more dominating than others among particular category of farms. It varies from farm to farm. The author has tried to investigate the important factors influencing the cropping pattern of the sample farmers in the study region. The 82 sampled farmers were asked questions, relating to the various factors influencing them in the selection of crops. We tried to persuade them to point out only one factor, which influenced them most. But most of the farmers insisted that only one factor was not responsible but there were more than one factor. We have taken all those factors, which were pointed out by the sample farmers. These were then arranged in descending order and the top ten factors were taken into consideration (Table 11.4).

The factors which were affecting the decision-making process of the sample farmers are discussed below:

Market Prices of the Crop Grown: Generally, the sample farmers consider farm harvest prices, before making any decision regarding the selection of crops. These prices are the average wholesale prices at which the commodity is disposed of by the producer to the trader at the village site. However, vegetables and *chara* have highly variable prices largely determined by its demand and supply channels. Prices of crops were found to be the most influencing factor in determining the choice of crop grown by the farmers. This shows the commercialization of agriculture in rurban fringe, whereas the region as a whole still has subsistence orientation in farming activity (Fazal, S., 1994). Sampled farmers (39%) were influenced most by the prices. The farmers prefer to grow those crops, which are profitable to them, which fetch them higher market prices and higher monetary benefits. Prices of crops were influencing the cropping pattern of mostly those farmers who are economically strong because these farmers can invest on costly inputs and they can also take risk of changing their cropping pattern. Medium (53.3%) and large (47.8%) farmers were found to be influenced maximum by prices.

Yield: Yield of the crops, emerged to be the second most important factor (29.2%), which influenced the cropping pattern of the sample farmers. Farmers from all the categories of farm sizes were equally concerned, they prefer to grow those crops, which gave them better yield.

Table 11.4: Factors influencing the changes in the cropping pattern of the sampled farmers in the fringe areas of Aligarh city

Large Farmers			*Medium Farmers*			*Small Farmers*			*Total Sampled Farmers*		
Rank	*Factors*	*No. of Farmers*	*Rank*	*Factors*	*No. of Farmers*	*Rank*	*Factors*	*No. of Farmers*	*Rank*	*Factors*	*No. of Farmers*
1.	Price	11	1	Price	16	1	Irrigation Facilities	10	1	Price	32 (399%)
2.	Yield	9	2	Yield	10	2	Financial Problems	9	2	Yield	24 (29.2%)
3.	Crop Prospect	8	3	Crop Prospect	9	3	Availability of H Y V	8	3	Crop Prospect	22 (26.8%)
4.	Labour	8	4	Irrigation Facilities	7	4	Prices	5	4	Irrigation Facilities	21 (25.6%)
5.	Irrigation Facilities	4	5	Availability of H Y V	3	4	Yield	5	5	Availability of H Y V	11 (13.4%)
6.	Traditions	3	5	Labour	3	4	Crop Prospects	5	5	Labour	11 (13.4%)
7.	Physical Factors	3	6	Financial Problems	2	5	Traditions	4	5	Financial Problems	11 (13.4%)
8.	Governmental Policies	2	7	Physical Factors	1	6	Physical Factors	3	6	Traditions	8 (8.5%)
9.	Availability of H Y V	–	7	Traditions	1	7	Govt. Policies	2	7	Physical Factors.	7 (8.4%)
9.	Financial Problems	–	7	Govt. Policies	1	8	Labour		8	Governmental Policies	8 (6%)

Note: Figures in brackets are percentages to total respondents. These figures are more than the total respondents as more than one reason were pointed by the respondents.

Source: Based on Field Survey (2008).

Because higher the yield more will be the production and more will be the income. This again shows that farmers in rurban fringe try to maximize their income from their lands. Again large (39.6%) and medium (33.7%) farmers were found to be influenced more than the small (17.2%) farmers. This is because small farmers are concerned more with other factors related with their poor economic conditions.

Crop Prospects: The farmers generally expect that they will get a certain quantity of produce from the crops they grow. But, some crops are more susceptible to pests, diseases and climatic changes and the risk of crop failure in these crops are high. So the farmers prefer growing those crops in which the risk of crop failure is low. In the selection of crops farmers kept an eye on the prospects of that particular crop. Large and medium farmers consider this factor significantly before selecting any crop for cultivation. On the other hand, small farmers keep themselves away from those crops in which the risk of crop failure is high. Again the prospect of crop is influencing more large (34.8%) and medium (27.2%) farmers. These farmers try to draw maximum income from their agricultural land and that is why their cropping pattern is influenced by price, yield and prospect of the crops they grow. A good balance of these three factors determines greater profit margins from their farming activity.

Irrigation Facilities: Availability of irrigation facilities, mode of irrigation, cost of irrigation, timeliness and adequacy of supply of irrigation water etc. were taken into consideration. Irrigation is one of the important and crucial inputs in agriculture because the modern technology and inputs works only with higher watering to the plants. This factor was influencing 25.6 per cent of the sampled farmers. The cropping pattern of small farmers (34.5%) were the worst affected because irrigation facility is not in their hands. They have to hire water, which is quite expensive, or they depend on urban sewage or waste water for irrigating their farms (there are five drains around the city, which carries cities sewage and waste water).

Availability of High Yielding Variety of Seeds and Chemical Fertilizers: Timely availability of high yielding variety of seeds and chemical fertilizers was also one of the most important consideration for the sample farmers. The small farmers (27.6%) were much influenced by this factor. Due to their poor economic condition they can't purchase these inputs from the market. The government gives subsidies on these inputs but it was observed that almost all these facilities were availed by the large and medium farmers because they are socially, economically and politically strong. Moreover, the investments for these inputs have to be made at the beginning of the season and small farmers with their hand to mouth situation cannot have capital for investing in agriculture. So the small farmers have to rely on local seeds and manures, which results in poor yield and low returns from their lands.

Financial Problems: These days with the introduction of new technology the cost of production has increased considerably. Inputs are quite expensive and apart from economically well-off farmers, it is very difficult for most of the farmers to invest heavily for their crops. The small farmers (31%) were the worst affected by it. These farmers belong to the economically backward class of the society. They can't provide the necessary inputs in their farms and also can't take the risk of crop failure and all these factors collectively restrict them from going for commercialization of agriculture. Large farmers are not affected by financial problems, while medium farmers are marginally affected by this factor.

Labour: Availability of labour at peak season was a major problem and large farmers (34.8%) were the worst affected. These farmers require hired labour because they themselves are not full time associated with farming activities and their family members also do not work in the field, so to manage their large holding, they have to depend on hired labour. This also prevents them from cultivation of labour oriented crops. On the other hand, small farmers are not at all affected by this factor. Every working person is engaged in agricultural activities including women and children in these farms.

Traditions: The farmers are bound with the age-old traditions of farming and they hesitate to make changes in their cropping pattern. Farmers cultivate crops according to their taste and preference. They like to cultivate those crops, which they have been eating traditionally, till some drastic changes come. Their customs and cultural background also plays crucial role in the selection of crops. Most of the farmers, which were affected by this factor, are illiterate. They are bound with the age-old traditional pattern of farming and hesitate to make changes in their cropping pattern.

Physical Factors: Physical factors were also seen affecting the cropping pattern of the surveyed farmers. This region is best suited to agriculture. It has good climatic conditions, flat alluvial plains and fertile soils. That's why the farmers of this region have not given much importance to this factor. However, in some surveyed areas the problem of salinity-alkalinity and waterlogging was observed.

Governmental Policies: Governmental policies regarding the distribution of loans, giving of subsidies on fertilizers and high yielding variety crops, improvement in irrigation systems, land development policies, land reforms, agricultural schemes for the benefit of small farmers, price control and establishment of credit societies are some of the governmental policies which influence the farmers' decision in selection of crops. These days with improved communication linkages and easy access has led to greater awareness for various governmental policies. Although the sampled farmers were not directly influenced by it but author found that the farmers were voicing their concern for improvements, urban proximity is one important reason for it.

The above discussed factors, which were influencing the decision-making process of sampled farmers regarding the choice of crops clearly points towards the concern among farmers for maximizing their returns from their farms. This commercial feature among them is largely due to the urban influence as they live in close proximity with Aligarh city. The subsistence farming system has been significantly transformed into commercial farming system. The urban proximity has given exposure to a larger and better marketing facility. The sampled farmers were found highly responsive to factors such as prices, yield and prospects of the crop. This suggests farmers try to ensure, higher level of production for crops of their choice, which would fetch them higher monetary benefits. Similarly, the urban forces have also made them aware of different governmental policies and modern inputs associated with agricultural activity. The influence of their cost and easy availability was also rated highly by the sampled farmers.

The striking feature of the sample survey was that, although large farmers have greater capacity to invest their resources but they were found to have lesser intensity of cropping in their farms. This is because of improper management of their large holdings. The sample survey also found that despite of strong urban forces, level of commercialization is lesser as they do not devote all their resources in agricultural activity. Medium farmers take advantage of better management of resources in agricultural activity. The intensity of cropping was highest among medium farmers, similarly, the intensive use of inputs has resulted in high productions in their farms. They were found to be more responsive to urban forces. They devote more land to remunerative crops and the degree of commercialization was found to highest among medium farmers. Small farmers were least responsive to the urban forces. They are socially and economically backward section of the society and these farmers have very limited access to modern inputs of agriculture. Thus, small farmers are unable to make much adjustment to their farming system. They were also observing the urban forces, but could not react to it because of their hand to mouth situation.

Factors Influencing Land Use among the Sampled Households Outside Agricultural Sector

The study also tried to study the landowner's decision-making process. Decision about the use of land involves a multiplicity of factors: the objectives of land user, the process by which he reaches on the decision and the socio-economic factors that consciously or unconsciously influences the decision and above all the proximity of the growing urban centre too exerts pull force. The sample survey conducted on 52 households, where land transformation (agriculture to other uses) has taken place. The sampled landowners were divided into *three* categories on the basis of disposed landholdings by them:

- *Large*: landowners disposed of more than 2 hectares of agricultural land.
- *Medium*: landowners disposed size of 0.5 to 2 hectares of agricultural land.
- *Small*: landowners disposed less than 0.5 hectares of agricultural land.

To know the factors, which lead to their decision of disposing of agricultural land, landowners were asked to state the reasons for their decision. Their answers were then arranged in descending order (Table 11.5). The factors which were affecting the decision-making process of the sampled landowners are discussed below:

Change in Employment: Urbanization has generated employment opportunities with increased and assured wages and landowners with better education have obtained jobs outside agricultural sector. These farmers, if their family allows are quick to dispose of their lands to get extra money. Landowners from large (34.8%) and medium (26.6%) category were found to be disposing their lands because of change in economic activity (Box 11.2).

> **Box 11.2**
>
> Land in India is generally inherited in the family, which is divided among son and daughters in different proportions (variation is found in different religion, caste and regional traditions). The division of land is mostly not properly documented and is rather verbal. It leads to conflict among the family members. Sometimes these conflicts extend among families from different generations.
>
> Another issue related to this division of land among the family members is shrinking of landholding. This lead to transformation of landholdings into uneconomic landholdings within a period of few generations. In India, where law of inheritance prevail, reduction in the size of operational land is adversely affecting agricultural activity.

Instant Money: Agricultural activity is being depressed activity, the cost of production is increasing and the profit margins are stagnant. The small (27.5%) and medium (20%) landowners with relatively poor economic conditions are disposing of their lands to get instant money. These farmers get some labour oriented jobs in the city and they dispose of their lands. The disposal of land is basically because their lands are not productive enough to sustain their family needs, so their entire family does work in city in different capacities while low productive lands are sold to get instant money.

Uncertainty of Profit Margins: Uncertainty of profit margins in the agricultural sector due to variation in natural-social-economic conditions also led to land transformation. The urban shadow effect has led to lower productivity, resulting in lesser priority to agricultural activity. Large (21.7%) and medium (18.4%) farmers were found to be disposing of their lands because of this reason.

Social Status: The urban forces have transformed the social-cultural mindset of the population. Owning agricultural land was once considered to possess higher social status but now social status is higher for jobs in urban area because of the higher wages. Again the large (21.7%) and medium (20%) landowners were found to be disposing of their agricultural land and disassociate themselves from rural connections. The younger population is found to be more responsive to this factor.

Protecting Future: Economic returns from the agricultural sector are lower and protecting agricultural lands from encroachment and litigations are difficult. So landowners dispose of their land when real estate prices are high and try to protect their future. The large and medium landowners who either have jobs in other sectors or feel no future in

Table 11.5: Reasons for disposal of agricultural land among sampled landowners in the fringe areas of Aligarh city (2008).

Landowner category	*Reasons for disposal of agricultural land*								
Large (land disposed of more than 2 hectares)	Reasons	C.E.	S.S.	U.P.	O.P.	I.M.	P.F.	U.L.	Fr.
	Rank	1	2	3	5	6	7	8	8
	Land-owners	8	5	4	4	4	3		
Medium (Land disposed 0.5 – 2 hectares)	Reasons	C.E.	P.F.	LM.	S.S.	U.P.	O.P.	U.L.	Fr.
	Rank	1	2	3	4	6	7	8	9
	Land-owners	8	6	6	6	5	4	1	—
Small (land disposed less than 0.5 hectares)	Reasons	LM.	FR.	U.L.	U.P.	O.P.	C.E.	S.S.	P.F.
	Rank	1	2	3	4	6	7	8	9
	Land-owners	8	5	4	2	1	1	—	—
Total	Reasons	CE.	LM.	U.P.	S.S.	P.F.	O.P.	U.L.	Fr.
	Rank	1	2	3	4	6	7	7	8
	Land-owners	17 (32. %)	17 (32%)	12 (23.%)	11 (21.1%)	10 (19.2%)	9 (17.3%)	5 (9.0%)	5 (9.0%)

Note: Based on Field Survey (2008).
Figures in brackets are percentages to total respondents. These figures are more than the total respondents as more than one reason were pointed by the respondents.

C.E.– Change in Employment., I.M.– Instant Money., P.F.– Protecting Future., S.S.– Social Status., U.P.– Uncertainty of Profit. Margins., O.P.– Operational Problems., U.L.– Uneconomic Landholding., Fr.– Forced.

agricultural sector dispose of their lands and invest it in other sectors. Another reason which contributes in selling their lands is the tradition of joint land possession, the landowners also dispose of land to avoid family dispute and get whatever money they can get which may not be possible if the dispute for division of land happens.

Operational Problems: Due to urban shadow effect landowners faces several operational problems in agricultural activity in the rurban fringe. Garbage dumping, unauthorized traffic, interfering with water troughs, vandalism and higher labour costs etc. are the common problems in farms close to urban settlements. Large landowners were worst affected by this problem due to lack of labour and management in their farms and this also led to disposing of their agricultural land.

Uneconomic Landholding: Small landowners are unable to sustain their family from the small-uneconomic landholding so they dispose of their land. The cost of production is high while the returns are lower. The small landowners work as labourers in the unorganized sector of urban centre and dispose of their unproductive-uneconomic lands.

Forced: Property dealers and land developers pressurize small landowners to dispose of their land as these people needs big areas for developing colonies. Small landowners because of their poor economic and social background could not resist the pressure and forced to sell their agricultural lands.

The sample survey shows that unlike the agricultural sector, all sections of the society belonging to different categories of landowners were observing the pressure of urban forces in the rurban fringe. But their responses to urban forces are different because of different economic and social background.

Large landowners (outside agricultural sector) were found to be more responsive towards the urban forces. The reason was that since they have distanced themselves from direct agricultural activity. This poses managerial and operational problems in farming activity, thus they are offering their lands in the fringe areas for urban development. Medium landowners were found to be resisting to urban forces outside agricultural sector. Socially, this section of the society has still associated themselves with farming community, but since they are also the progressive and dynamic section of the society, where they change occupation and this instigate them to dispose of their agricultural lands. Small landowners are also responsive to urban forces for disposing of their agricultural land. But their decision is due to their poor and miserable economic background. They are unable to sustain themselves in agricultural sector and the lure of getting instant money goads them to sell-off their agricultural lands.

Conclusion

The analysis of the 134 households belonging to the various categories of landholdings shows the existence of significant urban forces in the rurban fringe areas of Aligarh city, which is a fast growing urban centre in north India. The landowners who are in the agricultural sector were found to be performing intensive agriculture and a significant degree of commercialization in their farms. They were found to be making necessary adjustments to their farming pattern to attain maximum income from their lands. However, the magnitude of response to urban forces in the agricultural sector is varied and largely dependent on their respective socio-economic class to which they belong. The large farmers belong to the high and sound economic status. The economic background of the large farmers contributes substantially in the decision-making process. They can take risk in changing their cropping pattern and they grow those crops, which give them higher monetary benefits. These farms suffer from the problem of indifference and uncertainty of hired labour, this restricts them of intensifying their agricultural activity, which otherwise they are capable of doing it. Medium farmers have also great capacity to invest their own resources; this has contributed towards the increase in productivity. But there is slight difference between the large and medium farmers. Medium farmers are in a position to take advantage on both the counts, i.e. greater access to technology and more concentration on their farms. The intensity of cropping is highest on these farms. The intensive utilization of land coupled with the intensive use of inputs has resulted in high yield and productions. The degree of commercialization is greater as compared to large farmers. Conditions of the small farmers are not similar to the medium and large farmers. They have smaller landholdings and they are economically and socially very poor. There is intensive utilization of land and every member of the family work in the fields but the returns are poor. On these farms, the cultivation of crops requiring lesser inputs are preferred, these farmers do not have access to modern inputs and their poor economic condition does not allow them to have higher degree of commercialization in their farms.

The development of secondary and tertiary sector in Aligarh city has lured the population in the fringe areas to make changes to their livelihood. The result shows that urban forces have significantly changed the socio-economic values of landowners. Sampled household who reported of disposing of their agricultural lands and switching from agricultural to other occupation in the rurban fringe of Aligarh city. They alarmingly showed distraction from agricultural activity. People are switching from agricultural activity due to lesser profit margins, lower status in the society, uncertainty of profit margins, operational problems etc. This raises a very crucial issue in a predominantly agrarian economy that is endowed by fertile agricultural setting. The people are shedding their agricultural land and getting instant money but becoming landless, giving rise to the problem of unemployment. The urban sector is also unable to cope with large unskilled population looking for jobs. This ultimately results in emergence of different socio-economic problem. The livelihood of these unskilled populations, who do not have agricultural lands, opting for urban living are at great risk and stress. They constitute a new social group living in pathetic condition and their living conditions are even worse than rural areas. They have to bear higher cost of living in the city, while they cannot afford access to city's amenities, facilities and infrastructure. This ultimately culminates into serious social and economic crimes.

On the basis of the findings from the present study, following features of rurban fringe in Indian context can be stated:

- Rurban fringe are characterized by a large diversity representing a complicated system of living-working relationship, observing rapidly increasing land value, rapid changes in the size of build area, changes in the functionality of the area and changes in the composition and activities of the population.
- Rurban fringe is very disorder, because of lack of effective planning resulting in haphazard urban expansion and degradation of resources.
- Rurban fringe is located in city-country combinative area that is no longer rural but it is not yet urban.
- Rurban fringe is a dynamic zone, transforming due to its proximity with the city, the contradictory of city's expansion and farmland is very significant, incurring heavy loss of prime farmland of the region.
- Most significantly, the rurban fringe structure is not stable, economic system is very complex and economic activities and resources tend to focus on short-term benefits.

References

Amitabh, (1997). *Urban land markets and land price changes: A study in the Third World Context* Aldershot: Ashgate.

Bryant, C.R., L.H. Russwurm & A.G. Mclellan, (1982). *The city's countryside; Land and its management in the rural-urban fringe.* London: Longman.

Dupont, V. (1997). Les 'rurbains' de Delhi, *espace, populations, societes,* 2-3, pp. 225-240, Paris: Orstom.

Fazal, S., (1994) Factors Deciding Farmer's Choice of Crops. *Asian Profile,* Canada, Vol. 22, No. 5.

Fazal, S., (2001). "The Need for Preserving Our Farm Lands. A Case Study from a Predominantly Agrarian Economy". *Landscape and Urban Planning,* Vol. 55, No. 1, Elsevier Science Publication, United Kingdom.

Fazal, S., (2004). The Role of Accessibility in Land Transformation: A GIS Based Study of a Growing Urban Centre in a Developing Economy. *Asian Profile,* Vol. 32. No. 1. Canada.

Kundu, A., (1989). The dynamics of city hinterland relationships: The Indian case. In: P. Vennetier, ed., *La péri-urbanisation dans les pays tropicaux,* Centre d'Études de Géographie Tropicale, Valence, pp. 306-325.

McGee, T.G. (1991). The emergence of Desakota regions in Asia: Expanding a hypothesis. in: N. Ginsburg, B. Koppel & T.G. McGee, eds., *The extended metropolis, settlement transition in Asia.* Honolulu: University of Hawaii Press, pp. 3-26.

Nangia, S., (1976). *Delhi Metropolitan Region: A study in settlement geography.* New Delhi: K.B. Publishing House.

Observer Research Foundation (1998), India 1998. *Observer Statistical Handbook,* New Delhi.

Ramachandran, R. (1989). *Urbanisation and urban systems in India.* Delhi: Oxford University Press.

Schenk, H., (1997). The rurban fringe: A central area between region and city: The case of Bangalore, India. In: M. Chatterji & Y. Kaizhang, *Regional Science in Developing Countries,* New York: MacMillan, pp. 212-223.

Swindell, K., (1988). Agrarian change and peri-urban fringes in tropical Africa. In: D. Rimmer, ed., *Rural transformation in tropical Africa.* Ohio University Press, pp. 98-115.

Thakur, B., (1991). *Land utilization and urbanization, the rural-urban fringe,* Deep & Deep, New Delhi.

Wehrwein, E.G. (1942). The rural-urban fringe. *Economic Geography,* Vol. 18, pp. 217-228.

Yadav, C.S., (1987). *Rural-urban fringe.* New Delhi: Concept.

12

Changing Environs and its Impact on Peri-urban Zone of Varanasi

Neelam Pal and *Rana P.B. Singh*

Introduction

The term 'peri-urban' is basically used for an area on the city's peripheral location shows a marked variation in its land use pattern, demographic characteristics and other infrastructural facilities.

The terms 'urban' and 'rural' are still often used in ordinary conversation but most of the people have clear mental conceptions of some ideal-type landscape corresponding to each of the connotations. Due to rapid urban population growth and expansion of the built-up area, technical change, global economic restructuring, opening of new educational institutions, transportation and industrial establishment, the adjoining villages are gradually changing their rural character into urban landscape in all cities of India and not within limit of well-defined boundary. Now there is no dividing line where the city meets to the rural landscape. Cities have spread rapidly but commonly not in uniform nature and there is no circular ripple outward to the outer side. Instead, the process has been differentiated according to the combination of the following factors:

- The size and structure of the existing city.
- The composition of the urban and migrated population in terms of age, sex, family and household structure (including multi-local household), ethnic, cultural and religious diversity, educational and income levels, urban experience, and so forth.
- Circular migration with multi-local household often spanning rural areas and different categories of urban centre.

- Physical terrain and environmental barriers beyond the existing built-up area.
- The orientation, accessibility, and affordability of transport network.
- Land tenure system, land values, and land uses surrounding the city.
- Occasionally substantial differences between administrative urban and non-urban local authority.

Consequently, this process creates different transition zones between city and countryside. Some have uniform sprawl, others honeycomb structures or spines of growth along specific corridors. These transition zones generally known as peri-urban areas varying in width and nature and have rapid change with increasing population pressure. This population pressure captures many villages around the city have experienced immigration, growth change in population composition land use and economic base. As a consequence, the closer part of the city get transition from rural to urban and become built up part of urban area obtains a complex mixture of formal houses, mud structures, huts and other dwellings may be rebuilt in more urban style over time, these areas often retain distinct identities and even traditional chieftaincy structure. The result of this rapid peri-urban growth may cause and change their administrative boundary also (cf. Duncan 2008, and Duncan *et al.*, 2006).

The term 'peri-urban' now well established in the English lexicon, is also expressed in different languages and cultural contents. In Dutch, it is *halfstedig* (Semi-urban), in German, *Urban-landlichen Zonen* (Urban-rural zones) in Afrikaans, *Buitestedilik* (outer city or beyond the city). In East Asia and parts of South-East Asia, a new form of 'EMR' (Extended Metropolitan Region) has emerged as a process named as *deshkota* (city village) (Ginsberg, *et al.*, 1991). Latin America's large metropolises, which is due to particular farms of their close integration with the world economy as identified 20 years ago by Armstrong and McGee (1985) have also involved into "Urban archipelagos" with diffused boundaries and weakened official planning controls.

Thus, the peri-urban zone or Peri-Urban Interface (PUI) defined by NRSP (Natural Resource System Programme, 1995-2005) is as follows: "The peri-urban interface is characterised by strong urban influences, easy access to markets, services and other inputs, ready supplies of labour, but relative shortage of land and risks from pollution and urban growth" (cf. Phillips *et al.*, 1999: 5). Theoretically, a peri-urban zone may be different in width and steepness, which we can represent its rural-urban gradient over quite short interval of time, depending on the nature of pressure within the growing metropolis and of migration towards it. "The peri-urban denotes the 'sub-urban' or none urban population of the territory in urbanised areas outside the central cities. The urbanised area contains the three components – 'central city', 'suburb', and 'urban fringe'" (cf. Duncan, 1956: 372). For many purposes, it is important to consider the peri-urban zone as an extension of the city rather than as entirely separate area.

Objective and Approach

Overcrowdedness and development pressures are shifting permanently the socio-cultural fabric of Varanasi city, known as the cultural capital and heritage city of India. Due to fast galloping population and increasing traffic the space in old city area is shrinking fast and urban area is modifying its characteristic with high migration rate. This population pressure capture many villages around the city have experienced immigration; growth and change in population composition and land use. Varanasi city reveals impact on its three outer heterogeneous peri-urban concentric zones. This essay deals with the following major objectives: (i) delimiting the peri-urban areas, (ii) understanding the intensity of urban impact on the peri-urban zone, (iii) analyzing the variation in demographic factors of the peri-urban areas, and (iv) analyzing the impact of urban sprawl and consequential problems.

The present study presents village level demographic variables of Varanasi district and its adjacent districts surrounding Varanasi city. This study is based on procured data from the secondary sources from 1991 to 2001 and their representation by several cartographic and statistical methods. The results are presented through various maps and tables generated in ArcGIS, and interpretations are sought accordingly, taking into account:

1. General Population Tables, Census of India, data 1991 to 2001;
2. District Census records, 1961-2001; and
3. Population growth, Density, Literacy, Occupational structure, Sex-ratio, Land-use and other demographic variables of Varanasi and adjacent districts (village level).

Concept and Delimitation of Peri-urban Areas

Peri-urban areas or the extension of city area are flexible and extending immediately beyond the city limit. This peri-urban belt is a dynamic area, which fluctuates in span of time. It continues shifting outward from the city with sprawl of urban novelty in the surrounding localities. The International Urban Research Unit (IURU), University of California, following the U.S. Bureau of Census, has recommended the enclosure in the peri-urban zone as all those areas which have at least 65 per cent of labour working in economic activities other than agriculture may be included in peri-urban zone. Singh (1966) and Dubey (1976: 99) differentiate the peri-urban (rural-urban fringe) by placing over a series of maps covering several geographical factors, i.e. built-up area and house type, pattern of streets, occupational structures, sites for long institutions and industrial establishment, presence of lime and brick kiln, and limit of essential services, etc. An attempt has been made here to delimit the peri-urban areas of the Varanasi City based on the analysis of primary data through field survey, and Master Plan of the city and their extended projections. Here, a few determinants selected for further investigations include perspectives of spatial, occupational and demographic characteristics.

Spatial Determinants

To see the land use pattern of the surrounding urban sprawl areas, its spatial expansion, and characteristics of adjacent villages outside the present Municipal Corporation limit the boundary of Varanasi Development Region as demarcated in the Master Plan is assumed as the tentative peri-urban zone. Of course, for delimitation of peri-urban area of Varanasi city many facts of Varanasi, and of the nearby districts of Chandauli and Mirzapur which recording higher than the average values making urban tendency were superimposed over on a map and on the basis of that joint factor intensity was delineated (cf. Fig. 12.1).

On the basis of personal observation and land use pattern, it is clear that the expansion of the city in all directions is very high, except in the east. The extension of the city is more rigorous along all the transport routes, especially Varanasi-Allahabad road, Lanka-DLW road, Varanasi-Jaunpur road, and Varanasi-Ghazipur road. Additionally towards south-east and eastern side expansion also started due to expansion of three towns, viz. Ramnagar, Mughalsarai and Mughalsarai Railway

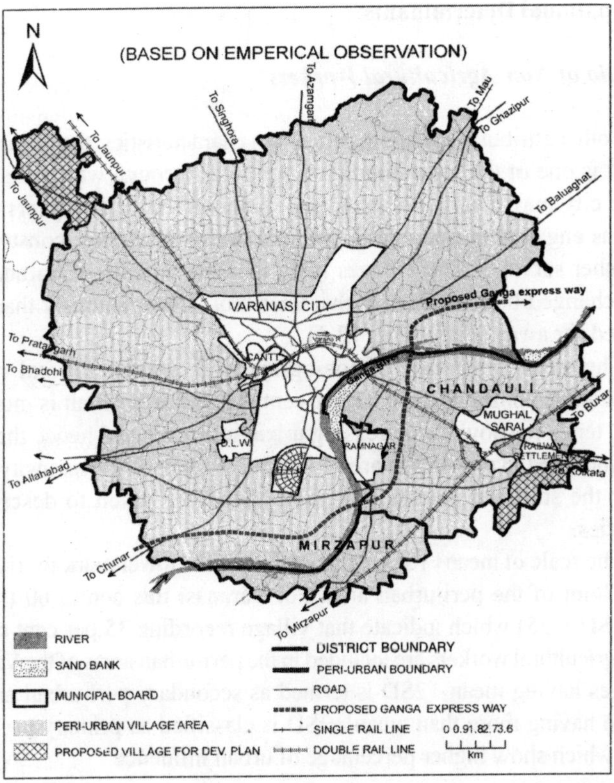

Fig. 12.1: Varanasi and its Peri-urban Area.

settlement along G.T. road, in addition with proposed Ganga Express Way. This results in expanding peri-urban areas through additional growth of residential colonies, industries, commercial activities, educational institutes, link roads resulting to new linkage and accessibility. On Jaunpur road near Tarna village a few heavy industries like BHEL's Heavy Equipment Repair plant, liquid petroleum gas filling plant of Indane near Babatpur are further changing the face of urban land use pattern. The development of heritagescape of Sarnath is attracting private and public sector for construction of residential colonies and rest houses that promote tourism trade. New residential development is causing the establishment of brick kiln in the peri-urban areas which is more profitable than farming. Similarly, the proposed Ganga Express Way will also change the total scene of the south and eastern part of Varanasi and adjoining villages of Mirzapur and Chandauli districts in near future.

Occupational Determinants

1. Ratio of Non-Agricultural Workers

Of all other attributes revealing peri-urban characteristics, the occupational aspect is one of the most important attributes through which the impact of the city may clearly be visualised. Non-agricultural workers are the persons engaged in household, manufacturing industries, constructions and other services. The villages lying in close vicinity of Varanasi city have changed their economic character more conspicuously than those situated far away (Figs. 12.2, 12.3).

The mean percentage of non-agricultural workers to total workers for Varanasi comes near 60.23 per cent. This share, which is more than mean, tends to show the increasing urban influence and hence they have been included in peri-urban areas. For the grading of the intensity of this factor the standard deviation method have been taken to describe the activities.

The scale of mean+1SD is being taken as the lower mark for fixing the outer limit of the peri-urban area. For Varanasi this comes 60 (mean = 35+1 SD = 25) which indicate that village recording 35 per cent or more non-agricultural workers are included in the peri-urban areas of the Varanasi. Villages having mean +2SD is termed as secondary peri-urban area and village having more than mean +3SD is classified as primary peri-urban areas which show higher percentage of urban influence.

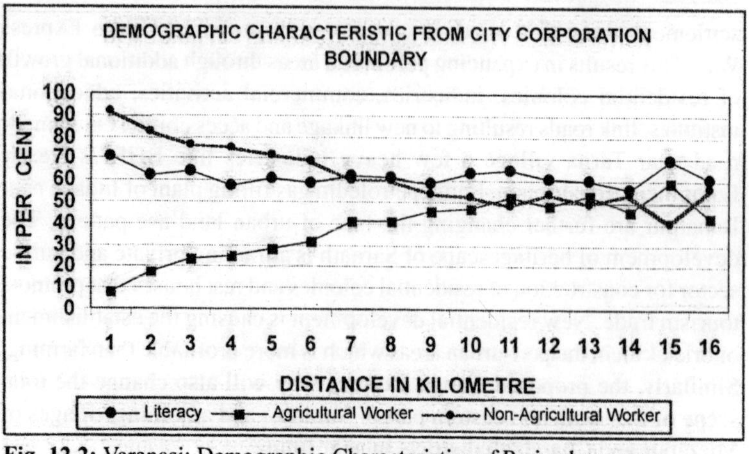

Fig. 12.2: Varanasi: Demographic Characteristics of Peri-urban areas.

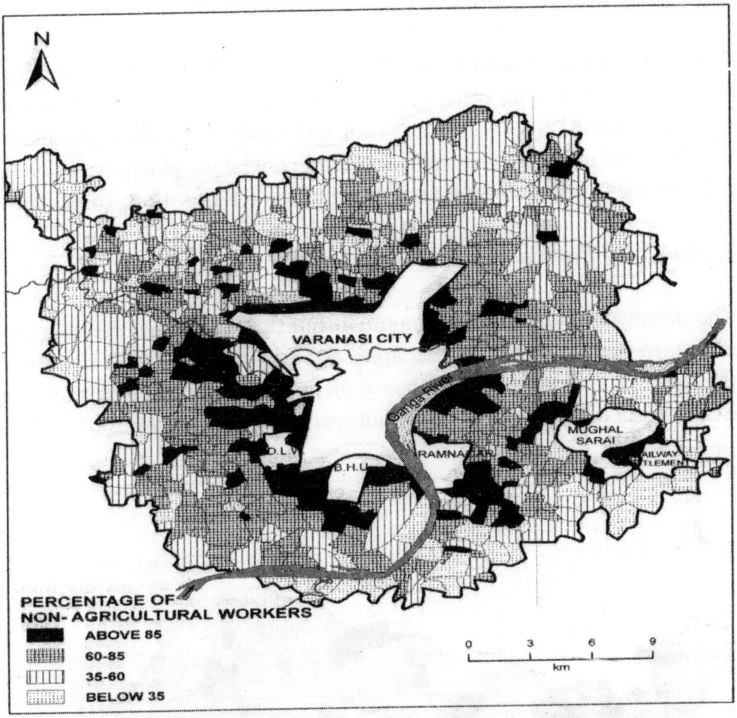

Fig. 12.2: Peri-Urban area of Varanasi: Share of Non-Agricultural Workers.

Fig. 12.3 clearly shows the extension influenced by the road and railway lines. Out of total 635 villages, 122 included in primary, 234 in secondary and 195 villages included in the outer limit of peri-urban areas.

2. Agricultural Workers

Agricultural workers are those persons who are engaged in cultivation and agriculture as their primary occupation; their ratio increases in distance from the city limit positively, as illustrated in terms of percentage share and its spatial pattern (Figs. 12.2 and 12.3). This may be categorised into four groups: 20-40 per cent in primary peri-urban, 40-60 per cent in secondary and above 60 per cent in the outer limit of peri-urban areas. This index gives the satisfactory result and demarcates the peri-urban area of the city in a more rational way. On the basis of this descriptive method 635 villages are counted in close spatial interaction with Varanasi city.

Demographic Determinants

Some demographic determinants of population like growth, density, literacy, sex-ratio, etc. were selected to set the limits of the peri-urban areas of Varanasi city (Figs. 12.2, 12.4, and Table 12.1). In the process of urban sprawl many demographical changes are taking place like growth-rate, sex-ratio, population-density, and literacy (cf. Fig. 12.4, Table 12.1).

1. Density of Population

The density of population is the most significant factor to evaluate the city influence on its peri-urban areas. Wehriwien (1942) has delimited the fringe of Indianapolis city, based on population density variable, for example not exceeding 388 inhabitants per sq. km. As per the 2001 Census

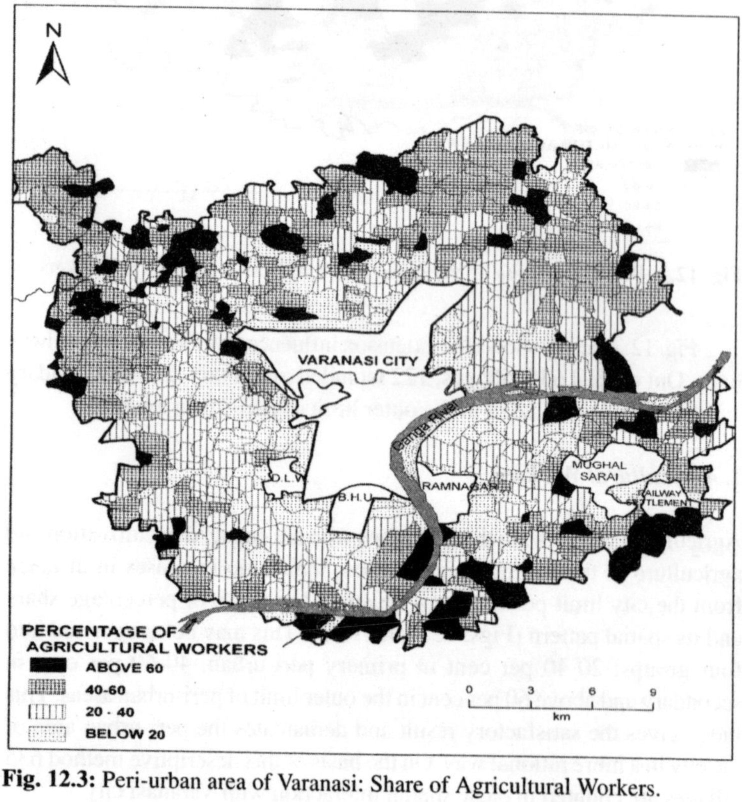

Fig. 12.3: Peri-urban area of Varanasi: Share of Agricultural Workers.

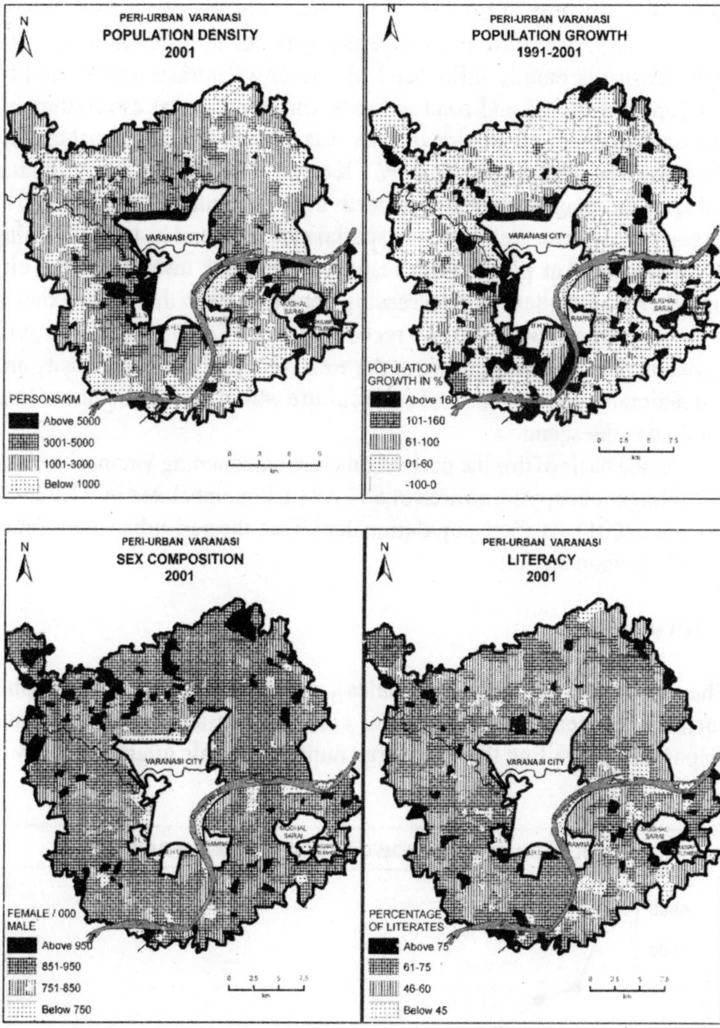

Fig. 12.4: Peri-urban area of Varanasi: Demographic Characteristics.

average density of population in Varanasi city is 12,622 persons per sq. km., followed by primary peri-urban area above 5,000 persons per sq. km., secondary peri-urban area 3,000-5,000 persons per sq. km. while the outer limit of peri-urban area records density of 1,000-3,000 person/ sq. km., and in the belt of periphery it fell down to below 1000 persons/

per sq. km. (cf. Figs. 12.4 and 12.5). Obviously, the peri-urban villages exhibit a large variation in population densities in different areas. The high density is mainly influenced by the city's infrastructural facility, development of rail and road network and commercial establishments and similarly high population density was noticed around townships like Mughalsarai, Ramnagar, D.L.W., Kotwa, Shivdaspur, and Lohata. Kakarmatta village near D.L.W. records highest population density 23,011 persons per sq. km. mainly due to spatial character and historically being an outside market place. With respect to distance away from the city limit there is a tendency of decreasing density even in the towns existing in the peri-urban zone. The two recently defined (2001) urban units, viz. Kotwa in the east and Kandwa in the west, record the lowest density and still maintain predominance of rural culture where more agricultural land dominates the scene.

On the basis of this the peri-urban areas surrounding Varanasi include 622 villages occupying an area of 647.25 sq. km., inhabited by 11,72,953 persons (2001). Average population density of the peri-urban area comes to 1822 person/sq. km.

2. Sex-Ratio

The sex ratio (females/1000 males), another effective demographic variable, presents the population composition and socio-economic disparities prevailing therein. Large number of male migrants to city in

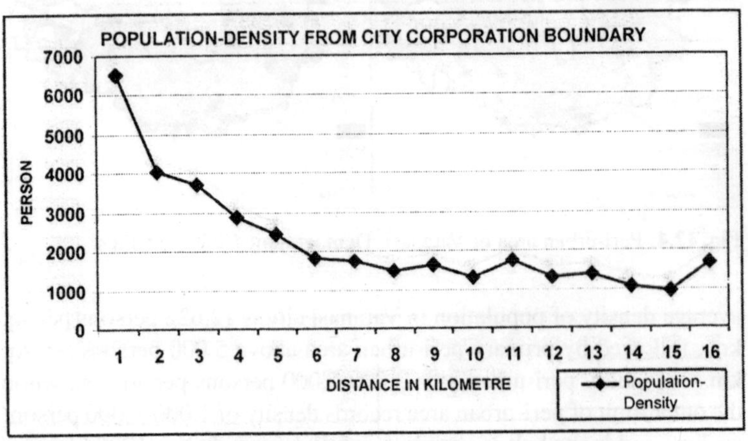

Fig. 12.5: Varanasi: Distance and Population Density relationship.

Table 12.1: Demographic Condition of the three Peri-urban Zones

Sr. No.	*Peri-urban Zones*	*No. of Vill.*	*No. of towns*	*Total*	*Area (sq km), Vill. Town = Total*	*Population*	*Den. of population*	*Growth, 1991–01*	*Lit. (%)*	*Sex-Ratio*	*Agri-Workers*	*Non-Agri. Workers*
1	Primary	186	7	193	289.84–102.96= 186.88	4,69,491	2,512	49.14	59	854	25	75
2	Secondary	237	1	238	225.91 – 4.34 = 221.57	3,21,119	1,449	102.25	58	875	38	62
3	Rural Peri-urban	199	1	200	251.09 – 12.29 = 238.80	3,82,343	1,601	38.64	53	877	56	44
—	Total (average)	622	9	631	647.25	11,72,953	1,822	63.34	57	869	40	60

Note: Density of population refers to persons/sq. km.

search of jobs leaving their families in rural areas is main reason of this composition. This type of ratio decreases towards the city side, and *vice versa*. Most of the poor, uneducated, and labour class prefer to live in peri-urban areas due to cheap residential and other facilities, in addition with proximity to their job areas in the city. Presently, a number of poor people are living in this situation with their families because their wives are also getting various types of jobs in the city. This living status generates the difference in sex-ratio (cf. Table 12.1 and Figs. 12.4, 12.6).

At peri-urban zonal level the sex ratio indicates continuous increase as one goes far from the city boundary, i.e. inverse relationship exists clearly. This is in support of the migrant labour in the city where the male dominancy suits to the labour requirement, and at other end in a more rural dominant economy relatively high sex ratio exists (cf. Table 12.1). However, at village level there exists contrasts and variation, which can be spatially represented with three categories, 751-850 females/1000 males, 851-950, and above 951; nevertheless this pattern also supports the earlier generalisation.

3. Literacy

It is a general observation that people living in the villages near the city will be more literate than the far away villages. The highly educated society of the city affecting and transforming the traditional

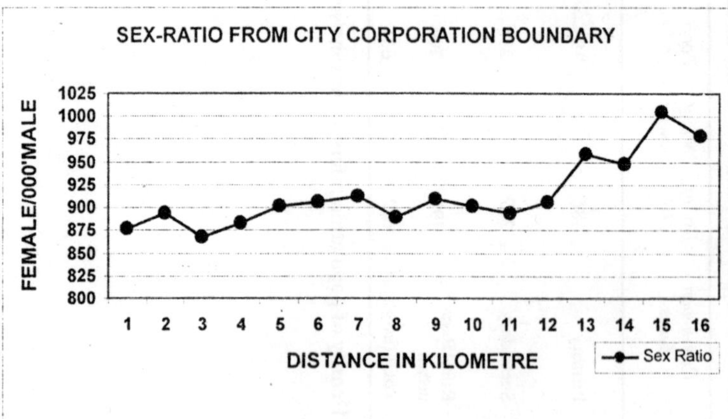

Fig. 12.6: Varanasi: Distance and Sex Ratio in Peri-urban areas.

and old living style of the villagers. The surrounding area is gradually changing in literacy pattern of all age groups. The average literacy rate in the village area is 60 per cent and this has been taken as outer limit of peri-urban. Villages falling in between mean (60 %) to mean +1SD (60+15) e.g. 75 per cent of literates are taken as secondary peri-urban and village and villages falling mean +above 1SD (60+15) e.g. above 75 per cent literates population are in the primary peri-urban area. In this way total 623 vi!iages lay in the peri-urban area of Varanasi city. Two villages of Mirzapur near Varanasi had recorded the highest literacy rate, i.e. above 90 per cent are Sherpur and Damodarpatti. In general context, the ratios of literary vary from 59 close to the city limit, 58 in the succeeding vicinity and 53 at the peri-urban border. This also supports the statement that going away from the city limit the literary decreases.

4. Growth-Rate

Like population density, population growth is also an important determinant to delimit the peri-urban area. The study of city wards and sample villages explain that the population of the peri-urban has higher increase than the population of the city. The average population growth during 1991-2001 has been taken as one of the indicators of peri-urban area. The population growth is high in peri-urban area due to regular immigration of the population to the fringe belt from different parts of the countryside. The high growth is also due to the improvement of medical facilities in Municipal Corporation area illustrate high birth and low death rate with the help of better convenience to the city centre by regular cheap transportation. The people find better scope for business, more employment opportunity, and relatively cheap and spacious land suitable for housing and outer socio-economic activities.

Under the impact of these factors the area having strong interaction with around the city approximately eight kilometres from the city is established as Municipal Corporation boundary. This peri-urban area occupies about 613.27 sq. km. apart from Municipal Corporation which occupied 86.51 sq. km. of area, and also BHU (5.78), DLW (3.54), Cantonment (4.47), Ramnagar (7.12), Mughalsarai (12.33) and Railway settlement (4.43 sq. km.). Within the peri-urban area exist eight towns, some of which are directly part of Varanasi Urban Agglomeration (cf. Table 12.2).

Table 12.2: Towns in Peri-urban Zone of Varanasi

Towns	*Area (sq. Km.)*	*Population, 2001*	*Density of Pop./ sq. Km.*	*Growth rate, 1991–01 (%)*
Varanasi MC	86.51	10,91,917	12,622	10.83
Lohata (CT)	1.09	19,706	18,079	52.56
Dulhipur (CT)	0.45	7,744	17,209	22.60
Shivdaspur (CT)	1.28	11,420	8,922	50.08
Mughalsarai (MB)	12.33	88,387	7,168	32.85
Mughalsarai Rly. Settlement	4.43	27,921	6,303	11.79
Ramnagar (MB)	7.12	40,619	5,705	34.87
Kotwa (CT)	2.81	12,411	4,417	25.34
Kandwa (CT)	4.34	7,555	1,741	21.80
Total Area (sq. km.)	120.36	13,07,680	10,865	—

Source: Census Handbook of Varanasi 2001, and Singh, Rana P.B. 2009, p. 30.

Classification and Types of Peri-urban Villages

The peri-urban landscape is the area where the cultural development takes place outside the boundaries of central cities and extends to the areas of the predominantly agricultural activities. All the determinants of delimitation of peri-urban areas when plotted on the city map of Varanasi superimposed over the other to give a clear implication of the city. The area immediately next to the city where most of these variable resemble like rural-type and the middle zone is the mixture of the both instinct. Thus, the extension of the peri-urban areas begin from the Municipal Corporation boundary and reaches up to rural tangential areas. On the basis of this process, the peri-urban zone of Varanasi city may be classified into three zones (cf. Fig. 12.7): (i) Inner or Primary Peri-urban Zone; (ii) Middle or Secondary Peri-urban Zone; and (iii) Outer or Rural Peri-urban Zone.

This division is a little different what suggested by Phillips (1999) into two peri-urban zones, of course they refer to the two ends and leaves the transition:

1. A zone of direct impact, which experiences the immediate impact of land demands from urban growth, pollution and the like,
2. A wider market related zone of influence, recognizable in terms of the handling of agricultural and natural resource products.

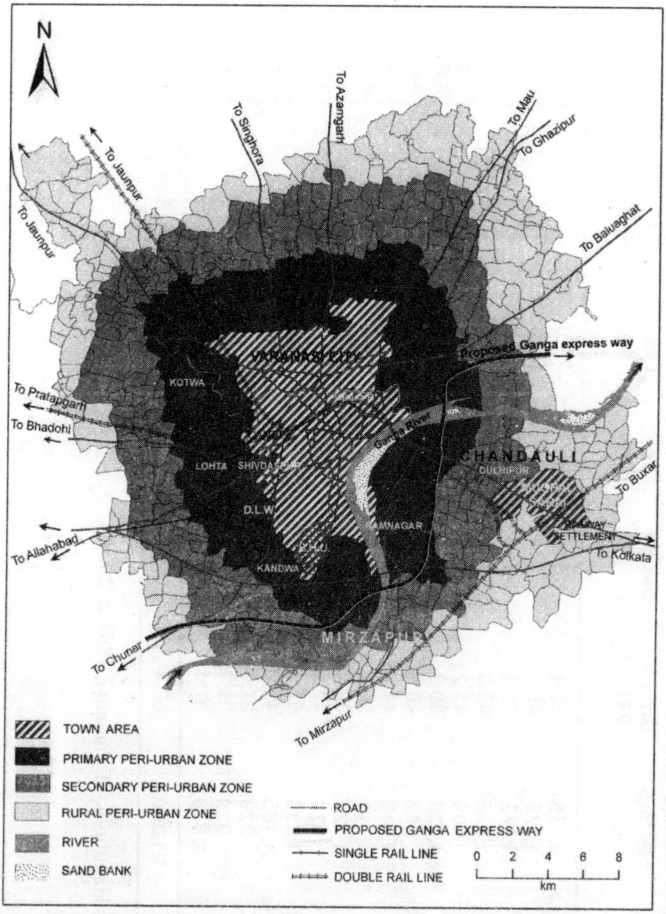

Fig. 12.7: Peri-Urban Zones of Varanasi.

On the basis of spatial, occupational, and demographic determinants, the peri-urban area of Varanasi city consists of 622 villages with an area of 647.25 sq. km. The primary peri-urban includes 192 villages with 186.88 sq. km. area, secondary peri-urban area includes 237 villages with 221.57 sq. km. area whereas rural peri-urban include 199 villages with 238.8 sq. km. of area (Fig. 12.4, Table 12.3). Peri-urban area is not a concentric zone around the city but a star shaped and it extends between 6 km. to 18 km. from the city centre. Towards the east and west the city extension is approximately 12 km, while in

Table 12.3: Varanasi: Variation in Demographic Condition of the Peri–urban Area

Distance from City, km.	*Tot. No. of Vill.*	*Total Pop. 2001*	*Total Pop. 1991*	*Growth, 1991–01*	*Density*	*Sex Ratio*	*Liter-acy*	*Agri. Worker*	*Non-Agri. Worker*
5	9	6,396	2,135	56.4	6,534	877	71.3	7.8	92.2
6	21	3,938	1,522	45.1	4,034	895	62.5	17.7	82.3
7	36	3,178	1,672	50.1	3,714	869	63.9	23.9	76.1
8	44	2,532	1,536	49.3	2,890	883	57.6	25.2	74.8
9	65	1,539	999	45.2	2,455	901	61.0	28.6	71.6
10	77	1,486	1,130	49.3	1,818	906	58.9	31.6	68.8
11	65	1,281	953	46.5	1,759	912	62.5	41.4	59.9
12	65	1,377	1,042	44.4	1,494	889	61.6	41.4	60.1
13	62	2,809	1,111	55.9	1,629	909	58.6	46.0	54.0
14	56	1,473	1,120	32.4	1,299	902	63.7	47.5	52.5
15	47	1,234	974	47.3	1,733	895	64.8	52.7	48.5
16	36	1,425	1,036	51.1	1,319	907	60.5	48.8	53.9
17	18	1,202	1,185	42.9	1,385	959	60.4	53.6	49.2
18	14	1,525	1,328	27.0	1,069	947	55.9	45.7	54.3
19	4	1,303	939	31.7	942	1004	69.7	59.5	40.5
20	3	3,218	2,518	37.1	1,661	979	60.6	43.4	56.6
Total	622	35,916	21,200	69.4	2,233	915	62.1	38.4	61.6

Source: Compiled from District Census Handbook of Varanasi, 1991 & 2001.

north-west along Jaunpur road it extends 21 km. In the north side along Azamgarh and Ghazipur route it extends 22 km. and 20 km. towards south-east side on Kolkata, Mughalsarai route. This shows the strong influence of transport network that widened the peri-urban zone while other area shrinks.

The primary peri-urban zone includes 186 villages lying around 6 to 9 km. at the periphery from the city centre. In this zone about 70 per cent working strength engaged in non-agricultural activity having population density of 2,798 persons per sq. km. The average growth rate of 49.14 per cent, average literacy rate of 59 per cent, and sex-ratio of 854 females per thousand males are some of the general characteristics of this zone. This zone touches the boundary of Municipal Corporation of Varanasi and six towns Kotwa, Shivdaspur, Lohata, and Maruadih Railway Settlement, Ramnagar, and Kandwa also existing in this zone. Therefore, in near future the villages existing in this zone will be part of the city.

The secondary peri-urban zone is just after the boundary of primary peri-urban zone in the periphery of 9 to 11 km. from city centre. According to 2001 census, the population density in this zone was lower than 1,775 persons per sq. km. and population growth 129.25 per cent which is higher than the inner zone. In comparison to inner zone literacy rate becomes low up to 58 per cent. The sex ratio was 875 females per thousand.

The extant of outer peri-urban zone is in 11 to 14 kms. towards periphery with some zigzag widening due to passing of the road and railway tracks. The average population density in this zone was 1,523 persons per sq. km. that is relatively less in comparison to inner zone. This zone records low literacy rate, population growth and non-agricultural workers (Table 12.3). It is obvious from the statistical information that close to city boundary there exist relatively larger population size of villages, and *vice versa*. Similarly, far from the city limit there is high sex ratio as also explained at zonal level.

Urban and Peri-urban Interaction

According to Dubey (1976), urban fringe is part of that land which can be most suitably released for further urban expansion under housing, industry and the like because they are the areas of close daily interaction with the city and generally using in character. It is clear that peri-urban zone is an extension of the city rather than an entirely separate area. 'Cultural development that takes place outside the boundaries of central cities and extends to the areas of predominantly agricultural activities', thus formed a zone of transition to be called peri-urban (Alpake, 1942). In this zone the two ways interaction and influence can also be seen. On the one side, urban development of city's outgrowth owing to increasing population pressure, opening of new educational, medical, transformational, industrial, and residential sectors are gradually changing their rural character into urban character. On the other side, city's surrounding rural areas are fulfilling the urban demand of milk, vegetables, cereals, and daily and economical supply of wages. Both the interactions are changing the face of the surroundings gradually.

Singh (1955: 116) has already remarked that "The city as a living organism depends for its vitality not only on its capacity to tap the sap for its growth from a vast region surrounding it, but also intensively on the surrounding areas." This is the endless process that an organism is required for its existence and development.

The peri-urban villages of Varanasi represent the changing land use pattern and proceeding crop diversification. The population residing in slum area of Varanasi is about 12.55 per cent of total city population, against 23.86 per cent for 26 million cities of our country. The absence of obnoxious industrial units, higher price of landholdings, smaller landholder, lack of entrepreneurial skill to venture to non-traditional sector have contributed to slow growth rate and low slum proportion.

In the process of interaction some bad land left over by the brick kiln owners within the peri-urban zone. And the developers are developing good residential colonies with all urban amenities. Village publication's enterprising nature is also an important factor. According to the new demand of the city in order to get benefit to villagers in general, particularly landholders are adjusting their crop structure and farm activity. Accessibility towards city from villages is increased due to improved transport facility. Urban work like marketing, storage, processing is also flourishing. A large number of workers are earning from the city activity but they are residing in the peripheral zone.

Decline of cultivated area is the result of increasing area under settlement and paths. The non-farm workers in proportion of total workers are increasing. The two-way interaction and influences between urban and peri-urban areas are changing the land use pattern, ratio of non-agricultural workers, population density, population growth, sex-ratio, literacy, house type, street, transport and commercial activity and many more.

Impact of Urban Sprawl

The peri-urban zone and its daily interaction with the city experience significant changes from time to time in terms of area and functional land use. Urban sprawl of Varanasi city expanding fast beyond municipal boundary in their immediate neighbourhood area substantial changes is observed. In this process due to friction of space, increasing land value congestion, crowding, air and noise pollution in the centre people tend to move from centre to the outskirts in the attraction of open space, fresh air, cheap value and an urban sprawl to taking place considerably with the growth of the city and built-up area. The earlier extensive tracts of area are changing under the threat and sprawling pace of urban expansion from their predominant rural to urban economy.

The impact of urban sprawl can be revealed through its land use pattern occupational structure, literacy, population growth, housing, urban amenities and public utility services. These processes of change firstly take place along the main roads radiating from the city. New building activities, increased trade and commerce, concentration of educational, health activities and expansion of civic function manifest this process. In the process of urban sprawl landscapes of peri-urban converts into semi-urban landscape.

Impact on Land Use Pattern

The impact of Varanasi city on the peri-urban area is highly reflected through the dynamics of land use changes. The existing land uses among all the 16 sample villages of peri-urban area of Varanasi city expose a mixed pattern. Due to urban sprawl the intensity of land use changes are relatively reciprocal to the distance from the city area. Non-agricultural activities become prominent near the city and decreases towards outskirts. The traditional agriculture is converting into cash crops due to increase in modern irrigation facilities, provision of various manure and high quality seeds affecting the mixed and multi-cropping pattern. In the primary peri-urban zone, cultivated land is involved in horticulture and cash cropping whereas outer peri-urban is prominent for foodgrains. On the basis of sample studies made in villages, it is clear that around six to eight kms. towards periphery 60 per cent of agricultural land was covered with vegetable and fruits like potato, tomato, onion, jackfruit, ladyfinger, green peas, cauliflower, salad, spinach, and 10 per cent of the agricultural land covered with cash crop. A case study of three villages in Chamaon

Gram Sabha was made in 2001 (cf. Singh and Sen, 2001). The secondary peri-urban zone is covered with 70 per cent cash crop and 30 per cent foodgrain whereas the outer zone having 10 per cent cash crop and 90 per cent foodgrain.

Farmers nearer the city grow cereals only for the home consumptions. But the marketed surplus of cereals increases with the increasing distance from the city. In fact, more than 80 per cent of vegetable produced by farmers is used for market purposes in all the locations. Marketed surplus of cereals and vegetables is recorded with respect to increasing tendency by the increasing size of holding. The cereals production records the tendency of constantly more surplus that is marketed from adjacent to city to the outside. While the tendency is opposite in case of vegetables, the share of surplus marketed is as high as 89 per cent close to the city and it is 84 per cent at the margin of peri-urban area. This indicates the vegetables are produced on commercial basis (cf. Singh and Sen, 2001). This is similar in other villages in peri-urban zone.

In the process of urban sprawl, the non-agricultural land uses are gaining ground and the traditional agriculture is being converted into cash crops and mixed farming. Establishment of several brick kilns along the roadside is also a major consumer of large fertile cultivable fields changing into derelict land. Due to cheap transportation facility people living close to city (9 kms) coming daily and even on foot and earning greater profit by immediate selling of their farm product and return to their villages by the late evening. Many educational institutes, veterinary hospitals, transport agencies, and agricultural seeds shops are opening along the roadside. The percentage of irrigated land is increasing near the city and in most belonging cultivated land is converting into residential settlements and other land uses.

Impact on Economy

Due to the urban sprawl the impact on the economy of peri-urban villages of Varanasi has been observed mainly along the axial route. The urban economic functions have affected the firm of agriculture. The land which was once devoted to the cropping of cereals is now converting into the intense cash crop farming, i.e. fruit, vegetable, and some remunerative crops such as lemon, guava, pumpkin, potato, flowers, cranberry (*karaunda*), cucumber, grewia (*phalsa*). sugarcane, groundnut, tobacco, and oilseed. In this production certain crops like sugarcane, cotton, and oilseed form the basic raw material for small scale cottage industry. In the two villages of peri-urban zone, viz. Ramgarhwa and Kapar Phorwa, one of the most prominent cottage industries is jiggery. In this reference the observation of Chamon Gram Sabha villages are notable. "Due to increasing area under irrigation, total cropped area and fertilizer, the latter exhibited by an increase in area under cash crop, in some cases introduction of relatively more remunerative crops. The rural sector becomes diversified and there is increase in area under settlement and paths resulting further decline in total cropped area" (cf. Singh and Singh, 2003: 26-27). In the process of urban sprawl the area under non-farm uses may increase further resulting in further decline in the total cultivated land. Agriculture in general and crop production in particular is likely to use ground because of further increase in land values and many yield place to secondary and tertiary activities. In this way, the village near city of Varanasi transforming its economy and may be incorporated in the urban agglomeration.

The development of industrial activities especially household nature can be seen in the peri-urban villages of Varanasi. These cottage industries can be seen in every direction along roadside in the peri-urban of Varanasi. In the west side of Varanasi Bhadohi is famous for carpet industry and given rise to carpet work along Varanasi-Bhadohi road some small scale industries like poultry farm, rice and flour mill, saw mill, dairy farm, local cigarette (*biri*) making, etc. are important. Along the Jaunpur road many saw mills, timber shop, roadside restaurants (*dhabas*), fish keeping aquarium, flour mills brick kiln, on the Ghazipur road a village Chiraigaon is famous for fruits based industry like jam, jelly, squash and pickles making apart from these industries like water lifting, rice and flour mill, *biri* making, handloom basket making developed on this road. G.T. Road towards Allahabad many filling stations, motor garages, *dhabas* (roadside eateries), furniture and carpentry works, big saw mills, tea restaurants, general stores, pottery, hosiery work, handloom, powerloom, bakery and basket making can be seen. The Lohata market of wholesale *sarees* in the west is also famous for bead, *biri*, and ticukly making.

Impact on Social Structure

The population is constantly growing due to medical and health facility and the immigration from rural areas. However, death rate is reasonably low in peri-urban zone because of medical accessibility. Increasing literacy rate is also one of the most important aspects of social structure. The females are now acquiring equal status gradually and are also being provided with the opportunities and facility for receiving higher education through establishment of many prestigious public convent schools also mass awakening towards education. A large number of District Board Schools, junior schools, and many technical colleges have been established in the peri-urban zone; these altogether improve the literacy conditions.

The study of sample village reveals that in the peri-urban areas houses are gradually changing their old structure and building materials due consequences of urban sprawl. Although in the middle part of peri-urban zone majority of houses are *kuccha* and mixed but along the roadside about 60 to 70 per cent houses are *pukka*. Electricity has reached almost all the villages in peri-urban zone. Beside this extension of newspaper supply, facility of telecommunication and postal services also further supported positive changes.

Concluding Remark

The impacts of urban sprawl upon peri-urban society will inevitably enhance the economic efficiency of its people and accelerate their living standard as in the past too. The continuity of these impacts will be in full swing; then undoubtedly these peri-urban villages will be able to join the mainstream of the city life. Life in the villages of this zone is in a phase of transition—the characteristic of peri-urban areas. That is, continuing the age old traditions and, at the same time, adopting the changing socio-economic system and the values associated with it through urban influence, which will be more crucial in the near future trying to achieve a balance with a foot in both camps, i.e. traditional village life and urban life. The traditional life and ethical values, which once well-known framework of harmonious life in Indian villages are now transformed to cope with the new waves of changes and valuation of life in which consumerism, individualism and market-oriented lifeways are the common consequences (cf. Singh and Sen, 2001).

References

Alpake, F. (1942). Land use control in the urban fringe of Portland Oregon. *Journal of Land and Public Economics,* 18: 463-478.

Dubey, K.K. (1976). The Use and Misuse of Land in the Kaval Towns (UP). *N.G.S.I.,* Varanasi, Research Publication. No. 15.

Duncan, O.D. and Reiss, Jr. A.J. (1956). *Social Characteristics of Urban and Rural Communities.* John Wiley & Sons, New York.

Phillips, D., Williams, K., Andrews, G., Clark, J., Carter, M., Kinsman, P., Smith, D., Wills, K., Bradbury, I., Wu, K. and Hillyer, A. (1999). Literature Review on Peri-urban Natural Resource Conceptualisation and Management Approaches, Final Technical Report, *DFID Natural Resource System Programme (NRSP),* Project R6949, University of Nottingham and University of Liverpool.

Simon, David, (2008). Urban Environments: Issues on the Peri-urban Fringe. *Annual Review of Environment and Resources,* 33: 167-185.

Simon, David; McGregor, Duncan, and Thompson, Donald (2006). Contemporary perspectives on the peri-urban zones of cities in developing areas; in their (eds.) The Peri-urban Interface: Approaches to Sustainable Natural and Human Resource Use. *Earthscan,* London/Stirling, VA: pp. 1-17.

Singh, R.B. and Singh, B.N. (2003). Land Use Transformation and crop substitution in Peri-urban fringe of Varanasi. *National Geographical Journal of India,* 49 (1-2): 31-36.

Singh, R.L., (1956). *Banaras: A Study in Urban Geography.* Nand Kishore Publisher, Banaras. 116.

Singh, Rana, P.B. (2009). Banaras—Geographical Personality: setting and Landscape; in, his: *Banaras: Making of India's Heritage City.* Planet Earth & Cultural Understanding, Series Pub. 3. Cambridge Scholars Publishing, Newcastle upon Tyne U.K.: 17-48.

Singh, Rana, P.B. and Sen, Chandra (2001). The Structure of Peri-urban Agricultural Environment in Varanasi Development Region. *National Geographical Journal of India,* 47 (1-4): 61-72.

Singh, Ujagir (1966). Urban Fringe in Kaval Towns; in, Singh, R.L. (ed.) *Applied Geography.* N.G.S.I., Varanasi, pp. 41-48.

Wehrwien, G.S., (1942). The Rural-Urban Fringe. *Economic Geography,* 18: 217-228.

13

Rapid Urban Sprawl in Large Cities and its Swift Encroachment on Agricultural Fringe Land of Uttar Pradesh

S.S.A. Jafri and *Milita Haldar*

Introduction

Urban sprawl may be defined as the scattering of new development on isolated tracts, separated from other areas by vacant land (Ottensmann, 1977). It is also often described as leapfrog development (Gordon and Richardson, 1977) as observed in all the major cities across the world. The cities are growing in all directions resulting into changes in urban land use, reflected on the border or peripheral rural areas as compared to that of the city centre. In the midst of urban and industrial expansion, there is increasing pressure on important resources predominantly in the metropolitan cities. Urban spread out has been blamed for disorganized use of land resources and energy and large scale intrusion onto the agricultural lands. As the cities enlarge, agricultural land and habitats like forest etc. are transformed into land for housing, roads, industry etc. The result is increase in the built-up area and related changes in the land use patterns, causing loss of productive agricultural lands, forest cover, other forms of greenery, loss in surface water bodies, depletion in groundwater aquifers and increasing levels of air and water pollution; causing environmental problems.

How much land is actually transitioning from farm to non-farm use? This is a question that needs to be addressed if we actually need to analyze the land use pattern of any state and how actually the urban areas have manufactured and modified its fringe areas "The government itself puts the figure at 1.5 per cent of net sown area between 1990 and 2003, or more than 21 lakh hectares have gone to non-farm activity. The actual figures could be much higher. If we accept that 21 lakh hectares of crop land have been diverted for non-agricultural use, and if this area were brought under wheat, it would amount to a mind-boggling 57 lakh tonnes of produce which could have fed more than 4.3 crore hungry people every year. Had there been the political will to prevent this diversion, the number of hungry would have declined by over 12 per cent. Since the area diverted is more than 21 lakh hectares, it is clear that policy-makers are implementing a blueprint to put India on the path to food insecurity" (Bhaskar Goswami).

"In the past decade or so, there has been a major diversion of land meant for wheat and rice cultivation into commercial crops such as oilseeds and cotton. Further, as per one estimate, 7.5 lakh hectare of agricultural land are being diverted to other uses for urbanization and industrialization such as real estates, roads, SEZs, industrial parks every year. A revitalization process for wasteland available in plenty in the country is necessary, but it has not yet started in a big way" (Indra, 2007). "According to the latest Economic Survey (2009) conducted by Centre for Monitoring Indian Economy (CMIE) "Decline in acreage and expected fall in yield will lead to a 16 per cent drop in *kharif* foodgrain production. It is expected to fall to 98 million tonnes from 117.7 million tonnes produced in *kharif* 2008." Further if we analyze just the production rate of wheat one of the major food crops we observe that its production per hectare was 2708 kg. in the year 2000-01 but it decreased to only 2602 kg. per hectare in 2004-05 that is at the national level the per hectare production of wheat has dipped 106 kg." This is when as well-known that the population growth have till now shown an upward trend.

The above-mentioned data analysis brings to the fore line the decline of the fertile agricultural land that are being driven away from the agricultural land use pattern to the urban land use pattern. Thus, the problem of expanding of city centres to its peripheral region is both complex and complicated. And this land use change is the end result of numerous interacting factors arising from different levels of associations of human-environment systems, which differs in time and space. Driving forces can be slow with long turnover times, which decide the boundaries of sustainability. Changes are generally driven by a combination of factors that work progressively and factors that happen irregularly. Thus, it is necessary to measure and monitor land use changes over space and time for sustainability.

Land Utilization in Uttar Pradesh

The condition of Uttar Pradesh, one of the most populous and the fourth-largest state of India with a total geographical area of 2,40,918 sq. km. accommodates 166.2 million population with a density of 690 persons per sq. km. The economy of the State to a great extent directly or indirectly depends upon agriculture. But, still the data analysis prove that out of 24.2 million hectares of reported area 68.6 per cent is cultivated land. Approximately 31.4 per cent of fertile land is being used for non-agricultural uses. Only less than 7 per cent is forest land and that too is not effectively covered by forests, when according to forest policy there should be one-third forest cover for healthy environment. Adverse environmental impact is now reflected in falling yield and increasing other than fallow and current fallow lands as it is becoming uneconomical to cultivate. For example, in Sultanpur, Pratapgarh, Lucknow and Unnao districts other than current fallow lands have increased up to 15 per cent. In U.P. cereal production was 41.76 million metric tonnes in 2001-02 which has fallen to 37.57 million metric tonnes in 2004-05 due to land degradation. During the last 50 years we have treated most of the wastelands and added mostly with agricultural land, but it is reported that after few years of cropping, land is again becoming infertile and uneconomical. Expert opinion is that after treatment of wasteland, it should be brought under plantation rather than bringing under cultivation. Industrialization, urbanization and globalization are the world phenomenon. Uneconomic agriculture, landlessness among rural masses and quest of modernization has created momentum to migrate from rural to urban areas that too towards metropolitan cities, where congestion and pollution is unimaginable. During last fifty years the land under non-farm use related to mainly urban has almost doubled, which would continue to grow. More than 50 per cent districts are showing above the state average, i.e. 10.6 per cent land under non-farm use. In Ambedkar Nagar, Kushi Nagar, Sant Ravi Das Nagar and Ghaziabad districts, the land under non-farm use has crossed beyond 15 per cent and many other districts are on the same trend.

If we analyze the land utilization during 2002 and 2005 we find that during these five years the land put to non-agricultural uses has risen 5.3 per cent and the current fallow has risen to 18.6 per cent and as a result the land which is lifeline, i.e. forest land and net area sown has decreased to 0.1 per cent and 0.8 per cent respectively. The land put to non-agricultural uses is occupying about 10.9 per cent area and in most of the cases it is expanding on most of the fertile lands when this land is important for foodgrain production for feeding the teeming millions. We are in deficit of 23 per cent of forest cover which is necessary to meet the National Forest Policy and as well to provide the better environment and retain the fertility of the soil urbanization and industrialization are the dialectal phenomenon which cannot be stopped but we must have certain policy to control their haphazard growth. China is the example before us where urbanization and industrialization is far ahead but they are progressing in controlled manner, most of the Chinese town and cities are growing vertically and not horizontally like India also unlike India the smaller towns are growing faster but horizontally whereas the big metropolitan cities are stagnant in population and land growth (see Table 13.1).

Table 13.1: Land Utilisation in Uttar Pradesh: 2002 & 2005

Land Use	*Percentage Area*		*Percentage Growth*
	2002	2005	*2002 & 2005*
Total Area of U.P.	2,42,02,000 (100.00)	2,42,01,000 (100.00)	
Forest Land	6.98	6.97	–0.06
Land Put to Non-Agricultural Uses	10.38	10.94	5.33
Barren & Uncultivable Land	2.46	2.19	–10.92
Pasture and Grazing Land	0.29	0.26	–9.86
Miscellaneous Trees	1.47	1.42	–3.38
Cultivable Wasteland	2.14	1.88	–12.36
Fallow/Other than Current Fallow	2.58	2.37	–8.16
Current Fallow	4.24	5.03	18.62
Net Area Sown	69.47	68.94	–0.77

Source: (a) Based on Statistical Abstract of U.P., 2006.
(b) Sankhyakiya Patrika of U.P.

Annual Growth Trend of Land Put to Non-Agricultural Uses

The annual growth rate of land put to non-agricultural uses in Uttar Pradesh is not uniformed. During 2001 and 2002 the growth rate was 3.2 per cent which dropped to 1.6 per cent during 2002 and 2003 but again it has risen to 2.1 per cent during 2004 and 2005. It is expected that during recent years the growth rate is much faster (see Table 13.2).

Table 13.2: Annual Growth Trend of Land Put to Non-Agricultural Uses in Uttar Pradesh, 2001–05

Year	*Land Put to Non-Agricultural Uses*	
	Percentage from Geographical Area (2005)	*Percentage Growth (2001–05)*
2001	9.82	—
2002	10.39	3.16
2003	10.55	1.59
2004	10.72	1.60
2005	10.94	2.09

Source: Based upon Statistical Abstract of U.P., 2007.

Land Put to Non-Agricultural Uses in Regions of Uttar Pradesh

Since Uttar Pradesh is one of the largest States, the land put to non-agricultural uses in rural and urban areas has been worked out according to its four geographical regions:

[(i) Western region, (ii) Central region, (iii) Bundelkhand region and (iv) Eastern region] during 2001 and 2008. Comparatively Western region is highest urbanized in Uttar Pradesh but its growth rate during 2001 and 2008 is less than the State average in both rural and urban land put to non-agricultural uses. The Central region has recently (2008) surpassed the State average in its rural and urban land put to non-agricultural uses. The growth of land put to non-agricultural uses in rural areas has risen to 19.1 per cent whereas in urban areas the growth was 43 per cent during 2001 and 2008. Similarly, in Bundelkhand during the last eight years the growth rate has gone up to 17.6 per cent in rural areas and 30.6 per cent in urban areas. In case of Eastern region the growth rate in rural and urban areas of land put to non-agricultural uses was higher than the Western region but quite far behind than the Central region and Bundelkhand, i.e., 11.3 per cent and 4.8 per cent respectively. Overall the growth rate of total land put to non-agricultural uses was below the State average in only Western region but in Central region, Bundelkhand and Eastern regions it was quite high, i.e. 22.2, 18.5 and 10.7 per cent respectively. The growth of rural and urban land put to non-agricultural uses is alarmingly high in Central region and Bundelkhand which needs an urgent policy and control (*see* Table 13.3).

Table 13.3: Land Put to Non-Agricultural Uses in Regions of Uttar Pradesh, 2001 & 2008

Region	*Percentage from Geographical Area*								
	Rural		*Percentage Growth*	*Urban*		*Percentage Growth*	*Total*		*Percentage Growth*
	2001	2008	2001–08	2001	2008	2001–08	2001	2008	2001–08
Western Region	9.50	10.23	7.72	2.19	2.20	0.45	11.69	11.96	6.34
Central Region	9.10	10.84	19.13	1.36	1.94	43.02	10.46	12.78	22.23
Bundelkhand Region	6.98	8.21	17.61	0.49	0.64	30.58	7.47	8.85	18.46
Eastern Region	10.54	11.74	11.32	1.11	1.16	4.79	11.65	12.90	10.70
Total Uttar Pradesh	9.51	10.67	12.17	1.41	1.42	0.50	10.93	12.09	10.65

Source: Based on Sankhyakiya Patrika of U.P. (upgov.up.nic.in/engspatrika).

Districts of Fast Growth (Above Average) Land Put to Non-Agricultural Uses

During 2008 there are districts in Uttar Pradesh where rural land put to non-agricultural uses has gone up quite high than the State average 10.7 per cent. For example, highest proportion of land put to non-agricultural uses are occupied in districts like Ghaziabad 18.4, Ambedkar Nagar 17.6, Kushi Nagar 17.4, Sant Kabir Nagar 15.3, Ballia 14.8, Ghazipur 14 per cent. While calculating the growth rate during 2001 and 2008 we worked out the average annual growth rate of rural areas put to non-agricultural uses and the State average comes 1.5 per cent there are districts where the annual growth rate is manifold than the State average, for example, Chitrakoot 10.4, Faizabad 8.7, Mahoba 6.6, Kanpur Urban 6.5, Unnao 5.6 and Ambedkar Nagar 5 per cent. In most of the cases the land put to non-agricultural uses in rural areas is in fact influenced by neighbouring towns and cities which are in the process of transition to become urban land. For vertical industrial and urban growth or vertical settlements in rural areas there is an urgent need of government policy which should be strictly implemented through the town and country planning (*see* Table 13.4).

Block-wise Growth of Land Put to Non-Agricultural Uses

If you go to micro-block level to understand the fast growth of rural land put to non-agricultural uses, we find at least 29 blocks are showing very fast growth rate, there are blocks like Razapur block, Loni block in Ghaziabad, Morava block in Muzaffarnagar, Kashi Vidyapeeth block in Varanasi and Kaurihar block in Allahabad where land put to non-agricultural uses is occupying more than one-fifth of the total area of each respective block. There are blocks where annual growth rate is more than 10 per cent which are Dabri block in Gautam Budh Nagar, Sarojininagar block in Lucknow, Rasulabagh block in Kanpur Dehat and Bhitargaon in Kanpur Nagar (*see* Table 13.5).

Why We Need to be Concern About?

If we compare the urban growth of Uttar Pradesh with the rate of land use conversion from agricultural use to non-agricultural we find that with the growing trend of urban growth more and more land are being acquired for non-farm activities and the number of landholdings are decreasing

Table 13.4: Districts of Fast Growth (Above Average) Land Put to Non-Agricultural Uses in Rural Areas of Uttar Pradesh, 2001 & 2008

Districts	*Percentage of Rural Land Put to Non-Agricultural Uses (2008)*	*Percentage Growth of Land Put to Non-Agricultural Uses (2001 & 2008)*	*Percentage Average Yearly Growth (2001–08)*
Saharanpur	13.30	14.38	1.80
Meerut	12.60	16.62	2.08
Ghaziabad	18.38	19.30	2.41
Bulandshahr	11.08	21.65	2.71
Aligarh	9.50	13.97	1.75
Ferozabad	9.93	31.20	3.90
Pilibhit	11.31	13.54	1.69
Etawah	10.02	22.01	2.75
Hardoi	8.61	13.09	1.64
Unnao	11.60	44.52	5.57
Lucknow	11.65	46.23	2.03
Rae Bareli	13.00	24.92	3.12
Kanpur Dehat	8.53	23.50	2.94
Kanpur Urban	11.12	51.70	6.46
Faizabad	11.15	69.71	8.71
Mahoba	12.36	52.57	6.57
Lalitpur	8.00	26.59	3.32
Chitrakoot	8.98	83.39	10.42
Bahraich	12.65	25.27	3.16
Gorakhpur	12.91	17.42	2.18
Deoria	12.22	19.51	2.44
Ballia	14.82	19.34	2.42
Ghazipur	14.04	23.17	2.90
Varanasi	13.67	25.39	3.17
Kushi Nagar	17.37	12.36	1.55
Ambedkar Nagar	17.55	39.84	4.98
Mahamaya Nagar	10.06	24.00	3.00
Sant Kabir Nagar	15.28	32.98	4.12
Barabanki	13.83	16.09	2.01
Total U.P. Rural	10.67	12.17	1.52

Source: Based on Sankhyakiya Patrika of U.P. (upgov.up.nic.in/engspatrika).

our cultivation is in a major chunk done on area that are termed as Marginal that is they are below 1 ha. Tables 13.6 shows at length that how some of the major districts of Uttar Pradesh depend upon marginal landholdings for their food supply if we observe the table we can see that some of the districts like Sitapur and Hardoi has total landholdings to the number of 5,86,000 and 5,85,000 respectively and out of which about 77.5 and 78 per cent it is termed as marginal or below 1 ha. respectively. While only 15

Table 13.5: Block-wise Growth of Land Put to Non-Agricultural Uses, 1998 & 2008

District/Block	*Percentage from Geographical Area of Respective Block (2008)*	*Percentage Growth (1998–2008)*
Gautam Budh Nagar		
(a) Jewar Block	15.03	81.88
(b) Dadri Block	9.62	116.56
Ghaziabad		
(a) Bhojour Block	13.82	23.55
(b) Muradnagar Block	15.07	24.42
(c) Razapur Block	23.13	23.46
(d) Loni Block	36.80	23.46
(e) Dhaulana Block	16.31	23.48
(f) Hapur Block	14.53	23.52
(g) Simbhawali Block	13.45	23.77
(h) Garh Mukteshwar Block	13.46	23.53
Baghpat		
Binauli Block	11.31	17.44
Muzaffarnagar		
Morava Block	23.43	26.19
Meerut		
Hastinapur Block	18.93	18.56
Bulandshahr	13.81	55.48
Sikandrabad Block		
Aligarh		
Bijouli Block	16.27	42.96
Mathura		
Mathura Block	17.61	37.25
Saharanpur		
(a) Ballia Keri Block	18.21	33.03
(b) Sarsawan Block	14.93	14.89
Bijnore		
Nazibabad Block	8.73	44.00
Varanasi		
Kashi Vidyapeeth Block	24.82	90.72
Lucknow		
(a) Mal Block	10.01	30.00
(b) Bakshi-ka-Talab Block	12.92	21.54
(c) Chinhat Block	31.28	83.28
(d) Sarojininagar Block	18.83	109.82
(e) Gasaiganj Block	8.89	34.02
(f) Mohanlalganj Block	11.68	43.73
Kanpur Dehat		**2001–08**
Rasulabad Block	11.11	149.51
Kanpur Nagar		**1998–08**
Bhitargaon Block	18.28	150.82
Allahabad		**2001–08**
Kaurihar Block	22.56	40.92
Total U.P. (Rural, 2001–2008)	10.67	12.17

Source: Based on Sankhyakiya Patrika of U.P. (upgov.up.nic.in/engspatrika).

and 13.5 per cent of landholdings can be termed as Small or land area ranging from 1 to 2 has. only. (*See* Table 13.6)

The resultant impact is the decrease in the production and average yield of total foodgrains in Uttar Pradesh, if we observe just in Lucknow Division, we find that in 2004-05 an area of 24,20,134 hectare the production was 49,58,114 metric tonnes only while in the next 2005-06 the area did decrease to 23,14,603 hectare and with it the production also decreased to 47,21,101 metric tonnes. The decadal growth rate of population in Lucknow for the period of 1981-91 and 1991-2001, we find that the population growth rate shows an increasing trend from 37.14 per cent to 33.25 per cent. If the condition remains the same in the near future with the dependency of our agriculture will the food production rate be able to supply food to the growing number of mouths that is increasing at the rate to be more precise per second. (*see* Table 13.7)

Conclusion

It is high time that we come forward with ideas for having an all-round development of the economy the need of the hour is to have sound land use planning as population and human aspirations are increasing, land is becoming an increasingly scarce resource, calling for land use planning. Land use planning is important to mitigate the negative effects of land use and to enhance the efficient use of resources with minimal impact on future generations. It should be kept in mind that simply on the basis of availability of infrastructure or agricultural land we should not go for converting our fertile farm land into non-farm land; it would be a serious mistake which would be irreversible. Therefore, it is most essential to identify the non-agricultural infertile land through satellite imageries and the data that are available and it should be a compulsion to utilize these non-agricultural lands for the development of our non-farm activities. Million plus cities should not be allowed to further grow by putting ban on expansion of industries or any kind of activities which are not directly required for the cities. In this way urbanization would grow in un-urbanized areas and thus barren and wastelands would be easily available for its use. Agricultural land should not be allowed at any cost to be used for non-farm activities, there should be strict check and control on the basis of clear cut formulated policies at all costs at the state and local level so that an all-round sustainable development could be achieved and that too within short period of time.

Table 13.6: District-wise Number of Total Landholdings in Uttar Pradesh (2000–2001)

District	*Total (All Holding Group)*	*Marginal (Below 1.0 Ha.)*	*Small (1.0 to 2.0 Ha.)*	*Agricultural Labourers*
Saharanpur	220	140	41	146
Muzaffarnagar	295	197	52	181
Bijnor	317	208	62	171
Moradabad	458	348	68	148
Rampur	200	136	40	95
Jyotiba Phule Nagar	179	121	34	47
Meerut	192	124	43	67
Ghaziabad	177	128	30	40
Bulandshahr	290	199	53	93
Aligarh	268	167	57	94
Hathras	154	106	28	53
Agra	253	161	52	68
Firozabad	177	117	36	45
Etah	407	299	74	84
Mainpuri	282	219	44	38
Budaun	515	384	83	105
Bareilly	448	343	68	124
Pilibhit	202	131	42	61
Shahjahanpur	387	279	66	104
Kheri	570	414	99	153
Sitapur	586	454	88	136
Hardoi	585	465	79	130
Unnao	441	349	63	83
Lucknow	242	196	33	58
Rae Bareli	415	335	53	114
Farrukhabad	230	176	38	54
Fatehpur	393	297	62	126
Pratapgarh	480	411	41	89
Kaushambi	201	163	24	97
Allahabad	533	432	62	157
Barabanki	422	350	50	116
Faizabad	306	258	32	81
Ambedkar Nagar	306	269	27	80
Sultanpur	579	509	50	129
Bahraich	453	349	70	132
Gonda	484	409	50	92
Siddharth Nagar	370	306	47	102
Basti	310	259	35	72
Mahrajganj	390	335	38	116
Gorakhpur	465	403	43	117
Kushi Nagar	421	373	34	158
Deoria	373	323	34	70
Azamgarh	563	486	52	107
Ballia	345	287	36	123
Jaunpur	655	587	49	87
Ghazipur	398	331	43	105
Mirzapur	267	199	43	106
Sonbhadra	167	106	29	86
Uttar Pradesh	21668	16659	3087	5957

Sources: Economics and Statistics Division, Govt. of Uttar Pradesh.

Table 13.7: District-wise Area, Production and Yield 2004–06

District/Division/ Region	*2004–05*			*2005–06*		
	Area	*Production*	*Average Yield*	*Area*	*Production**	*Average** Yield*
Saharanpur Division	361817	982016	27.14	333445	913791	2740
Moradabad Division	1023410	2475373	24.19	924110	2233261	2417
Meerut Division	708406	2088703	29.48	7255710	2058732	2837
Agra Division	2020210	4873766	24.13	1899536	4782661	2518
Bareilly Division	1861584	4320082	23.21	1688274	4110568	2435
Lucknow Division	2420134	4958114	20.49	2314603	4721101	2040
Kanpur Division	1185361	2720898	22.95	1132592	2632331	2324
Jhansi Division	1128030	1612920	14.3	1125525	1451713	1290
Chitrakoot Division	1191481	1269492	10.65	1057554	1018955	1034
Allahabad Division	1264085	2203565	17.43	1317385	2319386	1761
Faizabad Division	1215120	2698478	22.21	1202721	2811338	2337
Devipatan Division	1262756	2192100	17.4	1259085	2281400	1812
Basti Division	777573	12311763	15.8	756705	1478120	1953
Gorakhpur Division	1239816	2663827	21.5	1226859	2420074	1973
Azamgarh Division	996458	1430453	14.4	978850	1852446	1892
Varanasi Division	1154597	1741948	15.1	1104024	2121200	1921
Vindhyachal Division	544527	533308	9.8	611899	727055	1188
Western Region	6675709	16415775	24.59	–	–	–
Central Region	3675178	7611202	20.71	–	–	–
Bundelkhand	2319511	2882412	12.43	–	–	–
Eastern Region	7684967	13087417	17.03	–	–	–
Uttar Pradesh	20355365	39996806	19.65	19658877	39934132	2031

Note: *: Value of Production of 2005-06 in Tonne.

**:Value of Yield of 2005–06 in Kg/Ha.

Source: Compiled from the statistics released by : Economics & Statistics Division, Govt of Uttar Pradesh and The Fertiliser Association of India.

References

Bansal, S.C. (1975). Town Country Relationship in Saharanpur City-Region—a Study in Rural-Urban Interdependence Problems, Sanjeev Prakashan, Saharanpur.

Bryant, C.R., I.R. Russwurm & A.G. Mclellan (1982). *The City's Countryside: Land and its Management in the Rural-urban Fringe*, Longman, London.

Das Gupta, K. (2000). Is the Joyride Over? *Down to Earth*, Centre for Science and Environment, Vol. 9(6), New Delhi.

Fazal, S. (1998). *Agricultural Production and Price Mechanism*, Chugh Publications, Allahabad.

Fazal, S. (2001). The Need for Preserving Our Farm Lands: A Case Study from a Predominantly Agrarian Economy. *Landscape and Urban Planning*, Vol. 55, No. 1, Elsevier Science Publication, United Kingdom.

Jafri, S.S.A. (2003). India's Rural Habitat in Need of Rejuvenation, *Geographical Review of India*, Vol. 65, No. 2, Calcutta.

Jafri, S.S.A. (2006). Levels of Civic Amenities in Urban Settlements of Avadh Region of Uttar Pradesh, *Urban Panorama*, Vol. V, No. 2, Lucknow.

Jafri, S.S.A. (2008). Urbanization in Uttar Pradesh, *Urban Panorama*, Vol. VII, No. 2, Lucknow.

Master Plan 2021. Lucknow, Town and Country Planning Department, LDA, Lucknow.

Nangia, S. (1976). *Delhi Metropolitan Region, a study in settlement geography*, K.B. Publishing House, New Delhi.

Ranade, A. and Dev, M.S. (1998). *Agriculture and Rural Development*, India Development Report, Oxford University Press, New Delhi.

Shafi, M. (1969). Land Use Planning, Land Classification and Land Capability: Methods and Techniques, *The Geographer*, Aligarh.

Schenk, H. (1997). The Rurban Fringe: a Central area Between Region and City: the Case of Bangalore, India. in: M. Chatterji & Y. Kaizhang, *Regional Science in Developing Countries*, New, MacMillan, New York.

Thakur, B. (1991). *Land Utilization and Urbanization, The Rural-Urban Fringe*, Deep & Deep, New Delhi.

Yadav, C.S. (1987). *Rural-urban Fringe*. Concept Publications, New Delhi.

14

Spatial Behaviour of Daily Commuters of Aligarh City and its Impact on Fringe

Abdul Munir, Deepika Varshney and *Arshi Azmi*

Introduction

India is undergoing radical changes in demographic patterns as streams of people migrate to regions which offer better opportunities than their home. Much of this improvement is from rural areas to urban with large cities and mega cities as strong loadstones, attracting people with the promise of better living (Kurukshetra, 2009). In rural areas, appalling poverty, unbearable unemployment, low and uncertain wages, uneconomic landholding and poor facilities for education, recreation and other services work as push factors. By contrast, the pull of urban areas may include better employment opportunities, regular and higher wages, fixed working hours, better amenities of living, facilities for education and socio-economic activities (Chandra, 1992).

Commuting is usually on a daily basis but can occur weekly. Majority of the commuters commute to work in the cities. There is a positive relationship between city size and commuting distance. In developing countries and particularly in India, a large section of population is migrating from rural to urban areas because there is less job opportunities in rural areas. Many do not get employment throughout the year and commute between urban and rural areas. Subsequently, the linkages between rural areas and cities get intensified. As a result, the amount of outgoing commuters from rural settlement to urban settlement increases. Daily commuters are also agents of change who bring new ideas from urban centres back to villages. A city or town may loose its status and function of being a regional centre if commuting practices cease to exist (Bansal, 1975).

In regional planning, it is often argued that regional deconcentration process and urban sprawl tend to increase the amount and distance of commuting (Vandermissen *et al.*, 2003). Due to improved traffic infrastructure and falling transport costs, the spatial division of labour and housing locations extends the travel to work areas and compensates for locational disadvantages associated with local labour markets (Moss *et al.*, 2004). Intensity and frequency of cities and its regions also depend on linkages in terms of distance and the available nature of transport and communication. The greater the distance between a city and dependents town, the lesser will be the interaction and similarly, the frequency of reaching to a city of people and commodities is also affected with the inter-distance (Verma, 2006). Travel distance is the single important factor that affects effectiveness of transport nodes and consequent commuter travel decision in urban areas (Makin *et al.*, 1997).

Several studies have been done by many scholars taking into consideration different aspects to each other. Ommeren (1998) derived a framework explaining the job search behaviour of employed individuals. He explicitly took into account commuting costs and residential moving behaviour. Theriault *et al.* (1999) presented another model and simulation procedure to evaluate optimal routes and to commute travel time for each individual trip of an Origin-Destination (OD) survey database. Gangrade *et al.* (2002) structured a nested logic model of activity scheduling behaviour suggesting two stage decision processes. Corvers *et al.* (2003) sub-divided functional regional labour markets by modelling the commuting behaviour of workers in Netherlands. Charren, M. (2007) provided a methodological framework in which the observed average commute is compared with theoretical commuting value: the minimum and maximum average commute. Harvey (2007) studied cyclist commute behaviour in relationship to facility disruption providing a basis for prioritizing future infrastructure improvements and undertaking the impacts of disruptions in neighbourhood of south Minneapolis. Patuellie *et al.* (2007) offered a network analysis of the spatial commuter's network in Germany by comparing two Spatial Interaction Model (SIM) specifications in order to replicate the actual network structure.

Objectives

In the present paper, an attempt has been made to analyze the commuting behaviour by using the distance travelled from home to the city. Following basic objectives have been taken to pursue the present research work:

- To examine the spatial behaviour of commuters by demarcating the areas from where people commute daily for getting work in the city.
- To find out the spatial difference in commuting behaviour by frequency of commuters and distance.

Hypotheses

Following general hypotheses have been formulated to find out the facts of commuting behaviour of the city:

- Whether the impact of distance from the city has bearing on frequency of commuters.
- Whether there is variation in frequency of persons and intensity of settlements within each and every demarcated zone.

Methodology

To accomplish the above objectives as well as to ascertain the above hypotheses, personal survey was made for gathering information regarding daily commuters through spread questionnaire, on *nine* entry points:

- Sarsaul on G.T. Road
- Mukundpur on Agra Road
- Pala Aisi on Mathura Road
- Nimri on Gonda Road
- Musepur Jalal on G.T. Road
- Kwarsi on Ramghat Road
- Manzoorgarhi on Anupshahr Road
- Panaithi on Sikandrarao Road
- Bijona Khurd on Khair Road radiating from the city at peak hours in between 6 a.m. to 9 a.m. throughout the year, 2008. A map of the district showing villages with their locations have been prepared with the help of Tahsil maps obtained from the Uttar Pradesh Administrative Atlas, Census of India, 2001. All the informations and data collected have been plotted on map and subsequently commuters zone were demarcated. For the delineation of zones, firstly, data have been divided into 3 categories of high, medium and low frequency zone with the help of quartiles which are as follows:

- Zoning has been drawn with the help of following formula—
- Q1 (25%) = value of (N+1)/4
- Q2 (50%)= value of N/2
- Q3 (75%)= value of 3(N+1)/4

where, Q = Quartile value
N= Number of Settlements

Further, each zone has been divided of equal distances.

Study Area

Aligarh city is located in north India in the western part of the State of Uttar Pradesh. It is located at 27° 53′ north latitude and 78° 4′ east longitude, 126 km from Delhi and 1408 km from Kolkata (Fig. 14.1). The city is located in the Lodha block of Koil Tahsil and it lies almost in the centre of Aligarh district. The fusion of historical and geographical elements in Aligarh city has given it a distinct personality. Introduction of railway line in March 1863 from Tundla to Aligarh has played an important role in the progress and prosperity of the district (Neville, 1926). Aligarh city is the focal point of Aligarh district from where communication arteries radiate to every corner of the district.

Spatial Behaviour of Commuters

A city tends to exert a dominant influence over a small area in its immediate neighbourhood by virtue of the provision of specialized services (Bansal, 1975). So far not much study has been made to this concept but labour sheds are beginning to receive increasing attention from urban analysis (Alexander, 1963). Aligarh city enjoys a central position as the district headquarters where there is an administrative function and their offices. Besides, the presence of individual units, transportation facilities, the social and cultural institutions have made it into a number of regional importance in and outside the district. Therefore, Aligarh city has been an important source of urban influence. It has become a hub of urban amenities and facilities for the people of the fringe areas. The workers from the surroundings, settlements are largely attracted to the city by large scale industries and by the commercial and residential areas. For assessing the spatial behaviour of commuters, it is necessary to demarcate the areas from where people are coming to the city. Workers who commute

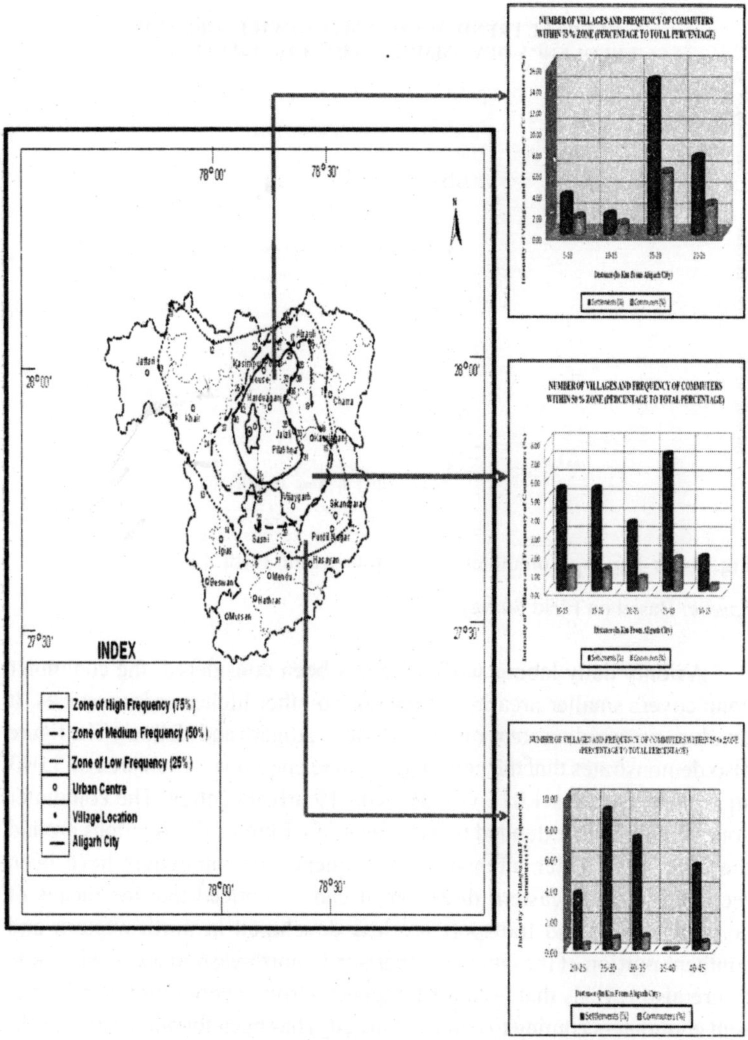

Fig. 14.1: Demarcation of Commuters zone at Varying distance from Aligarh City (2008).

daily using horse cart, auto rickshaws, buses, bicycle and as pedestrians for different purposes, have been surveyed for demarcating the sphere of influence. Fig. 14.2 reveals the spatial difference in commuting behaviour of daily workers with distance from the city. The entire commuting zone has been divided into three zones of varying distances.

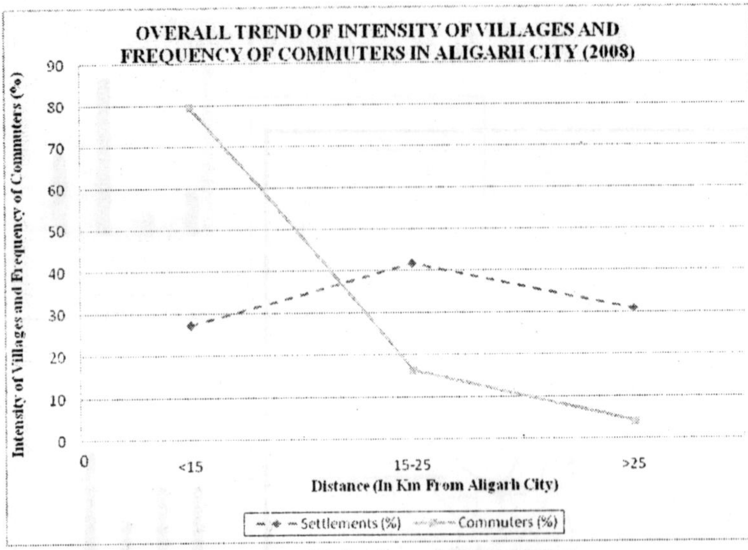

Fig. 14.2: Varying Commuters' Behaviour within Each Zone.

Source: Based on Field Survey.

As only daily labour workforce has been considered, the commuter zone covers smaller area in comparison to other higher order services. It involves surrounding areas of two districts—Aligarh and Hathras. The figure also demonstrates that the commuter's zone encompasses an area of 3,043 sq km and includes 1,011 villages with 19 urban centres. The commuter zone of the city is extended to a distance of 45 km in all directions around the city. The greater intensity and frequency of commuters have been recorded in north-eastern direction. It can be noticed that the means of communication and transport are less developed in north-western and southern portion of the city in comparison to north-eastern areas. The same figure also reveals that greatest frequency (from where more than 75 per cent commuters coming to and from the city) has been founded in the north-eastern portion of the zone comprising Atrauli and Dhanipur blocks within a distance of between 8 to 22 km. Within this zone, highest frequency value has been accounted in Madrak situated at 9 km away from the city followed by Jawan Vajidpur (16 km) and Mahrawal (8 km). On the other hand, 25 per cent zone having lowest frequency of commuters (from where only 25 per cent commuters commute to the city) is shown by outer boundary. There is a great bulge in its extreme western portion at Dharampur village (43 km) located in Chandausi Block. It represents the farthest point

Table 14.1: Overall Inflow and Outflow of Commuters in Aligarh City (2008)

Distance (Km)	*Name of Settlements and Their Location Code*	*Total Settlements*	*Total Settlements (%)*	*Total Annual Frequency (No.)*	*Total Annual Frequency (%)*
<15	Sahajpur(25), Jamalpur Siya(26), Lodha (27), Jiroli Dor (40), Madrak (41), Mahrawal (42), *Barautha, Morthal, Harduaganj, Darapur, Deosaini, Dhaurra Mafi, Chikaura, Kwarsi, Dhanipur*	15	27.273	580545	79.402
15–25	Ajahari (13), Kishenpur (14), Tikari (20), Sikargarhi (21), Sasni Dehat (22), Jawan Sikanderpur (23), Basai (24), Chapauta (28), Meergarhi (29), Jijharka(30), Akrabad (31), Soorajpur(32), Jalali (33), Gopalpur(34), Bhavigarh (35), Raipur (36), Jawan Vajidpur(37), *Narona Akapur, Daudgarhi, Ahmadpuri*, Shekhupur(38), Daupur (39), *Kalai*	23	41.818	105184	16.370
>25	Dharampur(1), Chandanpura (2), Jalalpur (3) Jamanpur (4), Madanpur(5), Bijauli (6), Charra Rafatpur(7), Bhadamai (8), Shri Nagar (9), Sahnaul (10), Mauhari (11), Dhorau Chandpur (12), Goverdhanpur(15), Northo (16), Atrauli (17), Nagaria Patti Chahram (18), Barla (19)	17	30.909	24175	4.229
Total		**55**		**709904**	

Source: Based on Field Survey.

Note: Italic Villages have shown 100 per cent frequency of commuters which have not been included in demarcated zones and not shown in the map.

having comparatively low frequency. Within this zone, higher frequency of commuters have been recorded in Charra Rafatpur (30 km) leaving behind Bijauli (32 km). Medium frequency zone has been shown by middle contiguous line.

Further, an investigation has been done to test the relationship between the commuter behaviour and distance within each demarcated zone. For this purpose, the data of each zone has been divided into different categories of equal distance from the city centre. Figure 14.1a and Table 14.2 show that within the zone of 75 per cent, higher frequency values of commuters and settlements (5.851 percentage to total percentage and 14.55 per cent settlements to total settlements respectively) have been figured out within the distance of 15-20 km which reveals the highest percentage value in all categories. It is mainly because all the settlements lying in this distance category are located within a dense network of roads. Therefore, commuters are moving to and from these villages on cheap and easy accessible transportation facilities. Relatively low trips of commuters and intensity of settlements (1.614 % commuters to total percentage and 3.64% settlements to total percentage) have been accounted within the distance of 5-10 km. It may be because of changing pattern of occupational structure. Most of the people of the immediate surroundings of the city are generally engaged in other varied primary and secondary services. Consequently, those who earn on daily basis are coming irregularly within a month or two only in needed conditions.

Higher percentage of commuters and settlements i.e. 1.768 per cent commuters to the total percentage and 7.27 per cent settlements respectively, have been found in more than 25-30 km distance category within the commuter zone of medium frequency (Fig. 14.1b and Table 14.3). It has been found out that Goverdhanpur, Northo, Atrauli, Nagaria Patti Chahram, Barla, all these villages lie in north-eastern direction where

Table 14.2: In and Outflow of Commuters within the Zone of High Frequency (75%)

Distance (Km)	Settlements (No.)	Settlements (%)	Commuters (No.)	Commuters (%)
5–10	2	3.64	11460	1.614
10–15	1	1.82	7100	1.000
15–20	8	14.55	41540	5.851
20–25	4	7.27	20320	2.862

Source: Based on Field Survey.

they are enjoying a very well developed transportation routes. The two categories of 10-15 and 20-25 km have more or less same percentage of settlements with a little bit variations in frequency of commuters

Figure 14.1c and Table 14.4 reveals that within the areas of 25 per cent, frequency of commuters and intensity of settlement have been found higher (0.769% commuters to total commuters' percentage and 9.09% settlements in between 25-30 km distance from the city). Within this distance, Charra Rafatpur and Sahnaul is situated in north-eastern direction. Two settlements of same categories, i.e. Shrinagar and Bhadamai lying in Hathras district in southern directions are benefited by Aligarh-Hathras and Aligarh-Sikandrarao routes. There is no village within the distance of 35-40 km. Therefore, it is interesting to note from the above going discussions that those categories of distances recording high frequency of commuters have such settlements which are located in north-eastern portion of the city.

Furthermore, it is evident from Table 14.1 and Figure 14.3 that there emerges inverse relationship between distance and number of commuters coming to the city. This relationship is sustained when all these three zones are combined together. All those settlements which record cent per cent frequency of commuters (according to quartiles) because of their favourable locations have not been incorporated in demarcation of zone. But now, to find out the clear cut picture of overall pattern of commuting behaviour over distance, all these settlements have also been included. The number of commuters (75%) decrease with increasing distance. Higher trips of commuters for working purposes are coming from less than 15 kms. distance from the city while it is lowest (7.22% to the total percentage) within the distance greater than 25 km. It can be clearly understood with the same figure that density of villages is comparatively low (18 in number) in between 0-15 km afterwards it increases up to 23

Table 14.3: In and Outflow of Commuters within 50% Zone of Aligarh City (2008)

Distance (Km)	*Settlements (No.)*	*Settlements (%)*	*Commuters (No.)*	*Commuters (%)*
10–15	3	5.45	8759	1.234
15–20	3	5.45	8234	1.160
20–25	2	3.64	5113	0.720
25–30	4	7.27	12550	1.768
30–35	1	1.82	2184	0.308

Source: Based on Field Survey.

Table 14.4: In and Outflow of Commuters within Less Frequency Zone (25%) of Aligarh City (2008)

Distance (Km)	*Settlements (No.)*	*Settlements (%)*	*Commuters (No.)*	*Commuters (%)*
20–25	2	3.64	2401	0.338
25–30	5	9.09	5460	0.769
30–35	4	7.27	6186	0.871
35–40	0	0.00	0	0.000
40–45	3	5.45	3640	0.513

Source: Based on Field Survey.

settlements within the distance of 15-25 km and then again decreases. Consequently, higher numbers of commuters are coming from smaller number of settlements.

Transportation used mainly depends on the distance covered by them. So in commuting activities, citizens have many choices in using public transport for their travelling (Tamin, 2005). Mainly commuters use buses, bicycle, auto rickshaws and by walking from their home to working places. Most of the people from within the distance of 6-7 km come as pedestrian for reaching at their working place for their daily earnings. Others who are covering distance of over 7 km use bus, cycle, auto rickshaws to reach their origin and destination. As Aligarh city is a centre of urban functions, it has great demand of labour work force. The main employment attractions are factories, shops, constructional sites etc.; one of the attractions is lock industry which has attracted thousand of workers. Therefore, there is strong relationship of city and its surroundings in this respect. It is observed that most of the commuting is from the places which are:

- Close to Aligarh city.
- Situated on roads radiating from the city.
- Settlements having comparatively efficient transportation facilities.
- Settlements having comparatively high proportion of poor persons.

Conclusion

The study reveals that large variations in commuting behaviour have been recorded from the city to varying distances. The analysis of the

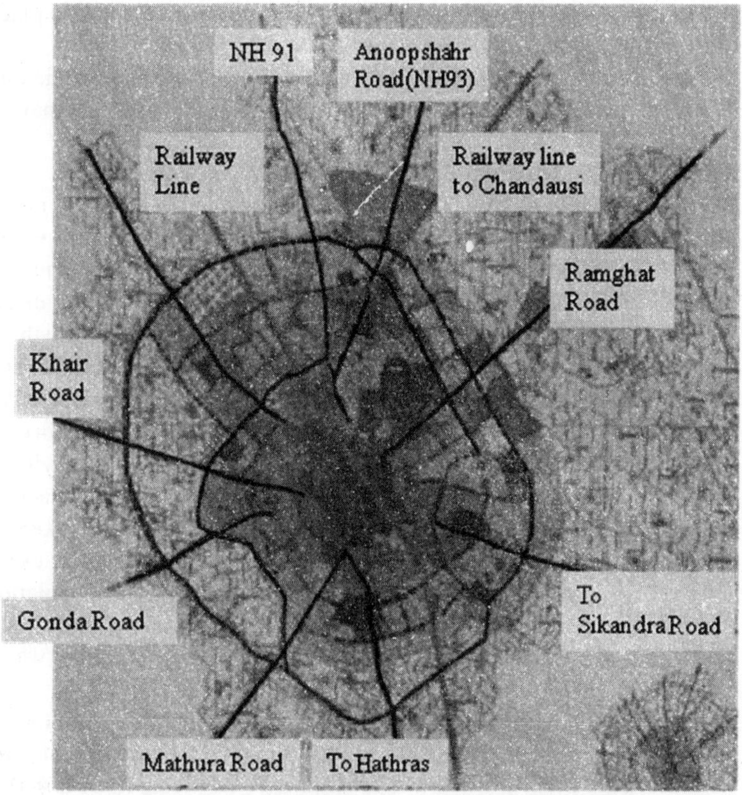

Fig. 14.3: Connectivity of Aligarh City.

study confirms the spatial behaviour of commuters with respect to distance from the city. It further reveals that variations are also recorded in commuter's frequency and number of settlements within each zone.

Problems and Suggestions

- Commuters assemble on roads at different areas such as near Gandhi Park, near Gandhi Eye Hospital, near Prakash Lodge in the city which in turn leads to traffic jams and congestion in morning. So there should be assembly points at the outskirts of the city.

- Simultaneously, they should be restricted to assemble any place where they are convenient.
- The entry points and roads should be managed and planned up to at least 50 km from the city centre so that congestion may be avoided.
- Roads should be much broader with pavements.
- As Aligarh city is more developed as compared to other urban centres, they get here much better output of their labour work. So they have limited choice for their earnings. It is evident that centres having large number of facilities induce pulling effect and become centres with greater chances of further growth by attracting and accommodating more people from surrounding areas. Therefore, since imbalanced regional development exists in other small and intermediate towns, great flow of working force move daily to the highly urbanized cities by paying a considerable higher transportation costs over longer distances. Thus, a comprehensive planning policy should be taken to promote urban growth to such an extent that each and every small and intermediate urban centre can serve its population and those living in surrounding rural areas. Consequently, their options for working purpose will be significantly increased which in turn will reduce pressure on urban centres.
- To cater the needs of domestic and inter-state commuters, Government of Uttar Pradesh has proposed development of outer Ring Road at Aligarh. The proposed Outer Ring Road is 45 km long. Out of this 27 km length has been taken up by NHAI separately and the balance length of around 18 km is being taken up by Awas Bandhu, Government of U.P. under IURP (Integrated Urban Rejuvenation Plan). Sikanderpur Bhukrawali, Mehrawal, Barai Suhangarhi, Haivatpur Sia, Mirzapur Sia, Alampur Subkara, Manzoorgarhi, Sikanderpur Cherat, Maheshpur, Dhorra Mafi, Nagla Mai Beg, Chikaura, Kwarasi, Asadpur Kyam, Yakootpur, Dhanipur, Gram Sidhauli villages are planned to be linked together by Outer Ring Road. With the development of 18 km, 6 lane outer Ring Road, city will be able to reduce the pressure on leading roads and provide comparable and reasonable safe services to the people within the city.
- In addition, for further investigation, the examination of special regional circumstances like polycentric or monocentric spatial characteristics will be a promising approach.

References

Administrative Atlas, *Census of India,* Uttar Pradesh, India.

Alexander, J.W. (1963). *Economic Geography,* Wisconsin, p. 556.

Bansal, S.C. (1975). *Town Country Relationship in Saharanpur City—Region—a Study in Rural-Urban Interdependence Problems,* Sanjeev Prakashan, Saharanpur, p. 23.

Corvers *et al.*, (2003). *The Regionalization of Labour Markets by Modelling Commuting Behaviour*, pp. 1-19. http://www.sre.wu.wien.ac.at/ersa/ersaconfs/ersa 03/cdrom/papers/199.pdf

Charron, M. (2007). "From Excess Commuting to Commuting Possibilities: More Extension to the Concept of Excess Commuting", *Environment and Planning,* Vol. 39, pp. 1238-1254.

Gangrade, *et al.* (2002). "A Nested Logic Model of Commuters' Activity Schedules", *Journal of Transportation and Statistics,* Vol. 5 (2/3), pp. 19-36.

Harvey, *et al.* (2007). "Commuter Bicyclist Behaviour and Facility Disruption: Final report", pp. 1-23. Website: http://www.conservancy.umn.edu/bitstream/5573/1/200715.pdf

Kurukshetra: A Journal on Rural Development (Rural Migration), Vol. 57 (8), June 2009.

Lampert, *et al.* (1998). *Commuting in Multi Nodal Urban Systems: An empirical Comparisons of Three Alternative Models*, pp. 1-26. Website: http://www.sre.wu-wien.ac.at/ersa/ersaconfs/ersa98/papers/252.pdf

Moss, J.E. *et al.*, (2004). "Employment Location and Associated Commuting Patterns for Individual in Disadvantages Rural Areas in Northern Ireland", *Regional Science,* Vol. 38(2), pp. 121-136.

Ommeren, J.V. (1998), "On the Job Search Behaviour: The Importance of Commuting Time", *Land Economics,* Vol. 74(4), pp. 526-540.

Patuelli, *et al.* (2007). "Network Analysis of Commuting Flows: A Comparative Static Approach to German Data", *Network Spatial Economics,* pp. 315-331. Website: www.springerlink.com/content/223185885v881112/fulltext.pdf

Tanim, O.Z. (2005). "Integrated Public and Road Transport Network System for Bunderg Metropolitan Area (Indonesia)", Proceedings of the *Eastern Asian Society for Transportation Studies,* Vol. 5, pp 1281-1300.

Theriault, M. *et al.* (1999), "Modelling Commuter Trip Length and Duration within GIS: Application to an O-D Survey", *Journal of Geographic Information and Decision Analysis,* Vol. 3(1), pp. 40-56.

Vandermission *et al.* (2003), "Analysing Changes in Urban Form and Commuting Time", *The Professional Geographer,* Vol. 55 (4), pp. 446-463.

Verma, V.L. (2006), *Urban Geography"*, Rawat Publications, New Delhi, p. 273.

15
Changing Scenario of Peri-urban Landscape Around Ballia City

Ram Kumar Chaturvedi and *Rana P.B. Singh*

Introduction

The word "peri-urban" could be used to denote a place, concept or process. As a place, it can refer to rural fringe areas surrounding cities. As a concept, peri-urban could be seen as an interface of rural and urban activities and institutions. As a process, it could be thought of as the two-way flow of goods and services and a transitional stage between rural and urban (Narain and Nischal, 2007: 261). Webber (1964: 116) defines it as groups of heterogeneous people who communicate with each other through space. Certainly, peri-urban is a concept referring to a zone or area where urban and rural development processes meet, mix and inter-react on the edge of the cities. It is often not a discrete area, but rather a diffuse territory identified by combinations of features and phenomena, generated largely by activities within the urban zone. The development of a peri-urban area is an inevitable consequence of urbanisation (cf. Nottingham and Liverpool Universities, 1998). These areas exist outside formal urban boundaries and urban jurisdictions typically split into a number of administrative areas which are in a process of urbanisation. As a specific and non-neutral space, a peri-urban area refers to a transition or interaction zone, where urban and rural activities are juxtaposed, and landscape features are subject to rapid modifications, inducing by human activities (Douglas, 2006: 18). The peri-urban interface constitutes an "uneasy" phenomenon, usually characterized by either the loss of "rural" aspects (loss of fertile soil, agricultural land, natural landscape, etc.) or the lack of "urban" attributes like low density, lack of accessibility, lack of services and infrastructure, etc. (Allen, 2003:

136). Landscape in peri-urban is environmentally unstable, and progressively assumes many of the characteristics of urban areas. The land area which can be characterised as peri-urban shifts over time as cities expand. It is also a zone of rapid economic and social structural change, characterised by pressures on natural resources, changing labour market opportunities and changing patterns of land use (Rakodi, 1998: 3).

The peri-urban interface is a dynamic zone both spatially and structurally. Spatially, it is the transition zone between fully urbanised land in cities and areas in predominantly agricultural use. Rapid expansion of peri-urban areas presents opportunities and challenges for urban and rural activities, institutions and sustainability. No longer solely seen in spatial terms, the peri-urban landscape is increasingly recognised in terms of dynamic flows of commodities, capital, natural resources, people and pollution. Although often seen as a transition zone, peri-urban areas are expanding rather than diminishing. The complex interactions between urban land use, environmental change, and socio-economic system in urban area and in peri-urban area generate changes in peri-urban landscape. It must be assessed because rapidly changing landscape of peri-urban areas have great ecological and socio-economic importance not only for their own but for future of urban area also.

Methodology

For collection of primary data, a comprehensive field observation and selected interviews with persons belonging to different social groups and occupations had been carried out. In fact, it is difficult to delimit the boundary of peri-urban area around Ballia city as there is no clear cut natural boundary which can be taken to limit it. Hence, for delimiting the peri-urban, only administrative boundaries of those villages have been included where some forms of urban elements (in contiguity of the city) have been noticed. Its boundary goes-off approximately one kilometre away from urban sprawl. Maps have been prepared with the help of Google Earth imageries using Computer Software Adobe Photoshop version CS2.

Study Area

Ballia city is located (25° 44′ to 25° 46′ N latitude and 84° 08′ to 84° 10′ E longitude) on the north bank of River Ganga and extended along both sides of Varanasi-Chhapra railway line and NH-19 (Ghazipur-Chhapra). It is a historical, cultural, administrative and commercial centre of eastern

Uttar Pradesh. It is located 150 km east of the Varanasi metropolis (cf. Fig. 15.1). It occupies an area of 16.11 sq. km. inhabited by 1,01,465 persons (Census, 2001).

Rural-Urban Forms and Land Use

Peri-urban area around Ballia city is characterised by mixed land uses, i.e. rural and urban (Fig. 15.2). The co-existence of rural and urban forms of land use indicates two way flows of goods, capital and services between the villages and town. As a result of the rapid urbanisation, pressure on land is rising because of migration from the core city and rural areas and natural population growth due to which rural character of peri-urban is constantly changing. The pressure on land transforms the use of land for urban purposes, such as construction of buildings, roads and lanes, and waste disposal. The result of increasing pressure on land in peri-urban is not only changing the land use pattern, but also causing degradation of natural resources, i.e. soil, water, vegetation, etc. (cf. Fig. 15.3). The growing urban population and their demand for food and other agricultural products have major impacts on land use in peri-urban areas and nearby rural areas (*see* report, UNESCO, 2000). Over the last decades, agricultural land has been acquired for non-agricultural purpose to fulfil

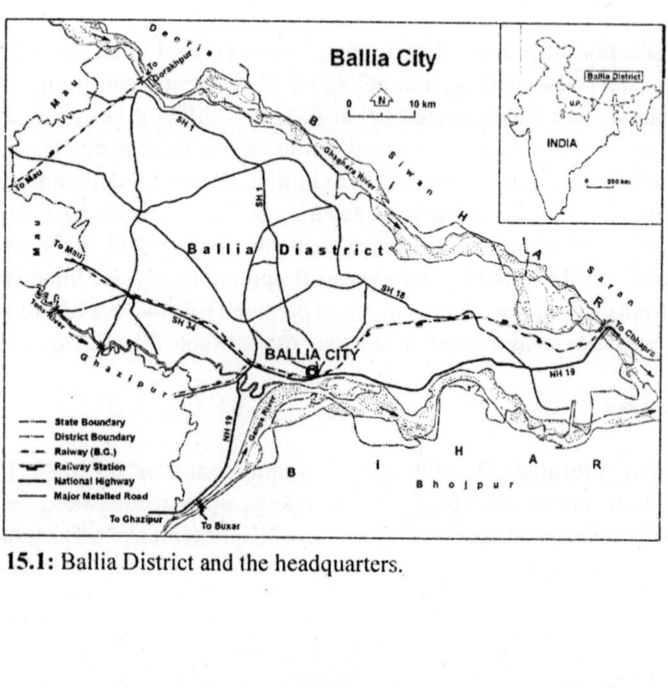

Fig. 15.1: Ballia District and the headquarters.

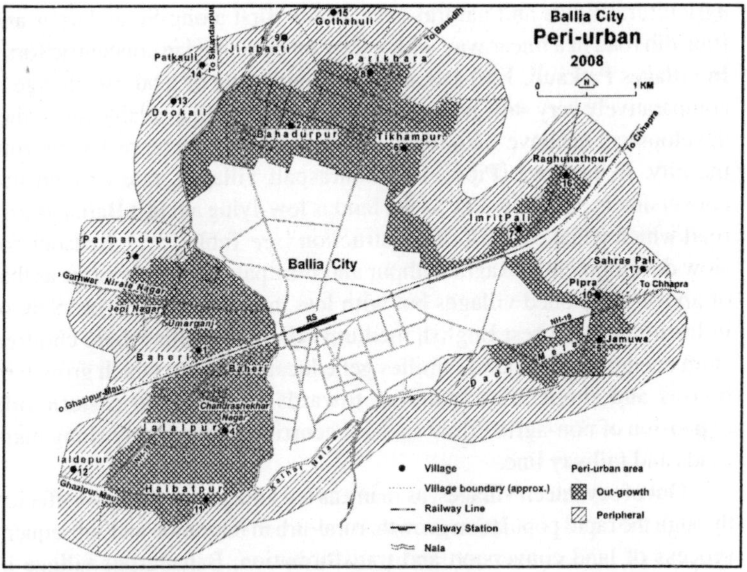

Fig. 15.2: Ballia Town: Peri-urban areas.

the needs of growing population. Most of these lands were private owned and sold by the farmers. High market prices of land allures landowners to sell-off their land and the amount of money they get is mostly utilized in marriages, education, upgradation of less fertile fields and agricultural infrastructure, construction of houses/shops for getting rent or for self-use. Conversion of agricultural land into other uses is resulting into diminishing size of landholdings and diminishing agricultural productivity.

The size of landholding is decreasing due to increasing population and subsequent fragmentation of landholdings between family members. At the same time, dearth of secure source of water supply declines opportunities of any agricultural based livelihoods. Such factors have greatly affected villages namely Bahadurpur, Tikhampur, Parikhara, Parmandapur, Baheri, Jalalpur, Haibatpur, Maldepur, and Imritpali which are located adjacent to city boundary. Though changes have been observed in all directions but most changes have occurred in north and west directions. In north, Bahadurpur, Parikhara and Tikhampur villages are the severely affected by the process of urbanisation. Baheri, Bahadurpur, Tikhampur, Jalalpur and Parikhara villages are highly and densely populated where rate of loss of agricultural land is found very high. Here, non-agricultural land uses and structures have encroached upon agricultural fields and natural vegetations, first along Sikandarpur and Bansdih road in a linear way which later on combined in concentric form. In villages Patkauli, Jirabasti, and Gothahuli, rate of land use change is comparatively very slow because plenty of land is still available for further development in above-mentioned villages and they are more distant from the city. In Jamuwa, Pipra, and Sahraspali villages, rate of land use conversion is relatively low as the land is low-lying against Ballia-Bairia road which enhances cost of construction (*see* Table 15.1). Reasons for slow development in Raghunathpur and Imritpali are mostly same as that of above-mentioned villages but with less intensity. Holy Cross School in Imritpali is the best English medium school of Ballia where children from economically sound families get education due to which growth of houses and shops are expanding towards Imritpali. In eastern side expansion of non-agricultural uses is occurring in linear way along main roads and railway line.

Out of seventeen villages, as many as ten villages are the most affected through the rapid population growth, rural-urban migration and subsequent process of land conversion and transformation. Bahadurpur village in north and Baheri in west is the severely affected by process of urbanization. Pipra and Jirabasti villages have witnessed comparatively less conversion of Agricultural land and Natural Vegetation into built-up area (*see* Table 15.1). Bahadurpur possessed Polytechnic College, a cinema hall, godown and warehouse. It is located contiguous to administrative zone of the Ballia district. A number of government employees have built their house

Table 15.1: Loss of agricultural land and natural vegetation in severely affected villages

S. No.	*Village*	*Area in ha (approx.)*
1.	Baheri	128.64
2.	Bahadurpur	90.31
3.	Parmandapur	27.49
4.	Jalalpur	25.64
5.	Jamuwa	24.55
6.	Tikhampur	20.50
7.	Imritpali	12.11
8.	Parikhara	9.16
9.	Jirabasti	6.71
10.	Pipra	3.20
	Total	348.31

Source: Personal Survey, 2008.

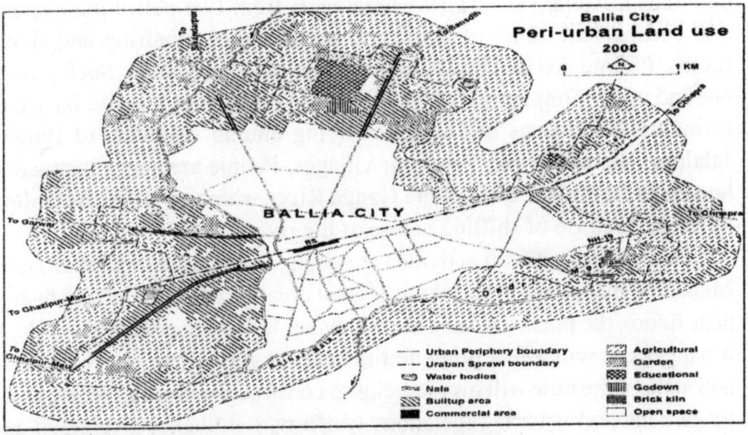

Fig. 15.3: Ballia Town: Land use in Peri-urban areas.

due to its nearness to their workplace; this subsequently resulted into rapid development of middle and high class residential colonies on agricultural lands of Bahadurpur, Tikhampur and Parikhara villages. Being in village jurisdiction, this area is devoid of any municipal taxes and laws. Presently, only about forty per cent of total agricultural land of Bahadurpur is available for cultivation. The morphology and architectural design of houses show urban resemblance. Some of the colonies are well planned with good sewerage facilities. In north, conversion of land use towards rural edge gets linear pattern along Sikandarpur and Bansdih road in villages of Devkali, Patkauli, Jirabasti, Parikhara, Tikhampur and Gothahuli where urban influence minimizes with increasing distance. In east, rural landscape is transformed rapidly on both sides of Garwar road. A number of shopping Katras and the Chandra Shekhar Nagar—a well planned residential colony, and semi-planned Nirala Nagar and J.P. Nagar residential colonies have developed in Parmandapur and Baheri villages on the cost of natural vegetation, water bodies and agricultural land. Chandra Shekhar Nagar colony is a well-planned high-class residential colony in the peri-urban area. Segregated residential areas along with railway line have also developed in Baheri village, where Umarganj and area around private taxi stand (west of Kathar Nala) are the most densely populated and congested areas in peri-urban zone. In the south-west, growth of houses and commercial establishment are growing incessantly from Kathar Nala to Maldepur village (about 2 km. from the city boundary). Along the NH-19 where apart from two petrol pumps, and one cinema hall, most of the shops are of motor repairing and show-rooms. Private taxi and bus stand have also developed here. Such growth has had greater impact not only on land use/land cover but also on socio-economic conditions and ways of living among residents of Baheri, Jalalpur, Haibatpur and Maldepur villages. People are also constructing houses in flood-free tract of the Ganga River which might be hazardous in future because of shifting nature of the river.

Such constructional activities are going on rapidly in and near Dadri Mela area that result in shrinking of total area for the fair due to which in near future, the place of Dadri Mela may be shifted to south of the Nala. If it happens, it will affect prime fertile land for agriculture into wasteland, and at the same time will give impetus to construction works, cutting down of gardens and natural vegetations which may influence livelihood and economic conditions of several families residing around the present location of Dadri Mela. The annual fair Dadri Mela, held on the full moon of Kartik (October-November) attracts about a million people. Dadri Mela site and contiguous area are also used as the major solid waste dumping ground for the city (Fig. 15.4). On the line of solid waste management by Municipal Corporation before one month of commencing the Mela, the site particularly from Shanichari Temple to Meena Bazar (central business area of the Mela) is dotted with refuse and waste plastics all-round. It not only pollutes food items in the market but also affect vitality of the historical Dadri Mela. Development of non-agricultural land uses takes turn in hazardous and unplanned way barring few constructions. Such process not only engulfing fertile productive agricultural land but also generating a number of vacant land plots. Thus, for economic reasons, most of the plots are neither used for residential nor for any other purposes and remains vacant and unused. Due to the unbalanced and haphazard growth, water supply to agricultural fields amidst such growth also obstructs consequently agricultural land that remains uncultivated and thus unused and vacant. Though in some areas, such land is used as playground and for social assemblies and ceremonies.

Apart from generating huge amount of vacant land, hotchpotch developments either deviate or obstruct natural drainage and sewerage facilities in the city. Of course in future, peri-urban area will be included in city area because at present about fourteen per cent area of the city (vacant land 6.8 per cent and 6.9 per cent agricultural land) that may be occupied for further urbanisation. It will have a great impact on structural configuration and morphology of once planned city like Ballia as most

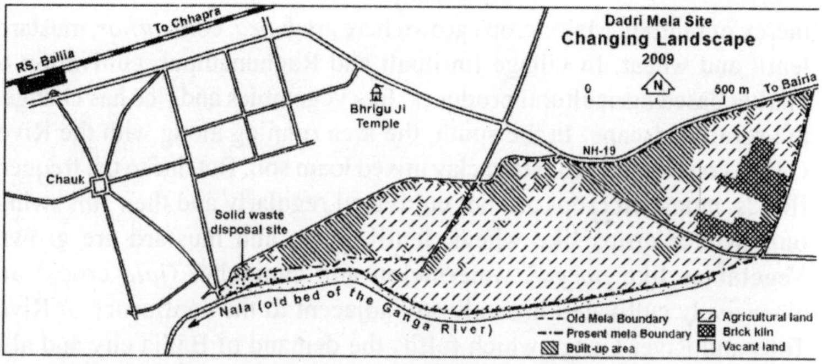

Fig. 15.4: Ballia Town: Land use in Dadari Mela site.

part of it is presently growing uncontrolled and unplanned that result into growth of slums and blights which are springing up here and there and creating several socio-economic problems to the city and also serving as obstacles in planning process and strategy for implementation. Peri-urban area has a great role to play in planning process and may serve as a major focus in making successful implementation of the future Master Plan of the city.

Agriculture and Livelihood

Peri-urban agriculture refers to farming near cities, generally intensive semi or fully commercial production (cf. UNESCO, 2000). In case of Ballia city, there is no substantial change in agricultural landscape in peri-urban area, mostly because of lack of awareness and entrepreneurship among farmers due to which they do not try to change their traditional farming. There are other reasons too, among which poor irrigation consequently results to promote vegetable farming on higher prices. Therefore, it follows typical cropping pattern of eastern Uttar Pradesh. The monsoon season crops include millets, viz., bajra, corn, rice and *arhar* and the winter crops like wheat, mustard, gram and lintel. Agricultural landscape in the study area displays three different patterns in the east, the south and the north-west directions which is an outcome of interplay between different types of soils, relief, mode of irrigation, and construction activities. The eastern part of the study area is a low lying flood-prone area particularly in south of Ballia-Baria road which was frequently flooded by River Ganga before changing its course a few years ago. That's why, here deposited highly fertile clayey loamy soil, but due to lack of developed irrigation facilities, all crops depend on mercy of rainfall. Major crops grown here are *bajra*, corn, *arhar*, mustard, lentil and wheat. In village Imritpali and Raghunathpur, cultivation of market based agricultural produces, like vegetables and rice has changed the rural landscape. In the south, the area running along with the River Ganga consists of high fertile clay mixed loam soil. But due to the frequent floods, monsoon crops are not cultivated regularly and their full swing; only winter crops like wheat, lentil, gram and mustard are grown. Vegetables like *parval*, watermelon and cucumber (*jaid* crops) are extensively cultivated in sandy soil adjacent to the confluence of River Tons and River Ganga which fulfils the demand of Ballia city and also the nearby towns. Irrigation depends on privately owned diesel pump sets scattered here and there. Due to historically famous Dadri Mela, approximately 100 ha. agricultural land goes uncultivated in monsoon seasons because it held in late October and *kharif* crops has to harvest before ripening of crops to make available room for Dadri Mela. Whereas it get too late for *rabi* crops which ultimately affect overall production of the seasonal crops. In the north-west, bore-wells are the main source of irrigation, but due to frequent cut of electric power, use of diesel-based pump sets is increasing gradually that consequently results to pollution. All crops and vegetables of different seasons are cultivated intensively in view of the demand and carrying capacity of the loam soil. It fulfils vegetable demand of Ballia to a great extent. In Jamuwa and Pipra villages, no substantial change in crop types has occurred but interruption in irrigation aroused out of walled open and built plots has been changing mode of irrigation, consequently decrease in production. Some of the small farmers have even left cultivation and adopted relatively better lucrative works in the city as substitute. They have either sold their land or have given on rent (*batai*) to others for farming.

Socio-economic Structure

As commonly noted, economic dependency on the city has been increasing. Members of households in the peri-urban adjust their socio-economic activities by intensifying agriculture or leaving it by seeking locally available non-agricultural employment and/or by out-migration to potential areas. This process of ongoing urbanisation has a selective impact on different types of households and on gender too. For some groups this means more options for living a better livelihood, while others are confronted more with negative aspects of this change. Gender disparity is narrowing down as literacy of both genders is increasing and female work participation in non-agricultural activities is also scaling up. Additionally, males and females have started working in the city. In accordance of urban demand dairy and cultivation of vegetables and fruits are increasing rapidly. People are availing their houses/*katras* on rent as an additional source of income. Farmers sell agricultural land to get money which is commonly invested in business, and construction of building for rental purposes. Such additional money is also spent on marriages, education and for livelihood.

At one hand, consequently economic conditions have improved, but on the other hand, societal harmonious interactions have been losing its fabric rapidly. In the purview of economic regions and social changes, the old system and ethical code of joint-family and community harmony has drastically transformed into nuclear family and individuality. These further turned into a critical stale through bad impacts of consumerism. Most of the poor families settled close to the urban boundary sell their houses/land on higher prices and settled down at much distance on comparatively low price land. At the other hand, well-off families settled far from the urban boundary are coming near to the city. Loneliness and crime are on the rise. Interest to higher and technical education among boys and girls has enhanced due to changing attitudes, ambitions and availability of better private and government colleges in the city.

Major Issues Directing Peri-urban Landscape Development

The occurring changes in peri-urban landscape have generated several issues to tackle with, which are crucial for proper development and planning of peri-urban area. These issues include environmental, social and economic ones those affecting the way of overall changes. Nature of land use/land cover change is one of the major issues reflecting in morphological structure, wherein, particularly in case of Ballia city, major difference lies in its size in different directions arising due to varying rate of land use/land cover change. Variation of land use/land cover change is mainly caused and determined by a number of factors including physical, socio-economic and infrastructural structures.

Environmental degradation in peri-urban area is another major issue which needs immediate attention from planner's side. Rapid changes in landscape is not only consuming fertile agricultural soil but also degrading its fertility due to unbridled waterlogging, sewerage and solid waste disposal. Mercilessly cutting down of trees and natural vegetation in peri-urban areas is a bid to growth of landscape and they having greater impact on city's life in future, e.g. total area under parks, and green area in the city is already fell down to only approx. 1.5 per cent. Brick kilns in peri-urban not only pollute air but also make the land waste where kilns is established permanently unproductive for agricultural, at the same time, upper fertile soil is used in brick kiln industry which exists comparatively less fertile lower level soil for agriculture. Consequently, the agricultural productivity has badly affected. Such environmental problems also affect human health, ways of landscape changes and above all bring changes in pattern of livelihood. Loss and degradation of fertile agricultural soil has altered agricultural pattern due to which the importance of agriculture in livelihood is diminishing. Consequently, small scale farmers and agricultural labourers are seeking other profitable avenues of livelihood. Consequently, agricultural sector is facing shortage of agricultural labourers which in turn has further caused changes in agricultural pattern.

Furthermore, besides scattered residential growth, encroachment and slum development have been degrading social environment wherein loneliness and increase in disputes and crime are becoming common practice. Due to unplanned and amorphous land use planning, lack of adequate civic amenities and in efficiency of the administrative system to handle the institutional and realistic problems of the changing peri-urban landscape, living conditions of the villagers have greatly been affected. In peri-urban area, the above-mentioned issues/problems have been intensified to a great extent, due to lack of guidance and proper planning as the area is governed by varying nature of Gram Panchayats which have not been able to control the growth of peri-urban landscape. The major obstacle in appropriate development in peri-urban is dearth of funds and planning under Gram Panchayats and prevalence of more or less homogeneous development policies in each village are the main reasons due to which these governing bodies have failed to control the physical growth. Therefore, the ambiguous peri-urban interface, split between urban and rural jurisdictional boundaries, presents significant governance challenges. There are often contradictory or absence of regulatory frameworks, and poor health, water and sanitation service provision. There is a haphazard mixture of planned and unplanned operations and a tendency to flout regulations. These features intensify pollution and land degradation, poor public health and sanitation, and are associated with an increasingly competitive labour market (Marshall, *et al.*, 2008: 1). On the other hand, urban administrative unit mainly concentrates on the management and planning of urban area itself only.

While urban regions, their state and development, constitute the major interaction of urbanization processes. Such regions comprise the urban core and its associated peri-urban and rural areas. Urbanization processes along the rural-urban continuum need to be monitored by a complex set of indicators (Banzhaf, *et al.*, 2009: 1675).

Conclusion

Ballia is a rapidly growing city with a small area which has not been extended since many decades; however, its peri-urban area is changing fast to cope with urban character with varying rates in different parts. Area along transportation routes are highly affected through process of urban sprawl. Highest changes in landscape have been occurred in the villages of Baheri, Parmandapur, and Jalalpur in the west; Bahadurpur, Parikhara, and Tikhampur in the north and Jamuwa and Pipra in the east. Loss of fertile land has reduced agricultural production which in turn has affected livelihood of many households. Even though city is progressing rapidly, but there are no substantial changes in crop pattern, and food crops still dominate the agriculture scene. A number of agricultural fields are turning into vacant lands together with haphazard and unplanned constructional activities that obstruct water supply for irrigation. Moreover, varying degrees and types of economic and educational improvements in peri-urban area, social and environmental degradations are emerging as resultant scenario. There are other unique problems also caused by unplanned and rapid urbanization that cause intense pressures on resources, including slum formation, lack of adequate civic and public services (e.g. water and sanitation). These problems need distinctive, innovative and inclusive approaches and solutions from planner's side which can only be brought into proper stream through people's participation and co-ordination. For this, the main task for urban and regional governance should be not only to check unplanned urban sprawl but to redirect the dynamics of urban development that support urban and peri-urban restructuring in future. Though the problems in peri-urban around Ballia city is not yet alarming but if proper steps are taken in advance then naturally it will be fruitful for the sustainable development of the city region in future. Owing to changing nature of peri-urban landscape around Ballia city, it needs either inclusion in city area or constitution of a peri-urban authority to look after major issues and planning and management processes.

References

Allen, A. (2003). Environmental planning and management of the Peri-urban interface. *Environment & Urbanization,* Vol. 15 (1): 135-147.

Banzhaf, E. *et al.*, (2009). Monitoring urban to Peri-urban development with integrated remote sensing and GIS information: a Leipzig, Germany case study. *International Journal of Remote Sensing,* Vol. 30 (7): 1675-1696.

Douglas, I. (2006). Peri-urban ecosystems and societies: traditional zones and contrasting values; in, McGregor, D. *et al.*, (ed.) *The Peri-urban Interface: Approaches to Sustainable Natural and Human Resource Use.* Earthscan, London: 18-29.

Marshall, Fiona, *et al.* (2008). *The Peri-urban Interface and Sustainability of South Asian Cities.* STEPS Centre, An ESRC Research Centre. 6pp. Web: http://www.docstoc.com/docs/18600317/PROJECT–OVERVIEW–The–Peri–Urban. <Accessed: 1 Dec. 2009 >

Narain, V. and Nischal, S. (2007). The Peri-urban interface in Shahpur Khurd and Karnera, India. *Environment and Urbanization,* Vol. 19 (1): 261-273.

Nottingham and Liverpool Universities (1998). Literature Review on Peri-urban Natural Resource Conceptualisation and Management Approaches. Initial Draft, Peri-Urban Production Systems Research, *Natural Resources Systems Programme,* DFID, London.

Rakodi, C. (1998). Review of the Poverty Relevance of the Peri-urban Interface Production System Research. Report for the *DFID Natural Resources Systems Research Programme,* 2nd Draft.

UNESCO (2000). United Nations Economic and Social Council Commission on Sustainable Development. Urbanization and Sustainable Agricultural Development. *Sustainable Agriculture and Rural Development Report of the Secretary-General, Eighth Session* 24 April-5 May; Addendum. Web: http://www.un.org/documents/ecosoc/cn17/2000/ecn172000–7add1.htm <Accessed: 09 Nov. 2009 >

Webber, M.M. (1964). The Urban Place and the Non-place Urban Realm; in, Webber M.M. *et al.*, (ed.) *Explorations into Urban Structure.* University of Pennsylvania Press, Philadelphia.

16

Glimpse of the Rural-Urban Fringe of Lucknow Metropolis

Dr. Archana Gupta

Introduction

In the past seven decades geographers have been paying great attention towards the aspect of economic and regional development. The process of economic development involves dealing with a number of regional geographical aspects and hence, the problem has attracted the attention of many geographers. During ancient times, the cities and rural areas were clearly defined — by walls or other protective structures around the city. In the cities people were engaged in non-agricultural activities and in the rural areas people were engaged in agriculture and animal husbandry. This distinction has persisted through time.

But now, the scenario has completely changed. The towns and cities are growing rapidly. Rapid industrialization along with an unprecedented increase in population has enhanced the scope of economic activities of urban centers both in magnitude and character. Hence, the cities are expanding beyond their administrative boundaries. It has created complexities and intricacies in their land uses associated with various problems. With the growth of metropolitan cities and large cities, the physical expansion of the built-up area beyond their municipal boundaries has been very conspicuous. Generally, their development happens to be in a haphazard, spontaneous and unplanned manner. In this type of development there is a revenue flow of people from city to the countryside. The agricultural lands are transformed for industrial and residential purposes.

> "The term rural-urban fringe has been used to designate such areas where we have a mixture of rural and urban land uses."

With the expansion of population and increase in number of migrants, the city is unable to accommodate all people and hence there is physical expansion of the city in two steps. The first step involves the occupancy of the vacant city areas and the second step includes the encroachment on land areas lying out side the city limits.

According to R. Ramchandran, the tentative definition of rural-urban fringe in India may be attempted:

> "The rural-urban fringe is an area of mixed rural and urban population and land uses, which begin at a point where full city services ceases to be available and the point, where agricultural land uses predominate or where some persons, at least, from the village community commute to the city daily for work or other purposes."

Classification of Rural-Urban Fringe

Various attempts have been made to classify the rural-urban fringe. R. J. Prior (1968) divided the rural-urban fringe into –

i. Urban fringe, and
ii. Rural fringe

'Urban Fringe' is contiguous with the central city, exhibiting a density of occupied dwellings higher than the medium density of the total rural-urban fringe, a higher proportion of residential, industrial and vacant units as distinct from farmland and a higher rate of increase in population density and land use conversion and community.

The 'Rural Fringe' is contiguous with an urban fringe exhibiting a density or occupied units lower than medium density of the total rural-urban fringe, a higher proportion of farms as distinct from non-farm and vacant land and a lower rate or increase in population density, land use conversion and community.

U. Singh (1966) recognized two types of fringes i.e.

i. Primary fringe
ii. Secondary fringe

'The Primary fringe' generally along the municipal limits and 'the Secondary Fringe' are along the regulated areas of towns and cities.

In the present study, the Fringe zone has been divided into two sub-zones:

i. Inner Fringe or the Urban Fringe
ii. Outer Fringe or the Rural fringe

'Inner Fringe' is characterized by land in an advanced stage of transition from rural to urban land use. It is an area just beyond the municipal corporation limits or political boundary of the city with the high value on the scale of urbanity. Here in this zone development is closer and more continuous, it gets almost all the facilities of an urban centre as - electricity, piped water, phone etc.

The second area in the fringe is 'the outer zone' which is an area in which rural land use continues to dominate the landscape but there is infiltration by those urban land uses which take up too much land to be easily located elsewhere. For e.g. airports, sewage works etc. The built up area may be discontinuous, marketing facilities partially available in the area itself and the percentage of the cultivable land relatively much higher. The major occupation is the production of goods in the town such as vegetables, dairy products etc. This belt is more rural than urban.

However, it will not be wrong to say that there is no physically discernible boundary between the two zones, became both are inter-linked and interdependent. An attempt has been made to divide the two on the basis of statistical calculation.

Area of Study

Lucknow lies almost in the centre of Uttar Pradesh. According to Indian Surveyor Journal it has an area of 2,544 square kilometers, which is 1.07 per cent of the states total area. Situated at an altitude of 125 meters above sea level, its position is between 26° 30' N and 27°10' N latitude and 80°30'E and 81°13' E longitude. To its south east and south west lie Barabanki and Unnao districts respectively. To the south of Lucknow is Raibarelly district and to its north-east and north-west are Sitapur and Hardoi districts.

River Gomti, Behta, Loni and Reth flow through the district. It has four tehsils - Malihabad, Lucknow, Mohanlalganj and Bakshi Ka Talab. It consists of eight development blocks namely Mohanlalganj, Gosaiganj, Sarojninagar, Chinhut, Kakori, Malihabad, Maal and Bakshi Ka Talab.

Lucknow is the meeting place of three National Highways, NH-24 runs from Delhi, NH-25 Kanpur-Bhopal and NH-28 to Gorakhpur. It is also connected by four state Highways leading to Hardoi, Raibarelly, Sultanpur and Kursi. It is also a meeting point of Northern Railway and North-Eastern Railway. Lucknow is connected by Air to Delhi, Patna, Kolkata, Mumbai and other important cities and internationally to Sharjah and Dubai. It is also connected by road with Kolkata (970 Km), Delhi (499 Km), Varanasi (317 Km) and Kanpur (78 Km).

According to 2001 Census the district has total population of 36.47 lakhs out of which 22.45 lakhs lived in urban areas. It's population density is 1,434 persons per square kilometer and male female ratio is 1000:891. The literacy rate of Lucknow is 69.39 per cent.

Determinants of Rural-Urban Fringe

(a) Structural Parameter

Demographic Structure

The demographic characteristics include various aspects of population growth and density of population. Population growth is nothing but the net change in the population of a given area during a specific period of time. Whereas density of population is the simple ratio between the total population and the total land area and is expressed in terms of persons per unit of area.

Growth of Population

Growth of population is the term used for the net change in the population of a region during a specific period of time. Largely, there are three factors that determined the population growth these are fertility rate, mortality rate and migration. Such a change can be measured both in terms of absolute numbers and in terms of percentage. Mortality rate is the most important factor in the population growth. This is simply because, over the years due to improved medical facilities, we have been able to counter the death rates. However, migration factor both in and out migration plays a vital role in the population growth of a region.

The rural-urban fringe depends upon the inter play of the push and pull factors of urban centers. Same is the case with the rural-urban fringe of Lucknow Metropolis. Every year a lot of people migrate from the rural to the urban areas, in the search of better facilities and luxuries of life available in the city. This is the major cause in the decrease of rural population growth.

The Table 16.1 shows various phases of population growth, in the Lucknow district as well as in the rural urban-fringe of Lucknow City. There were a lot of fluctuations in the population growth, before the year 1921. Although it seems quite impossible in the present time but the fact is that population graph was actually decreasing till 1921. However, after 1921 population growth was quite steady. Thus 1921 is known as "The Great Demographic Divide". Since then population of the country, as well as the Lucknow district is continuously increasing.

The latest census of 2001 estimated the total population of Lucknow district to be 3681416. This population data shows a 33 per cent decadal increase from the population of the year 1991, which were about 2762801.

The population of Lucknow can be broadly categorized into two-Rural and Urban population. Since 1921, the population of both the Rural and Urban areas of Lucknow is constantly increasing. But there is a difference in the rate of increase of population. Rural population, on one hand is increasing at a much slower rate, while urban population on the other hand is increasing at very high rate.

The year 1961, shows a fall in the decadal growth of the rural population. However, the year 1991, shows a tremendous decrease in the rural population and the urban population on the other hand shows a

Table 16.1: Decennial Variation of Population in Lucknow District

Decade	*No. of Inhabited Villages*	*Population*			*Decadal Percentage Increase*		
		Total	*Rural*	*Urban*	*Total*	*Rural*	*Urban*
1991	932	793241	500604	292637	-	-	-
1911	924	764411	478513	285898	-4.00	-4.00	-2.00
1921	934	724344	461364	262980	-5.00	-4.00	-8.00
1931	934	787472	487642	299830	9.00	6.00	14.00
1941	914	949228	534038	415190	21.00	10.00	39.00
1951	930	1128101	607577	520524	19.00	14.00	25.00
1961	907	1338882	565526	773356	19.00	11.00	27.00
1971	907	1617846	794376	823470	21.00	18.00	24.00
1981	899	2014574	954855	1059719	25.00	20.00	29.00
1991	824	2762801	1031577	1731224	37.00	8.00	63.00
2001	847	3681416	1435907	2245509	33.00	39.00	30.00

Source: District Census Handbooks

tremendous rise, within a period of ten years whereas the scenario has just changed in between 1991-2001. Among the various factors, which determine the population growth, such as: fertility, mortality and migration, such a tremendous rise in the urban population may be largely contributed to the factor of migration. Young youths from the rural areas migrate towards the city area, in search of better educational facilities. The attraction of better job opportunities and various luxuries of life, free them to migrate from the rural areas to the city proper.

Density of Population

Density of population concerned with the ratio between the size of the population and the area. The Geographers have been making more frequent use of the concept of density of population. This is because it is a simple concept relating population size to the land area with a view to assess the pressure of population upon the resources of the area.

The average density as per 2001 Census in the rural areas of Lucknow district is 472 persons per square kilometer. The observations of density of development blocks show that Malihabad is the most densely populated block, with a density of 574 persons per sq. km. Other blocks having high density include Bakshi ka Talab, Chinhat etc. The least densely populated block is Mohanlal ganj, with density of 399 persons/sq km (Table 16.2).

Land Use Pattern

A city can only grow when there is a favourable situation for a multitude of services and activities concerning trade, commerce and industries. It has been observed that the land use pattern, in the vicinity of Lucknow is partly urban and partly rural. Road and railways have played a significant role in the northward shift of urban area. Urban functions have spilled far

Table 16.2: Population Density (Persons/sq km)

Block Name	*1991*	*2001*
Malihabad	376	574
Mal	304	467
Bakshi Ka Talab	341	501
Kakori	381	467
Chinhat	338	481
Sarojani Nagar	327	476
Mohanlalganj	331	399
Gosainganj	307	464

beyond the compactly built city mostly along the arteries of communication.

The total geographical area of the district is 252.2 thousand hectares. Table 16.3 shows alarming trend in land use. Land use under forest has increased from seven thousand hectares in 1975-76 to 11.41 thousand hectares in 2007-08. This may be because of intensive and extensive afforestation programme undertaken by the Government. Kukrail Reserve Forest, protected forests near Musabagh are all evident by the forestation programme by the Government. Barren and uncultivated land decreased as it has been increasingly used due to massive development activities. The area under non-agricultural uses remains almost same, over the years. However, cultivable wasteland has decreased from 19.2 thousand hectares to 9.2 thousand hectares. Both the permanent pastures and miscellaneous tree crops and groves have registered a declining trend. A steep rise in trend in current and other fallow is observed which can be properly harnessed to meet demand pressure. Area under net sown area is slightly increased in 1990-91.

Trend of land utilization of 1990-91 and 2007-08, does not show much difference, except for cultivable waste, which has decreased; and current fallow and other fallow which have shown increasing trend.

(b) Functional Parameter

Isocommutations

Lucknow is an administrative city. It is the center of all the major medical and educational institution. The economic, social and cultural life of the

Table 16.3: Trend of Land Utilization, District Lucknow

Landuse Category	*Area (In Thousand Hectares)*		
	1975-76	*1990-91*	*2007-08*
Forest	7	11.41	11.41
Barren & Unculitvable Land	16.7	10.71	10.1
Land in Non-Agricultural Use	23.2	23.65	23.9
Cultivable Waste	19.2	11.04	9.2
Permanent Pastures & Grazing Land	4.4	3.38	3.1
Land Under Tree Crops & Groves	11.5	5.45	3
Current Fellow	11.3	20.17	32.5
Other Fellow	11.5	13.53	17.1
Net Sown Area	147.1	152.78	141.64

Source: Agricultural Statistics Bulletins.

surrounding countryside is guided by it. Over the years, commuting has become an important aspect of the fringe of Lucknow. The people from surrounding fringe areas come to Lucknow for different purposes. Some of them are daily commuters, who generally arrive early in the morning and return in the evening.

The commuting population may be grouped as regular and casual commuters. Regular commuters generally include students, service holders and labourers. Students make the daily up-down, for better educational facilities. However, service class people and poor labourers come to the city to earn their livelihood.

Casual commuters are those, who come to the city for the shopping purposes. Their purchasing items generally include: cloths, medicine, grains etc. however, some commuters just come to seek for their recreational purposes.

The commuting population largely guided by the transport facility available in the area. Properly constructed road joining fringe area and the city, as well as adequate transport facility enhance the commuting activity.

For delineation of the fringe of Lucknow metropolis, regular or daily commuters have been considered. The percentage of daily commuters out of the total population of the village has been plotted and lines have been drawn at an interval of ten per cent each, signifying the percentage of commuters to the total population. The commuter zone forms maximum along the Barabanki road, Kursi road, Raebareli road and Kanpur road and also along the railway lines towards Kanpur and Raebraeli. The second significant commuting zone is also found in the north along the Sitapur road and railway route. However, the commutation is less significant along the Hardoi road in the west and also along Sultanpur road (Fig. 16.1).

Literacy

The literacy rate in the city area of Lucknow is much higher than its fringe counterpart. This is mainly because the urban areas have got better educational facilities, which include - sufficient number of schools for children & Degree colleges, good library facilities etc. Rural areas, in turn suffer from lack of educational facilities. Rural people are quite unaware about the importance of education especially of girl child. This is also one of the reasons of low literacy level among the fringe dwellers. However, most of the surrounding villages and one which is well connected with the city has higher percentage of literacy. About seventy

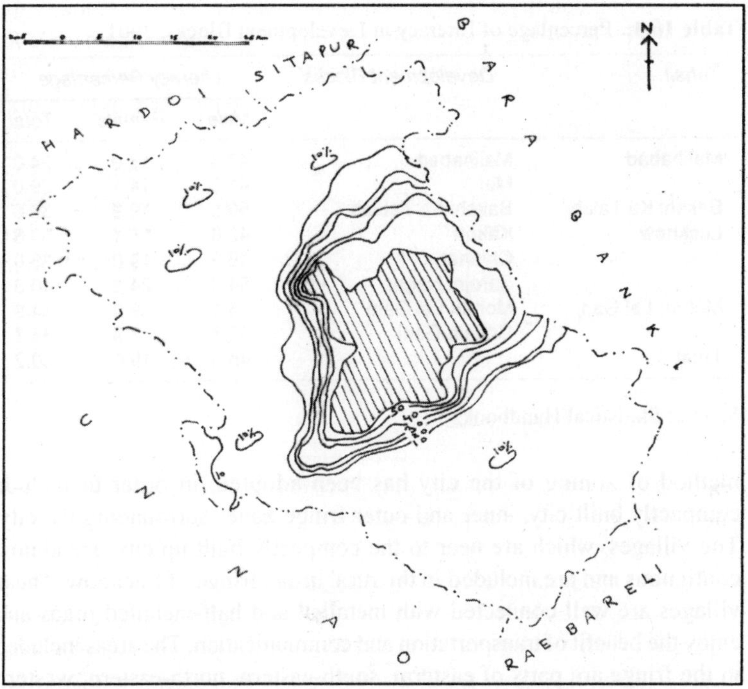

Fig. 16.1: Isocommutation: As Percentage of Total Population of the Fringe

per cent of the population in the city is literate and educated while the corresponding figures for fringe area is nearly thirty per cent.

As it may be enumerated that according to 2001 census the total rural literacy percentage is 30.2 per cent and in the urban area, it is 70.1 per cent. Among the development blocks, highest percentages of literates are present in Sarojninagar. It also tops, in the maximum number of literates both in male and female category. However, still much to be done, in order to improve the educational level of the region.

The least literacy percentage is found in Mal development block, where the female literacy level is worst in the district (Table 16.4).

Delimitation of Rural -Urban Fringe

The structural, functional and physical parameters together determine the extent and form of the fringe. Actually speaking, they co-exist in the space at the same time. To determine the limitation of the fringe, the

Table 16.4: Percentage of Literacy in Development Blocks, 2001

Tehsil	*Development Blocks*	*Literacy Percentage*		
		Male	*Female*	*Total*
Malihabad	Malihabad	47.3	18.0	34.0
	Mal	41.6	14.1	29.0
Bakshi Ka Talab	Bakshi Ka Tablab	50.5	19.9	36.6
Lucknow	Kakori	42.6	16.1	30.6
	Chinhat	49.9	19.0	36.0
	Sarojni Nagar	54.0	24.8	40.8
Mohan Lal Ganj	Mohan Lal Ganj	48.1	19.2	34.9
	Gosain Ganj	50.8	17.9	35.7
Total		48.6	19.0	30.2

Source: Statistical Handbooks

method of zoning of the city has been adopted, in order to include compactly built city, inner and outer fringe zones surrounding the city. The villages, which are near to the compactly built up city, are almost contiguous and are included in the rural urban fringe of Lucknow. These villages are well connected with metalled and half-metalled roads and enjoy the benefit of transportation and communication. The areas included in the fringe are parts of easterm, south-eastern, north-eastern, western and south-western parts of Lucknow tehsil. The fringe also includes southern and south-eastern parts of Bakshi Ka Talab tehsil and western parts of Mohanlalganj tehsil.

Recent trends in Land-use pattern show that land put to grow food crops are decreasing and farmers prefer to grow cash crops. It may be said on this base that percentage of land put to food crop growing decreased from 73.7 per cent to 66.8 per cent between 1991-2008. The net sown area decreased from 68.5 per cent to 55.88 per cent between 1991 and 2008 in the rural areas. This shows that more and more people are getting engaged in non-agricultural activities. The average percentage of non-agricultural labours existing in the urban fringe is 27 per cent and more, and between 12 per cent to 27 per cent in the rural fringe. There is a very slight increase in the land put to non-agricultural uses. It was 23.2 thousand hectares in 1975-76 while in 2007-08, the land area increases to 23.9 thousand hectares. Other functional characters that help in delimiting the fringe includes educational level, commutation etc. The average literacy in the fringe area is 30.2 per cent , whereas literacy percentage of the city population is nearly 70.1 per cent. The low level of literacy in the rural- urban fringe is largely due to the lack of sufficient educational institutes. As such, younger generation is bound to commute to the city for better educational opportunities. These, commuters include students, labourers servicemen etc. So in case of commutation more than 20 per cent is taken as limit for urban fringe and 10.5 per cent for rural fringe & less to it is the rural area.

The Rural-Urban fringe of Lucknow does not form concentric zones around the city but pretends differently in different direction. The maximum extend is towards the east, north-east and south-west, where physiographic attributes are highly favourable. The fringe extends along the lines of transport and axial routes but in inter-sectoral spaces, fringe tends to shrink.

The fringe thus, demarcated may be sub-divided into Rural Fringe and Urban Fringe, according to the intensity of urbanity. The urban fringe adjoins the Municipal limits of the city. Actually this zone is intimately connected with the city and is potentially more important for its future growth (Fig. 16.2).

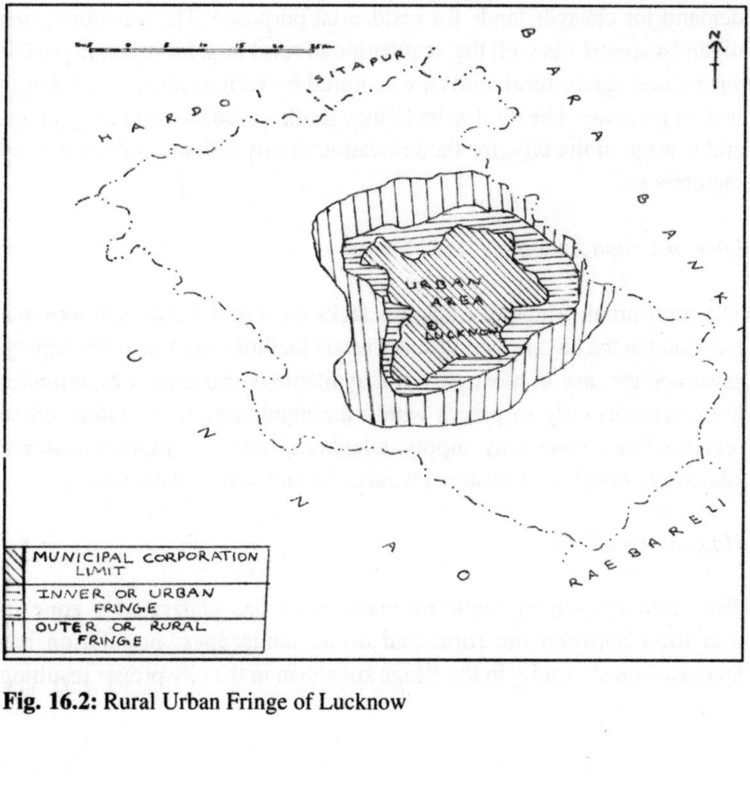

Fig. 16.2: Rural Urban Fringe of Lucknow

Problems of the Fringe

The rural-urban fringe is an area of rapid change in land use and population characteristics. Due to rapid urbanization process, the urban areas are expanding, in order to receive and accommodate urban population. These expansion create host of problems which are increasing daily with the gradual sprawl of the town on such premature lands some of these problems include—land-use problems, lack of urban amenities and services, housing problem, traffic congestion and transportation problem and administrative problems etc.

Most of the problems are related to the weaknesses of our present administrative framework and its inability to cope with the rapidly changing landscapes of the rural-urban fringe of Lucknow.

Land-Use Problems

Due to rapid urbanization process, the population of the Lucknow Metropolis is increasing at a faster rate. This in turn, has increased the demand for cheaper lands for residential purposes. The transformation of landscapes starts with the acquisition of rural land for urban uses. The vacant and agricultural lands are acquired by various agencies and built in their own way. The rural-urban fringe is often used for dumping garbage and sewage of the city, for the relocation of city's slums and location of factories etc.

Lack of Urban Amenities and Services

The rural-urban fringe of Lucknow lacks most of the civic services that are found in the city proper. Primary urban facilities, such as water supply, sewerage etc. are in most part, not available because the city provides these services only to places within the municipal limits. Other urban services like—electricity supply, telephone services, disposal systems, education, health care system etc. are also not very satisfactory.

Housing Problems

The rapid growth of Lucknow metropolis has generated a zone of transition between the rural and urban landscapes; population has increased most rapidly in the fringe zone than in the city proper resulting in an unplanned and haphazard growth of new residential colonies. Though middle class people could afford the housing charges, but it is the poorest people who suffer most, since the land prices are such a high that they cannot afford decent housing.

Transportation Problems

The lack of metalled roads joining fringe areas with the city, pose problems for the commuter. Those fringe dwellers that commute daily create traffic congestion, during the rush hour. To avoid this, number of by - passes are required to be built.

Thus rural -urban fringe of Lucknow faces a lot of problems regarding land use planning, proper residential planning, lack of urban amenities etc. So for the proper planning and development of fringe steps should be taken to provide solution to these problems.

Suggestions for Planning and Fringe Development

The present study makes on attempt to provide detail information about various aspects of the rural-urban fringe of Lucknow. However, the main objective of this study is to provide a detail base for the scientific planning for fringe development.

The problems and prospects of the fringe are ignored by both urban and rural authorities because they fall outside their territory. Thus, an independent separate authority should be developed and established to solve the problem of the fringe. Thus, there is need for efficient planning and control of the rural-urban fringe in full adjustment with the city planning. These include:

Land Use Planning

Land use planning is an important aspect of the fringe development. It involves allocation of land for different purposes, such as—residential colonies, recreational ground, disposal sites, Industrial area, etc. Planning should be such so that agricultural lands remain unaffected. Industries are set on that land inappropriate for the agricultural activities. Low lands have been suggested for building tanks and dumping garbage. Like-wise other public necessities such as—schools, dispensaries, and markets etc. should be constructed.

Residential Planning

The rapid growth of population both in the city and fringe area of Lucknow required a proper planning for residential areas. The residential area should be far away from the C.B.D., and be provided with the adequate public utility services, schools, dispensaries and small recreational centers. The inner fringe belt has been good for the low-income group, multiple family houses, whereas middle income group would prefer outer fringe belt. Besides this provisions should be made to link each house with road.

Medical Planning

Medical facilities are one of the basic amenities required for the fringe people. Each residential sector should have health centre, dispensaries and medical stores, so as to meet the emergent need of the fringe dwellers. There should be a clinic for the general and maternity purpose and should be accomplished with Doctors, Gynaecologist, nurses etc.

Educational Planning

Educational planning should be such as to include schools and colleges for every age group. A nursery school for every hundred families has been suggested at a place away from the busy road. Middle schools have been suggested for the children of age group of 12 to 18 years, for every thousand population and a High School for every three thousand population. Normally a College has been suggested for a radius of not exceeding three to flve kilometer.

Transport Planning

Properly constructed roads are required for joining fringe areas with the city proper. In order to provide better links between the city and the fringe, a number of link roads have been proposed which will almost inter-linked all the important places of the fringe with the city. The existing unmetalled roads of the fringe should be metalled and improved. A number of by-pass required linking important regional roads in the fringe.

Industrial Planning

The industries should be set up at a site, which is not good for agricultural purposes. Industries should be of such kind which raw materials used are easily and conveniently available from the area itself. It is proposed to establish agro based and agro fostering industries in agricultural areas such as rice, flour, & oil mills, fruit canning, dairy etc. There is U.P.State Industrial Development Corporation (UPSIDC) for the development and progress of industries in the area.

Agricultural Planning

Green belts include the parts of the open and cultivated areas of the fringe particularly of the outer part. Here, horticulture, pisiculture and other profitable agricultural pursuits can be carried on keeping in view the investment profit ratio. The existing pattern of agriculture has been transformed by introducing profitable cropping patterns. The plants and trees should be planted so as to cope with the increasing pollution.

References

Prior, R.J., (1968), *Defining The Rural Urban Fringe*, University of North Carolina Press, Vol. 47, No. 2, December.

Ramachandran, R., (1989), *Urbanization and urban systems in India*, Oxford University Press, New Delhi.

Singh, U., (1966), *Urban Fringe in KAVAL Towns* in R.L. Singh (Ed.), Applied Geograpjy, NGSI, Varanasi

17

Changing Pattern of Peri-urban Scenario Surrounding the Varanasi City

Pankaj P. Singh and *Rana P.B. Singh*

Introduction

Study of any society is incomplete and insufficient without a reference to the life in rural communities. According to the statistics by Census of India 2001, of the country's total population 27.8 per cent lives in urban areas, and the rest 72.2 per cent in rural India (cf. Rao, 2006), which comprises of 5,93,731 inhabited villages of different sizes (out of 6,38,596, including uninhabited). Chamaon Gram Sabha belongs to Pindra Tahsil and Lamahi Gram Sabha in Varanasi Tahsil—both in Harahua block of Varanasi district. One of them, viz. Chamaon Gram Sabha, was studied longitudinally and intensively by Singh and Singh since 1977. Harahua Block in Varanasi district lies in eastern Uttar Pradesh. Its major area is stretched towards the north and west direction of the Harahua block headquarters. The block is spread over an area of 142.50 sq km. This block is situated 6 km. away from district headquarters in north-east direction. The State Highway (NH 56) passes through the block, linking the study area with city and district headquarters of Varanasi, and adjoining districts of Azamgarh and Jaunpur (Fig. 17.1). Administratively, the block lies in two different Tahsils, namely Pindra and Varanasi Sadar, which is further divided into 15 Nyay Panchayats, consisting of 84 sub-units of Gram Panchayats that consist of 169 villages.

For the detailed study of changes in urban sprawl, two Gram Sabhas, namely Lamahi and Chamaon Gram Sabha were taken as samples. No claim will be made that these villages are in true sense the representative of the entire, but they represent the transition phase between urban sprawl and rural lifeworld. Chamaon and Lamahi Gram Sabhas are viable units of the "village council" defined under the government programme of village development on the line of the old tradition of co-operative system called panchayat, introduced in 1952 under the first land reformation in the Indian Republic (Gustafsson, Singh and Lejonhud, 2000: 204). Lamahi and Chamaon lie in eastern and western part of the urban sprawl, respectively. This essay is based on fieldwork conducted to ascertain demographic aspects, lifestyle and changing structure of farming. Some emphasis is also laid upon the impact of modernization on the life of people in the village and the price one has to pay for the pace of development.

Methodology and Scenario

It was not possible to restrict to a particular technique for collecting data for the present study and hence various techniques were adopted simultaneously according to the requirement of the local scenario. The behaviour of people is different in varied circumstances and hence it is difficult to follow some exact method. After selecting the Gram Sabha (unit of village council) nearby Varanasi city, impression of the people were collected by interviewing them on the issues of change, likely to experience in near future in lifestyle, land use, social and religious festivals. Proceeding with the field investigation, the information was collected with respect to land use pattern and cropping pattern. Information was also collected from households with respect to demographic and caste structure practices and implements used in agriculture, impact of technology on agricultural practices, folk culture, development and changes occurring in the villages.

A detailed questionnaire was filled up for fifty families in each of the two Gram Sabhas. The families were chosen so as to be satisfactory representation of the villages in question. Thus, in Chamaon Gram Sabha, the fifty families interviewed out of total 445 represent nearly 11.2 per cent of the total households of the Gram Sabha. Of these fifty families, 23 were Kurmi, 12 Rajput, 8 Yadava, 4 Harijan, 2 Musahar and 1 family was from Lohar community. In the context of occupation of the total surveyed households, 35 were farmers, 2 in government services, 8 dealing with business activities and the rest 5 belong to miscellaneous activities. Crops grown in the villages include paddy, wheat, grain, *jwar* (millet), maize and mainly vegetables for cash crop. Not all the families surveyed own their own land.

The fifty families from Lamahi Gram Sabha recorded 15.2 per cent of the total 328 households, of which 28 families were Kurmi, 8 Muslim communities, 4 Rajput, and the rest were mostly the Scheduled Castes. The average annual income per capita ranged from Rs. 1,000 to Rs. 20,000. Kurmi (Patel) families grow mainly vegetables because of their traditional expertise and their productive values as cash crop, which has high demand in nearby population of Varanasi city.

Chamaon Gram Sabha (CGS)

Since 1956 the CGS consists, from east to west, of three village settlements along the Varana river, which demarcates the southern boundary: Chamaon, Pachhimpur, and Shahabuddinpur, lying at 25°21′ north and 82°58′ east, and located at a distance of about seven kilometres from the main city of Varanasi adjacent to the National Highway 56 (Fig. 17.2). Spread over an area of 181.3 hectares, CGS has recorded a population of 2,421 persons (1286 males and 1135 females in 2001 census). It is bounded by Koirajpur Gram Sabha in the west, Koiran Gram Sabha in the east; a State highway passes in north direction.

Lamahi Gram Sabha (LGS)

Lamahi Gram Sabha is located on the busy Varanasi-Azamgarh Road and better known as the birthplace of noted Hindi novelist and story writer, Munshi Premchand (1880-1936), an otherwise non-descript village with its green fields and cluster of houses. It has a prominent place on India's cultural map. Lamahi Gram Sabha consists of two villages Lamahi and Banwaripur. It is located at 82°59′ E longitude and 25°23′ N latitude along State Highway 73 Varanasi to Azamgarh road, at the distance of 5 km. from the district headquarters of Varanasi (Fig. 17.3).

Population

The most important component in village life is the population characteristics. Population size determines the nature and pattern of human settlements. Keeping in view the close interrelationship between the population and the settlement, here discussed the growth, distribution, density, occupational structure and other demographic characteristics of the rural population (Singh, 1975: 14). The main causes of population growth were related to the social and economic development, resulting first from the agricultural revolution and followed up from the industrial revolution and finally from advances in the medical sciences, public health and environmental situations, which may also be attributed to economic development (Bhende and Kanitkar, 2006: 77). In this region urban to rural migration is more pronounced in the work of 'push' as well as 'pull' factors.

After 1971, improvement in educational and medical facilities, irrigation and green revolution had had a powerful impact on agriculture production and quality of life. As a result, decrease in out migration and death rate occurred. After 1991, Chamaon and Lamahi Gram Sabha were included in peri-urban region of Varanasi city due to spatial expansion towards the surrounding areas (Singh, 2009: 291). Consequently, number of commuters increased by the push factors to out migration. This period is also characterized with immigration because people who were in service, returned to their native place after having retirement and some families purchase land for settlement. As a result, a steep growth of population occurred after 1991. The increase in population has resulted into an increase in population density (persons per sq. km.) and today it is approximately doubled of what it was in the decade 1981. A tremendous

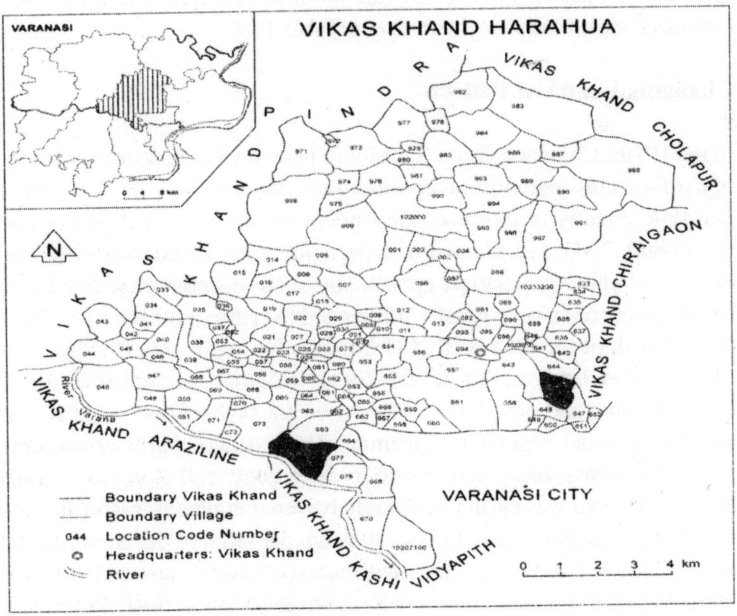

Fig. 17.1: Harahua Block of Varanasi district.

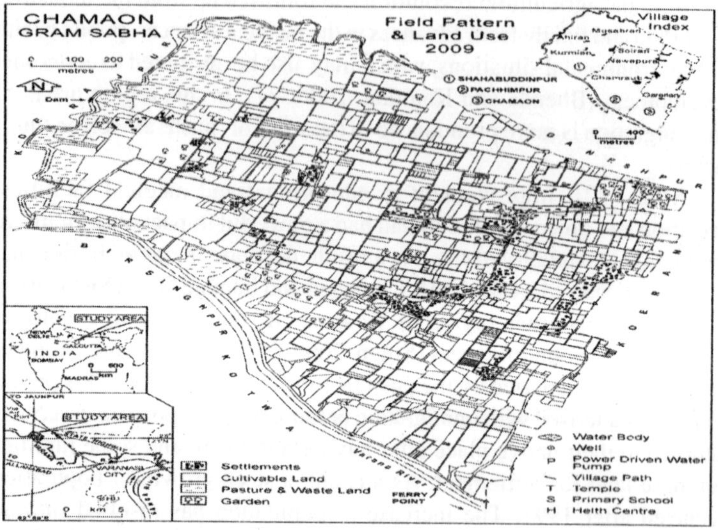

Fig. 17.2: Location of Chamaon Gram Sabha.

growth of 57 per cent in literacy rate has also occurred during the same period. Selected indices are shown in Table 17.1.

Changing Land Use Pattern

In the 1970s, Chamaon Gram Sabha was perceived as peaceful residence of medium class agricultural communities. Most of the villagers were at that time directly or indirectly dependent on farming for their survival (Lejonhud, 2003: 11). Chamaon is predominantly based on agricultural economy, where population growth and socio-economic-technological development have been greatly influenced the pattern of land use. About three-fourth of the total area (181.3 ha.) is net sown area (Table 17.2). Those land earlier were not suitable for agriculture (i.e., cultivable barren, current fallow and other fallow), are used for orchard and gardens, and also for seasonal vegetable gardening. The guava orchards grown only since last twenty years, and are flourishing quite well along the Varana River. This area was earlier cultivable barren, but now transformed into commercial gardening. It appears through the table of different periods that cultivable barren lands are continuously being reclaimed from 13.3 per cent to 6.8 per cent and used for cultivation since 1981. Vegetables are produced round the year because of high demand from nearby Varanasi

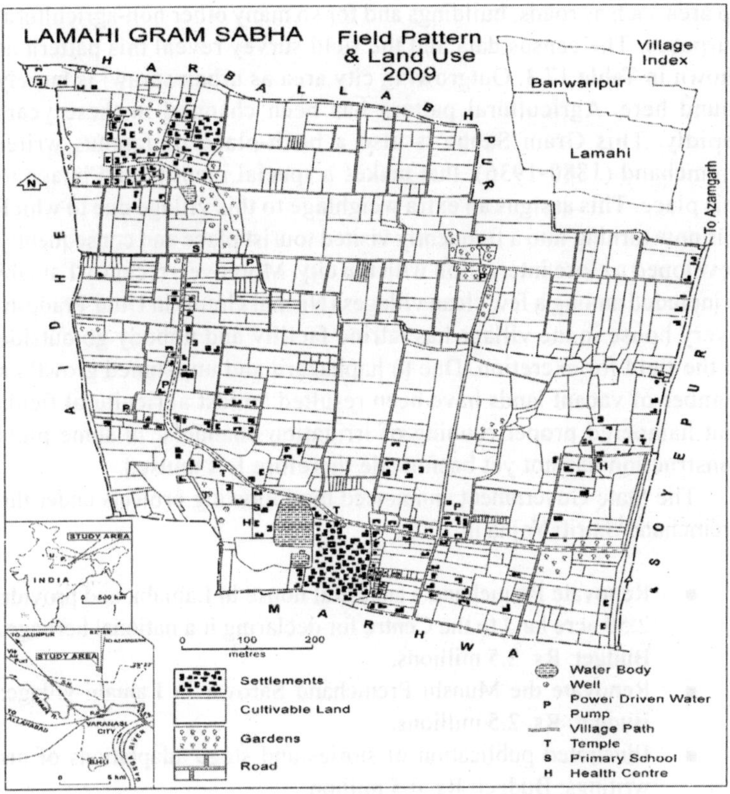

Fig. 17.3: Location of Lamahi Gram Sabha

city. Among vegetables grown brinjal, cauliflower, cucumber, spinach, potato and green been are much sought. The vegetable *Parval* had not ever sown in the village, but in 2007 it was introduced in the village by some farmers which vindicate the impact of market in agriculture. Development of transport and communicational facilities has made the market accessible to farmers. And at the same time increase in literacy rate has made farmers more aware about changes in market prices of produce.

Lamahi Gram Sabha has a total area of 82.97 ha. (Census, 2001). The data reveals that there is tremendous change in the land use pattern of the area (Table 17.3). The net sown area is declined at higher rates because of close proximity of the city Varanasi, resulting into a drastic pressure of population. Major portion of land is largely used for built-up area such as roads, buildings and for so many other non-agricultural purposes. The census data and the field survey reveal this pattern as shown in Table 17.3. Outgrowing city area as urban sprawl is largely found here. Agricultural pattern has been changed in these years rapidly. This Gram Sabha is also a birth-place of famous writer Premchand (1880-1936), that makes a special identity and image to this place. This assigns an extra weightage to this village due to which it is now turning into a frequently visited tourist place and consequently developed a close interaction with the city. Moreover, recently Lamahi is included among a few clean villages (Nirmal Gram) in Uttar Pradesh. Every house in the village has latrine facility and nobody go outside in the field for excretion. Due to haphazard and unplanned growth, a number of vacant lands have been resulted amidst agricultural fields that hampered proper running of irrigation channels. In some plots construction has not yet been made therefore left unused.

The State Government announced the following projects under the Premchand Smriti Yojna in 2005:

- Renovate Premchand's ancestral house in Lamahi, and provide 2.50 acre land to the Centre for declaring it a national heritage: Budget: Rs. 2.5 millions.
- Renovate the Munshi Premchand Sarovar in Lamahi village: Budget: Rs. 2.5 millions.
- Illustrated publication of stories and stage adaptations of his writings: Budget: Rs. 0.5 million.
- Canopy over Premchand's statue at Pandeypur crossing: Budget: Rs. 0.5 million.

Table 17.1: Population Variation

Gram Sabha	*Index*	*1981*	*1991*	*2001*	*2009*
Chamaon	Population	1,521	1,844	2,421	3,011
	Density	839	1,017	1,335	1,664
	Sex Ratio	880	911	883	879
	Literacy	34.65	31.56	52.74	66.3
Lamahi	Population	906	1,190	1,667	2,182
	Density	1,092	1,434	2,009	2,629
	Sex Ratio	697	836	863	869
	Literacy	35.87	44.36	62.09	69.5

Source: Census of India.

Table 17.2: Chamaon Gram Sabha, Varanasi, 1974 to 2009: Land Use Pattern

Category	*1974*		*1994*		*2004*		*2009*	
	Area (h)	% of a	Area (h)	% of a	Area (h)	% of a	Area (h)	% of a
Land Use	*1*	*2*	*3*	*4*	*5*	*6*	*7*	*8*
Total Area	181.3	100.0	181.3	100	181.3	100	181.3	100
Non-agricultural	11.7	6.3	19.2	10.5	26.7	14.6	30.5	16.8
Cultivable waste	35.6	19.6	24.2	13.3	16.8	9.3	12.3	6.8
Fallow Land	29.4	16.2	19.7	10.8	12.1	6.7	7.3	4
Irrigated Land	60.9	48.0	117.9	77.9	155.9	84.7	169.9	86.4
Net sown area	104.6	57.7	118.2	65.2	125.7	69.3	131.2	72.4

Source: Singh, Rana P. B. 2009 and field survey in June 2009.

- A 5 km road connecting Premchand's house in Lamahi, passing through Aidhe Adampur from Varanasi-Sindhaura road: Budget: Rs. 4.5 millions.
- Smriti Dwar and six pillars at the outskirts of Lamahi village on Azamgrah-Lamahi road: Budget: Rs. 1 million.

Of course, works are in progress, no substantial and expected results are sought till date, mainly due to lack of active people participation, misuse of funds and lack of administrative continuity and consistency in interest and implementation.

Changing Lifestyle of the People

Lifestyle is the way a person or a group lives. The people of village lead a simple but hard life. Earlier the costumes and ornaments of people were exotic, colourful and divergent but they have been replaced by modern dresses. There has been change of option of people regarding the dress. The younger generations don't even know about traditional garments like *dhoti-kurta*. Housing pattern in the village has also changed over the last forty to thirty years. Earlier the houses were *kachcha* (mud walled and tile roofed), having an attractive mud plaster and built on a rectangular plan using mud and *khapara* (tile-roofed). Presently, the house scenario is predominated by burnt brick-made walls and flat cemented roofs (*pacca*); and, more than half of the houses are single storied and the rest two storied. There were houses of Scheduled Castes, most of which are built with grass and straw roofs. The houses of the higher castes

Table 17.3: Lamahi Gram Sabha, Varanasi, 1981 to 2009: Land Use Pattern

Category of Land use	*1981*		*1991*		*2001*		*2009*	
	Area, a (h)	*% of a*	*Area, a (h)*	*% of a*	*Area, a (h)*	*% of a*	*Area, a (h)*	*% of a*
	1	*2*	*3*	*4*	*5*	*6*	*7*	*8*
Total Area	82.97	100.00	82.97	100.00	82.97	100.00	82.97	100.00
Non-agricultural	6.88	8.29	7.92	9.55	10.56	12.73	13.78	16.61
Cultivable Waste	4.23	5.10	3.80	4.58	2.56	3.09	2.44	2.94
Fallow Land	11.33	13.66	10.02	12.08	17.00	20.49	24.93	30.05
Net sown area	60.53	72.95	61.23	73.80	52.85	63.70	41.82	50.40
Irrigated Land	43.14	71.27	48.61	79.39	43.65	82.59	23.55	56.31

Source: Census of India, Lucknow and field survey in June 2009.

have roofs of stone slabs, concrete or burnt bricks. The *osara* (porch) of cattle shed have mostly straw roofs. But the scenario has changed in last thirty years. Now the people have constructed new houses but still maintained the old ones too, i.e. half of the house has turned into *pucca* and the rest still *kachcha*. Many people still have only *kuchcha* or semi-*pucca* house. In modern houses the construction pattern is different; here the rooms in ground floor are meant for guest and are used as sitting/drawing rooms. The rooms in upper storey are used as living rooms. But people were interrogated for the advantages and disadvantages of old and newly constructed houses. According to them the old houses were cool in summers and hot in winter and there was no need of using a fan in summers. Since these houses were made of wood and mud, the same provided insulation to the houses. But newly constructed houses are hot in summers and cold in winters. Before construction of new house priest is consulted who decides an auspicious day which is good for initiation rite for the construction of house. *Puja* is performed at the site before starting the construction. After the completion of house, a ceremony commonly known as *griha-pravesh* is performed and feast is given to friends and relatives. The availability of resources, likes and dislikes of people and time constrains are responsible for the change in housing pattern. People are more inclined towards ready to use and easily available material for constructing houses.

Food consumption patterns determine the nutritional status and lifestyle of a community. There has been a change in man's outlook and lifestyle after modernization and urbanization. Villagers choose food keeping in view its nutritive value and medicinal value and hot and cold nature. Some of these are consumed seasonally and some throughout the year for their special taste, medicinal value and for a change in taste. Some of these are different types of *achar* (pickles), *murabba* (jiggery), *ghee* (clarified butter), *gud* (raw sugar), *papad* (dried thin pasty) and potato chips. The methods involved in cooking and serving have evolved over a period of time and form a part of traditional wisdom of people of the village. The general as well as the traditional food items have been included, like *dal, bhat, roti, khichari, puri, sewai, halwa, sag, khir, sattu* and fruit vegetable, etc. The ethnic food is a part of culture and reflects the prosperity and rich cultural heritage of the village. But the food and food habits are changing. Earlier the people used *kodo* and *jwar* (rough small millets) in their staple food but now they are also switching over to other cereals such as wheat and even rice.

Fairs and festivals play a very significant role in the life of people. Not only do they great religious implications but are of economic importance for the people. People in the village actively participate in fairs and festivals and other community based functions. Festivals are linked with the agriculture, folk deities, nature worship and family interactions and these depict their simple lifestyle and proximity to nature. The festivals linked with agriculture and livestock are celebrated at community level. People cook special food on these occasions and make offerings to the folk deities. Some important festivals of the villages include Ramanavami, Nagapanchami, Rakshabandhan, Krishna Janmasthami, Dushahara, Ramalila, Dipavali, Makar Samkranti, Shivaratri and Holi. A number of colourful cultural programmes, including folk music and dance, are also organized on the Ramlila Ground in the village Lamahi, as performance of local artists reminded of the social and cultural transformation that were strongly portrayed in the characters of novelist Prem Chand's writings.

But with the arrival of modern means of entertainment like radios and TVs, all the traditional methods of entertainment and village fair and festivals, religious ceremonies, are becoming things of the past. People are getting more inclined towards the modern means of entertainment; these are consequences of the strong impact of media. People sit at homes and watch TV programme of their choice. New generation girls/women are least interested in learning and singing folk songs. Recreation for village folk is basically a group singing at a community place in homes and dancing together. Such kind of celebration takes place at least on marriage ceremony. But now-a-days these practices are superseded by the modernisation and Bollywood impacts. Not only this, elders also feel that the relationship between generations are getting worsen for which means of modernization and media are more responsible. Traditional values like respect for elders, mutual understanding and other warm feelings are also disappearing.

Changing Land Values

Although accurate information could not be provided on land sales, villagers were able to estimate the broad changes in the land costs. In cases where information was given as a range of values, the average has been calculated. Land near a highway is sold for more money; similarly, good cropped land has been more valuable than less cropped land. The figures for 1981, 1991 and 2009 (cf. Table 17.4), show marked variations among villages, although they do not appear to be closely related to the distance from Varanasi city. There is a general tendency of declining land values as go away from the nearness to the city boundary. Although Lamahi Gram Sabha had the highest averages in these years, there were substantial increases in land values everywhere during the decade.

Socio-economic *scenario*

The occupational structure of the peri-urban villages is similar to that of subsistence economy, has undergone some changes during the last decades. Formerly, most of the villagers worked within the area in accordance with village tradition and their caste affiliation (Lejonhud-2003: 43). Today, the villagers cannot rely only on their traditional occupations but have to find other ways of making living, using various kinds of strategies. There has never been a demand for qualified labourers within the area, so men with higher education have to search outside the area for employments that correspond to their qualifications. In most of the families who own some lands for farming, some of the members also seek work outside the area, and work in nearby industries, as trolley carriers, weavers or shop assistants due to small size of agricultural land. Village women, because of their responsibilities for the households and prevailing prejudices in mobility and education, are reduced to seek employment within the area. The opportunities for wage-earning work for women locally are mainly available in farm labouring. Some women work at home, producing small items for sale such as baskets, leaf-plates and artificial ornaments. If the family is not of high caste, the women in the family take care of animals also. In families that run a household

Table 17.4: Change in Land Values in Rupees per *Biswa**, 1981–2009

Villages	*1981*			*1991*			*2009*		
	Min.	*Aver.*	*Max.*	*Min.*	*Aver.*	*Max.*	*Min.*	*Aver.*	*Max.*
Chamaon	500	3,000	5,000	5,000	25,000	40,000	25,000	75,000	2,00,000
Lamahi	500	2,250	4,000	6,000	28,000	50,000	100,000	200,000	3,00,000
Average	500	2,625	4,500	5,500	26,500	45,000	62,500	137,500	2,50,000

Source: Based on Personal Survey.

*One Biswa equal to 1361.25 sq feet, i.e. 126.46 sq. metre.

industry or small business such as weaving or a shop, the women and their children in the families contribute with their work. A job outside the area is better paid than within the village area. Disparity in wages is such that in city areas it is Rs. 100 per day, while in rural areas, a farm labourer gets around Rs. 70 per day.

Conclusion

The village elders expressed their concerns on the changing scenario of village life. According to them the younger generation is either not aware of the rituals and traditions or they don't want follow them. The changing food habits led to a decline in the nutritional status. The utilization of land depends upon physical factors like topography, soil and climate as well as upon human factor such as density of population, duration of occupation in the area, land tenure and technical level of the people. There are spatial and temporal differences in land utilization due to the continued interplay of physical and human factors. The cultivable waste-land and fallow land experienced a considerable loss of land area over the period 1981-2009, while most other land use categories increased in area. The largest gains in land area are recorded in the categories of net sown area in the Chamaon Gram Sabha whereas a decreasing trend is shown in the Lamahi Gram Sabha. These reflect a competition between the agricultural activity and the growing demand for land for commercial purposes—the main consequential scenario in the peri-urban areas.

References

Bhende, A.A. and Kanitkar, Tara (2006). *Principles of Population Studies.* Himalaya Publishing House, Mumbai.

Census of India (2001). Number of Villages.

Web: http://censusindia.gov.in/Census_Data_2001/Census_data_finder/A_Series/Number_of_Village.htm <accessed: 5 January 2010>

Gustafsson, Gerhard, Singh, Rana P.B., Lejonhud, Kristina & Vålvik, Karl Ivar (2000). Change and continuity in village India: Crisis and Prospects in Chamaon, Varanasi. FENNIA, *International Jaurnal of Geography* (Geogr. Soc. of Finland, Helsinki). Vol. 178 (No. 2): pp. 203-214.

Lejonhud, Kristina (2003). Indian Villages in Transformation: A Longitudinal Study of Three Villages in Uttar Pradesh. *Karlstad University Studies,* 2003: 11. Karlstad University, Karlstad (Sweden).

Rao, S. (2006). *How many people live in villages in India?* Irrinki Roskilde University, Denmark.

Web: http://wiki.answers.com/Q/How_many_people_live_in_villages_in_India <accessed: 5 January 2010>.

Singh, R.L. and Singh, Rana P.B. (1977). Rural Development in Indian Environment: Assessment and Prospect: A Case Study of Chamaon Gram Sabha near Varanasi City, U.P. NGSI Pub. 29, for UNO-CHBP. *National Geographical Society of India, Varanasi.*

Singh, R.B. (1975). Rajput Clan Settlements in Varanasi District. *NGSI Pub. 12*. National Geographical Society of India, Varanasi.

Singh, Rana P.B. (2009). Urban expansion and changing peri-urban and rural landscape: case of Varanasi, India; in, Persi, Peris (ed.) *Contested Territories: Knowledge Fields, Local Identities, Institutions, Planning* (Proceedings of the 4th International Conference on 'Cultural Heritage': Pollenza-Macerata, Italy; 11-13 July 2008). Istituto Interfacoltà di Geografia, Università degli Studi di Urbino "Carlo Bo", Urbino (Italy), pp. 286-294.

18

Dynamics of the City Periphery in Aligarh and its Rural-urban Fringe

Ghazal Salahuddin

Introduction

The present study evaluates the urban problems and the quality of life in the periphery of an industrial city. The major industries of Aligarh city are the famous lock industry and the building-fittings industry.

(i) As these industries are labour-intensive in nature, they induce considerable migration from the neighbouring rural-urban fringe.
(ii) Here, I would like to submit a point to the learned teachers that the cities of labour-intensive industries may also have a relatively higher natural growth of population than the commercial and educational cities.

The city periphery is highly vulnerable to urban sprawl rather than to urban expansion and urban development. The city periphery under enquiry is largely inhabited by the Muslim minority groups. A city periphery is generally neglected in terms of civic and municipal facilities. But, if a periphery is inhabited by a minority group of meagre politico administrative gravity, it is all the more deprived part of the basic and essential necessities. Because of a higher rural-urban migration, as well as inherent poverty, there is a predominance of rural norms of living on the city periphery. There is also a lack of urbanism in their lifestyles which is evident from:

(i) Rural medium of cooking fuel (firewood and dung cakes)

(ii) Keeping of poultry birds and goats to subsist their surviving incomes.

Major Aspects of Enquiry

- Location, Extent and Civic Amenities
- Spatial Variation of Population and Social Structure
- Literacy Rate and Educational Levels
- Employment and Income Levels
- Built-up Environment and the Habitat
- Quality of Life and Social Well-Being

Objectives of the Study

- To assess the socio-economic conditions and poverty levels
- To examine the occupational structure and labour conditions
- To examine the health, longevity and quality of life
- To ascertain the distance-decay characteristics.

Location and Extent

Figure 18.1 shows the location and extent of the three wards on the south-western periphery of the city.

The total geographical area of these wards is 4.2 sq. km. It varies in extent from 2.544 sq. km. for the outer most Slaughter House ward number 21 and 0.893 sq. km. for Bhujpura to 0.763 sq. km. for A.D.A. Colony ward. Figure 18.1 also shows marked intra-city structural variation.

Demography and Social Structure

The total population of the three peripheral wards is 32,195 persons. Slaughter House has 10,472 persons. A.D.A. Colony has 10,845 persons. Bhujpura has 10,878 persons. The average population of these wards is 10,732 persons against an overall city average of only 9,558 persons. These peripheral wards have 13 per cent higher population over the average inner wards. A bigger population size of the peripheral wards is strange and contrary to the spatial law. A comparatively larger population of these peripheral wards can be attributed to excessive in-migration of labour to the industrial city.

The population density in the peripheral wards is generally lower the density of the inner wards. The population density of these wards shows a variation.

The average population density of these wards is 7,665 persons per sq. km. as against the average density of the city of Aligarh with 21,253 persons per sq. km.

Figure 18.3 shows the spatial variation of population density in the peripheral wards. These low population density figures are superficial and misleading because one has to distinguish that even though the population densities are much lower in the peripheral wards, the actual settlement and residential density is much higher due to poverty-stricken crowding.

Literacy Rates and Educational Levels

Literacy is the lesser god of development. Figure 18.4 depicts a comparative literacy at national, regional and local level. The peripheral wards of Aligarh do not have adequate educational infrastructure.

There is a highly gloomy picture of literacy in these wards.

(i) The average literacy in the Slaughter House Ward is 23.25 per cent.

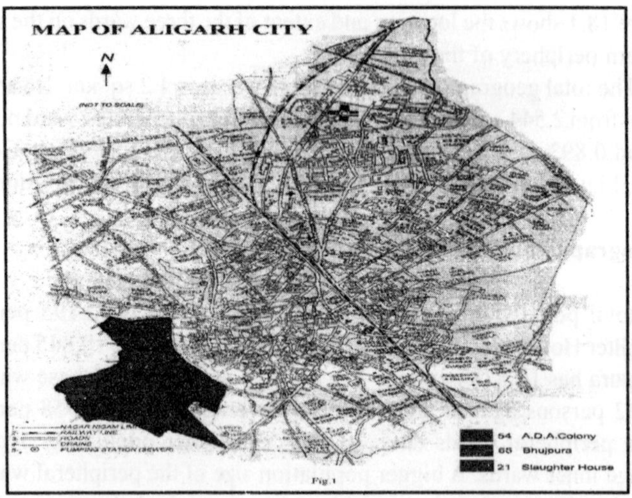

Fig. 18.1: Location and extent of the three wards on the south-western periphery of the city.

Source: Municipal Corporation, Aligarh.

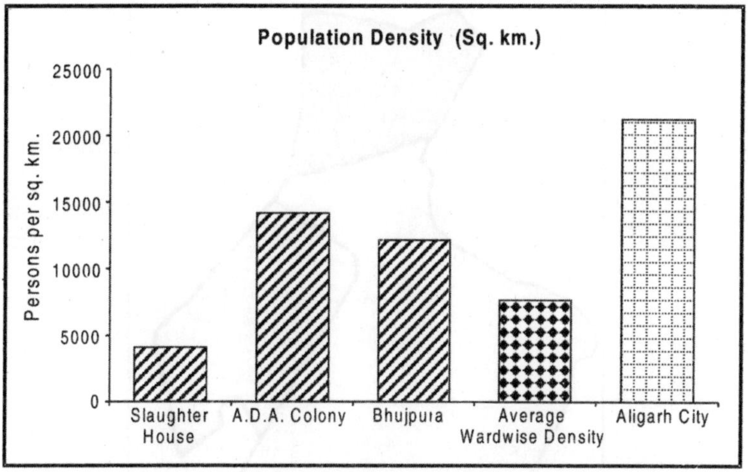

Fig. 18.2: Aligarh City: Peripheral Wards.

Source: Based on Primary and Secondary Data.

(ii) A.D.A. Colony Ward has still lower 19.72 per cent literacy.

(iii) Bhujpura Ward has a dismal 8.19 per cent literacy.

Bhujpura has lowest literacy because of maximum child labour. There is a gloomy scenario of Muslim literacy of 40.37 per cent in Aligarh city as against the average literacy of 53.39 per cent for Aligarh city. This is an alarming indicator of the educational backwardness of Muslims even in the city of Aligarh Muslim University.

There may be *two* major reasons for such a dismal Muslim literacy in Aligarh:

(i) There appears a feeble influence of Aligarh Muslim University in raising the literacy levels in Aligarh city.

(ii) The economic conditions of the wards are very poor which prevent the adoption of literacy. Figure 18.5 demonstrates the secondary, college and technical education levels.

Out of the already low literacy levels, the educational levels are also low. This is due to high drop-outs and educational unsustainability of the first generation learners under competition. The main reason of these dismal educational levels is that almost entire employment in these wards is in the unorganized private sector of daily wagers.

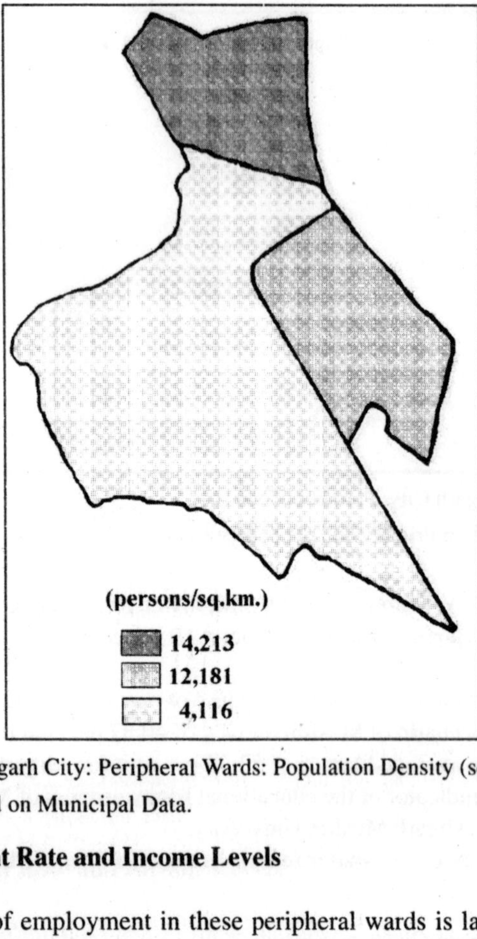

Fig. 18.3: Aligarh City: Peripheral Wards: Population Density (sq. km.).
Source: Based on Municipal Data.

Employment Rate and Income Levels

The nature of employment in these peripheral wards is largely labour oriented. From income perspectives, most of the manual labour is in the unorganized private sector. The entire economy of these wards is based on household industrial and business undertakings. Their economic ventures are small scale. There is a large concentration of marginal workers. There are also large employment uncertainties. Figure 18.6 shows the wage structure in the study area.

Bhujpura is relatively less peripheral ward. Hence, it has relatively earlier habitation as well as industrial units.

Because of this scenario:

(i) The percentage daily-wagers is the lowest 6 per cent.

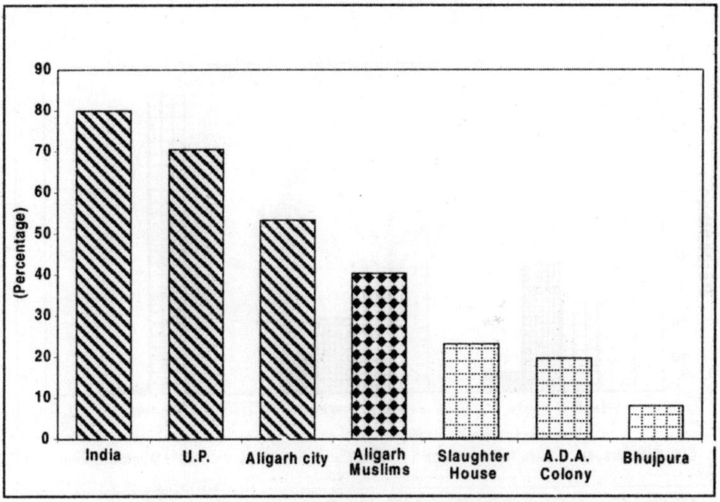

Fig. 18.4: Aligarh City: Peripheral Wards: Percentage Average Literacy.

Source: Based on Primary and Secondary Data.

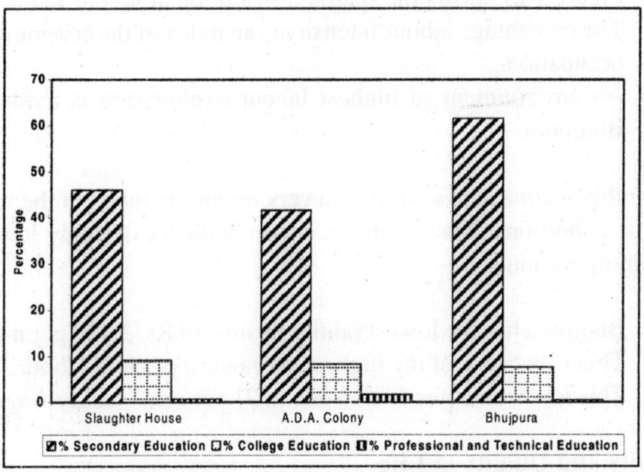

Fig. 18.5: Aligarh City: Peripheral Wards: Percentage Secondary, College and Technical Education.

Source: Based on Primary data.

(ii) The percentage weekly-wagers is the highest 91 per cent.

(iii) The percentage fortnightly-wagers is the lowest 2 per cent.

(iv) The percentage monthly wagers is also the lowest 1 per cent.

(v) This indicates that Bhujpura is the poorest labour ward.

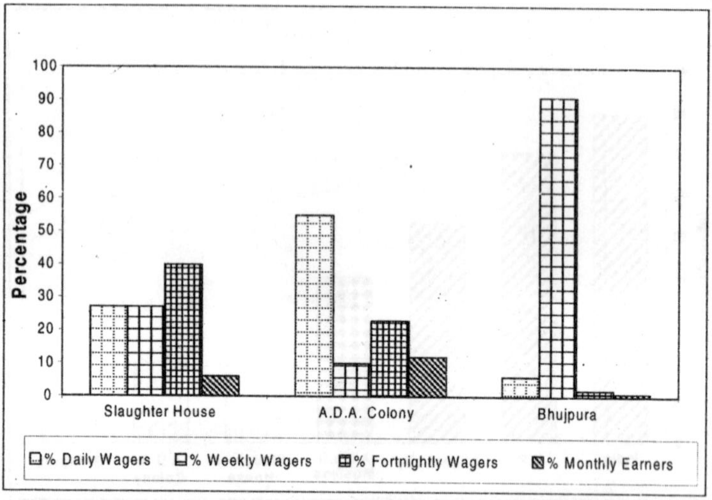

Fig. 18.6: Aligarh City: Peripheral Wards: Percentage Wage Structure.
Source: Based on Primary Data.

(i) Figure 18.7 shows the spatial distribution of labour intensity.
(ii) The percentage labour intensity is an index of the economy and occupation.
(iii) An environment of highest labour exploitation is evident at Bhujpura.

Monthly income and savings is a very important index of the socio-economic conditions. The income scenario depicts extremely low and unsustaining earnings:

(i) Bhujpura has the lowest family income of Rs. 3,430 per month.
(ii) This is because of the highest prevalence of child labour.
(iii) This lowest income is also due to 91 per cent weekly wagers.

Longevity and Quality of Life

Longevity is a composite index of the quality of life and ultimate well-being. There is a general rise of urban longevity in the last twenty-five years:

(i) Figure 18.8 shows the percentage longevity at 60+ and 65+ age group.

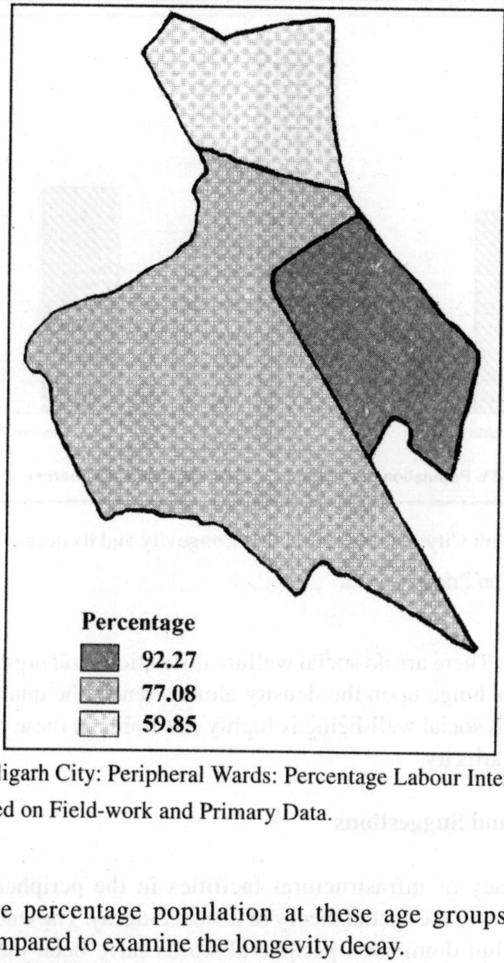

Fig. 18.7: Aligarh City: Peripheral Wards: Percentage Labour Intensity.
Source: Based on Field-work and Primary Data.

(ii) The percentage population at these age groups has been compared to examine the longevity decay.

(iii) It is alarming to note that there is a drastic fall in the percentage population at 65+ age.

In Bhujpura there were only 2.27 per cent people at 60 years +. This dropped to 0.52 per cent at 65 years+. The national longevity or senility is 7.4 per cent. The state longevity is also close to 7 per cent. The longevity gap and decay in these wards is very large in just five years of elderly age. This is evident from the poor nutrition, hygiene and health conditions in these Muslim inhabited wards. There is a high degree of socio-economic marginalization of these people. Social security is meager. Life is *ad hoc*

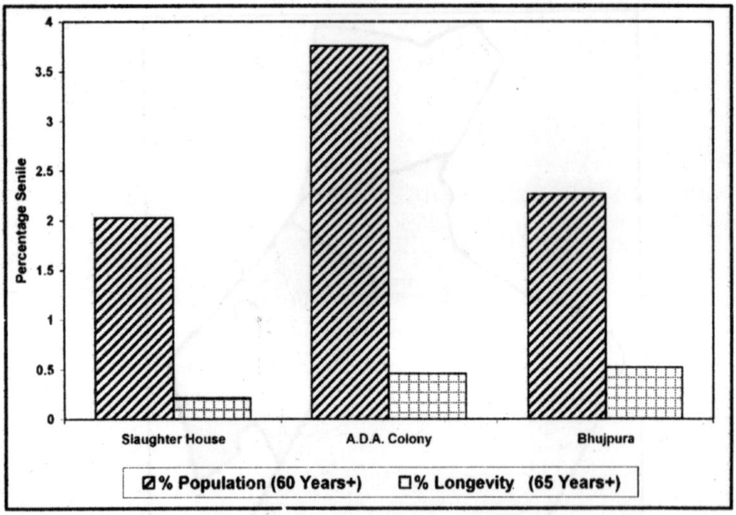

Fig. 18.8: Aligarh City: Peripheral Wards: Longevity and its decay.

Source: Based on Primary Data.

and uncertain. There are no social welfare institutions and organizations. Their fortunes hinge upon the density alone. Hence, the quality of life and the overall social well-being is highly miserable in these peripheral wards of Aligarh city.

Conclusion and Suggestions

The inadequacy of infrastructural facilities in the peripheral wards abundantly proves the spatial theory of distance-decay. The study reveals that the Muslim dominated peripheral wards have been municipally reduced to the Marginal Lands and economically rendered to Marginal Man. The stark poverty in the city periphery also proves that the rich-poor gap in the Indian cities is several times larger than the rich-poor gap in rural areas.

The private sector wage structure should be legally equated with the public sector in the cities. There is a need for the radical changes in the mode of payment. The daily and weekly wages should be abolished. The municipal water supply in the poor, peripheral wards should be twice that of the self-sufficient affluent wards.

References

District Revenue Records, Collectorate Office, Aligarh.

District Statistical Handbook, Uttar Pradesh, Census of India, 2001.

Gautam, Bhan, (2009). The Urban Poor and the Right to the City in Millennial Delhi, Environment and Urbanization, *International Institute for Environment and Development (IIED)* Vol. 21, No. 1, pp. 127-142, London.

Nevill, H.R. (1928). Aligarh: *A Gazetteer,* Vol. VI.

Shabahat, (2008). *Family Structure and Socio-Economic Conditions of Muslims in Aligarh City—A Geographical Analysis,* Unpublished Ph.D. Thesis, Aligarh Muslim University, Aligarh.

Statistical Abstract (2004). Central Statistical Organization, Govt. of India, New Delhi.

Part IV

Dynamics of Land Use in Rural-Urban Fringe

19

Urban Gravity, Rural Settlements and Land use Gradient: A Spatial Analysis

Salahuddin Qureshi

Concept of Rural-Urban Fringe

The term rural-urban fringe was first used by T.L. Smith in 1937 to signify the discontinuous built-up area just outside the corporate limits of Louisiana City. Subsequently, the concept of 'rural-urban fringe' was developed by Robin J. Pryor in 1968. Rural-urban fringe is a complex zone on the periphery of a growing urban area. Rural-urban fringe is a zone rather than a boundary. Hence, the rural-urban fringe cannot be precisely demarcated. In an attempt to understand and demarcate the rural-urban fringe it is imperative to measure the rural and urban interaction. Rural-urban differentiation can be examined in several aspects. For example, occupational differences, environmental differences, difference in the nature of housing and households, difference in the density of population, difference in social mobility and migration and the differences in social interaction and stratification.

Definition of Rural-Urban Fringe

Rural-urban fringe is a universal phenomenon. Hence, we should examine the Western and Indian definitions.

1. George S. Wehrwein was an American Land Economist who first defined the rural-urban fringe in Economic Geography in 1942. According to him, "Rural-urban fringe is a transitional area between the well recognised urban land uses and the area of agricultural land use."

2. Blizzard and Anderson in 1952 defined "the rural-urban fringe as the area of mixed urban and rural land uses where the full city services cease to be available and where the agricultural land uses predominate."
3. R.L. Singh in 1955 defined the rural-urban fringe of Varanasi as 'the area where the urban influences mingle with the rural forces without striking a line of distinction.'

Several definitions have been charted out in order to distinguish the rural-urban divide. Pocock believes that both village and the city are elements of the same civilization. Hence, neither rural-urban dichotomy, nor the rural-urban continuum is meaningful. Rao had projected that although both villages and towns are part of the same civilization, yet there are specific institutional and organizational ways which differentiate the social and cultural life between the village and the town. Thus, according to Rao, the rural-urban continuum makes more sense. Ghurye believes that as urbanization is the result of migration of the people from the villages, the migrants carry and retain their rural consumption patterns, traditions and value systems which tangibly demonstrate the rural-urban continuum, i.e. a lack of urbanism. It means that urbanization is a process much faster than urbanism. Urbanism is a much slower social, cultural and institutional transformation.

Origin of Rural-Urban Fringe in India

The rural-urban fringe did not exist even around the large cities of India, until the 1950. This is because the city growth in India was very slow. The fringe phenomenon in India appeared around the Green Revolution in 1965. The fringe phenomenon appeared with the emergence of rural-urban linkages. Linkage density determines the inner fringe and the outer fringe. In the ancient and medieval walled cities, there was no interface between the city and its surroundings. The physical limits of the city were defined by the walls, moats, gates and other protective structures. The city and the country sides were clearly divided by marked boundary features. Even today the boundary of small towns and 1 lakh cities can be demarcated in India. Hence, rural-urban fringe is a phenomenon around the large and fast growing cities.

It has become difficult to precisely demarcate as to where does the urban end and where does the rural begin. Moreover, the rural-urban fringe is such a dynamic zone of mixed functions that it is always changing.

In a zone of changing functions and land use it may not be necessary to demarcate the rural-urban boundary as well as the land use gradient. In this sense, Maclever points out that although the communities are divided into rural and urban, the line of demarcation in space is not always clear. There is no sharp demarcation line or gradient line to visibly depict as to where does the city end and where does the country begin.

As most of the rural migrants inhabit the city periphery, the older city periphery becomes inner part of the city in due course of time and the newer periphery grows outward. Hence, every city carries some elements and ingredients of the village. However, Sorokin and Zimmermann insist that the rural can be distinguished from the urban in terms of occupation, size, population density, social mobility, social stratification and social walks of life.

Nature of Land use in the Rural-Urban Fringe

The rural-urban fringe is a landscape interface between the city and the countryside. As the fringe is located under the sphere of urban influence, it has a wide variety of land use such as dormitory settlements, houses of middle income commuters, airports, sewerage works, cremation grounds, golf courses and riding clubs etc. The rural-urban fringe along the arterial roads has small residential colonies, partially developed housing plots, vacant lands and few factories along the inner fringe. Further away towards the outer fringe are land uses such as warehouses, cold storage, brick kilns and timber yards. Despite the urban uses, the fringe remains open with the majority of agricultural land, woodland or other rural uses. Rural-urban fringe is a dynamic zone of changing land use characteristics. The width and nature of fringe varies with the size and function of the city.

(i) In Netherlands, the fringe is difficult to recognize and delineate.
(ii) In England, the city fringe is defined by the Green Belt.

Rural-Urban Interaction and Social change

Urban gravity is a rural stimulus. Urban hierarchy and function determine the intensity of rural-urban interaction and social change. Near the larger cities, villages have smaller percentage of current fallow, old fallow and cultural wastes. India is traditionally an agricultural country with 70 per cent rural population. For the agricultural growth and development, priority for urban development is imperative. In India the areas which have relegated to the subsistence agriculture, there is very little urban stimulus. Large areas are agriculturally stagnant. For example, Bihar is the least urbanised state. Therefore, rural-urban interaction is very less. Hence, the agricultural development is lowest. A sustainable rural development planning calls for such programmes which can control and contain the rural-urban migration. There has been a rapid urban growth in the last two decades. Urban growth may have one type of impact on the rural-urban interaction whereas urban development may have another type of impact on rural-urban interaction.

Premises of the Study

The present study is based on the following assumptions:

- That urban gravity is in proportion to urban hierarchy.
- That the rural land use intensity is in proportion to urban gravity.
- The rural land use decreases as the distance from the urban centre increases.

Nature of the Study Area

The above assumptions have been tested in the rural landscape of Aligarh District. Aligarh District in the middle Ganga-Yamuna doab is one of the agriculturally developed districts of Uttar Pradesh. It has 5 tahsils and 12 development blocks.

Table 19.1 depicts the general geographical profile and the urban

Table 19.1: Geographical Profile of Aligarh District (2001)

General Profile	*Figure*	*Urban Profile*	*Population*
Total Area	3,700.4 sq. km.	Aligarh City	6,67,732
Total Population	2,992,286	Atrauli	43,845
Population Density	810	Chharra Rafatpur	40,826
Population Below 6 Years	4,78,766	Khair	27,661
Urban Population	25.7%	Jalali	17,451
Rural Population	74.3%	Jatari	17,038
Sex Ratio	861	Qasimpur	13,754
No. of Tahsils	5	Iglas	11,861
No. of Development Blocks	12	Harduaganj	11,564
No. of Villages	1212	Kauriaganj	10,581
Average Literacy	71%	Pilkhana	9,692
Male Literacy	79%	Vijaigarh	5,921
Female Literacy	61%	Beswan	5,459

Source: District Statistical Hand Book, 2001.

gravity of the study area. The district has a total geographical area of about 3,700 sq. km. with a total population of nearly 3 million rural-urban inhabitants. The population below the 6 years age group has now considerably decreased to a level of 16 per cent. The average population density according to 2001 census is around 810 persons per sq. km. The population density by 2010 is nearly 900 persons per sq. km. Hence, there is a considerable pressure of population on the land. On the other hand, the percentage urban population in the district is low, accounting to only 25.7 per cent. This urban percentage is above the state average of 21 per cent. However, the low urban gravity of Aligarh does not seem to be a good propellant of the agricultural market, infrastructure, land use intensity and land use diversity.

The average literacy of Aligarh district is 71 per cent. This is above **the natural and state** literacy levels. The male literacy of 79 per cent is higher than the female literacy of 61 per cent. The female literacy is not very low as compared to most of the districts of the state. The literacy indicates a growing awareness in the district. The awareness could also be attributed to a fairly good network of linkages and mobility due to nearness of the district and its headquarters to the National Capital. The agricultural fortunes and the progress of the district could have improved, had it been deservingly included in the National Capital Region. Aligarh City is only 132 kms. from Delhi. In Rajasthan, the National Capital Region has encompassed the places even more than 180 kms. away from the National Capital. However, towards Aligarh, the NCR limits its approach to a shortest extent of 80 kms. from Delhi. Hence, there appears a deliberate exclusion of Aligarh from the NCR.

Rural Settlement Hierarchy

Aligarh district has a total rural population of 21,54,001 persons (2001). This comprises 74.3 per cent of the total population of the district. There are a total number of 1,212 villages in Aligarh. A theoretical average size of the village is 1,777 persons. Fig. 19.1 shows the size hierarchy of rural settlements in the district. According to population size, there are six categories of villages in their rural hierarchy. The largest villages have over 5,000 persons. The large size villages have a population size of 1000-4999 persons. The medium size villages have 500-999 persons. The small size villages have 200-499 people. The smallest villages have

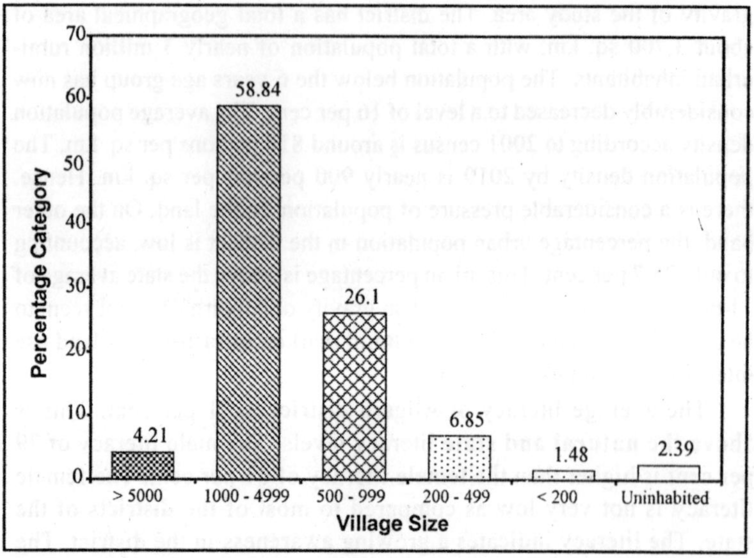

Fig. 19.1: Hierarchy of Rural Settlement in Aligarh District

a population size below 200 persons. The sixth category belongs to the uninhabited villages.

Out of 1,212 villages in the district, 51 villages belong to more than 5000 population size. They comprise 4.21 per cent of the total population. The villages of 1000-4999 persons had a largest number of 712 villages. These comprise 58.84 per cent of the total population. There are 316 villages of 500-999 persons. These represent 26.1 per cent of the total population. There are 83 small size villages of 200-499 persons. They constitute 6.85 per cent population. The smallest villages had less than 200 persons. There are 18 such villages, representing 1.48 per cent population. The uninhabited villages were as many as 29 in number.

The most characteristic size of rural settlements in the district is the large size villages of 1000-4999 persons. As far as the geographical distribution of the largest size of villages in more than 5000 category is concerned, there is a clear evidence of the impact of urban gravity on the very large size of villages. The development blocks namely, Jawan Sikanderpur, Gabhana and Koil have the highest proportionate concentration of the over 5000 population villages in relation to the centrality of their location. On the other hand, the development blocks of Atrauli, Bijauli and Gangiri are located on the periphery of the district.

These blocks are at a distance-decay location from the commanding district headquarters of Aligarh city. As a result of peripherality, these wards have the lowest proportionate concentration of more than 5000 size villages.

Conclusion

The present study of urban gravity and the rural settlement pattern has revealed the following characteristic features of the distribution of rural settlements. Most of the 51 villages with >5000 population were located along the accessibility corridors. Many of them were located near Aligarh city. Most of the 29 uninhabited villages were located along the Yamuna and Ganga flood plains in the Khadar belt. They were farthest from the city gravity. In the origin and evolution of rural settlements the nearness to the water body is generally considered an important determinant. The present study, however, reveals that along the river there are many uninhabited and very small population villages. On the other hand, the very large and large size villages are located along the canals. Thus, canals have a formidable influence in the growth of agricultural economy and the rural settlements than the rivers. This is because, rivers are seldom a direct source of irrigation and the sustainability of rural settlements.

References

District Revenue Records, Collectorate Office, Aligarh.

District Statistical Handbook, Uttar Pradesh, Census of India, 2001.

Gautam, Bhan, (2009). The Urban Poor and the Right to the City in Millennial Delhi, *Environment and Urbanization,* International Institute for Environment and Development (IIED) Vol. 21, No. 1. pp. 127-142, London.

Nevill, H.R. (1928). Aligarh: *A Gazetteer,* Vol. VI.

Provisional Population Totals, Uttar Pradesh, *Census of India, 2001,* Lucknow.

Shabahat, (2008). Family structure and Socio-Economic Conditions of Muslims in Aligarh City—A Geographical Analysis, *Unpublished Ph.D. Thesis, Aligarh Muslim University,* Aligarh.

Statistical Abstract, 2004. Central Statistical Organization, Government of India, New Delhi.

20

A Quest for Developing Agro-Processing Centres in Rural-Urban Fringe Areas: A Key for Sustainable Development and Propelling Rural Prosperity

Kamal Asif and *S. Hifzur Rahman*

Introduction

In the present state of affairs agro-processing enterprises constitute a pivotal position in the economy of India because it incorporate diverse commercial activities by using better unification of labour, materials, capital and technologies. But, this sector is still in infancy. Agricultural development is crucial to India's overall progress and this can be achieved by intensifying agricultural and allied activities through diversification and commercialization of agriculture. A strong and effective agro-processing sector plays a significant role in diversification of agricultural activity, improving value addition of the produce, ensuring employment generation and creates surplus for export. India ranks first in the production of milk, second in fruits and vegetables, third in fisheries, fourth in poultry and fifth in meat production. Besides it is also the world's largest producer of spices, dry fruits, tea, rubber and honey. But, the constriction is that only 2 per cent of the farm produce goes to processing sector and 30 to 40 per cent is recorded as post-harvest losses every year. Beyond this, there is a little share in world trade (less than 1%), low capacity utilization (less than 50%), low value addition (about 7%), high cost of production, inadequate infrastructure and poor quality are weaknesses of India's agro-processing sector (Ministry of Food Processing Industries, Annual Report, 2008, Government of India).

In this regard the government urges to develop the food processing sector in a comprehensive manner to provide self-employment opportunities and livelihood security to women, unemployed youths and under-employed farmers. Such ventures are planned to ensure livelihood security and rural prosperity through sustainable habitat utilization.

Thus, agro-enterprises have become valuable in bringing out harmoniously balanced and integrated socio-economic order between rural and urban economies. The economic development on sustainable basis that takes into account natural resources, environment and human health as the priority areas are the driving forces for establishing the agro-enterprises in the rural-urban fringe areas. Such ventures are planned to ensure the availability of raw material and labour. While, the nearby urban centre helps in providing new innovative technologies, skills and market exposure.

Rural-Urban Fringe Areas

The rural-urban fringe areas can be described as the 'hinterland between town and country' or alternatively, as the transition zone where urban and rural uses mix and often clash. Its definition shifts depending on the global location, but typically are intensively managed to prevent urban sprawl and protect rural areas. Therefore, rural-urban fringe is a continuous area that starts beyond the urban limits of cities. According to Herington (1984), "rural-urban fringe is an area with distinctive characteristics, which is only partly assimilated into the growing urban complex, which is still partly rural and where many of the residents live in the countryside but, are not socially and economically of it".

Agro-Processing Centres

Agro-Processing Centre is an establishment, where required facilities for processing, storage, drying of cereals, pulses, oilseeds, spices, fruits and vegetables are available. Processed and packaged food products are prepared and marketed with specific brand name (Kumar and Ilyas, 2003). The entrepreneurship of Agro-Processing Centre may be of an individual, community, cooperative or voluntary organization. The Agro-Processing Centre creates additional value to a product so as to increase marketability of surplus produce available in the village, cluster of villages or surrounding area (Singh, *et al.*, 2007).

Agro-Processing Activities

The foremost principle of Agro-Processing is 'the transformation of raw agricultural stuffs (i.e. plant's and animal's produce) into tastier, nutritious, safe, and value added products'. Agro-processing implies all the steps taken for the preparation of harvested agriculture produce for marketing, such as, handling, drying, shelling, cleaning, polishing, grading, treating and packaging. The processing activities encompass the methods of curing, grinding, pasteurization, preservation (sugar, salt, oil and spices, acids and chemicals), fermentation, aseptic packaging, irradiation and freezing. Today a wide variety of processing methods and combination of modern technologies of distribution, and marketing networks have made seasonal crops possible to be available round the year and all-over the world.

Government Emphasis for Second Green Revolution through Agro-Processing

The Prime Minister of India, Dr. Manmohan Singh during his address at Global Agro-Industries Forum (8-11th April, 2008, New Delhi) has

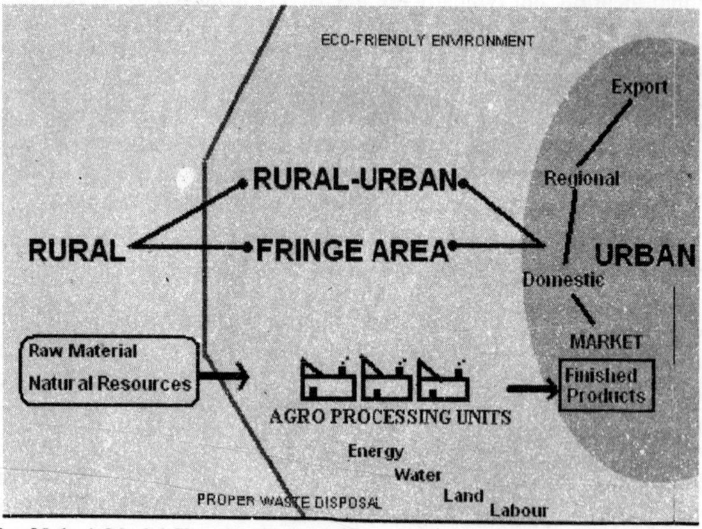

Fig. 20.1: A Model Showing Synergy between Urban and Rural through Agro-Processing Activities in the Rural-urban Fringe.

charged and rejoice the agro-processing sector with the intentions that, "It is our sincere desire and effort to take Indian agriculture to a new level of knowledge-based development; a development that is inclusive, a development that is equitable, a development that is environmentally sustainable and a development that is regionally balanced. It is our goal to ensure both livelihood security and food security for all our people, paying particular attention to the needs of small and marginal farmers. We need a Second Green Revolution. We need new technologies, new organizational structures, new institutional responses and, above all, a new compact between farmers, technologists, scientists, administrators, businessmen, bankers and consumers. I would like to see greater and wider engagement, especially in providing long-term solutions to the problems faced by small and marginal farmers, particularly for poverty alleviation, for risk mitigation and access to finance. For promoting agri-business and agro-industries, we need a model that can combine the economics of small farms with the economics of mass production and modern marketing. We in India, wish to promote agro-industries and offer people living in rural areas new avenues of employment close to the place they work and live. We need much greater global and national effort to increase investment in rural areas in agriculture and agricultural technologies, in-farm and off-farm economic activities. I hope we can all work together to make this possible."

Research Needed and Importance of Agro-Processing in Fringe Area

The study argues to establish agro-processing centres in the rural-urban fringe areas for economic integration of the rural and urban economies, and to open new avenues of employment for the fringe dwellers close to the place where they live, this will help to minimize the pressure on urban centres. The functions of cities also incorporate in shaping the agricultural and food policies related with production and marketing. In India, there has been a trend towards the formation of large metropolis or urban agglomerations. The development of such cities has accompanied the consolidation and concentration of agro-processing industries in rural-urban fringe areas rather than the far away remotely located rural ones. The post-harvest and agro-industrial developments in general are always favoured by urbanization.

Agricultural products like fruits, vegetables, cash crops, dairy and poultry products etc. are most profitably produced in the fringe areas of the urban centres. Processing of farm produce can also play an important role in the conservation of farming systems and effective utilization of the produce. This adjustment may enhance the growth of agro-processing centres in the nearby fringe areas (Fig. 20.1), based on the available resources and agricultural situation of the fringes. Such clustering of agro-processing centres can provide research applications required for sustainable planning and development.

Implications of the Study

The Rural-urban fringe area plays a key role in feeding the people residing in urban areas while acting as a playground for the rural areas. In almost all the developing nations including India, rural areas are the centres of cultivation and agricultural production, while the urban as consumers. The conversion of raw agricultural produce into edible and or marketable products takes place often in the rural-urban fringe areas which has equal access to the raw material and the urban markets. In this process of adding

Fig. 20.2: Major Agro-Processing activities for Rural-urban Fringe areas of India.

the value to raw agricultural produce, the rural-urban fringe areas play a prime role. The growing demand for processed and semi-processed agricultural products accompanied by a rapid transformation of the traditional marketing system into more diversified system of retailing through supermarkets have created the urges of concentrating food industries in the nearest possible locations.

Urbanization affects all sectors of the food system. As the urban population increases more and more food is needed and that has to be transported and distributed. Therefore, an easy accessibility to the fringe areas is also another advantage for developing agro-industries. The developments in the post-harvest sector over the past decade and modifications attempted in marketing, processing and distribution systems ensure the availability of food in urban areas. Thus, the agriculture of urban fringe areas become more market oriented, that fills the food diversity gap and generating employment opportunities for the fringe dwellers.

Today more and more people live in and around cities than in rural areas. Educated youth are migrating from rural areas to the urban centres, especially in the fringe areas, in search of employment. This has resulted in urban sprawl, i.e. the emergence of rural-urban fringes. Introducing agro-processing ventures (Table 20.1), in rural urban-fringes, resulted in value addition and processing, that provide regular source of income directly and indirectly at the place of living. People, who are engaged in procurement, processing and marketing of the agriculture produce, will directly benefited by this sector. Farmers and the weaker section of the society, especially women who are underemployed or unemployed, will try to increase their income and farm productivity. This adjustment may stimulate the growth of agro-processing sector according to the availability of resources and agricultural situation of a region/area (Fig. 20.2).

Recommendations

- The foremost upshot is to establish 'Fringe Area Development Authorities (FADA)' for each rural-urban fringe.
- Micro level planning for effective development of rural-urban fringes through agro-processing sectors.
- Location: Land and land development, financial credits, infrastructure, market (domestic and export), and increasing awareness.

Table 20.1: Sustainable Agro-Processing Activity in Rural-Urban Fringe of Major Cities in Different Agro-Climatic Regions of India

Urban Fringe City/UT	*Cereal*	*Pulses*	*Fruit & Veg.*	*Dairy*	*Meat*	*Sugar*	*Veg. Oil*	*Fishery*	*Tea*	*Spice*	*Honey*	*Herbs*	*Coir/Coconut*	*Sericulture*	*Floriculture*
Jammu	–	–	–	–						–	–	–			–
Srinagar			–	–								–			–
Chandigarh	–	–	–	–	–		–				–				
Ambala	–	–	–	–	–		–								
Kullu			–						–	–		–			–
Shimla			–									–			–
Bilaspur	–		–	–		–	–				–				–
Delhi	–	–		–	–		–								
Panipat	–	–	–	–	–										
Faridabad	–	–		–			–								
Hissar	–	–	–	–			–				–				
Dehradun			–							–	–	–			–
Pantnagar	–	–	–	–	–	–	–				–	–			
Saharanpur			–		–	–					–				
Ghaziabad	–	–	–		–	–	–								
Kanpur	–	–	–	–	–		–								
Pratapgarh		–	–			–					–	–			
Muzaffarpur		–	–								–				–
Siliguri			–				–		–	–	–	–		–	–
Darjeeling			–						–	–	–	–			–
Kolkata	–	–	–	–	–		–	–					–	–	–
Gangtok			–							–		–			–
Guwahati	–	–	–	–				–	–	–	–	–		–	
Shilong			–								–		–		–
Itanagar			–						–	–		–			–
Kohima			–									–			–
Imphal			–							–	–				–
Aizawal			–							–					–
Agartala			–									–	–		–
Ranchi	–											–		–	
Cuttack								–					–	–	
Raipur	–									–	–	–			
Bikaner		–								–					
Jodhpur		–								–					
Udaipur		–	–				–			–	–				
Indore		–	–												
Khandwa		–	–			–									
Ahmedabad	–	–	–	–	–		–			–					
Surat	–	–	–	–	–		–	–		–		–			
Vadodra	–	–	–	–	–		–								
Daman & Diu							–	–							
Mumbai	–		–	–	–		–	–					–		–

(*Contd.*)

Urban Fringe City/UT	*Cereal*	*Pulses*	*Fruit & Veg.*	*Dairy*	*Meat*	*Sugar*	*Veg. Oil*	*Fishery*	*Tea*	*Spice*	*Honey*	*Herbs*	*Coir/Coconut*	*Sericulture*	*Floriculture*
Pune			–	–			–				–				–
Nagpur	–	–	–		–	–	–				–				
Ratnagiri			–					–		–	–				–
Vishakha-patnam							–	–					–	–	
Hyderabad	–	–	–	–	–		–					–			
Panaji			–					–					–		–
Bangalore	–	–	–		–					–	–	–		–	–
Mysore			–						–	–	–	–			–
Mangalore					–			–		–		–	–		
Pondicherry								–					–		–
Salem	–	–	–	–	–	–	–			–	–	–	–		–
Coimbatore	–	–	–	–					–	–	–	–		–	–
Madurai			–			–	–		–	–	–	–		–	–
Calicut			–		–			–		–		–	–		–
Idduki			–						–	–		–			–
Ernakulam	–	–	–	–	–	–	–	–	–	–		–	–		–
Trivandrum	–		–					–		–		–			–
Andman & Nicobar								–		–		–	–		–

Source: Based on the information from Statistical Data Book for Agricultural Research and Development in SAARC Countries, and Ministry of Food Processing, Government of India.

- Empowerment of rural masses through promotion of agro-processing activities.
- Encouraging group entrepreneurs for small Agro-Processing Centres at village level.
- Establishing the facilitation centres at least one in each urban fringe area for helping farmers and processors in all sorts of knowledge.
- Farming systems that are ecologically and economically sustainable for a particular fringe (as shown in Table 20.1).
- Application of the proposed 'Multi-spectral Model for developing sustainable Agro-Processing Enterprise' (as shown in Fig. 20.3).
- Easy and quick transportation and storage facilities in the fringe areas.

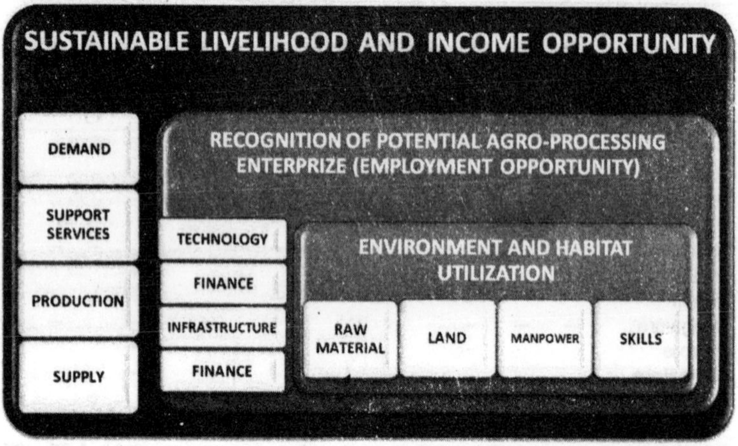

Fig. 20.3: Multi-spectral Model for Potential Agro-Processing Centre.

Conclusion

The present study begins with the question: Can Agro-Processing centres be located in the rural-urban fringe areas?, unleash the synergy between the environmental, agricultural and economic development. The analysis of internal working and external environment of the centres affirms the answer in positive. However, these centres are at different levels of development and have assorted ability of contribution to sustainable development. The agro-processing centres can and do contribute for preserving the local agricultural systems and economic development, and also the sustainable environment in the rural-urban fringe areas.

Bibliography

Anbumozhi, V. (2007). Eco-Industrial Clusters in Urban-Rural Fringe Areas—A Strategic Approach for Integrated Environmental and Economic Planning, *Business and the Environment Research Project, Kansai Research Centre,* Hyogo, Japan.

Asif, K. (2009). Place Perception on an Exurban Agricultural Landscape of Aligarh City, paper presented at *National Conference on Land Degradation, Soil Quality and Land Productivity,* University of Meerut.

Asif, K. (2009). Enterprising Agro-Processing Activities in Rural-Urban Fringe Areas—A Key for Sustainable Development and Propelling Rural

Prosperity, paper presented at the *9th Agricultural Science Congress,* SKUAST, Srinagar, 22-24 June.

Borbora, Saundarjya and R. Mahanta (2003). Food Processing Industries in the North-East India: Status and Prospects, *Indian Journal of Agricultural Economics,* July 2003.

Chengappa, P.G. (2004). Emerging Trends in Agro-Processing in India, *Indian Journal of Agricultural Economics*, Vol. 59, No., 1 pp. 58-74.

Government of India. *Economic Census 2005, All India Report, Ministry of Statistics and Programme Implementation,* New Delhi.

Hanif, M.Z. and M. Agarwal (2005). Agriculture Produce and its Processing, In: *Sustainable Development: Opportunities and Challenges, (ed. R. Dayanand),* Serials Publication, New Delhi, pp. 244-250.

Hite, J. (1998). Land Use Conflicts on the Urban Fringe: Causes and Potential Resolution, Strom Thurmond Institute, www.strom.clemson.edu/publications

Hoffman, N., (2001). Urban Consumption of Agricultural Land, Rural and Small Town, *Canada Analysis Bulletin.* Vol. 3, No. 2. www.statcan.ca

Iqbal, B.A. (2006). Agro Industries: Key to Economic Progress, *Kurukshetra,* Vol. 54, No. 4, pp. 4-7.

Kabir, W. and Akter, N. (2007). *Statistical Data Book for Agricultural Research and Development in SAARC Countries,* Vol. 5, 2006/2007.

Khan, B.A. and Basharat, S.P. (2006). Economic Variability of Vegetable Production in Kashmir, *Agricultural Situation in India*, Vol. 62, No. 10 pp. 677-684.

Mathi, K.M. and Jino Chacko (2005). Food Processing in India—The New Dawn, In: *Sustainable Development: Opportunities and Challenges,* (ed. R. Dayanand), Serials Publication, New Delhi, pp. 215-221.

Nelasco, Shobana (2005). Entrepreneur: The Key for Sustainable Development, In: *Sustainable Development: Opportunities and Challenges, ibid.*, pp. 369-376.

Singh, Akath, K.D. Babu, R.K. Patel and Utpal Barua. Temperate Fruit Plants Gaining Momentum in the Subtropical Areas of the North-East, Division of Horticulture, *ICAR Research Complex for NEH Region,* Umiam-793103, Meghalaya.

Singh, Manmohan (2008). India Needs a Second Green Revolution, *Prime Minister of India Address to Global Agro-Industries Forum (Highlights),* April 10, 2008, New Delhi.

Swaminathan, M.S. (2009). *Report of a Round Table on Global Economic Slowdown and Indian Agriculture,* IARI, New Delhi, 24th April.

Thorat, Y.S.P. (2006). *Annual Report 2006, National Bank for Agriculture and Rural Development* (NABARD), Mumbai.

Tripathy, K.K. (2006). Processed Food Industry in India: Potentials and Constraints, *Kurukshetra,* Vol. 54, No. 6, pp. 12-16.

UNCHS. (2001). The State of the World's Cities Report 2001, www.unchs.org

Vishwanathan, P.K. and G. Shivakoti (2008). Integration of Tribal Economies in the Era of Globalization: Perspectives of Rubber Based Farming Systems in North-East India, *Asian Profile*, Vol. 36, No. 3, pp. 281-298.

Waibel, H. and Schmidt, E. (2000). Feeding Asian cities: Food Production and Processing Issues", *Regional Seminar organized by F.A.O. on Feeding Asian Cities, Bangkok*, 27-30th November.

Webliography

Microsoft Encarta: *Reference Library 2005.*

Wikipedia: The Free Encyclopedia—*www. wikipedia.org*

Google Image: Maps and Images—*www.google.co.in/images*

National Horticulture Board: Ministry of Agriculture, Govt. of India—www.hortibizindia.org

Ministry of Food Processing Industries: Govt. of India—*www.mofpi.in*

Agricultural and Processed Food Product Export Development Authority: *www.apeda.com*

National Bank for Agriculture and Rural Development: *www.nabard.com*

21
Trend and Pattern of Vegetable Cultivation in Rural-Urban Fringe of Aligarh City

Nizamuddin Khan, Mohammad Sadiq Salman and *Anisur Rehman*

Introduction

Vegetable cultivation is one of the important value added crops which have been cultivated since long period. Earlier, it was cultivated as subsistence crops along with cereals, pulses and oilseeds and occupied a meagre share of total cropped area especially in developing countries like India. The cultivation of vegetables was traditionally confined to certain castes and still persists in larger parts of the country. This kind of cropping system could not get proper attention by policy-makers as well as by Indian farmers to exploit the national and international economy in the form of agri-business of vegetables, despite wide range of agro-climatic conditions favourable for production of different varieties of vegetables of the world.

After independence, the planners emphasized and stressed for improvement in agricultural economy through technological change. Green revolution was introduced during 1968s in order to overcome the problems of food starvation in the country and attain self-sufficiency. Foodgrains especially wheat and rice grew up both horizontally and vertically in area expansion, cropping intensity as well as yield per hectare of land after adopting capital intensive technocratic equipped with HYV and irrigation facilities. Many policies were formulated for agricultural developments but not for the farmers which resulted in very pity condition of farmers. More than 40 per cent of the farmers as evident from sample survey 2009, are willing ready to leave their land and farming if provided with alternative employment for their survival. The implementation of

WTO and liberalization of agriculture and agri-business also aggravated the plight of Indian farmers. Cereal based traditional farming system became uneconomical for marginal and small farmers, which constitute about 80 per cent of farming community. Under this stress, the agricultural planners and the government urged the farmers to diversify the agriculture system with value added crops like vegetables to increase their income, employment and consequently their socio-economic transformation in recent decades.

The vegetables cultivation has been emerging as very promising poverty alleviation option among the poor farmers. It can be grown in almost all agro-climatic regions, i.e. tropical, temperate, wet, dry, semi-arid, hilly and plain tracts. But they are practically often growing in niches, places more related to market and population centres than to suitable agro-climatic conditions. The vegetable cultivation, in larger proportion, earlier and still, has been developed in peri-urban areas of the world and with special reference to developing countries. The urban population has rather high daily demand for fresh vegetables. Being a perishable commodity, it is not ideal to grow vegetables far away from market centres unless an efficient refrigerated transport network is developed. Von Thunen Agricultural Land-use Model recognized the concentric rings or zone around the urban centre taking into account the economic rent or return per unit volume of production. Thus, peri-urban areas around all towns/cities have a good potential for development of vegetable cultivation and feed the burgeoning urban population with micro-nutrients of food.

Peri-urban agriculture is recognized for potential role in increasing food security, employment, income generation, poverty alleviation, community resource development, waste development and environment sustainability. Urban agriculture is becoming a growing global phenomena practiced by an estimate of 800 million people which produce 10 per cent of world food supply (UNDP). About two billion people especially women and children are affected by micro nutrient deficiencies. A minimum level of daily intake of vegetable (200 g/day) is required to meet the micro nutrient deficiencies of the body but the vegetable intake in most of the developing countries is far below this level.

However, the urban population is expanding at a faster rate which encroached much cultivable fertile land in their fringe area. The establishment of new pattern of vegetable shopping centres, especially retailing, regulated markets, co-operative institution, agri-business export centres and internal consumer's demands which has been continuously expanding due to increasing disposable income, health consciousness and vegetarian food habits, have put greater pressure on limited small vegetable farms mainly controlled by marginal and small farmers, in urban-rural interface or fringe area. The rich social and economic variability and dynamics offers opportunities to researcher to make an analysis of existing socio-economic behaviour of vegetable cultivation and their effect on socio-economic transformation of vegetable growers in peri-urban area as well as the food security level improvement in urban area and sustainability of the environment.

Objectives of the Study

The above-mentioned conditions and significance of vegetable cultivation in peri-urban areas, urged the researcher to understand the following objectives—

1. Spatio-temporal pattern of vegetable cultivation in peri-urban area.
2. Socio-economic profile of vegetable growers/workers.
3. Marketing pattern of vegetable supply from production point to urban centres.
4. Level of employment generation and their effect on socio-economic development.
5. Existing constraints and remedial suggestions.

Study Area Profile

Aligarh city and the villages around it are selected as study area. Aligarh is one of the historical city and known for Aligarh Muslim University and lock industries. It is located in upper Ganga plain of western Uttar Pradesh near Agra and Delhi. Aligarh expanded at very fast rate, both horizontally and vertically during last two decades. Residential as well as industrial areas are well expanded. At present, the city covers an area of 54 sq. km. inhabiting around 8 million persons. There are one regulated market, one periodic market and six retail markets where vegetable transactions are mainly taking place everyday. There are approximately 500 villages in the fringe area of 20 km. distance from the centre of the town, from where vegetables are supplied to vegetable markets of Aligarh city.

Research Methodology and Database

In the present study, the demarcation of fringe area for vegetables is made on the basis of preliminary survey of vegetable suppliers from surrounding areas. 20 kms. redial distance from the centre of the city is taken, which covers approximately five blocks with 500 villages. Five villages from different directions at different distances have been selected for detailed study for understanding the aforesaid objectives. Research work is based both on primary and secondary data. Primary data were collected through field survey of 50 per cent households of vegetable cultivators from selected villages from peri-urban area. Secondary data were collected from District Statistical Bulletin, Aligarh. The collected data were processed and interpreted for required result.

Interpretation of Results

The peri-urban area of Aligarh city is found to be very important region for vegetable cultivation. All the five blocks cultivated about 12,304 hectares of land contributing 7.05 per cent of the total gross cropped area. The percentage of vegetable area is not uniform but varying from

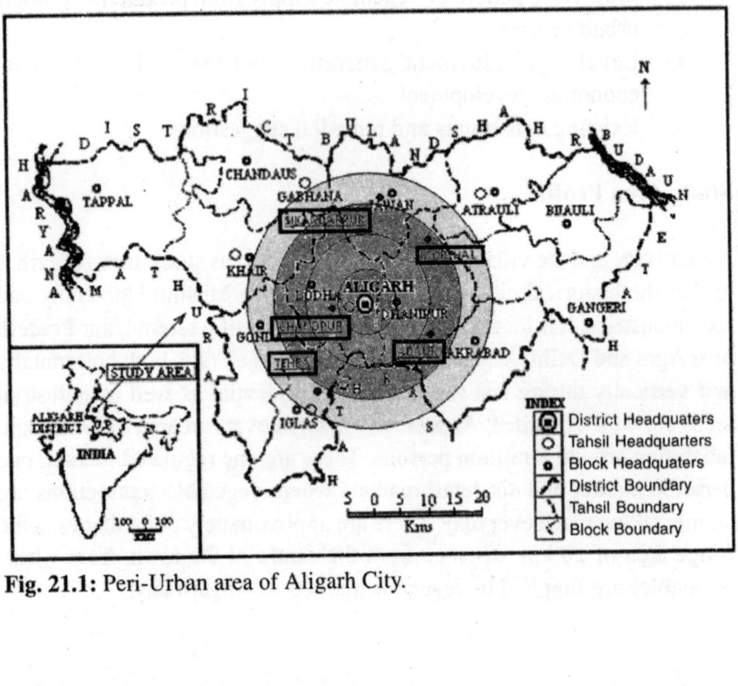

Fig. 21.1: Peri-Urban area of Aligarh City.

Table 21.1: Area under Vegetable Cultivation in Selected Block and Villages in Fringe Area of Aligarh City

Name of Blocks	*Gross cropped Area (In Hectares)*	*Vegetable cultivation*	
		Area (In Hect.)	% to Gross Cropped Area
Khair	45,152	1,915	4.24
Jawan	41,133	510	1.24
Lodha	13,899	1,775	12.77
Dhanipur	38,582	972	2.52
Iglas	35,842	7,132	19.90
Total	1,74,608	12,304	7.05

Source: District Statistical Bulletin (2004).

1.24 to 19.90 per cent in different blocks under study. The variation in the vegetable area is attributed to the availability of irrigation facilities, composition of the caste, size of holding as well as the level of accessibility for the transaction of vegetables in the Aligarh vegetable markets. Iglas and Lodha recorded rather high area due to availability of sewage water for irrigation as well as establishment of regulated markets repectively. The canal irrigation is also well developed in Lodha block which has played a favourable role while the Jawan block experience wide range of Aligarh expansion and the vegetable area has been reduced due to urban encroachment. Besides soil is also saline which discourage vegetable cultivation.

Analysis of Table 21.2 showing change in area under vegetable cultivation during 2004 to 2009 in sample villages indicated a very positive growth in peri-urban area of Aligarh city. During the said period on average 19.09 per cent vegetable area expanded. The highest growth, i.e 27 per cent is recorded in Tehra sampled village due to highly accessible to Aligarh city and accessibility of irrigation water from sewage water. Ninety per cent of cropped area of this village is under vegetable cultivation which supplies vegetable to Aligarh. It is followed by Morthal (23%), Chandpur (19%), Sikandarpur (15%) and Adoun (10%).

Socio-economic Profile of Vegetable Cultivators

Vegetable cultivation in the study area is controlled by social stratification. In general, the vegetable growers belong to low social profile specially Other Backward Classes and Scheduled Castes. Table 21.3 shows that OBCs accounted for the largest share followed by Scheduled Castes. The

Table 21.2: Temporal Change in Area under Vegetable Cultivation in Sample Villages of Peri-urban Area of Aligarh City

Name of sampled villages	*Area under vegetable cultivation (In Acres)*		*Change During 2004-08*	
	2004	*2009*	*Area (In Acres)*	*Percentage*
Sikandarpur	117.7	135.35	17.65	15
Morthal	232.5	285.97	53.47	23
Adoun	209.7	230.67	20.97	10
Chandpur	112	133.33	21.28	19
Tehra	189	240.03	51.03	27
Total	860.9	1025.36	164.41	19.09

Source: Field Survey (2009).

important castes/regions involved in vegetable cultivation are Kachi, Lodha, Baghel, Jatav and Muslims. The high caste groups are almost negligible. Similarly, the vegetable growers are also poor farmers who have less than 4 hectares of land. Marginal farmers shares 37.23 per cent, landless 22.15 per cent and small 22.07 per cent of the total vegetable growers (Table 21.4). The highest share of poor and backward group of the farmers for vegetable cultivation is found due to the fact that they have abundant household labour to employ for the vegetable cultivation as this requires abundant labour. Socially, the female participation is also free rather than among the rich farmers with high social status.

Marketing Process of Vegetables

Marketing is very important post-harvest operation of vegetable cultivation as vegetable requires immediate transaction to the consumers. The study reveals that the villages in the peri-urban area have good accessibity to the Aligarh city. The farmers sell their marketable surplus to the vegetable traders either at farmhouse or to the wholesellers in regulated or town market. Out of total vegetable transacted, at farmhouse it is 1.62 per cent while at the rural market it is 24.09 per cent, town market 17.45 per cent and regulated markets constitute 56.83 per cent. They follow the following channels:

1. Producer—consumer
2. Producer—retailer—consumer
3. Producer—village trader—wholeseller—retailer-consumer

Table 21.3: Social Profile of the Vegetable Cultivators in the Sampled villages of the Peri-urban Area of Aligarh City

Castes	*Number of Respondents*	*Percentage of Total*
Kachi	116	35.50
Lodha	66	20.40
Baghel	59	18.40
Jatav	55	16.70
Muslim	29	9.00
Total	**325**	**100.00**

Source: Field Survey (2009).

Role of Vegetable Cultivation in Socio-Economic Development of Vegetable Cultivators

The vegetable cultivation has high potential of employment generation and poverty alleviation in both urban and urban fringe area through involvement of different kind of activities like growing, plucking, harvesting, sorting, packaging, transportation and marketing. Table 21.6 shows that 92 per cent of the sample households replied social change has taken place through the vegetable cultivation. Increase in purchasing power is answered by 83.69 per cent of the respondents. Similarly, self-dependence (80%), income generation (80%) and employment generation (68%) was answered by the respondent households.

Problems in Vegetable Cultivation and Marketing

Vegetable growers in Peri-urban areas suffer from the following problems, as observed during field survey:

1. The producer's share in the consumer price is quiet low.
2. Lack of storage facility.
3. Lack of regular availability of agricultural labourers in the fringe area.
4. Inadequate marketing space.
5. Irregular availability of water for irrigation.

Suggestions

The following suggestions are recommended for improvement of

Table 21.4: Landholding-wise Participation in Vegetable Cultivation

Sampled villages	*Landless*	*Marginal (1–2)*	*Small (2–4)*	*Medium (4–10)*	*Large (>10)*	*Total Household*
Sikandarpur	12	19	16	5	2	55
	(21.8)	(34.5)	(29.09)	(9.09)	(3.63)	(100)
Morthal	18	33	19	5	0	75
	(24)	(44)	(25.33)	(6.66)	(0.00)	(100)
Adoun	21	29	22	10	8	90
	(25.33)	(32.22)	(24.44)	(11.11)	(8.88)	(100)
Chandpur	9	19	14	3	0	45
	(20)	(42.22)	(31.11)	(6.66)	(0.00)	(100)
Tehra	12	21	17	6	4	60
	(20)	(35)	(28.33)	(10)	(6.66)	(100)
Total	72	121	88	29	14	325
	(22.15)	(37.23)	(22.07)	(8.92)	(4.30)	(100)

Source: Field Survey (2009).

Table 21.5: Marketing Process of Vegetable

Name of Sampled Villages	*Farmgate (In %)*	*Rural Markets (In %)*	*Unregulated Town Market (In %)*	*Regulated Markets (In %)*
Sikandarpur	1.36	22.25	12.28	64.11
Morthal	1.45	23.45	17.09	58.01
Adoun	1.80	25.89	13.89	58.42
Chandpur	2.10	21.77	19.09	57.04
Tehra	1.43	27.09	24.9	46.58
Total	1.63	24.09	17.45	56.83

Source: Field Survey (2009).

vegetable cultivation and vegetable farmers in the peri-urban area of Aligarh city:

1. The government should allot adequate space for marketing of vegetables.
2. Proper storage facilities should be maintained in the market centres of the city.
3. Direct marketing and contract marketing should be encouraged.
4. The producer should be given incentives through adequate supply of water for irrigation.

Table 21.6: Role of Vegetable Cultivation in Socio-Economic Development of Vegetable Cultivators

Sampled Village	*Employment*	*Income Generation*	*Social Change*	*Increase in Purchasing Power*	*Self-Dependence*
Sikandarpur	47 (85.45)	52 (94.55)	53 (96.36)	46 (83.64)	45 (81.82)
Morthal	45 (60.00)	60 (80.00)	71 (94.67)	66 (88.00)	61 (81.33)
Adoun	65 (72.22)	58 (64.44)	83 (92.22)	75 (83.33)	70 (77.78)
Chandpur	22 (48.89)	40 (88.89)	40 (88.89)	39 (86.67)	36 (80.00)
Tehra	42 (70.00)	50 (83.33)	52 (86.67)	46 (76.67)	48 (80.00)
Total	221 (68)	260 (80)	299 (92)	272 (83.69)	260 (80)

Source: Field Survey (2009).

Conclusion

The study reveals that the vegetable cultivation is mainly practiced due to its remunerative value, fast returns and regular demand. It has become a major source of income and employment to urban poor. The beneficiaries are not only the producer and traders but all the people involved from production to marketing of the produce. The major problems regarding the vegetable cultivation is negligible incentive to the producer, improper marketing facilities and inadequate place for transaction of vegetables. Thus, there are many issues to be addressed for the sustainable development of vegetable cultivation in the rural-urban fringe of the Aligarh city.

References

Acharya, S.S. and Agarwal, N.L. (1987). *Agricultural Marketing in India*, New Delhi.

Acharya, S.S. (2009). *Agricultural Economics Research Review*, Vol. 22, January-June, pp. 1-19

Arya, P.S. (2002). *A Text Book of Vegetable Culture*, New Delhi.

Behra, V. Kad Mahapatra, I.C. (1998). Income and Employment Generation for Small and Marginal Farmers through Integrated Farming System, *Indian Farming,* Vol. 48, No. 3, pp. 16-25.

Das, P.C. (2003). *Vegetable Crops of India*, New Delhi.

Deshmukh, P.D. and *et al*., (1970). Marketable Surplus and Marketing Cost of Important Cereals in Western Maharashtra, *Agricultural Situation in India*, Vol. 43, No. 10, January, pp. 675-678.

Joshi, N.N. (2006). Rural Markets—Miles to Go, *Yojna*, Vol. 50, April, pp. 21-23.

Khan, Nizamuddin and *et al*., (2003). Market Participant's Behaviour in Rural Market Centre in North India: A Study in Cultural Geography, *Asian Profile*, Vol. 31, No. 3, June, pp. 239-255.

UNDP (2006). *Urban Agriculture: Food, Jobs and Sustainable Cities.*

22

Rural-Urban Fringe and Socio-Economic Structural Analysis of Vegetable Traders: A Case Study of Uttar Pradesh

Mushir Ali

Introduction

The outward expansion of urban centres along with their peripheries is a typical phenomenon of urban landscape generally in developing countries and particularly in India. The fringe zones of a city not only provide fresh vegetables, cereals, and greeneries but also adjustments in between rural and urban ways of life. Vegetables are important ingredient of diets in urban areas due to nutritional and therapeutic values. The marketing of fresh vegetables has a significant role to enhance their production and consumption for urban population that provides ample opportunities for the growers to earn better returns per unit area of land. Moreover, the vegetables are mainly produced at outer limits of a city by farmers who have strong interaction with parent city. That is why vegetable producers/traders of the fringe areas bear urban reflection on the physical, occupational and demographic characteristics. By and large, they enjoy the urban services but at grass roots their livelihood level and socio-economic conditions are not satisfactory which is the subject for research (Dixit, 1984; Jean-Joseph *et al.*, 2003; AERC, 2005; Ali and Khan, 2007).

Objectives

Keeping in view the importance of socio-economic conditions of vegetable sellers, the study has following objectives—

(1) To assess the size of landholdings, income, mobility and literacy of the vegetable traders of rural-urban fringe.
(2) To analyze age, gender and caste structure of vegetable traders and distribution of basic amenities among them.

Data and Methodology

The work is based on the primary sources of data. They were collected through field surveys from villages and the outer settlements which were situated 3, 5, and 7 km. from the centre of Shahjahanpur city in 2005-06. On the basis of random sampling method, 6 villages and 4 outer wards of the city were selected where 50 per cent households (of 326 vegetable producers/traders) were sampled for detailed study. Direct questionnaire method was used to collect information from the respondents pertaining to their socio-economic characteristics. The collected data were analyzed with simple statistical and geographical techniques.

Study Area

Rural-urban fringe of Shahjahanpur city has been selected as a study area. It is situated (27°54′N latitude and 79°57′E longitude) in the tract between the Ganga and foothills of the Himalayas in Uttar Pradesh. The major section of population of rural-urban is engaged in agricultural, service as well as trading activities and more or less dependent on selling and purchasing of agricultural and non-agricultural commodities, especially perishable goods and livestock. Such type of marketing activities provides employment to workers of unorganized sector and their source of livelihood. Population of Shahjahanpur urban centre and its urban areas, railways settlements Rosa, Shahjahanpur Municipal Board, and Cantonment Board is 3.33 lakh and covers an area of 21.6 sq km.

Results and Discussion

Vegetables are the main products of transacted crops in daily and periodic markets because of their freshness and perishable nature, which discourage the long distance for the transaction. The traders usually transact these perishable commodities in 2-9 km. radius around their production region (Ali, 2009). Due to high demand and easily reachable markets of the city as well as its fringe areas, marginal and small holders produce the vegetables. They dispose of these perishable surpluses (vegetables) at

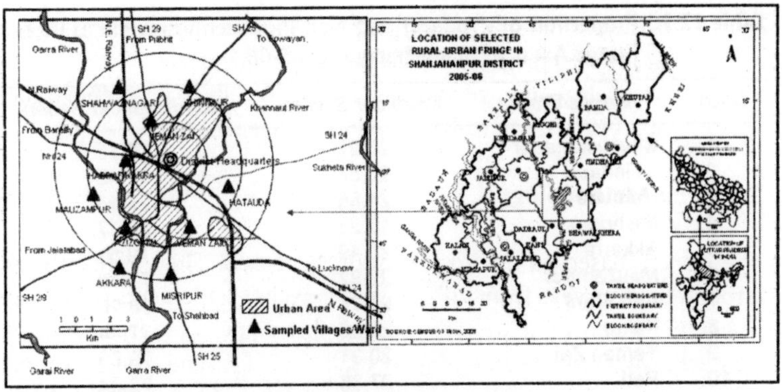

Fig. 21.1: Rural-urban Fringe of Shahjahanpur City.

remunerative prices because of ever increasing dietary requirements in urban areas (Mukherjee and Jayaswal, 2006). Commonly the study region is backward in context of storing, freezing, and transporting facilities at grass roots level. Therefore, the adjoining areas of city are considered as ideal centres for the transaction of Potato, Cabbage, Cauliflower, Brinjal, Tomato, Onion, Garlic, Peas, Green beans, Bittergourd, Bottlegourd, Lady'sfinger, Pumpkin, Jackfruit, Radish, Carrot, Green chilli, and Lemon etc. (Arya, 2002).

Producer and Non-Producer Traders

Table 22.1 shows that the average participation of crop non-producer sellers (77.48 %) is in selected rural-urban fringe. It is due to prevailing unemployment and underemployment in the study area. The 3/4th of workforce of the study area is engaged in agricultural activities and a lion's share of them is marginal workers (landless and casual labourers). They trade vegetables as non-producer sellers for their livelihood and supplement for income to sustain their lives.

Their proportion varies from 72.64 per cent in ward of Reti to 80.77 per cent in village of Mishripur. The highest participation of non-producer sellers (80.77%) lies in Mishripur where they purchase these marketable commodities from the regulated markets or producers from the fringe areas of the city and sell in the markets of 10.7 km radius (Ali *et al.*, 2007). It happens because mostly vegetables are cultivated in the nearest concentric zone of town/city (Von Thunen, 1886). Urban sellers carry vegetables from the regulated market as well as different parts of the

Table 22.1: Proportion of Producer and Non-Producer Vegetable Traders in Fringe Areas of Shahjahanpur, 2005-06

S.No.	Villages/Wards	Producer Sellers	Non-Producer Sellers
1.	Shahwaznagar	23.27	76.73
2.	Chinnaur	22.57	77.43
3.	Hatauda	24.86	75.14
4.	Mishripur	19.23	80.77
5.	Akkarra	20.49	79.51
6.	Mauzampur	22.82	77.18
7.	Aziz Ganj	21.74	78.26
8.	Kakra	22.56	77.44
9.	Yeman Zai	20.31	79.69
10.	Reti	27.36	72.64
	Total	**22.52**	**77.48**

Source: Field Survey, 2005-06.

district to sell in adjacent regions of the city. Unemployment and underemployment are main push factors in the rural-urban fringes to force their residents to trade vegetables for earning the livelihood and supplement to their income (Verma *et al.*, 1999). However, it has been noted during the field investigations that non-producer traders visit to the markets those are held along the roads for purchasing and selling vegetables.

Holding-wise Vegetable Traders

The study has revealed that nearly 20 per cent vegetable traders are producers (Table 22.1). Among them about 64 per cent traders are the marginal and small farmers who have less than 1 ha. size of landholdings. It is followed by small holders (27.24%), semi-medium (7.67%) and medium as well as big farmers 1.57 per cent (Fig. 22.2). The figure also highlights the facts that among 6 villages/wards out of 10, no producer-seller belongs to medium and big farmer category.

The share marginal and small farmers 84 per cent presents a description that cultivation of vegetables and their marketing have been main source for income of marginal and small farmers in the peri-urban region (Haque, 1996). That is why FAO has accepted that vegetable farming is considered as a next revolution in agriculture after green revolution for the food and nutritional security. It is a boon for these farmers because increasing population reduces size of landholdings (FAO, 1999).

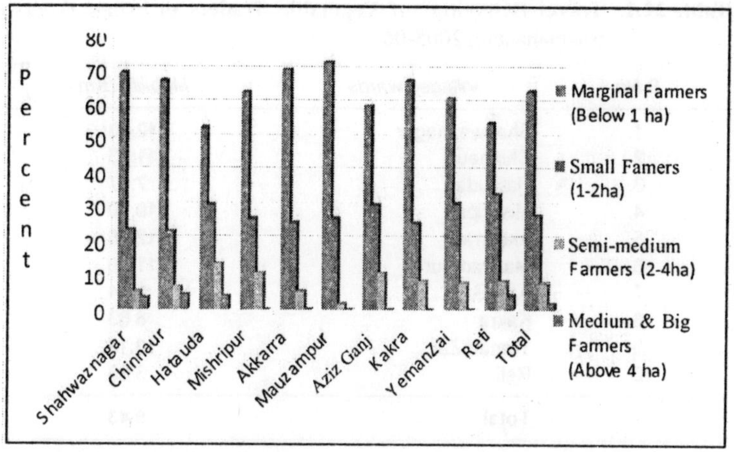

Fig. 22.2: Holding-wise Proportion of Vegetable Producer Traders in Fringe Areas of Shahjahanpur, 2005-06.

Source: Field Survey, 2005-06.

Mobility of Vegetable Traders

The mobility for trade is an important factor for the development of a region or country. The threshold and range of goods decide the length of travelling distance and visiting frequency of traders (Khan and Qureshi, 2004).

Table 22.2 reveals that the vegetable traders of rural-urban fringe move nearly 10 km for the selling and purchasing of the vegetables. The perishable nature of the commodities and lack of refrigerating facilities, generally, limit distance for marketing of local vegetables. The average mobility of vegetable traders is not homogenous and varies from 3 kms. to 12.43 kms. (Table 22.2). The traders of Shahwaznagar are more mobile (12.43 km) than that of the others. It is because they visit the periodic markets of fringe and remote areas for the marketing of vegetables.

Income Level of Vegetable Traders

Table 22.3 shows that 18.49 per cent vegetable traders earn below Rs. 3,000 per month. The income of the traders depend upon their input cost or investment in the trade, size of landholdings, mobility of the traders, and demand of vegetables (Amani and Khan, 1993).

Table 22.2: Travel Behaviour of Vegetable Traders in Fringe Areas of Shahjahanpur, 2005-06

S.No.	*Villages/wards*	*Mobility (Km)*
1.	Shahwaznagar	12.43
2.	Chinnaur	11.83
3.	Hatauda	7.57
4.	Mishripur	10.70
5.	Akkarra	12.36
6.	Mauzampur	11.30
7.	Aziz Ganj	5.64
8.	Kakra	8.63
9.	Yeman Zai	10.15
10.	Reti	3.65
	Total	**9.43**

Source: Field Survey, 2005-06.

Average 65.84 per cent vegetable traders earn between Rs. 3,000-6,000 per month and 15.68 per cent traders make earning more than Rs. 6,000 per month. Higher proportion of the traders nearly 85 per cent lies in the category who earn Rs. 6,000 per month shows that although the vegetable business do not offer a very good earning, it provides employment to casual, landless labourers as well as marginal farmers throughout the year by engaging in producing and marketing activities (Ali and Khan, 2007).

Literacy Level of Vegetable Traders

Literacy level is an important index of socio-cultural advancement and economic transformation of a society. Table 22.4 shows that literacy of the vegetable traders is higher (71.13 %) than that of district average (63.4 %).

At least 29 per cent vegetable traders are under primary and got education below 5 standard classes. It is followed by primary (20.9 %), 12.65 middle (8 standard classes) and secondary and above (9.69%). The table describes the facts that higher proportion of the traders belong either illiterate or lower grade of the education level. It is because that study region is socio-economically backward and people like to earn income for bringing up the family than getting higher education (Ali, 2009).

Table 22.3: Income Level of Vegetable Traders in Fringe Areas of Shahjahanpur, 2005-06

S.No.	*Villages/wards*	*Below 3000*	*3000–6000*	*Above 6000*
1.	Shahwaznagar	17.00	61.57	21.43
2.	Chinnaur	32.57	51.71	15.71
3.	Hatauda	17.86	69.29	12.86
4.	Mishripur	15.71	70.65	13.63
5.	Akkarra	17.00	70.00	13.00
6.	Mauzampur	18.57	72.57	8.86
7.	Aziz Ganj	17.14	54.29	28.57
8.	Kakra	11.43	78.57	10.00
9.	Yeman Zai	21.43	65.00	13.57
10.	Reti	16.14	64.71	19.14
	Total	**18.49**	**65.84**	**15.68**

Source: Field surveys, 2005–06.

Age Structure of Vegetable Traders

Figure 22.3 illustrates that working-age group of traders 15-59 years (77.42 %) are dominated in the transaction of vegetables in the selected rural-urban fringe. It is followed by the senile above 60 years (14.56%) and juvenile population 0-14 years (8.02 %) respectively.

Involvement of the senile and child population in the transaction of vegetables indicates that it is livelihood which compels them to trade vegetables for sustaining their lives and supplement for the family income (Teltscher, 1994; Haque, 1996). The highest participation of the child and old traders in the transaction of vegetables has been recorded nearly 10 per cent and 18 per cent in the ward of Kakra. It is because that this locality has high concentration of other backwards classes of Muslim community. They are engaged in this profession throughout the year for *Rozi* and *Roti* (employment and income).

Gender Structure of Vegetable Traders

Cultivation and trade of vegetables are considered a revolution for the generation of employment among women in which females get job round the year for production and process of vegetable marketing to earn cash (Michael, 2009). It has been noted during the field surveys that about 9 per cent women were engaged in the trade of vegetables in urban and peri-urban areas (Table 22.5).

Table 22.4: Literacy Level of Vegetable Traders in Fringe Areas of Shahjahanpur, 2005-06

S. No.	Villages/wards	Illiterate	Under Primary	Primary	Middle	High School+
1.	Shahwaznagar	37.14	32.15	12.54	10.81	7.36
2.	Chinnaur	22.47	29.52	19.47	14.87	13.67
3.	Hatauda	26.67	28.46	18.43	15.79	10.65
4.	Mishripur	30.75	24.39	22.03	12.88	9.95
5.	Akkarra	35.71	21.07	27.14	12.51	3.57
6.	Mauzampur	36.67	20.00	23.33	10.00	10.00
7.	Aziz Ganj	19.23	34.62	19.23	15.38	11.54
8.	Kakra	24.29	31.26	20.09	13.16	11.20
9.	Yeman Zai	33.33	33.33	15.38	10.00	7.96
10.	Reti	22.46	32.14	23.26	11.11	11.03
	Total	**28.87**	**28.69**	**20.09**	**12.65**	**9.69**

Source: Field Survey, 2005-06.

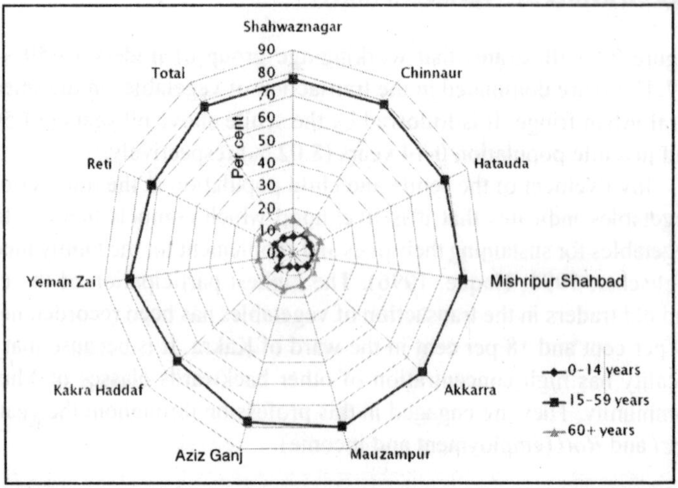

Fig. 22.3: Age Structure of Vegetable Traders in Fringe Areas of Shahjahanpur, 2005-06.

However, it is a tiny proportion in comparison of involvement of male traders. But the fact is that it is the trade of vegetables which provide platforms to women for participation in the tertiary economic sector otherwise their sharing was absent from business class in the selected rural-urban fringe (Momesen and Townsend, 1987; Dixit, 1999; Hapke,

Table 22.5: Proportion of Male and Female of Vegetable Traders in Fringe Areas of Shahjahanpur, 2005-06

S.No.	*Villages/wards*	*Male*	*Female*
1.	Shahwaznagar	90.48	9.52
2.	Chinnaur	92.66	7.34
3.	Hatauda	90.78	9.22
4.	Mishripur	89.86	10.14
5.	Akkarra	87.78	12.22
6.	Mauzampur	90.17	9.83
7.	Aziz Ganj	91.19	8.81
8.	Kakra	96.06	3.94
9.	Yeman Zai	95.15	4.85
10.	Reti	87.67	12.33
	Total	**91.18**	**8.82**

Source: Field Survey, 2005-06.

2001). The highest participation of women (12.33 per cent) lies in Reti. This village is situated near the district regulated market (rosa) as well as daily market that exists in the village along the road where women participate actively in the transaction of vegetables.

Marital Status of Vegetable Traders

Table 22.6 highlights that 76 per cent vegetable traders are married. It is followed by 20.65 per cent unmarried and 3.34 per cent widow/separate. The married life is accepted as a life of responsibility and the urban when the persons are married they need money for sustenance of their family life smoothly.

At this situation the vegetable transaction is a suitable option for the residents of rural-urban fringe where the empire of poor condition of education and either no land or marginal and small size of landholdings exists. The proportion of the single and separate traders also describes that the vegetables trading is the attractive business at grass roots level in the rural-urban fringe (Gosh and Gupta, 2005).

Caste-wise Participation of Vegetable Traders

The caste system, with its social stratification and restrictions continues major impact on the Indian socio-economic profile. This system, generally, identified with Hinduism is also prevalent among Christians, Sikhs, and Muslims. Working castes now known as Other Backward

Table 22.6: Marital Status of Vegetable Traders in Fringe Areas of Shahjahanpur, 2005-06

S.No.	Villages/wards	Married	Single	Separate/Married
1.	Shahwaznagar	70.86	25.02	4.12
2.	Chinnaur	74.44	21.68	3.88
3.	Hatauda	72.14	24.95	2.91
4.	Mishripur	75.19	21.30	3.51
5.	Akkarra	84.33	13.76	1.91
6.	Mauzampur	75.67	22.00	2.33
7.	Aziz Ganj	71.57	26.27	2.16
8.	Kakra	74.26	22.17	3.57
9.	Yeman Zai	81.23	14.62	4.15
10.	Reti	80.44	14.70	4.86
	Total	**76.01**	**20.65**	**3.34**

Source: Field Survey, 2005-06.

Class (OBC) and Scheduled Castes (SC) were always poor and considered at bottom in the Verna system[1] and were kept away from opportunities (Jacob, 2009).

This fact lies in Table 22.7 that vegetable traders belong to general (13.77 %), OBC (70.66 %) and SC (15.56 %) in the rural-urban fringe. The higher proportion of OBC traders presents a reality that vegetable trading is the main source of the livelihood, especially for socially backward people (*Kachhi, Saini, Kujra* and *Bhatiyara* who are traditionally sellers of vegetables), casual workers, and agricultural labourers. The traders of higher caste are involved in vegetable trade, first one who have medium and big size of landholding they sell vegetables in bulk. Second, those are economically weak they consider this profession as the source of the income for survival. Scheduled Castes people have proportion nearly 16 per cent. Many of them are traditionally growers and sellers and do the job of vegetable marketing as a lucrative business for the livelihood and employment (Srinivas, 1994).

Housing Conditions of Vegetable Traders

Fig. 22.4 highlights housing conditions of vegetable traders to total traders of the selected rural-urban fringe. The vegetable traders who live in semi-concrete houses are on top position 58.43 per cent. It is followed by *pucca* householders (20.22 %), *katcha* householders (15.18 %) and hut/slum dwellers (6.17 %).

Table 22.7: Caste-wise participation of Vegetable Traders in Fringe Areas of Shahjahanpur, 2005-06

S. No.	*Villages/wards*	*Gen*	*OBC*	*SC*
1.	Shahwaznagar	19.57	73.77	6.67
2.	Chinnaur	10.71	75.00	14.29
3.	Hatauda	17.14	75.71	7.14
4.	Mishripur	17.14	64.29	18.57
5.	Akkarra	8.30	83.57	8.12
6.	Mauzampur	11.43	57.14	31.43
7.	Aziz Ganj	22.86	48.57	28.57
8.	Kakra	10.57	71.43	18.00
9.	Yeman Zai	11.43	81.43	7.14
10.	Reti	8.57	75.71	15.71
	Total	**13.77**	**70.66**	**15.56**

Source: Field Survey, 2005-06.

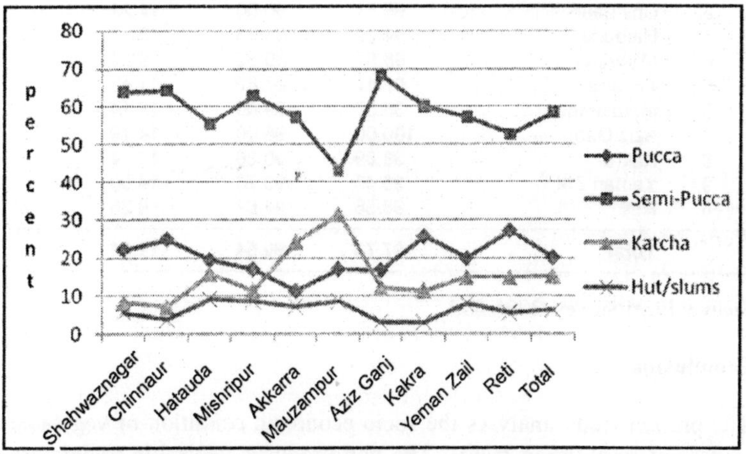

Fig. 22.4: Disribution of Basic Amenities among Vegetable Traders in Fringe Areas of Shahjahanpur, 2005-06.

The highest share of semi-concrete dwellers among the vegetable traders reflects their poor economic and social conditions that these traders do not have all season houses. That is why their houses often become causes of casuality in the rainy season and disease prone in the transaction of the atmospheric seasons (WHO, 2004).

Distribution of Basic Amenities among Vegetable Traders

Table 22.8 reflects the distribution of basic amenities among the vegetable traders in the selected rural-urban fringe. Health facilities provided by the government is very poor, nearly 12 per cent vegetable traders beneficial, in spite of being the seasonal disease prone conditions of their houses. At least 3 per cent traders do not get safe drinking water and about 10 per cent traders do not have any kind of toilet facilities (Park, 2002). It has been noted during the field surveys that mostly available toilet facilities were unhygienic and service type.

Table 22.8: Distribution of Basic Amenities among Vegetable Traders in Fringe Areas of Shahjahanpur, 2005-06

S.No.	*Villages/wards*	*Safe Drinking water*	*Toilet*	*Govt. Health facilities*
1.	Shahwaznagar	97.14	83.14	8.56
2.	Chinnaur	95.71	90.00	14.29
3.	Hatauda	94.29	88.33	13.57
4.	Mishripur	98.57	89.82	9.71
5.	Akkarra	97.14	87.82	11.43
6.	Mauzampur	98.57	89.00	12.14
7.	Aziz Ganj	100.00	96.00	14.29
8.	Kakra	98.89	90.86	12.14
9.	Yeman Zai	98.43	93.73	14.00
10.	Reti	98.56	96.67	9.26
	Total	**97.73**	**90.54**	**11.94**

Source: Field Survey, 2005-06.

Conclusion

The present study analyses the socio-economic condition of vegetable traders of rural-urban fringe. The non-producer vegetable traders are common in the fringe areas and their share is nearly 77 per cent. The proportion of producer-cum-traders is at least 23 per cent in which more than 84 per cent producers belong to marginal and small farmer categories. It is due to prevailing unemployment and underemployment conditions. These traders earn money and supplement for their income. 85 per cent vegetable traders of rural-urban fringe earn below Rs. 6,000 per month. The illiteracy and backwardness in education among the vegetable traders is widespread because the percentages of illiterate and primary as well as under primary are nearly 28 and 48 respectively. The proportion of traders of working age is about 77 per cent but availability of the children and old person reflects their poor socio-economic profile. Male traders are in majority marketing of vegetables at least 80 per cent are married. Nearly 90 per cent traders belong to OBC and SC categories because they are traditionally growers and sellers of vegetables. However, they have not only limitedland size holdings for the vegetable farming but also their majority about 80 per cent live in hut/slums, *katcha*, semi-*pucca* types of dwellings. At least 3 per cent traders do not get safe drinking water and nearly 10 per cent are far away from any kind of toilet facilities. A chunk of traders (88%) is not under reaches of government health facilities while the nature and unhygienic environment of their houses always invite many diseases generally and particularly at the transition of atmospheric seasons.

Moreover, it has been found that vegetable traders face social, economic, infrastructural and institutional difficulties. There is an urgent need to reduce these problems, which will help for socio-economic well-being of vegetable traders, thereby helping in development of rural-urban fringes. Taking into consideration the prevailing conditions of the traders a number of steps should be taken for their betterment. These are as follows:

(1) A major section of vegetable traders (non-producer sellers) belong to marginal, small farmers and labourers of unorganized sectors. So, micro credit facilities should be provided to them.

(2) Vegetables are the commodities of perishable nature so storing, freezing, and quick and fast transportation facilities should be provided. By these facilities marginal and small holders can dispose of their vegetables at remunerative prices.

(3) Majority of the farmers in the study area operate small farm units and produce only small marketed surpluses that require marketing facilities at nearby places. So cooperative marketing system should also be started and government and private purchase centres (formal agencies) should be set-up in rural-urban fringe. They should have linkages among the each level in the hierarchy of market yards with telephone, fax and internet facilities, and allowing electronic trade.

(4) The problem related to health and basic amenities, is big issue among the vegetable traders. So health services, and all seasons *pucca* houses should be provided properly and awareness should be developed among them about the health and education. Because without proper basic amenities and awareness, infectious diseases can't be defeated.

The agro-based industries should be established in rural-urban fringe areas. It will increase the price of commodities and provide job for the population of surrounding areas directly and indirectly to promote the well-being and socio-economic development among the people of the rural-urban fringe.

Notes

1. Varna system was the source of present caste hierarchy in India which divided population into four classes, Brahmins, Kshatriayas, Vaishays, and, Shudras. It was based on the occupation of the people and the complexion of the skin. In this hierarchical order Brahmins were on the top ranking followed by Kshatriayas, Vaishays, and Shudras. In due course of time, it became extremely rigid and high caste people exploited to low caste people.

References

AERC (2005). Fruits and Vegetables Mandies Located in Urban and Semi-Urban Areas of Delhi. *Agricultural Situation in India,* Vol. 61(1), pp. 799-801.

Ali, M. (2009). *Geography of Agricultural Marketing at Grass Roots Levels*, Pacific Publication, Delhi.

Ali, M. and Khan, N. (2007). Transaction of Vegetables through Rural Markets in Jalalabad Tahsil of Shahjahanpur District. *The Geographical Review of India,* Vol. 69 (1), pp. 55-61.

Ali, M. *et al.* (2007). Hierarchy of Periodic Market Centres in Shahjahanpur District, Uttar Pradesh: A Geographical Analysis. *Indian National Geographer,* Vol. 22 (1&2), pp. 185-195.

Amani, K.Z. and Khan, N. (1993). Spatial Behaviour of Consumers and Traders in Periodic Markets in North Indian State: A Case Study. *Asian Profile,* Vol. 21(3), pp. 227-46.

Arya, P.S. (2002). *A Text Book of Vegetable Culture*, Kalyani Publishers, New Delhi

Dixit, R.S. (1984). *Market Centres and their Spatial Development in Umland of Kanpur*. Kitab Ghar, Allahabad.

——(1999). *Geography of Markets and Commercial Activities in India*. Concept, New Delhi.

FAO, (1999). Urban and Peri-Urban Agriculture. *Committee on Agriculture 15th Session*, Rome.

Gosh, G.N. and Gupta, S. (2005). Agricultural Diversification Opportunities for Small Farmers. *National Centre for Agricultural Economics and Policy Research*, New Delhi.

Haque, T. (1996). *Sustainability of Rural Small Holders Agriculture in India.* Concept, New Delhi.

Jacob, K.S. (2009). *Caste and Inequalities in Health,* The Hindu, 132 (200). p. 10.

Khan, J.H. and Qureshi, S. (2004). Spatial Patterns of Internal Migration in Shahjahanpur District. *The Geographer,* Vol. 51 (2), pp. 1-22.

Michael, H. (2009). Marketing Plan for the Tasmanian Vegetable Industry, *Vegetable Centre of Tasmanian Institute of Agricultural Research,* Tasmania.

Momesen, J. and Townsend, J. (1987). *Geography and Gender in the Third World,* Hutchinson, London.

Mukherjee, N. and Jayaswal, M. (2006). *Chained by Food Marginalized Voices from Peri-Urban India.* Concept, New Delhi, pp. 6-17.

Park, K. (2002). *Man and Medicine: Towards Health for All Park's,* Textbook of Preventive and Social Medicine, 17th Edition, Banarasidas Bhanot Publishers, pp. 5-15.

Srinivas, M.N. (1994). The Indian village: Myth and reality. In: *The Dominant Caste and Other Essays.* Oxford University Press, Oxford.

Teltescher, S. (1994). Small Trade and the World Economy: Informal Vendors in Quito, Ecuador, *Economic Geography,* Vol. 70, pp. 167-87.

Verma, R.V. *et al.* (1999). Some Perspectives of Educated Unemployment in Rural India: A Micro Level Study. *Regional Symbiosis,* Vol. 7, pp. 11-24.

Von Thunen, J.H. (1886). Dev Isoleirite Staat in Beziehung and Land Wartscaft and Nationalo Konomie, Rostok. In Bradford M.G. and Kent W.A. (1977) *Human Geography,* Oxford University Press, pp. 29-34.

WHO (2004). Facts & Figures, Sanitation and Hygiene Links to Health, http:// sanitationupdates.wordpress/11/17 (accessed 30/01/2009).

23
Sustainable Development and Urban Sprawl of Kanpur Nagar

Pratima Ghosh

Introduction

The concept of rural-urban fringe has emerged due to engulfment of the adjoining rural tract from time to time by the increasing unscientific encroachment of urban functions. The fringe area of the district towns which was neglected before the commencement of railways and roadways is being used for the new development of the congested towns. These areas may justifiably be called zone of urban invasion. After the establishment of petrol pumps garages, stores and the like the farmers get profitable gain by selling their surplus perishable goods, i.e. vegetable, milk and others.

Von Thunen (1826) in his major work 'The Isolated State' has discussed the importance of location. Every landowner wants the maximum monetary return from a particular piece of land. Ricardo's rent theory is also more or less similar to Von Thunen idea of rent. He believes that the type of use of land would depend upon maximum return to owner who would select whether it is useful for industries, housing or agricultural production. Not only would this even poor grade land be used with an increase in town population.

In the fringe area changing the farm land into non-farm uses will create new problems. The pressure on land has to shift in some other alternative direction so as to give employment to the farmers whose land has thus ceased to be agricultural. Residential development in the fringe area must rely on rural forms of government to furnish urban services.

Natural resources are under increased pressure in this area because of the use of land for *inter alia*, clay pits, quarries, sewage disposal tanks and garbage dumps and as a result of air and water pollution from local industrial and urban sources (Dhawan and Singh, 1994).

The process of urbanization operating (urban sprawl) in the fringe of Kanpur Nagar has also given rise to typical land use associations. Dynamic land use pattern is developing side by side in the old villages. New residential extensions, commerce, industry, city service and farming are not nearly sorted out into homogenous areas but are intermingled in a random fashion which gives a distinctive quality to the land use pattern of rural-urban fringe. The haphazard development of slums, unauthorized colonies, piecemeal commercial development, intermix of conforming and non-conforming uses of land coupled with inadequate services and facilities have become common features in the fringe. The dynamic change from rural to urban land use is so fast that the resultant need and complex uses coupled with shortage of land have led to speculation and increase in land values. The ever-growing difference between the demand and supplies of house sites and units coupled with B.D.A's restriction on other forms of supply and very high cost of land in the city have increased the pressure on fringe area tremendously which has given rise to proliferation of unauthorized development of land uses—residential and industries etc. The fringe areas are generally within the jurisdiction of Panchayat which has neither the financial resources nor the technical expertise to plan and manage the rapidly developing fringe.

Against this backdrop, the present paper examines the impact of urban sprawl of Kanpur Nagar on land use change, food security, basic amenities and residential scenario.

I. Objectives

The major objectives of the study are:

(i) To review the trend of land use patterns.
(ii) Identify areas under crops and analyze the situation of food security in the district.
(iii) Examine the cost of housing in the urban fringe.
(iv) Analysis of basic amenities provided in the district's fringe areas.

II. Hypotheses

Following hypotheses have been formulated to be tested:

(i) As the land under non-agricultural uses increases net sown area is reduced as well as forest land also decreases leading to less sustainable development.

(ii) Food security is endangered due to urban sprawl.

(iii) Residential houses are cheaper in the fringe areas which means that people will be more settled in the fringe areas.

(iv) Basic amenities are expected to increase due to urban sprawl.

III. Methodology

(i) Selection of indicators representing land use as identified by the revenue department has been made.

(ii) The secondary data pertaining to Kanpur Nagar of the year 1990-91 to 2008 have been taken from Economics and Statistics Department, Kanpur as well as Town and Country Planning Department, Kanpur.

(iii) Trends of different land use and agriculture have been analyzed with the help of correlation, regression methods.

(iv) Data provided by secondary sources of Statistical Department regarding basic amenities and housing have been analyzed.

(v) Land under non-agricultural uses has been used as an indicator of urban sprawl.

IV. Urban Sprawl of Kanpur City

Urban sprawl of Kanpur can be defined by the increase in number of blocks in Kanpur city. Total number of blocks in Kanpur city has increased since 1998. The name of the blocks included in Kanpur city has been given in Table 23.1. Within the period of ten years urban sprawl has undertaken ten blocks in the same district. There were 278 villages in the Census of 1991 in Kanpur district which have increased to 1003 in number. The new blocks added to this city have been shown in Figs. 23.1 and 23.2.

In Fig. 23.2, the present Kanpur district is shown along with the new blocks added to it.

V. Trends of Land Use

In order to find out the impact of increase in land under non-agricultural uses on forests, permanent pastures and miscellaneous trees in Kanpur

Table 23.1: Blocks in Kanpur City

Year	*1994*	*2007–08*
	Kalyanpur	Kalyanpur
	Bidhnu	Bidhnu
	Sarsaul	Sarsaul
		Bilhaur
		Kakwan
		Shivajpur
		Chaubepur
		Bhitargaon
		Ghatampur
Population	3,81,154	41,67,999
Villages	278	1003

Source: *Statistical Diary*, Economics and Statistics Division, Kanpur Nagar.

Map 23.1: Blocks added to Kanpur Urban District.

Nagar attempt to plot correlation between all the land uses, has been made. Certain inferences have been drawn based upon the correlation matrix in Table 23.2. The results are based upon the time series analysis of land use of Kanpur Nagar from 1991-92 to 2007-08.

Land under non-agricultural uses is positively correlated with all the other land uses. This category of land use depicts a coefficient of correlation of 0.56 with forests and a high correlation of 0.93 with net

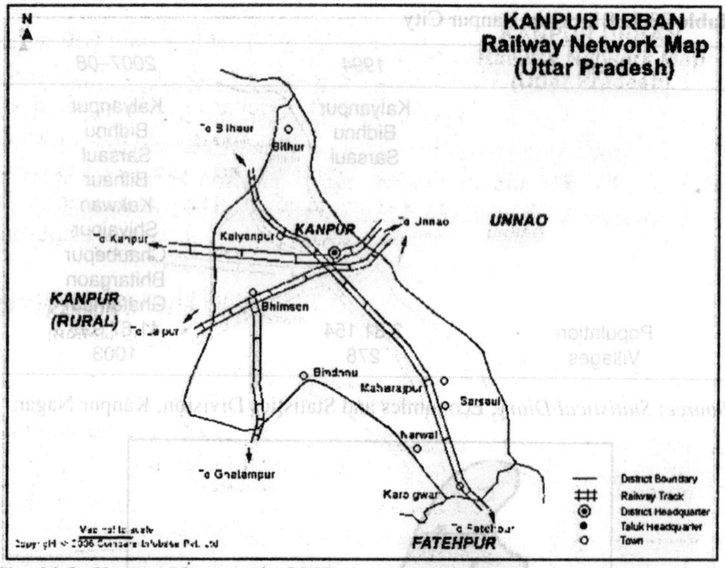

Fig. 23.2: Kanpur Nagar as in 2008.
Source: Railway Network Map.

sown area. Definitely, the coefficient of correlation is low but positive with permanent pastures (0.4) and (0.1) with miscellaneous trees.

Thus, it is depicted in the Table that environmentally significant land in Kanpur city have been used for non-agricultural uses to a lesser degree and the proportion of permanent pastures, forests and net sown area in the reporting area is almost constant. This scenario is presented in Table 23.3.

Table 23.3 presents the analysis of changes in the proportion of land uses in the total reporting area. The Table also tries to analyze whether increase in the land under non-agricultural uses has resulted in a decrease in forests, net area sown and permanent pastures and miscellaneous trees.

According to the Table the entire time period of 1992-93 to 2007-08 can be divided in three phases. It has been found that during the period 1992-93 to 1997-98, forests had remained to at around 1.55 per cent. But the per cent decreased to 0.53 when more blocks were included. During this period culturable waste showed a trend of decline from 5.77 per cent in 1992-93 to 3.85 per cent in 1996-97. Current fallow also showed a decline of 4.94 to 3.67 per cent. Land under other fallow almost remained constant at 6.52 per cent. During this time period, proportion of barren

Table 23.2: Correlation Matrix of Nine Fold Classification of Land Use in Kanpur Nagar (1992–93 to 2007–08)

Land use calegories	*Forest*	*Cultivable Waste*	*Current Fallow*	*Other Fallow*	*Barren land*	*Land under Non-Agricultural Uses*	*Misc. Trees*	*Permanent Pastures*	*Net sown Area*
Forest	1.00								
Cultivable Waste	0.12	1.00							
Current Fallow	0.56	0.63	1.00						
Other Fallow	–0.01	0.64	–0.03	1.00					
Barren land	0.12	0.97	0.70	0.59	1.00				
Land under Non-Agricultural Uses	0.56	0.78	0.94	0.23	0.82	1.00			
Miscellaneous Trees	–0.12	0.28	0.07	0.15	0.21	0.19	1.00		
Permanent Pastures	–0.09	0.62	0.35	0.37	0.58	0.44	0.12	1.00	
Net sown Area	0.34	0.94	0.83	0.47	0.97	0.93	0.18	0.53	1.00

Source: *Statistical Diary*, Economics and Statistics Division, Kanpur.

land was hovering around 5.3 per cent. Land under non-agricultural uses increased marginally from 14.14 per cent to 14.89 per cent in 1995-96. Proportion of land under miscellaneous trees increased from 3 per cent in 1992-93 to 4 per cent in 1995-96. Permanent pastures reduced from 2.21 to 1.71 per cent and net area sown also showed a fluctuating trend between 56 to 54 per cent.

In the time period of 1998-99 to 2000-01 it has been found that 7 new blocks have been included in Kanpur Nagar. This resulted in lowering of percentage of land put under non-agricultural uses. The addition of new blocks resulted in an increase of total reporting area. There was no development in these blocks and the larger portion of land was under agricultural practices. Thus, there was an increase in the proportion of net area sown to 64.85 per cent. All the other land uses had lower proportion than the previous year except barren land (7.0 %). However, urban sprawl began to increase land under non-agricultural uses which increased marginally from 10.38 per cent to 10.41 per cent. As the data in the Table suggests that only two land uses which showed a decline during this time period were land under permanent pastures and net sown area.

Table 23.3: Percentage of Various Land uses in Total Reporting Area of Kanpur Nagar

Year	*Land use Categories*									
	Forest	*Cultivable Waste*	*Current Fallow*	*Other Fallow*	*Barren land*	*Land under Non-Agricultural Uses*	*Miscellaneous Trees*	*Permanent Pastures*	*Net sown Area*	
1992–93	1.55	5.77	4.94	6.52	5.36	14.14	3.00	2.29	56.43	
1993–94	1.55	5.16	4.44	6.22	5.16	14.40	3.10	1.73	57.30	
1994–95	1.55	6.21	3.92	6.45	5.30	14.89	3.10	1.71	56.87	1st Phase
1995–96	1.55	6.94	3.88	7.04	5.30	14.89	4.06	1.71	54.63	
1996–97	1.50	3.85	3.67	6.00	7.46	10.38	1.20	1.09	64.85	
1997–98	0.53	3.54	7.28	3.05	7.48	10.41	1.20	0.02	64.69	
1998–99	0.53	3.84	6.39	3.58	7.48	10.41	1.20	1.87	64.70	
1999–2000	0.53	3.83	6.51	3.61	7.48	10.41	1.20	1.87	64.57	2nd Phase
2000–01	0.53	3.83	6.55	3.65	7.48	10.41	1.20	1.87	64.48	
2001–02	0.53	3.73	6.94	3.02	7.42	11.26	1.20	1.42	64.48	
2002–03	0.53	3.69	6.86	3.03	7.00	11.34	1.29	1.40	64.88	
2003–04	0.53	3.36	9.15	3.00	7.01	11.64	1.20	1.56	62.55	
2004–05	1.88	3.39	9.60	2.72	5.97	11.61	0.97	1.06	62.80	
2005–06	1.89	3.18	10.27	2.46	5.85	12.11	1.23	1.01	62.01	3rd Phase
2006–07	1.88	3.22	8.89	2.23	5.57	12.95	1.21	1.04	63.01	
2007–08	1.88	3.06	9.83	2.31	5.63	13.59	1.22	1.04	61.44	

Source: Statistical Diary, Economics and Statistics Division, Kanpur.

During the third time period 2001-02 to 2007-08 it has been found that land under non-agricultural uses increased by 1.25 per cent, i.e. it increased from 10.41 per cent to 11.26 per cent in the year 1996-97. But net area sown remains at 64.48 per cent in 2000-01. It increased to 64.88 per cent in the next year. During these two years of 2000-01 and 2000-02 non-productive uses of land like cultivable waste decreased. But by the year 2007-08, it has been found that proportion of land under non-agricultural uses increases to 13.59 per cent. It tends to reduce net sown area from 64.88 per cent in 2000-01 to 61.44 per cent. This shows the impact of urban sprawl.

The positive aspect of the inclusion of new blocks is that land under forests have increased from 0.53 per cent in 2001 to 1.88 per cent in 2008. Cultivable waste have reduced to 3.06 per cent in 2007-08 from 3.73 per cent. Other fallows have also reduced from 3.02 per cent to 2.31 per cent during the same time period. Proportion of barren land have also reduced from 7.48 per cent to 5.63 per cent in 2007-08. Land under miscellaneous trees has also increased from 1.20 per cent to 1.22 per cent. However, land under permanent pastures have reduced from 1.4 per cent to 1 per cent during the same time period.

From the above analysis following inferences can be drawn:

(i) Urban sprawl of Kanpur Nagar has resulted in the reduction of net sown area. Though the per cent of decline is very small.

(ii) The effect of urban sprawl has not able to reduce the forest percentage from the level of 1992-93. In fact, percentage of forests, permanent pastures and miscellaneous trees have slightly increased.

VI. Urban Sprawl, Land Use and Food Security

The above background paves the way to find the effect of increase in the land under non-agricultural uses on the productive, non-productive and productivity of land, i.e., food security. In Table 23.4 time-series data of the three variables have been juxtaposed. It is assumed that increase in land under non-agricultural uses fairly denotes urban sprawl. Productive land uses are sum of land under forests, net area sown and permanent pastures and miscellaneous trees. Non-productive land use comprise of the summation of land under barren land, cultivable waste, land under current fallow and land under other fallow. Food security in this case has been measured by productivity of net sown area under the crops like cereal and pulses.

The hypothesis to be tested are:

(i) Is urban sprawl associated with productive land uses in negative manner?
(ii) Urban sprawl is a danger to food security.

The coefficient of regression between the land under non-agricultural uses and productive land uses is 6.4 which is significant. This indicates the degree of urban sprawl is positively related to land under productive uses. The change in land under non-agricultural uses by 1 unit would increase the land under productive uses by 6.4 units. The expected negative association between urban sprawl and productive land uses did not get support from the analysis of the empirical data.

This is depicted in the Table 23.5 also where we find net sown area to have increased in the year 2007-08 as compared to 1998 in absolute terms. This increase has been found in the villages namely Kalyanpur, Shivrajpur and Patara which are more close to Kanpur city.

Regression analysis of land under non-agricultural uses and non-productive land uses also show a positive but very less in the sense that if 1 unit of land under non-agricultural uses is increased non-productive

Table 23.4: Land Under Non-Agricultural Uses, Productive, Non-Productive Land Use and Productivity in Kanpur City

Year	*Land under Non-Agricultural Uses*	*Productive Land uses*	*Non-productive Land use*	*Production (Quintal per Hectare)*
1992–93	14814	66266	23669	192.07
1993–94	15021	66441	21889	173.93
1994–95	15532	65977	22819	176.07
1995–96	15532	64637	24159	189.85
1996–97	31157	206006	62954	21.34
1997–98	31157	198935	63916	240.39
1998–99	31159	204512	63764	190.56
1999–2000	31159	204107	64169	22.15
2000–01	31159	203836	64440	21.1
2001–02	33725	202512	63198	22.4
2002–03	33952	203875	61608	21.55
2003–04	34864	197160	67411	23.61
2004–05	34759	199742	64934	19.59
2005–06	36267	198036	65132	21.21
2006–07	39025	202322	59979	21.04
2007–08	40958	197580	62788	20.45

Source: *Statistical Diary*, Economics and Statistics Division, Kanpur.

Regression between land under non-agricultural uses and productive land uses

Productive Land uses	*Coef.*	*Std. Err.*	*t*	*P>t*	*[95% Conf.*	*Interval]*
Land under Non-Agricultural Uses	6.402107	0.6269007	10.21	0	5.057539	7.746676
_cons	–20536.44	19202.09	–1.07	0.303	–61720.83	20647.96

Note: Results based on Table 4.

Regression between land under non-agricultural uses and non-productive land uses

Non-productive Land use	*Coef.*	*Std. Err.*	*t*	*P>t*	*[95% Conf.*	*Interval]*
Land under Non Agricultural Uses	1.91332	0.192158	9.96	0	1.501182	2.325458
_cons	–2680.672	5885.836	–0.46	0.656	–15304.54	9943.191

Note: Results based on Table 23.4.

Regression between land under non-agricultural uses and Productivity

Production(Quintal per Hectare)	*Coef.*	*Std. Err.*	*t*	*P>t*	*[95% Conf.*	*Interval]*
Land under Non-Agricultural Uses	–0.007119	0.0017992	–3.96	0.001	–0.0109779	–0.0032601
_cons	295.3096	55.10966	5.36	0	177.1112	413.5081

Note: Results based on Table 23.4.

Table 23.5: Land Used for Net Area Sown in Blocks of Kanpur City

Blocks / Villages	*1998*	*2008*
Kakwan	7341	7325
Chaubepur	12064	11995
Kalyanpur	**12263**	**12712**
Shivajpur	**13920**	**12900**
Bilhaur	18141	16023
Bidhnu	18683	18774
Sarsaul	19529	18930
Patara	**20434**	**20617**
Bhitargaon	25477	22833
Ghatampur	39779	36337
Total	**187631**	**178446**

Source: *Statistical Diary*, Economics and Statistics Division, Kanpur.

land uses increased by 1.9 units, which is much less than the productive land uses.

Regression between land under non-agricultural uses and productivity presents the coefficient of –0.00719 which is negative and its impact is less. This implies that urban sprawl is a danger to food security.

VII. Amenities available in Kanpur Urban

The urban sprawl of Kanpur City has not resulted in increase in all the amenities. Though some of them have increased. Table 23.6 depicts that the number of police stations in 1994 in Kanpur city was 61 which have reduced to 33 in 2006-07. Primary schools have increased from 1614 to 1757 in 2006-07. Hospitals (Allopathic) have reduced in this district from 186 to 96. This can be due to two reasons. Either non-operational hospitals have been closed or some Homeo and Ayurvedic hospitals have increased. Family welfare centres have increased from 22 to 30 in the year 2006-2007. Rural banks have increased marginally from 4 to 5 in number in Kanpur city. Post offices have reduced in the district from 236 in 1994 to 122 in the year 2006-07. Public call offices have increased from 3810 to 4548 in the year 2006-07.

VIII. Urban Sprawl and Housing

In Kanpur Urban KDA and UP Housing Development Board develop land and allot plots for construction of HIG, MIG and LIG houses. As per

Table 23.6: Position of Amenities available within Ten Years

Basic amenities	*1994*	*2006–07*
Police station	61	33
Primary school	1614	1757
Hospitals, primary health centres	186	96
Family Welfare	22	30
Rural Banks	4	5
Post offices	236	122
PCOs	3810	4548

Source: *Statistical Diary*, Economic and Statistics Division, Kanpur.

the latest data available UPHDB has 1126.32 hectare area in possession and out of which only 688.54 hectares have been developed. About 5 to 10 per cent residents carry out tiny activities in the unorganized sector like grocery shops, barber shops etc. at their residential areas people prefer flats or apartments over here.

Kanpur has a housing stock of about 5 lakh dwelling units as shown in the Table 23.7. Out of total houses, about 85 per cent of the houses are in urban area and remaining 15 percentages falls in the rural areas of Kanpur (Kanpur Vision Document, 2004). The *pucca* houses are 75 per cent whereas remaining 25 per cent are either semi-*pucca* or *kutcha*. As far as type of material is concerned, 82 per cent houses are made of RBC/RCC whereas 18 per cent are made of grass, leaves, mud etc.

Up to March 2006, U.P. Housing Board has developed 26,690 houses in Kanpur (Table 23.8). The vacant houses are mostly in Yojna No. 2 which are lying vacant mainly due to their location at the remote places and poor connectivity with the main city. The break up of unsold property are meant for EWS/LIG category and the major reason due to which houses remain unsold are remote location, lack of infrastructure and increase in the cost of houses due to which they become unaffordable for the poor. Fig 23.3 explains that most of the houses are vacant which have been constructed under Ashray schemes and 37 per cent houses which have not been sold belong to economically weaker sections. The unsold commercial land properties are as less as 3 per cent. Thus, the above analysis presents the picture of basic amenities and housing facilities provided in Kanpur Nagar after its urban sprawl.

Table 23.7: Type of Houses

Distribution of Census Houses by Pre–dominate Wall Material	Number	Percentage
RBC/RCC & Burn Brick Houses	415,370	82.01
Houses of grass, leaves, mud, unburnt bricks, etc.	91,105	17.99
Total	**506,475**	**100.00**

Source: Kanpur Vision Document—2020.

Table 23.8: Houses not allotted in various schemes in Kanpur city

Scheme	Year of starting the scheme (under section 32)	Acquired land (in acre)	Developed Houses	Allotted Houses	Acquired Houses	% of Acquired Houses
Yojana No.1	20.09.1980	519.74	7617	7195	5498	72.2
Yojana No.2 Phases 1&2	20.09.1980	818.34	11818	10279	8341	70.6
Yojana No.3	25.06.1982	470.30	7255	6936	4535	62.5
Total		**1808.30**	**26690**	**24410**	**18374**	**68.8**

Source: Data collected from U.P. Housing Board, 2006.

IX. Conclusions and Policy Suggestions

In conclusion, it may be mentioned that productive and non-productive uses of land are positively correlated to increase in urban sprawl in Kanpur Nagar. The impact of urban sprawl is more on non-productive land uses which is restricted to increase by lesser proportion than the productive land uses. The hypothesis that urban sprawl is a danger to food security of course, seems to be correct from the analysis of the data. Many factors may be responsible for this. Firstly, the spatial growth pattern reveals that high growth has taken place in the core area and steps to decongest the inner core are required.[1] Secondly, it may be that area under industries has increased marginally (6.42% to 6.93%) which can be due to the closure of many large scale industries in recent times. The area under public utilities has increased marginally from 6.59 per cent to 6.9 per cent recently.[2]

Thirdly, the net area sown or the agricultural land is being used for the production of leafy vegetables and all such perishable agricultural items which are used in the cities. The agricultural lands may also be used for commercial crops.

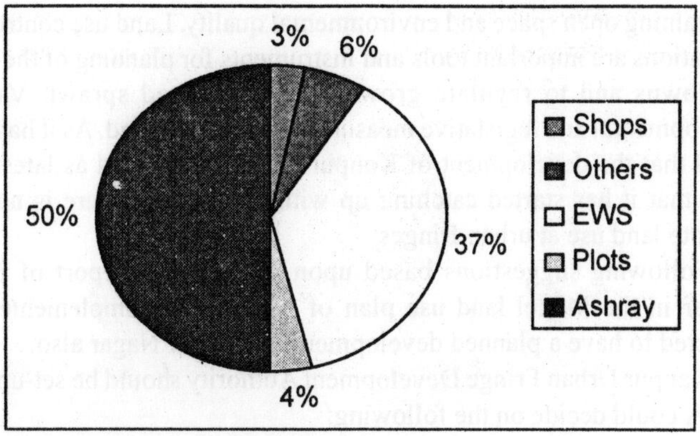

Fig. 23.3: Nature of Unsold Property.

Source: Data collected from KDA 2006, Final Report on Kanpur City Development Plan

Fourthly, as it had been hypothesized that basic amenities are not provided in rural-urban fringe, we find the proposition to be correct to some extent.

Lastly, urban sprawl results in many unsold property meant for EWS/LIG category and the major reason due to which houses remain unsold are remote location, lack of infrastructure and increase in the cost of houses.

It can be said that in spite of its Industrial characteristics Kanpur has not shown drastic problems in its fringe areas like in Gautam Buddha Nagar or Lucknow. Yet an estimated 75,000 hectares of land are being used each year which by and large mainly come from agriculture. In the fringe, there are tendencies for spot developments. Such spot growth is wasteful and is often of a sub-standard nature. The scattering of small settlements necessitates the residents to commute for a longer distance besides stretching of public utility services. Obviously, such a state of affairs is neither in the interest of public authorities nor in the interest of individual. It is, therefore, suggested that the spot development should be discouraged and compact development encouraged which is one of the major issues which needs to be considered. Decisions made today will either ensure future generations a choice of how they use the land or effectively limit their actions. Because many land use activities, specially in urban areas, result in irreversible changes, it is essential that the needs of future generations is considered. The dilemma in the regulations lies in balancing present *versus* future needs. Preservation of prime agricultural lands on the periphery of expanding cities and towns are necessary for maintaining open space and environmental quality. Land use control and regulations are important tools and instruments for planning of the cities and towns and to regulate growth and associated sprawl. Various developmental and legislative measures are to be adopted. As it has been found that the development of Kanpur Nagar has started as latest data show that it has started catching up with other cities, there is need to regulate land use at urban fringes.

Following suggestions based upon the research report of Bimal Kumar in the Model land use plan of Allahabad, if implemented are expected to have a planned development of Kanpur Nagar also.

Kanpur Urban Fringe Development Authority should be set-up. The UFDA could decide on the following:

(i) Conservation of green areas such as orchards, agriculture, social forestry and allied activities.

(ii) Development of water management and drainage system. Ponds and other water retention structures be revived. Any encroachment on such land should be identified and legal proceedings against encroachers be initiated.

(iii) The provisions made under Zamindari Abolition and Land Reforms Acts (specially sections 143 and 154) and Consolidation of Holdings Act be used effectively to check diversion of agricultural land for non-agricultural purposes.

(iv) Heavy fine should be imposed (say ten times the cost of the land) in case of such diversion on the owner of the land.

(v) In addition to it, if the agricultural land had been sold then capital gain tax should be imposed on purchaser of the land. Because huge capital gain accrues to the builders who develop colonies in such lands.

(vi) The first priority be given to development of social services in the fringe area which will include hospitals, educational centres, training centres for farmers and agro-based barren and uncultivable land should be identified for development of micro-industrial estates and then for developing multistoried residential complexes which are land saving as well.

Notes

1. Final Report, Kanpur City Development Plan Under JNNURM.
2. *Ibid.*

References

Bajpai, B.K., Fahimuddin, Tyagi, R.C., Model land use Plan for different Districts of U.P., *GIDS*, 2004.

Dhar, T.N. (2001). Resource Management and Environment, *IIPA*, U.P., Lucknow

Draft Eleventh Five Year Plan (2007-12) *Volume 1 Part 11, Annual Plan 2007-08,* p.16, Govt. of Uttar Pradesh, State Planning Commission.

Kumar Bimal, Project on Land Use Optimization in Allahabad, *G.B. Pant Social Science Institute,* Allahabad.

Mishra, G.P., Bajpai, B.K. (2004). *Development Induced Displacement: A Package for Rehabilitation in Uttar Pradesh,* New Royal, pp. 91-103.

Mishra, S.P. (2001), Management of Land Use Patterns in U.P.: Need for a Participatory Framework.

Singh, A.K. (1997), *Perspective Plan for Conservation, Management and Development of Land Resources for Central Zone of India, GIDS*, Lucknow.

Singh, Mridula, Murarilal (2004). *Land Use Planning with Special Reference to Degraded Land*, pp. 3.1-3.3.

Vaidya, B.C. (1992), Geographical Analysis of Agricultural Land Use at Kachangaon in Yashoda Basin in Maharashtra (Hindi).

24

Agricultural Dynamics of Panjoopur Village in the Rural-Urban Fringe of Aligarh

Sahila Salahuddin

Introduction

The present enquiry of the agricultural dynamics of Ramgarh Panjoopur village in the rural-urban fringe of Aligarh takes into consideration the following aspects of the study area.

Outlines of the Enquiry

(i) Location of the village in the inner fringe.
(ii) Demographic structure and social change.
(iii) The size, structure and the impact of landholdings.
(iv) Land use pattern in relation to landholdings.
(v) Size of landholding, irrigation intensity and cropping intensity.
(vi) The size of landholding has been taken as an independent variable and the agricultural dynamics as dependent variables.

Objectives of the Study

The paper enquires the spatial variation of agriculture at a sub-micro level, within a large village:

(i) In proportion to different size of landholdings.
(ii) In response to technology, inputs and social inheritance.
(iii) In relation to socio-economic conditions of the people.

Characteristics of the Inner Fringe

Rural-urban fringe is a dynamic area of:

(i) Enhanced agricultural opportunities induced by the market impulses of the city.

(ii) Urban encroachment on the docile and less sustainable village lands.

Location of Ramgarh Panjoopur

The village Ramgarh Panjoopur is located within a distance of 3 km. from the Civil Lines periphery of Aligarh city in Jawan Sikandarpur Development Block. It is a large village with a total geographical area of 406.46 sq. hectares.

Contrary to the Nearest Neighbour Analysis in Fig. 24.1, the size of the village is comparatively larger. This is because the village is located on the historically sparsely populated periphery of the Civil Lines. On the other hand, most of the villages located along the periphery of the old city are small to medium size in accordance to the theory of city and urban spacing.

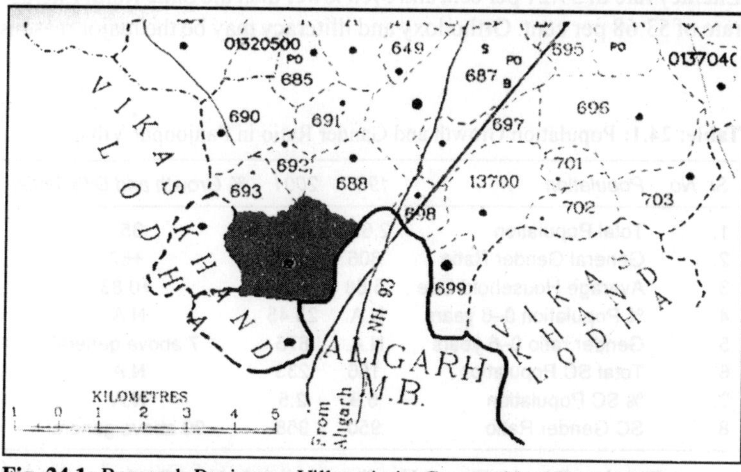

Fig. 24.1: Ramgarh Panjoopur Village in its Geographical Surroundings.

Source: Based on the Census of India, 2001.

Demographic Structure of the Village

The total population of Panjoopur including Nagla Qila and Nagla Patwari was 9,312 persons in 2001 census. The population of the village increased from 2,653 persons in 1981 to 9,312 persons in 2001. Such an exponential growth is due to the inclusion of the population of Nagla Qila and Nagla Patwari.

Table 24.1 shows a female population growth of 1.84 per cent from 44.63 per cent in 1981 to 46.47 per cent in 2001. The sex-ratio in 1981 was 806 which increased to 868 in 2001. This female population growth is a favourable sign of gender tolerance and rising status of women in the social order of the village. A higher sex-ratio of 875 in 0-6 years age group indicates a recent trend of female child acceptance. A still higher Scheduled Castes gender ratio of 950 in 1981 to 958 in 2001. This could be due to the fact that among the conservative social groups such as Muslims, Roman Catholics and the Scheduled Castes, there is a lesser degree of gender engineering and gender bias. They scarcely manipulate their natural population growth.

Low Literacy Level

The literacy level in the village so close to the city was inexplanably low at 38.82 per cent in 2001. It is considerably below the National Rural Literacy rate of 59.21 per cent and even lower than the State Rural Literacy rate of 53.68 per cent. Orthodoxy and illiteracy may be the major reasons

Table: 24.1: Population Growth and Gander Ratio in Panjoopur Village

Sr. No.	*Population*	*1981*	*2001*	*% Growth and Differential*
1.	Total Population	2,653	9,312	351
2.	General Gender Ratio	806	868	+62
3.	Average Household Size	5.88	6.71	+0.83
4.	% Population 0–6 years	N.A.	23.45	N.A.
5.	Gender ratio 0–6 years	N.A.	875	7 above general
6.	Total SC Population	156	233	N.A.
7.	% SC Population	5.9	2.5	N.A.
8.	SC Gender Ratio	950	958	90 above general

Source: Based on District Census Handbook, Aligarh, Uttar Pradesh, 1981 and 2001.

of a low gender ratio and women empowerment. Literacy of Panjoopur as a social welfare indicator is much below the average.

Structure and Impact of Landholdings

Table 24.2 and Fig. 24.2 depict the primary data of landholding structure. A total number of 405 landholdings cover 312 hectares of agricultural land in the village. Out of this, nearly 47 per cent of the landholdings are smaller than 1 hectare in size. This indicates that the largest number of fields are cultivated by the marginal farmers. About 33 per cent of the total number of landholdings are cultivated by small farmers of 1-2 hectare land. Only 18 per cent of the total number of landholdings are cultivated by the medium farmers of 2-4 hectares field. However, the largest 119 hectares of the cultivated land is under this category. A small 1.5 per cent of the total number of landholdings are cultivated by large farmers of 4-10 hectare holdings.

These large landholdings account for as much as 21.4 hectares of the land. It is critical to note that 76 per cent population of Panjoopur is landless workers. Many of them periodically to regularly come down to the next door city of Aligarh. This large percentage of landless labourers suggests that closer is a village to the city, higher is the percentage of landless people due to the higher value of land beyond their reach. Cultivation on some of the marginal farms is rendered unremunerative. Hence, they sell out their meager land and compulsively become landless workers. Many of the landless workers daily go to Aligarh city or to other villages as agricultural labourers. However, for economic and prestige reasons they do not work in their own village.

Table 24.2: Average Size of Landholdings and Land Use in Panjoopur Village

Sr. No.	*Landholding Category*	*No. of Land-holdings*	*% Land-holding*	*Average Size*	*Holdings Hectarage*	*% Area of Holdings*	*Avr. Family Size*
1.	< 1 Hectare	191	47.16	0.32	61.12	19.61	7.0
2.	1–2 Hectare	135	33.33	0.82	110.07	35.32	6.9
3.	2–4 Hectare	73	18.03	1.63	118.99	38.19	7.4
4.	4–10 Hectare	6	1.48	3.57	21.42	6.88	7.5
5.	> 10 Hectare	Nil	Nil	Nil	Nil	Nil	Nil
	Total	**405**	**100.00**	**1.58**	**311.60**	**100.00**	**7.2**

Source: Computed from Primary Data.

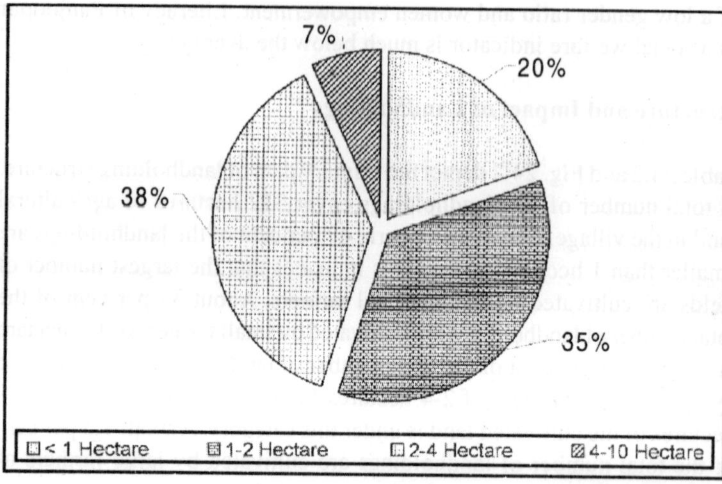

Fig. 24.2: Percentage Area to Each Landholding Category in Panjoopur Village.

Source: Based on Primary Data and Field Survey.

Major Findings

As much as 74.5 per cent of the cultivated land in Panjoopur is under the control of medium and small farmers. There are only 3 government tube wells and 4 private tube wells in the village. This speaks of inadequate irrigation facilities and low irrigation intensity. As a result, the double cropped area to the net sown area is not very large. Hence, the cropping intensity is also low. Such an infrastructural inadequacy reveals that Panjoopur is not a developed village. About 76 per cent of the population is landless and 10 per cent is marginal farmers. Hence, there is growing evidence of marginalization in Ramgarh Panjoopur. Only 5 per cent population of the village represents the medium and large farmers.

Conclusion and Suggestion

As per our understanding of the Yon Thunen's model of location of agricultural activities and zonation of agricultural intensity, we had an expectation of: (i) High infrastructural facilities, (ii) Resultant agricultural development. It appears that the village is not properly integrated to the city gravity. There is a marked heterogeneity in land assets and a telling socio-economic disparity in the village.

The large farmers often have ownership landholdings bigger than the operational landholdings. Hence, the surplus land is rendered unused in the form of old fallow and culturable wastes. This renders a lower per unit area productivity of large landholdings. The lands left uncultivated for more than 5-7 years may be transferred to the landless people in the village. There should be at least 1 efficient tube well of the Gram Panchayat for every 20 hectares of the agricultural lands in the villages. Farm produce exploitation by the middleman should be minimized. The rural marketing system should evolve a mandatory "Protection Prices" particularly for the perishable produce.

References

Administrative Atlas, Uttar Pradesh, Vol. I, *Census of India,* 2001, Directorate of Census Operations, Uttar Pradesh, Lucknow.

District Revenue Office, Collectorate, Aligarh.

District Statistical Handbook, Uttar Pradesh, Census of India, 1981.

District Statistical Handbook, Uttar Pradesh, Census of India, 2001.

District Level Household and Facility Survey, *Fact Sheet,* Uttar Pradesh, Ministry of Health and Family Welfare, Govt. of India, 2008.

Provisional Population Totals, Uttar Pradesh, *Census of India,* 2001, Lucknow.

Statistical Abstract, 2004, *Central Statistical Organization,* Govt. of India, New Delhi.

25

Common Land Resource Utilization for Socio-Economic Development in the Fringe Areas of Allahabad: A Case Study

Mohammad Sadiq Salman and *Abdul Munir*

Introduction

India is basically an agricultural country where a major of its population lives in rural areas with agriculture as basic means of livelihood. Therefore, livelihood of majority of the people depends upon the land resource. As the population is continuously increasing there is an immense pressure on the land resources of the country, especially on the agricultural land. The share of landless and small farmers is largest among the total farmers. As their own land resources are insignificant they rely upon the Common Land Resources (CLR) for their livelihood. Scholars of various discipline specially Sociologists, Economists and Geographers have done research in various aspects of common land resources. Many scholars have done research in the various dimensions of Common Property Resources (CPR) in general and CLR in particular. Hardin (1968) in his paper entitled 'The Tragedy of Commons' has rightly stated 'ruin is the destination towards which all men reach, each pursuing his own interest in a society that believes in the freedom of the Commons'. The same concept of common property resources has been advocated by Jodha (1986) where he has defined Common Property Resources (CPR) as the resources owned in common by an identifiable group of people regulated by social conventions and legally enforceable rules. In India, the Common Land Resources (CLR) have been broadly classified by Mohammed (1981) into forest, barren and uncultivated land, pasture and grazing land, culturable wastelands and fallow lands other than current fallow.

Since the common land resources are by and large no one's exclusive property they are exploited and improperly utilized for the private benefit. Hence, proper management of CLR is essential. As far as utilization of common land resources is concerned, this is an important aspect while taking into consideration the economic value or the economic gains of the people by the proper and optimal utilization of CLR. A number of studies have been undertaken in this respect. Bajpai (2005) has studied the factors promoting wasteland and the methods to reclaim them. Besides, many studies have been undertaken to observe the degradation of forests, grazing lands etc.

The fringe area is the zone of transition. There is a continuous change in the utilization of resources and services in this zone. The people of the fringe experience the rural as well as urban influences. Many studies have been undertaken regarding the concept, delineation, and land use change in the fringe areas in India and abroad the notable ones are Galster G. *et al.*, (2001), Srivastava B. and R. Ramachandran (1974). Some studies regarding the socio-economic status of the inhabitants of fringe areas have also been undertaken by scholars but they have not studied the role of CLR in the socio-economic development of the people in the fringe area.

The above review of literature clearly reveals that a number of studies have been conducted to study the concept, delineation, land use change in the fringe areas. Also the use and misuse of Common Property Resources (CPR) in general and Common Land Resources (CLR) in particular have been undertaken by many scholars but there are very few studies related to the role of CLR on socio-economic development of the inhabitants in the fringe area. As the utilization of CLR is economically beneficial there is a need for its role in the socio-economic development of the people in the fringe areas. Thus, the present study is an attempt to focus the role of CLR on the socio-economic development of people in general and particularly landless and small farmers in the fringe areas of Allahabad City.

Objectives

The present study has the following objectives:

(1) To study the spatio-temporal distribution of common land resources in the Allahabad District.

(2) To analyse the dependency of inhabitants of sampled village on the common land resources.

(3) To examine the role of common land resources upon the socio-economic development of people in the sampled village.

(4) To make few suggestive remarks for the optimal utilization of CLR.

Data Base and Methodology

The study is based on the primary data collected through field survey supplemented with secondary information obtained from various sources like, (i) Statistical Abstract of India, (ii) Statistical Abstract of Allahabad District, (iii) Agricultural Statistics at a Glance, (iv) State Land use and Board, Lucknow, and (v) Directorate of Statistics and Economics, Lucknow.

The field study has been conducted in the sampled village Kathaula in 2007. The village was selected on the basis of population size and accessibility. Total number of households in the village is accounted for 250. Thus, 50 per cent of households, i.e. 125 were taken as sample for the pilot study. The data regarding the population of the sampled village and the social structure was obtained from the village *pradhan* (Political head of Gram Panchayat). The collected data have been processed using simple percentage technique and have been represented using suitable tables and diagrams.

Study Area

The district of Allahabad selected as the study area is located in the eastern part of Uttar Pradesh. Allahabad is located between 24° 47' North and 25° 43' North latitudes and between 81° 31' East to 82° 21' East longitudes. It covers an area of 5482 sq. km. The total rural area is 5339.28 sq. kms. and the urban area is 142.72 sq. km. This district lies in the southern part of the state in the Ganga plain. River Ganga and Yamuna flow through the district. From administrative point of view, the district has been divided into 8 Tahsils and 20 blocks which include 3065 villages (District Statistical Abstract, 2005). The Ganga, the Yamuna and the Tons are important rivers of the district. River Yamuna joins Ganga at Sangam in Allahabad. Besides these rivers, there are many lakes also. On the basis of physiography, the district can be divided into Gangapaar, Yamunapaar and Doab region. The Gangapaar region has "Khadar" soil formed by floods. The Doab region has fertile alluvial soil whereas the Yamunapaar region possesses light sandy soil full of granules.

Common Land Resources of Allahabad District

The common land resource includes forests, pastures and grazing lands, culturable wasteland, barren and uncultivated lands other than current fallow and fallow lands. The share of total area under the common land resources is calculated to be 16.49 per cent of the total geographical area of the district. It has been observed that the share of other fallow land is largest followed by barren and uncultivable land. On adding the area under other fallow land and barren and uncultivated land their total share becomes 56.03 per cent of the total common land resources in the district. The next important category in the common land resources is forest and cultivable wasteland. The area under permanent grazing and pasture land

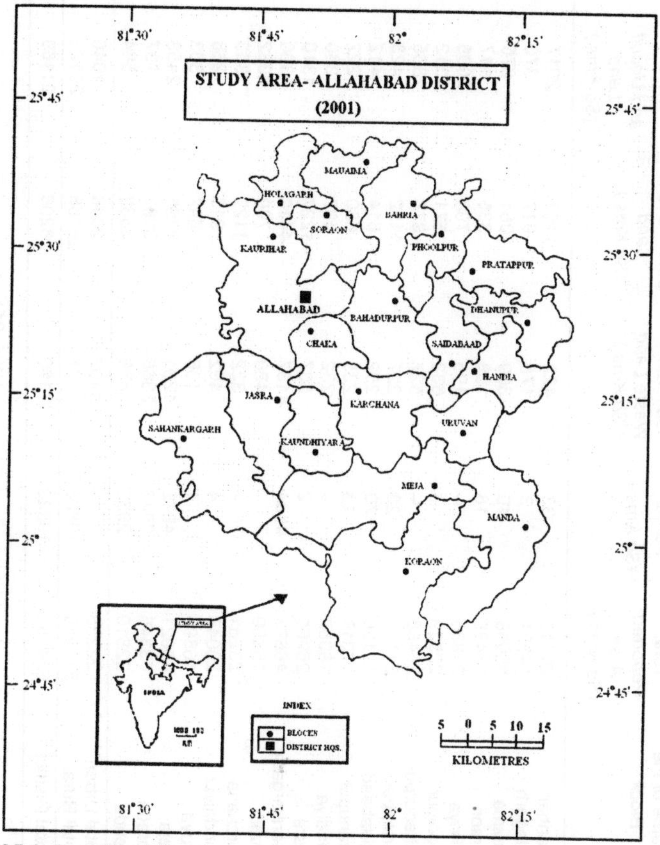

Fig. 25.1: Location Map.

Table 25.1: Block-wise Share of Different Categories of Common Land Resources in Allahabad District (1995-96)

Name of the Block	Total Reported Area (Sq.Kms.)	Forest (Sq.Kms.)	Culturable Waste Land (Sq.Kms.)	Other Fallow Land (Sq.Kms.)	Barren and Uncult. Land (Sq.Kms.)	Permanent Pasture/ Grazing Land (Sq.Kms.)	Share of Common Land Resources (In %)
Koarihar	20713	33	422	1463	2017	76	19.36
Holagarh	14831	3	178	917	370	105	10.61
Mauima	15058	40	309	1061	670	93	14.43
Soraon	13485	18	108	335	147	14	4.61
Bahriya	24835	–	195	798	2005	125	12.57
Phoolpur	22529	–	632	571	1312	175	11.94
Bahadurpur	26468	–	527	876	2865	2	16.13
Partappur	21101	23	227	1152	423	26	8.77
Saidabaad	19126	70	252	614	412	7	7.08
Dhanupur	17317	13	235	680	222	12	6.71
Handiya	16067	–	232	497	330	7	6.63
Jasra	26960	2	507	1227	1310	5	11.32
Shankargarh	46673	4804	4137	4410	1300	12	31.41
Chaka	15359	–	480	730	2032	–	21.10
Karchana	23281	–	322	1127	363	2	7.79
Kondhiyar	20046	4	402	913	268	61	8.22
Uruva	16890	1	136	697	303	1	6.74
Meja	45021	4872	1281	2395	2453	3	24.44
Koraon	73346	7013	3366	3063	737	983	20.67
Manda	32810	2932	1839	2632	584	11	24.37
Total Urban	22235	–	1403	2048	1046	6	20.25
Total Rural	511916	19828	15787	26158	20123	1720	16.33
Total District	534151	19828	17190	28206	21169	1726	16.49

Source: Statistical Booklet of Allahabad District (1995-96).

is just 2 per cent which is of great concern because the existence of the livestock in the district is largely dependent upon the grazing land and pastures.

Spatial Distribution of Common Land Resources

The share of common land resources vary from 4.61 per cent in Soraon to 31.41 per cent in the Shankargarh block. Thus, there is a large range of distribution of common land resources. The share of various categories of the common land resources also varies in different blocks. The block-wise share of different categories of Common Land Resources (1995) is shown In Table 25.1 whereas the block-wise distribution of Common Land Resources (1995) is shown in Fig. 25.2.

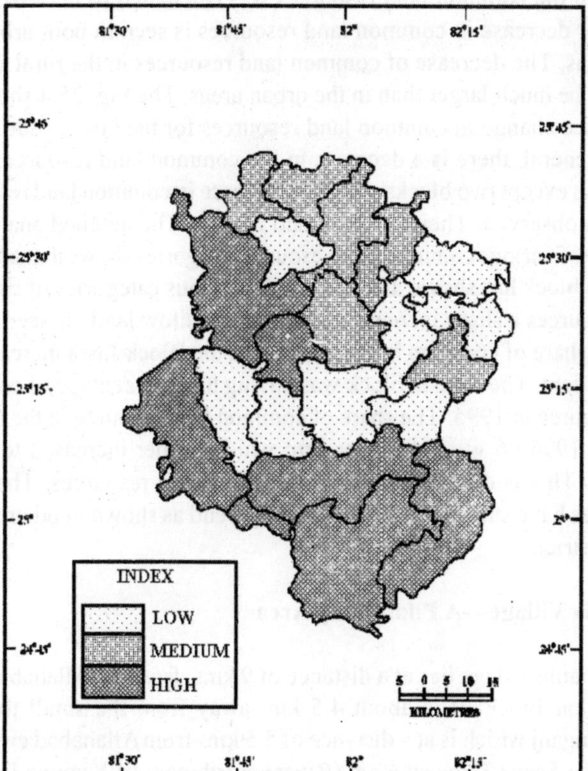

Fig. 25.2: Spatial Distribution of Common Land Resources in Allahabad District (1995).

The common land resources are being utilized indiscriminately by the people to get the maximum benefit. Thus, these resources are continuously depleting. The block-wise distribution of common land resources in 2005 shows a change in the share of common land resources in all the blocks. The block-wise share of different categories of common land resources (2005) is shown in Table 25.2 whereas the block-wise distribution of common land resources (2005) is shown in Fig. 25.3.

Temporal Change of Common Land Resources in Allahabad District

After analyzing the common land resources of the Allahabad district between 1995-96 and 2005-06 it has been found that there is an overall decrease in the common land resources during the last decade. The decadal change in the common land resources was calculated to be—10.98 per cent. The decrease in common land resources is seen in both urban and rural areas. The decrease of common land resources in the rural areas is found to be much larger than in the urban areas. The Fig. 25.4 shows the block-wise change in common land resources for the last decade.

In general, there is a decrease in the common land resources in all the blocks except two blocks where an increase in common land resources has been observed. They are Jasra and Manda. The detailed analysis of the share of various common land resource categories shows that although the Jasra block has shown a decline in the various categories of common land resources a sharp increase in the "other Failow land" is seen. Thus, the total share of common land resources in the Block Jasra increased by 4.20 per cent. The Manda block was having high percentage of common land resource in 1995. The share of common land resource in the Manda block in 1995-96 was 24.37 per cent which further increased to 26.63 per cent. This is due to the increase in the forest resources. The other categories have shown a similar declining trend as shown in other blocks of the district.

Kathaula Village—A Pilot Study Area

The Kathaula village lies at a distance of 9 kms. from the Allahabad City in Kaurihar block. It is about 4.5 km. away from the small town of Dhoomanganj which is at a distance of 5.5 kms from Allahabad city (Fig. 25.5). The *Sasur Khaderi Nadi* (River), a tributary of Yamuna is about 6.5 kms. away from the village. The village is well connected with Dhoomanganj town, Bamrauli air strip, Subedarganj railway station, G.T.

Table 25.2: Block-wise Share of Different Categories of Common Land Resources in Allahabad District (2005-06)

Name of the Block	*Total Reported Area (Sq.Kms.)*	*Forest (Sq.Kms.)*	*Culturable Waste Land (Sq.Kms.)*	*Other Fallow Land (Sq.Kms.)*	*Barren and Uncult Land (Sq.Kms.)*	*Permanent Pasture/ Grazing Land (Sq.Kms.)*	*Share of Common Land Resources (In %)*
Koarihar	42035	132	483	4017	1784	84	15.46
Holagarh	14846	0	170	739	250	105	8.51
Mauima	15060	12	240	622	658	84	10.73
Soraon	13485	10	214	280	123	18	4.78
Bahriya	24875	0	195	733	883	125	7.78
Phoolpur	22529	0	628	342	1183	175	10.33
Bahadurpur	26468	0	527	885	2149	2	13.46
Partappur	21101	1	79	604	367	26	5.10
Saidabaad	19142	2	84	458	454	7	5.25
Dhanupur	17322	18	102	318	191	12	3.70
Handiya	16067	0	215	191	340	9	4.70
Jasra	26958	0	502	2402	1276	5	15.52
Shankargarh	46908	4818	4137	4003	1525	12	30.90
Chaka	15359	0	401	782	1801	0	19.42
Karchana	23281	0	360	474	131	2	4.15
Kondhiyar	20046	0	325	764	113	61	6.30
Uruva	16890	0	136	590	301	2	6.09
Meja	44221	3983	1269	2140	2400	1	22.14
Koraon	71942	6115	365	1702	55	918	12.72
Manda	34643	4765	1735	2273	450	3	26.63
Total Rural	533178	19856	12167	24319	16433	1651	13.96
Total Urban	22235	0	1307	2185	815	0	19.37
Total District	555413	19856	13474	26504	17248	1651	14.17

Source: Statistical Booklet of Allahabad District (2005-06).

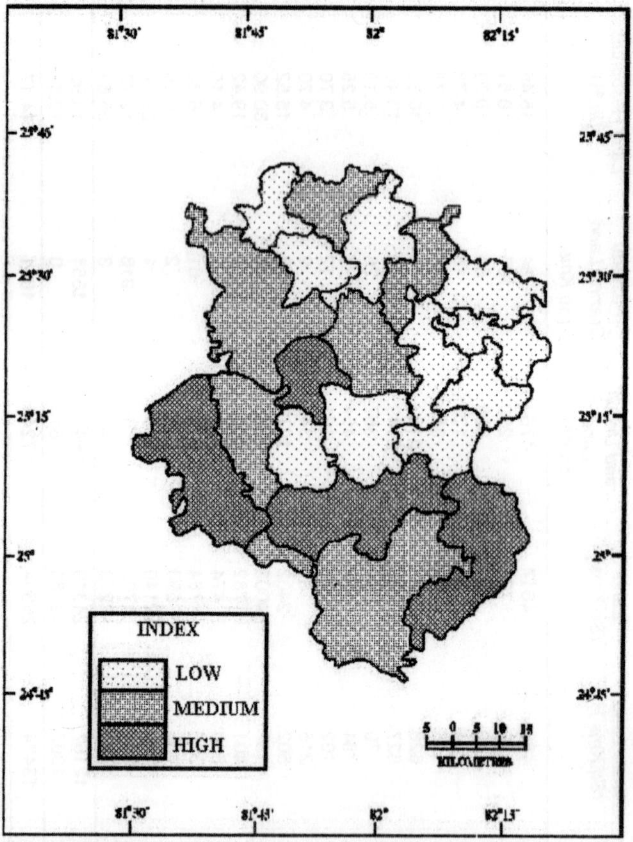

Fig. 25.3: Spatial Distribution of Common Land Resources in Allahabad District (2005).

road and the nearby villages with metalled as well as unmetalled road. Total population of the village is reported to be 1700 and the approximate number of households is 250. Kathaula village is having two major religious communities, i.e. Hindus and the Muslims living in harmonious relationship in socio-cultural sphere. People of the different castes of Hindus residing together in the village are Chamar, Dhobi, Harijan, Kushwaha and Madari. Majority of the people are found to be illiterate and large section of them is not having any land. Besides, those having own land have either small or marginal farms. A very few of them have big size landholdings.

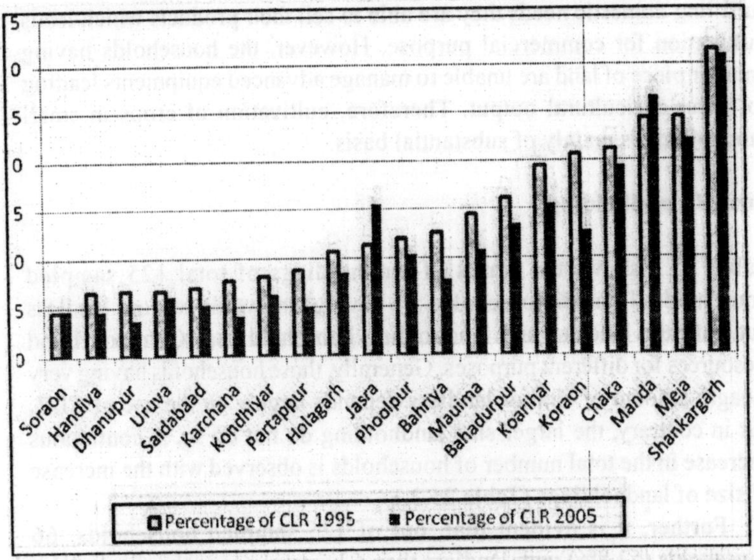

Fig. 25.4: Block-wise Decadal Change in Common Land Resources in Allahabad District (1995-2005).

Socio-Economic Profile of the Households

People from most of the major caste groups like Chamar, Dhobi, Harijan, Kushwaha and Madari and Muslims have been surveyed for the present study. In the village, largest share of Harijan (28%) followed by Chamar (21.2%) and Muslims (19.3%) have been reported. Majority of the households are having joint family with varying family size accounting family members from 3 to 20 persons in some cases. The people are not inclined towards education rather are interested in earning at early age to assist their family. Consequently, lower rate of literacy prevails there.

Although agriculture is the major economic activity of the people of Kathaula village but other activities like, private shop or marketing of goods and rearing of cattle and livestock are important means of livelihood. Those who are educationally better are engaged in clerical jobs and teachings are also involved in agricultural activities. However, landless people are involved in very low earning activities like rickshaw pulling, agricultural labouring, labour in non-farm sector, private business and shop keeping etc.

It is observed that the families having very large size of landholdings are utilizing modern and advanced farm mechanization, therefore, after fulfilling domestic needs they are able to sell their products which leads cultivation for commercial purpose. However, the households having smaller piece of land are unable to manage advanced equipments leading to lower agricultural output. Therefore, cultivation of crops in small landholding is mainly of substantial basis.

Size of Landholding

Table 25.3 shows the status of landholdings of total 125 sampled households. Total 86 households are having land while rest are landless but both the landless and landholding household uses Common Land Resources for different purposes. Generally, those households having very meagre amount of land or landless depends largely on the use of CLR, but in contrary, the larger size landholding do not do so. A continuous decrease in the total number of households is observed with the increase of size of landholdings (Table 25.3.)

Further, it is evident that, out of 125 sampled households, 66 households (52.8%) with landless than 6 hectares are categorised under small landholdings (Table 25.3). However, only 8 households, i.e. 6.4 per cent of the village with land more than 12 hectares are large size of landholdings. It is interesting to note that 82.05 per cent (32 households) of the landless households utilizes CLR for different purposes to maintain domestic expenditure partially or entirely. Besides, more than 62 per cent of the households of small size landholdings are using CLR. In contrary, 25 per cent of the large size landholding households use CLR as a supplementary to their different activities. Therefore, it is revealed that,

Table 25.3: Landholding-wise Share of Total Respondents Using CLR in Kathaula Village (2007)

Category of land-holding	*Size of Landholding (Hectares)*	*Sampled Household*		*Household Using CLR*	
		Number	*Per cent*	*Number*	*% to Sampled Household*
Landless	0	39	31.2	32	82.05
Small	<6	66	52.8	41	62.12
Medium	6–12	12	9.6	04	33.33
Large	>12	08	6.4	02	25.0
Total	—	125	100	79	63.2

Source: Based on Field Survey (2007).

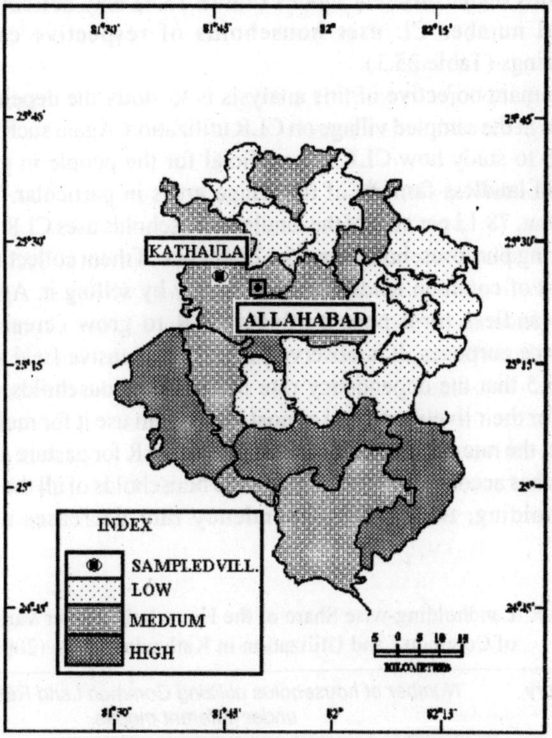

Fig. 25.5: Sampled Village (2005).

79 households, i.e. 63.2 per cent of total 125 sampled households of Kathaula village are reportedly using CLR (Table 25.3).

Mode of Utilization of Common Land Resources

The households were found to utilize the Common Land Resources in various ways. The most common mode of utilization is grazing and pasture followed by agro-forestry and crop cultivation. CLR were also found to be used as manure pits, cemeteries, storage grounds, playgrounds, temporary construction of sheds for animals, storage of fodder and storage of agricultural produce etc. Table 25.4 reveals the share of the households under various modes of Common Land (CL) utilization. It is worthy to mention that, a household uses CLR for more than one purpose. For instance, a household may use CL for pasture and grazing, for agro-forestry and for crop cultivation also. Therefore, total number of CL user households under different modes (Table 25.4) may not correspond to the total number CL user households of respective category of landholdings (Table 25.3).

The main objective of this analysis is to study the dependency rate of people in the sampled village on CLR utilization. Again such an analysis will help to study how CLR is beneficial for the people in general and small and landless farmers of the fringe areas in particular. Table 25.4 reveals that, 78.12 per cent of the landless households uses CLR for pasture and grazing purposes, however, 65.12 per cent of them collect wood from the forest of common lands and earn money by selling it. Again 50 per cent of landless rural poor cultivate CLR to grow cereal crops for subsistence purposes. It is observed from the intensive field survey and Table 25.5 that the dependency rate of landless households on CLR is highest for their livelihood and almost all of them use it for multipurpose. However, the rate of dependency on the use of CLR for pasture and grazing purposes has accounted highest among the households of all the categories of landholding, though the dependency rate decreases among the

Table 25.4: Landholding-wise Share of the Households under Various Modes of Common Land Utilization in Kathaula Village (2007)

Category of Landholding	*Number of households utilizing Common Land Resources under different modes*				
	Total Households	*Pasture & Grazing*	*Agro-Forestry (Fuelwood collection)*	*Crop Cultivation*	*Other*
Landless	32	25 (78.12)	21 (65.62)	16 (50.0)	06 (18.75)
Small	41	28 (68.29)	07 (17.07)	23 (56.10)	05 (12.19)
Medium	04	02 (50.0)	0 (0)	01 (25.0)	01 (25.0)
Large	02	01 (50)	0 (0)	0 (0)	01 (50.0)
Total	79	56 (70.88)	28 (35.44)	40 (50.63)	13 (16.45)

Source: Based on Field Survey (2007).

Note: Figures in bracket show percentage of total households under concerned mode to total number of households of respective category of landholding.

households with increasing size of landholding. It is evident that, 17.07 per cent household of small size landholding depend on CLR for collecting forest wood for sale, earning and assisting domestic expenditure, however 56.10 per cent household of this category depend on CLR for crop cultivation to fulfil their family needs. No one household of medium and large size landholding category depends on CLR for forest wood collection, while 1 household (i.e., 25%) of medium size landholding and no one of large size landholding category uses CLR for crop cultivation (Table 25.4). It may be argued that the availability of CLR is significant for the socio-economic development of landless and households with small landholding. They use it for rearing the cattle and collecting forest wood for maintaining family expenditure, and crop cultivation to sustain family needs of foodgrains.

Cost-Benefit Analysis

As the agricultural activity in India is no longer subsistence one rather it has become an economic activity where farmers are more concerned with cost-benefit analysis of their agricultural produce. Thus, an attempt has been made to estimate the landholding-wise cost-benefit analysis of agricultural activity of the sampled households.

The farmers having small landholdings get a benefit of 121.05 per cent over their input cost per hectare while the farmers of medium and large size landholdings get a benefit of 116.53 and 115.53 per cent respectively (Table 25.5). Here we can easily see the decreasing trend of benefit with the increasing size of landholding. The main reason for this seems to be the different land use pattern among the various farmers in different categories. The farmers of small landholdings tend to cultivate wheat and rice only for subsistence purposes and other crops are not cultivated much, while the farmers having large size landholdings cultivate sugarcane, bajra, maize, potato etc. The farmers of medium size landholdings have to employ more numbers of agricultural labourers than those in the small size landholdings resulted into the increase of output cost. The farmers having large size of landholdings generally use tractors and machines in the agriculture thus their input cost per hectare is lesser than farmers having medium size landholdings.

Therefore, small size landholders are much gainer than medium and large size landholders. It may be said that for the enhancement of ratio of benefit, planning should be made for the modernization of farm mechanization.

Table 25.5: Cost–Benefit Analysis of Agriculture on Own Land (excluding the use of CLR) in Kathaula Village (2007)

Category of Land-holding	*Average Input/Hect. (A) (in Rs.)*	*Average. Output/Hect. (B) (in Rs.)*	*Average. Income/Hect. (C) (in Rs.)*	*Ratio of Benefit D=(C/A) X 100*
Landless	0	0	0	0
Small	6,230	13,771	7,541	121.04
Medium	8,970	19,423	10,453	116.53
Large	9,755	21,005	11,250	115.33

Source: Based on Field Survey (2007).

Cost-Benefit Analysis of Use of Common Land Resources

Here an attempt has been made to analyse the relative difference of benefits of utilization of common land among the households of different size of landholdings. It is well-known that, no input cost is incurred for pasture and grazing, and forest wood collection. In such modes of utilization, individual get only output, therefore, total output is profits. But in the analysis, for convenience, total input (wherever incurred for crop cultivation only) and output has been taken and their average has been computed over households of respective category. Table 25.6 reveals that highest ratio of benefits, i.e. Rs. 170.20 per cent has been recorded by households of small size of landholding, which is followed by landless households getting a benefit of Rs. 165.64 per cent. However, large size landholdings get a benefit of Rs. 102.43 per cent which is much lower than small landholding and landless households. It is mainly due to the higher dependency of landless and small size landholding households on the common lands for pasture and grazing and for forest wood collection purposes in which they don't need to invest money as input cost but only earn money though in very meagre amount. Their earning from it is the means of livelihood. Therefore, with very little earning is the misery of their life and level of living. It may be argued that, higher dependency and higher ratio of benefit from the use of CLR reveals poor socio-economic condition of the inhabitants, as its utilization is the only way of their livelihood.

Comparative Analysis of Agricultural and C.L.R. Income

Again it is evident from Table 25.7 that entire income from utilization of land for livelihood of landless households come from common land

Table 25.6: Cost-Benefit Analysis of Use of Common Land Resources

Category	*Average. Input/Hect. (A) (in Rs.)*	*Average. Output/Hect. (B) (in Rs.)*	*Average. Income/Hect. (C) (in Rs.)*	*Ratio of Benefit D=(C/A) X 100*
Landless	4700	12485	7785	165.64
Small	3510	9484	5974	170.20
Medium	2935	6675	3740	127.43
Large	2960	5992	3032	102.43

Source: Based on Field Survey (2007).

resources, however, households of large size landholding marginally depend on it. Whatever the share of income of households of large size landholding is accounted from CLR, is only by means of saving the amount from rearing cattle on the CLR, i.e. pasture and grazing. In comparison to agricultural income, 100 per cent share of income of landless households come from the utilization of CLR, however, it shares 21.23 per cent among the households of large size landholdings (Table 25.7).

The analysis clearly reveals that the landless households are highly dependent upon the common land resources for their sustenance while considerable share in the total income of small farmers also comes from it. Thus, the common land resources significantly contribute to the socio-economic development of landless and small farmers.

Conclusion

The foregoing study reveals that the Common Land Resources are accounted for 16.49 per cent to the total geographical area of the district. The maximum users are landless people followed by people having small, medium and large landholdings. The maximum share of income from CLR is recorded among the landless households, which accounts 100 per cent followed by households with small landholdings (44.20%). Thus, it becomes evident that there is a significant role of common land resources in the socio-economic development of the people in the fringe areas of Allahabad city. The optimal use of Common Land Resources is necessary.

The study regarding role of common resources on the socio-economic development of landless and small farmers reveals that the common land resources have significant impact upon socio-economic development of the people in the fringe areas of Allahabad city. As the share of income from CLR is quite significant in the total income of the landless and small farmers there is a need to utilize the CLR properly for the sustained

Table 25.7: Comparative Analysis of Agriculture and Common Land Resources

Category of landholding	*Income from Agriculture on own land (in Rs.)*	*Income from CLR (in Rs.)*	*Total Income (in Rs.)*	*Share of CLR to total Income (%)*
Landless	0	7785	7785	100
Small	7541	5974	13515	44.20
Medium	10453	3740	14193	26.35
Large	11250	3032	14282	21.23

Source: Based on Field Survey (2007).

socio-economic development of these deprived classes in the fringe areas of Allahabad in future. The proper utilization of the CLR can only lead to sustainable socio-economic development of the people in the fringe areas. Thus, few suggestions have been put forward to achieve this goal are as follows:

1. The proper survey of the Common Land Resources should be undertaken by the government.
2. The present state of the Common Land Resources should be analysed.
3. The poor and landless people of any area should be allotted these lands for small period of time.
4. The forests and pastures should be protected from misuse and overuse.
5. The government should encourage social forestry and agro-forestry.

References

Bajpai, M. (2005). 'Utilization of Wasteland in Ganga-Yamuna Doab' in Pandey, B.W. (ed.) *Natural Resource Management*, Mittal Publications, New Delhi.

District Statistical Abstract, Allahabad (1995).

District Statistical Abstract, Allahabad (2005).

Galster, G., R. Hanson, M.R. Ratcliffe, H. Wolman, S. Coleman, and J. Friehage. (2001). Wrestling sprawl to the ground: Defining and measuring an elusive concept. *Housing Policy Debate* 12(4): 681-717.

Hardin, G. (1968). The Tragedy of Commons, *Science*, Vol. 162, No. 3859, pp. 1243-1248.

Jodha, N.S. (1986). 'Population Growth and Decline in Common Property Resources in Rajasthan, India', *Population and Development Review*, Vol. 11, No. 2.

Mohammad, N. (1997). 'Agricultural Development and Environmental Degradation in Sonipat District, Haryana', *National Geographical Journal of India,* Vol. 43(3), Banaras Hindu University, Varanasi.

Mohammad, N. (1981). 'Perspectives in Agricultural Geography—Framework of Agriculture', Vol. III, Concept Publishers, New Delhi.

Mohammad, N. (1998). 'Participatory Management of Common Land Resources in Saryupar Plain: Some Issues and Problems', Paper presented at *Seminar on Participatory Management of Natural Resources,* October 29-30, 1998, Lucknow, Uttar Pradesh.

Srivastava, B. and R. Ramachandran (1974). 'The Rural-Urban Fringe', *The Geographical Journal of India,* Vol. XLIX, p. 19.

Part V

Land Acquisition and Livelihood Issues

26

Land Acquisition Problems under Special Economic Zones (SEZs): Experiences and Evidences from India

N.M.P. Verma and *Vinit Kumar*

Introduction

The logic of SEZs is based on several propositions. They may attract large-scale foreign capital and modern technology, strengthen export orientation by boosting net export earnings and create employment in labour intensive export industries and rural-urban fringe. After India's Independence in 1947, the Indian Government accepted planned economy where the "Commanding heights" were to be occupied by the government. Liberalization was a far cry and not the demand of the day not even for the industrialists who drew up the so-called "Bombay Plan" in 1944-45, in anticipation of Independence, leading industrialists issued what they called "A Plan of Economic Development for India". In the early stages of industrialization, industrialists such as illustrious G.D. Birla, J.R.D. Tata, Kasturibhai Lalbhai, A.D. Shroff and John Mathai said that, "The state should exercise in the interests of the community, considerable measure of intervention and control," where, "An enlargement of the positive as well as the preventative functions of the state is essential to any large scale planning".

The development of Special Economic Zones (SEZs) is one such element which is currently leading to a great deal of conflicts between various actors—either political or societal.

The previous Commerce and Industry Minister's answer to this was to improve the climate for exports with FDI as he realized the need for domestic enterprises and manufacturers for India to be competitive globally—as well as raising the infrastructure base also in hitherto underdeveloped regions of India. Since 2000, the government has been seriously thinking of promoting Indian Special Economic Zones, which the aforementioned Minister, Mr. Murasoli Maran, once described as, "Our best dream projects" and as "Magnet and glue-magnet to attract FDI and glue to identify and plan strategies that will benefit a large number of people and organizations. The objective of the present paper is to give the theoretical background of the Rural-Urban development to examine the developmental issues under expansion of SEZs in various States including Uttar Pradesh, shifting problem of land from agricultural to industrial like SEZs and the changes thereof. For this, there would be shifting of land from agriculture/rural to industry/SEZs/urban sector.

Rural-Urban Transformation Model

The relationships between the urban and rural areas of a developing economy like India encompass the terms of trade between rural wages of labour in the two sectors, the intersect oral transfer of saving, the relative sectoral returns to investment, the relative sectoral contributions to tax revenue and benefits from public expenditure and the extent to which government policies favour on sector over the other. There are at least three sets of theoretical frameworks for the analysis of these relationships:

(a) The Lewis model of economic growth with surplus rural labour,
(b) The 'coercive', or 'price-scissors',
(c) Model of economic policy is subject to 'urban basis (Knight and Song, 1999).

(a) Lewis Model

The industrial sector expands by drawing on abundant rural labour in perfectly elastic supply and reinvesting industrial profits. With industrial development in a market economy, the supply curve of labour eventually becomes inelastic owing to a rising Marginal Product of Labour (MPL) in agriculture and a relative improvement in the price of agricultural goods; in a competitive labour market, the urban wage begins product of labour in agriculture and a relative improvement in the price of agricultural goods; in a competitive labour market, the urban wages begins to rise. Thus, the model implies an eventual improvement in the rural-urban terms of trade, an intersect oral transfer of labour but not of capital, and intersectoral equality in labour income. (Also see, Krishnamurty, 2008).

(b) Scissors Model

It is possible for government to finance the growth of the industrial sector in a socialist economy by reducing the producer price of agriculture in relation to industrial goods. By coercing rural people and depressing their real consumption, government can effectively transfer rural saving to finance industrial capital accumulation. This is the model that was followed in the Soviet Union. It implies an initial deterioration in the rural-urban terms of trade an intersectoral transfer of both labour and capital, and government policies with regard to pricing, tax and investment that favour industry over agriculture (also see, Mittal).

(c) Urban Bias

In economic policies, government systematically favours the urban over the rural sector owing to the political power of urban-dwellers. It is argued that, although they normally form a minority of the population of poor countries, urban-dwellers exercise an influence on government policy which is disproportionate to their numbers. This may be because of urban residence, *per se*, the proletariat being politically more aware, more militant, and better organized than the peasantry; or it may be that certain dominant groups, such as the industrialists, the bureaucrats, or the educated, are mainly urban. The forms of urban bias might include credit, trade, exchange rate, tax and government expenditure policies to favour industry or urban areas. The government is seen to encourage or permit the emergence of a wage differential in favour of urban employment. This relative increase in urban private and public consumption, in turn, induces rural-urban migration in excess of the absorptive capacity of the urban sector. There will be rise to urban unemployment and poverty, unless the migration is controlled to protect urban-dwellers. Thus the model implies excessive intersectoral transfer of labour and capital, and relatively high urban wages.

The Lewis and Price-scissors models have been depicted in Figure 26.1. The horizontal axis, OO', measures the supply of labour in the economy, assumed to be fixed. The curve MPL_a shows the marginal product of labour in the agricultural (here equated with rural) sector. Industrial (urban) employment is measured leftwards from O'. The Indian

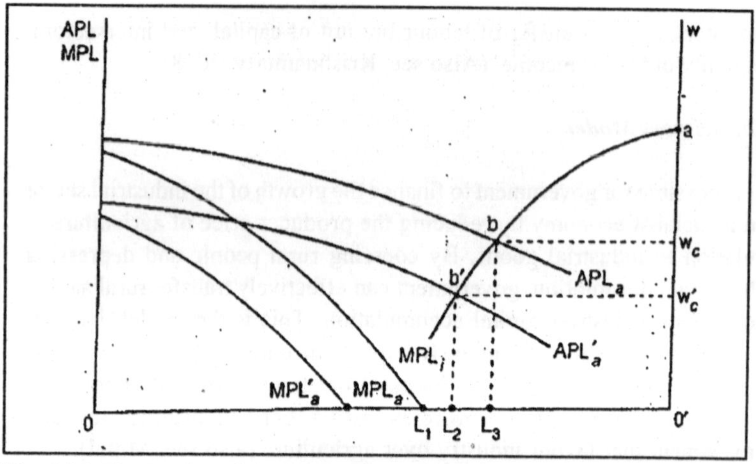

Fig. 26.1: The Lewis and the Price-scissors Models.

economy is characterized by surplus labour, it is a labour surplus economy par excellence. This is reflected in the low marginal product of labour in agriculture ($MPL_a = 0$ beyond OL_1). Under these conditions, the rural supply price is dependent on the average product of labour. In a competitive labour market in which the rural supply curve is given by APL_a and the urban demand curve by MPL_i, the competitive wage would be w_c and labour allocation OL_3 in the rural and L_3O' in the urban sector. Profits, shown by the area abw_e, are reinvested. This produces dynamic growth of the industrial sector, a transfer of labour from agriculture to industry and an eventual increase in the competitive wage, initially held down by the elastic APL_a curve.

The price scissors model requires only minor modification of the figure. Government intervention to reduce the price of the agricultural product reduces APL_a and MPL_a to APL_a' and MPL_a' respectively. The rural supply price falls. This produces a lower wage, w'_c, in the urban sector. Industrial employment is expanded to L_2O' and the higher industrial profits, $ab'w'_c$, permit faster industrialization.

The urban bias model has been depicted in Figure 26.2. In this case government sets the urban wage higher than the competitive wage, at w_u. In a market economy this would imply urban employment L_5O'. In the framework of probabilistic migration models the 'expected wage'—w_u multiplied by the probability of obtaining it—equals the rural supply price with the probability equals the rural supply price. With the probability equal to the ratio of urban employment to urban labour that the curve

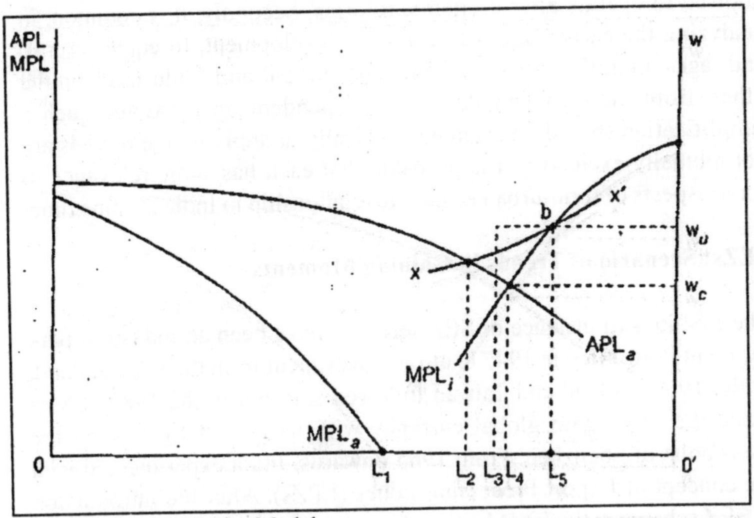

Fig. 26.2: The urban bias Model.

xx', passing through the point b, is a rectangular hyperbola, urban open unemployment equal to L_2L_5 is created.

A government pursuing urban bias policies might oppose this outcome, Government can prohibit open unemployment by controlling rural-urban migration and by creating surplus jobs, L_3L_5, in the state sector. Thus the labour force is divided in to OL_3 (rural employment) and L_3O' (urban employment). Discontent in the urban sector is reduced by raising the urban wage above the competitive level and by sharing unemployment in disguised form among the urban labour force. Discontent in the rural sector is reduced by sharing out the land equally and so also sharing disguised unemployment among the rural labour force (evidenced by L_1L_3). Urban bias in the form of investment allocation has the dynamic effect of raising MPL_i relative to APL_a.

These models offer potential frameworks for addressing rural-urban economic divide in India. As a result, the regional fringe transformations. Each of them has been the subject of an extensive literature of exposition, criticism, and debate. Rather than present a review at this stage, we prefer to draw on the literature only if and when it becomes relevant to our application of a particular framework to the Indian economy.

Thus, first, insofar as they rely on market forces, the models should be treated with caution. The Indian economy has been primarily a mixed economy in which strong market forces have until recent years been allowed to operate after economic reforms. Secondly, it is common, in analyzing the early stages of economic development, to equate 'rural' and 'agricultural', on the one hand, and 'urban' and 'industrial' on the other. Both the Lewis model is less dependent on it. Again, such a simplification should be examined critically in applying the models are not mutually exclusive: it is probable that each has some relevance to some aspects of rural-urban economic relationship in India at some time.

SEZs: Scenario of Trends in Gaining Moments

The first known instance of SEZ seems to have been an industrial park set-up in Porto Rico in 1947 to attract investment from the US mainland, in the 1960, Ireland and Taiwan followed suit, but in the 1980s China made the SEZs gain global currency with its largest SEZ being the metropolis of Shenzhen. From 1965 onwards, India experimented with the concept of Export Processing Zones (EPZs). After the introduction of SEZ scheme in the EXIM policy from 1.4.2000, all existing FTZ/EPZ have been converted to SEZ. These did not quite deliver as much as was expected, however. Thus, in 2000, the New Export and Import Policy allowed for SEZs to be set-up in the public private or joint sector or by state governments. Eight EPZ were converted into SEZs. Altogether, a total of 19 SEZs were established prior to the promulgation of the SEZ Act, which were latter in 2005—legally deemed as SEZs under the new Act. SEZs have been enabled with a view to providing an internationally competitive and hassle free environment for exports. Units may be set-up in SEZs for manufacturing goods and rendering services. All the Import/Export operations of the SEZs units are on a self certification basis. Sales by SEZ units in the domestic tariff area are subject to payment of full custom duty and to the import policy in force. Furthermore, offshore banking units may be set-up in the SEZs.

India is one of the first countries in Asia to recognize the effectiveness of Export Processing Zone (EPZ) model in promoting exports. Asia's first EPZ was set-up in 1965 in Kandla. The proposal for setting up the Kandla Free Trade Zone (KAFTZ) was marked in 1961for following reasons.

(i) To facilitate the development of the Kutch region,
(ii) To ensure greater utilization of Kandla Port, and
(iii) To create employment opportunities in the Kandla Gandhidham area.

(i) Uniqueness:

Uniqueness of SEZs is: Special Economic Systems and Policies. In other words the control government gives to the Special Economic Zones, special policies and flexible measures, allowing them to utilize a special economic management system such as:

(a) Special tax incentives for foreign investments in the Special Economic Zone
(b) Greater independence on international trade activities
(c) Economic characteristics are represented as "4 primacies"
  (i) Constructions primarily rely on attracting and utilizing foreign capitalists.
  (ii) Primary economic forms are Sino-foreign joint ventures and partnerships as well as wholly foreign-owned enterprises.
  (iii) Products are primarily export-oriented.
  (iv) Economic activities are primarily driven by market.

(ii) Objectives of SEZs Policy are:

1. Attract Foreign Direct Investment (FDI)
2. Earn foreign exchange and contribute to exchange rate stability
3. Boost the export sector, especially non-traditional exports
4. Create employment opportunities
5. Introduce new technology
6. Develop backward region
7. Stimulate sectors such as electronics, information technology, R&D, tourism, infrastructure and human resource development that are regarded as strategically important to economy of India
8. Create backward and forward linkages to increase the output and raise the standard of local enterprise that supply goods and services as to the zone.

(iii) Salient features of SEZs:

(i) No license is required for import
(ii) Manufacturing, trading or services activities allowed
(iii) Full freedom of subcontracting
(iv) No routine examination of export-import cargo by customs authorities

(v) SEZ Units to have positive net foreign exchange earner
(vi) Financial incentives, like tax, holidays, duty free imports and exports
(vii) Single window clearance
(viii) High quality infrastructure
(ix) Strategic location and market access.

Special Economic Zones in India are governed by provisions of Special Economic Zone Act, 2005 and Special Economic Zones Rules, 2006.

Land Acquisition under SEZs

Land especially agricultural land in India, is a very delicate subject and has been an emotive issue ever since the Zamindari days. Land is livelihood of millions of people. Not only the immediate owners of the land are affected, but also sharecroppers or daily wage labourers who eke out their living through a scant, but reasonably reliable source of income. The farmers of Jamnagar district in Gujarat moved the High Court of Gujarat and later even the Supreme Court to challenge the setting up of a 10,000 acre SEZ by Reliance Infrastructure in November 2006. They alleged that the acquisition of large tracts of Agricultural Land Acquisition Act of 1894 but was also in breach of the public interest, this led the government to 'consider' putting a coiling on the maximum land area that can be acquired for the multiproduct zones and decide to 'go slow' in approving SEZs'. In this context, the left wing parties started demanding a cap on at least the IT SEZs or even putting a final ceiling on the total number of SEZs to be permitted some small scale protest against land acquisition in Maharashtra were put down by the police, which according to some—'served to increase the frustration, anger and suspicion about the state machinery being the agent of the corporate. This can lead to militancy and worse' was dark forecast in an article in a left-leaning weekly, concurring with the introductory remark made by the former Prime Minister of India, V.P. Singh. Decision making on SEZs has generally been non-transparent. SEZs are imposed on the local people without any prior consultation. Whenever the displaced persons opposed the location of an SEZ, their dissent had been termed "anti-development" and crushed mercilessly with the iron hand of the state. The selection process of the promoters of SEZs is in itself highly non-transparent. There is not a single case of SEZ in which the promoter is selected through well established competitive bidding procedures this has provided enormous scope for consumption and political patronage. SEZs displace people on a large scale. The displacement is both physical and occupational. In some states like Andhra Pradesh, some SEZs are located along the sea coast, cutting off fisherman's access to the sea from which the latter eke out their livelihood. In many places, small agriculturists are thrown out of their homelands and along with them, those that depend on agriculture, such as artisans and rural workers have also lost their livelihood. In the past the land acquisition law which is indeed a draconian one had been used to acquire lands for genuine public purposes such as schools, hospitals etc. it had rarely been used to further private interest, as is the case now. (Mukherji, 2007).

The regulatory framework for acquiring land under the Land Acquisition Act (LAA, 1894) is ill suited for serving a rapidly growing economy. The Land Acquisition Act allows the government to acquire land for public purpose. Public purpose was defined for an age when the government used to carry out many development activities, which are in the domain of the private sector today. An SEZ is a case of Public Private Partnership (PPP Model) in building township, which will be run and administered largely by the private sector for generating export oriented and profit making activities. All a time when displacement, relief and rehabilitation issues were not clearly resolved for government projects such as dams, roads and bridges, SEZs posed a serious challenge to the regulatory framework governing the acquisition of land. Most of the farmers do not want to sell their land; following are a few statements by the farmers of the villages affected by the SEZ. Farmers were paid Rs. 20 lakh per acre by the government. But the market price for the land on the fringes of bustling Gurgaon is at least 2 crore per acre. "None of us wanted to give our land. The government took it away by force and then gave it away to private companies, i.e. Reliance. We were cheated, we should have got much more money because the market rate is ten times of what we got", said a farmer of Mohammedpur village outside Gurgaon. (Mukherji, 2007).

"The land is very fertile. Farmer used to grow wheat, rice, cotton, sugarcane, mustard and millets. We might have got the money now but how will our coming generation feed their children without land. Land is everything", said the village headman. "Water is plentiful now, but villager's fear it will be sucked away by the industries in the SEZ". Reliance has opened offices in Jhajjar, Bahadurgarh and Gurgaon to purchase the land directly from the farmers. But there is ambiguity as the *bayana* or agreement papers contains the name of not RIL but Nariman Point Company whose authorized signatory is on Rajeev Aggrawal. What if something goes wrong? Whom do we sue! Ask the farmers. (Mukherji, 2007).

Satpal, a youth of Mundakhera village who works in Delhi, says his family has 12 acres of good agricultural land. Asked whether they are considering selling the land, he says firmly, "We do not intend to give away the land. Let us see what happens when the state government comes to us". (Mukherji, 2007).

Praveen, a youth who himself is not engaged in farming activities, says he will not give his land to Reliance, but the state government has the power to take it over. He adds that if opposition parties decide to take up the issue and mobilize people here in protest against the acquisition move, people will certainly extend their support. At the time of land transferring in Nandigram SEZs in West Bengal (150 kilometers from Kolkata) in January and March 2007, which posed a substantial threat to the success of SEZs in India. The West Bengal government was working with an Indonesian foreign investor, the Salim group, to set-up a petrochemical SEZ in Nandigram. Local people were informed by the use of force to evict people from their places of residence and agricultural livelihood. Political forces to the extreme left such as the Maoists and the more moderate Trinamool Congress helped to organize a social movement under the banner of Bhoomi Ucched Pratirodh Committee to prevent the setting up as the SEZ. The Congress party, which faced criticism on a variety of development issues from its coalition ally, did not lose this opportunity to project this lapse in the commitment to the rural poor. The situation in Nandigram continued to be tense till central forces were deployed to ease the situation. Land acquisition in Nandigram may have been affected by the power of absentee Landlords, whose interests coincided with the political opposition groups in the area. Land acquisition and SEZs earned a bad name after these incidents and the Central Government needed to recalibrate its policies on land acquisition. Chief Minister, Buddhadeb Bhattacharya has reassured the people of Nandigram in late December 2007, that there will be no SEZ in Nandigram and that the violence caused due to land acquisition is deeply regretted and of the issue like. Janadesh 2007, the long March of the 25,000 landless and tribal people from Gwalior in Madhya Pradesh to New Delhi in October 2007, has raised the issue of Land Reforms and access to common property resources, especially among the tribal and disadvantaged people. It has led to the setting up of the National Land Reforms Council with the

Prime Minister as Chairman. Inequitable distribution of land and natural resources and attention to marginaiized sections as part of relief and rehabilitation policy has gained attention as a result of this non-violent struggle initiated by a Gandhian Non-Governmental Organization called Ekta Parisad Council of Unity and aftermath of violence in Nandigram, SEZ produced a freeze on "in principle" SEZ approvals between January and May 2007. (Mukherji, 2007).

The question of displacement of farming communities to acquire land for industrialization has assumed great political importance, primarily because of the strong resistance offered by these communities in Ghaziabad in Uttar Pradesh and the SEZ at Nandigram. Land acquisition has become a prime objective of the State governments, as they climb over each other to seek the graces of global capital. The peasants are resisting such virtual eviction in many places, but the state governments are using or threatening to use a Colonial Land Acquisition Act. Which allows the government to acquire for public purpose? Any land on payment of "compensation" even though the owner may not be willing to port with the plot. The acquired land is then handed over to the enterprises at a subsidized rate. That is compensation that is given to the peasants.

This is just a modest beginning of new phase of capitalist expansion. In this policy, the compensation being offered is not "adequate". That those who are not landowners but depend on agriculture for their livelihood are not compensated; that agricultural production will go down as the proposed SEZs or industrial estates are largely located on prime agriculture land. The recent spate of state violence against farmers to force them of their land in order to hand it over to global capital for real estate business or for setting up industrial enterprises.

Marx quotes Bacon on an Act of Henry VII, promulgated in 1533 and comments on it. The device ...... was profound and admirable, in making firms and houses of husbandry of a standard; that is maintained with such a proportion of land unto them as may breed a subject to live in convenient plenty, and no servile condition, and to keep the plough in the hands of the owners and not mere hirelings what the capitalist system demanded was on the other hand, a degraded and almost servile condition of the mass of people, and the transformation of them into mercenaries and of their means of labour into capital [Marx 1954, p. 674]. The features of agricultural land are to produce crops. That is why when the government takes over agricultural land for construction of industry or amusement parks the peasants oppose such moves.

Modern economic growth generates refugees of development by constructing industry or housing resorts for the rich on agricultural land; by the loss of fertility caused by modern farming that cannot be replenished; by the loss of occupation of the fisherman caused by the discharge of chemical effluents into water bodies, by displacement of forest dwellers and agriculturists on account of construction of large dams. The displaced migrants crowd cities in search of livelihood. All metros face such problems.

SEZs vs. Land Issues—Experiences and Evidences

In the following description and the development of local periphery and other impacts of SEZs are being provided:

(a) Dadri SEZ in Uttar Pradesh

The Reliance Energy has plans to build the world's largest gas based power plant of 3500 MW in Dadri, in Ghaziabad. The investment outlay is more than Rs. 10,000 crore. However, the real investment is the 2500 acres of land in the most fertile region. At the launch of the project on February 22, 2004, the government had announced that rate given to the farmers for the acquired land would be Rs. 350 per sq. mt. while the prices in the market around was 13,500 per sq. mt. Further, The government of UP had waived off all the stamp fees and other related costs for buying the land for Reliance, along with the subsidy in which the Reliance would pay only 40 per cent of the costs and government would pay the rest. Land in Dadri (Delhi) is worth Rs. 13,500 per sq. mt. whereas farmers are being offered only Rs. 120 per sq. mt. Further the power project only needs 700 acres, but 2500 acres have been acquired because of high real estate value. And finally no legal procedure has been followed in acquiring the land. (Tyagi, 2007).

(b) HSIDC SEZ in Jhajjar—Gurgaon

One of the first laws passed by the Congress led Bhupinder Singh Hooda government was the Haryana Special Economic Zone Act and thus came into existence one of the biggest SEZs of the country in Haryana. This multi-product Delhi-Jaipur Highways. It is being jointly set-up by Reliance Ventures, a wholly owned Infrastructure Development Corporation, in a 90:10 ownership basis between the former and the later. Reliance claims it to be of the standards of Dubai and Singapore. According to the RIL chairman, the SEZ would come near National Highway No. 8 in Gurgaon and extended up to Jhajjar district, adjacent to proposed Kundli Manesar-Palwal Express Highway. The government had acquired 1395 acres of land near Garhi-Harsaru in Gurgaon district and on 19th June, 2006, it has transferred this land to the joint venture company. This land would in open market cost around Rs. 10 crore per acre, and the SEZ has got it for undisclosed prices, which are bound to be very low, as state is also partner in the SEZ. So it has already got the land worth Rs. 13,950 crore for throwaway price/free and even if it is sold, it has a straight profit of Rs. 8,756.9 crore from the deal without even starting any business there. But as it is mentioned earlier the state is hand in glove with the corporation in this case, the land for a long time was surprisingly not bought by Reliance Ventures but by a company based in Nariman Point known as Central Commercial Private Limited, because the Reliance—HSIIDC company was not registered till then, it was only by mid of October that the company came into existence and then all the land was transferred to Reliance Ventures, so even if there was no company formed even after knowing it kept silent on this issue. What is interesting in this context is that before the project, like the Reliance SEZ in Haryana had even come up for approval before the BoA, the state government has already offered Reliance 25,000 acres (10,000 hectares) and even acquired some land. So what validity of BoA procedures has when a SEZ promoter starts functioning without formal approval? In speculation of much higher prices a lot of people are not selling all their land, they are just selling a part of it and keeping the rest for the future, so the company is buying land in small pockets over the whole stretch of 25,000 acres and thus killing any possibility of a people's resistance, as they will never get united and there is already a psychological victory of the company as a lot of land has been bought. Then there is a clause in the SEZ Act that to get a contiguous area, the State might use its power for acquiring land. The people who are selling the land are told that the area having "abadi", i.e. population will not be touched. So that they don't have a fear of displacement, but is it ever possible that a contiguous area of 25,000 acres is acquired without displacing any "abadi"? Another aspect was regarding the compensation paid. It is paid to the owner of the land, while the Land Acquisition Act mentions "person affected" should be paid the compensation. Thus, the agricultural labourer who would be badly affected by it, would not get a penny in lieu of snatching away their livelihood and would be most vulnerable group, if we see the State's statistics 52 per cent of the population is involved in agriculture—36.34 per cent are cultivators and 15.22 per cent are agricultural labourers and they are much more in this region accounting for at least 50 per cent of the population. There is a common myth that the landless farmers will not be affected in terms of livelihood, as new industries are coming in the SEZ which would provide more and more options of livelihoods. But the people are dislocated from their own bases from the SEZ from where the access to the SEZ might be difficult. And the kind of livelihood options created out of the capital-intensive industries of an SEZ will not match with the skills of the local labourers. (Tyagi, 2007).

(c) SEZ at Kancheepuram

Kancheepuram, Tamil Nadu, is vital production bases of international industrial groups like; Ford, Hyundai and Sant Gobin. The district of Kancheepuram has got many benefits. It is in proximity to the International airport and two seaports of Chennai and Ennor and road connectivity through the East coast road and the upcoming upgrade NH 4 and 45. It has also no dearth of talented skilled manpower being in metros. Mahindra World City is corporate India's first Special Economic Zone that has been approved for three sectors-specific SEZs, IT (Services & Manufacturing) Apparel & Fashion Accessories and Auto Ancillaries. The Mahindra World City is just 30 minutes away from Chennai. International airport has been established in prime agricultural land which is surrounded by small hills and rivers. The Mahindra's have established a 'real estate' SEZ by which they will sell out the property acquired from the farmers to other companies for establishing their commercial and industrial units at a price which is 10-20 times more than what they have given to the farmers. (Tyagi, 2007).

(d) POSCO SEZ

In the past three years, the Orissa Government has signed more than 40 MoU with companies, both domestic and foreign. On June 22nd POSCO signed an MoU with the Orissa Government for construction of the world's first overseas integrative steel works and the development of a mine at Bhubaneswar, the capital of Orissa. POSCO proposes to construct first the steel works from 2007 to 2010 on about 4500 acres of land at Kujang tahsil near Paradip of Orissa. Out the total land only 20 per cent is individually owned and the rest comes under government/community land. And out of this POSCO has been given prospecting licenses or direct lease for mining over a total area of about 2000 hectares. With the coming in of the company 3 panchayats—Dhinkia, Nuagaon and Gadakujanga compromising of 11 village/hamlets with about 22,000 people (3500 families) will be directly affected. The estimates of those whose agricultural land would be affected are the only ones who get recognized in terms of lost livelihood. There is no estimate of those who would be indirectly affected in terms of their livelihood. These include those engaged in grazing, collection of firewood, forest produce, fishing etc. Kujang block where the plant is set to come up is also unique since it is the area where the best quality betel (pan) is grown. With the plant coming up the whole 'pan' belt would also be ruined. The livelihood of those engaged in the 'pan' cultivation which ranges from the young to the old would also be compelled to give up their livelihood. On the other hand, the company is proposing to build a port at Jatadhari, which also evoked concerns of damage to the coastline and also the nesting habitat of the endangered Olive Ridley Turtle giving rise to intense opposition. It would also destroy the complex system of myriad natural creeks, *nalas* and waterways, to create a vast backwater of Mahanadi and its associates especially during the rainy season and floods. The POSCO project will occupy large areas of public and private lands. The proposed plant is near the Bhitarakanika Mangrove forests (which has now got the status of a sanctuary). Apart from fears that land for the plant will encroach upon the mangroves there is also a fear that the plant will draw water from a watershed that also feeds the sanctuary. Mangroves act as natural protection against super cyclones and coastal cyclones, and destroying these forests will leave Orissa's coastline vulnerable. All this has raised the fundamental questions relating the industry-induced displacements on one hand and to the government's commitment to promote the interests of the corporation world. (Tyagi, 2007).

(e) SEZs in China vs. India

The SEZ policy can thus be thought of as ushering in a third generation of economic reforms. The first two phases were dominated respectively by efforts to liberalize the macro policy environment, and by the creation of institution for regulating a market economy Phase three has a special emphasis on facilitating a global presence for India's largest private sector firms and rapidly enhancing the physical infrastructures which such firms operate. India's SEZ Act is different in at least three key respects from the Chinese 'model' which was said to have inspired Murasoli Maran at the beginning of this decade. First is whereas in China it was the public sector that was overwhelmingly responsible for developing the SEZs, in India this task has been assigned to the private sector. Private sector promoters of SEZs have in many cases partnered with government entities, but by far the greatest share of the investment capital is coming from the private sector. The second difference between India's SEZ policy and the internationally recognized paradigm for SEZ development is the lack of emphasis in India on using SEZs as a mechanism for promoting underindustrialized areas. India's SEZ are because of the incentives created by the policy design and the fact that they are far the most part, not initiated by government bodies—overwhelmingly located in areas. that are already highly developed. Almost SEZs were approved in the vicinity of major cities. Some cities like Ahmedabad, Chennai, Delhi, Gurgaon, Hyderabad, Kolkata, Mumbai, Manglore and Pune. This is a far cry from what took place in China. The Ministry of Rural Development began working on a relief and rehabilitation policy, which had been discussed within the Cabinet. A new Bill had been introduced in the Parliament, which could lead to an amendment of the LAA, 1894. Given the investment and employment opportunities that lay ahead, the SEZ policy moved faster than government legislation.

(i) The processing area within SEZ was decided by MOCI would be 50 per cent of the total SEZ area rather than 35 per cent of the same, as was the case before.
(ii) The Board of Approval headed by the Commerce Secretary was looking for 100 per cent consent from the local people before approving SEZs. This provision was to ensure that another Nandigram type violent protest would not be repeated as a consequence of forced land acquisition by invoking the LAA of 1894.
(iii) The Relief and Rehabilitation Policy (2007), enunciated by the Ministry of Rural Development, discouraged investors from acquiring land that were fertile. Displacement was to be kept at a minimum social impact assessments based on rigorous surveys of the area and public hearing were proposed. Land acquired for one purpose should not be used for other purposes. (Mukherji, 2007)

Rehabilitation Package and Compensation

There is a consensus that no development can be accepted at the cost of social equity. Land acquisition needs total reform and rehabilitation package has to be an integral part of the Land Acquisition Act. Land-owner, should get adequate compensation of their land. There is also a need to think proactively to make partnership under SEZs with such landowners to bring the social equity. Therefore, rehabilitation package needs to include continuous/ongoing sharing of income. It was heartening to note that some of the developers have offered not only employment guarantee of one person per family but certain percentage of lease rental so that landowner will continue to get benefit lifelong. The compensation package needs to address the issue of reinvestment of such compensation as to avoid the misuse of unexpected funds due to lack of entrepreneurship. Social study has proved that such compensation has resulted not only family disturbances and has totally ruined the families on account of spending on unnecessary/perishable luxuries. It has also widened the difference amongst the family members over the distribution of wealth some time resulted into criminal activities and therefore, it is very important, to make the law to prevent misuse. NGOs can play a vital role for education and helping such illiterate farmers. The compensation and rehabilitation packages announced by the concerned states lack credibility as there are thousands of families displaced by previous projects still awaiting compensation payments. In a few cases those displaced in early 1970s are yet to receive compensation. In many cases, the true beneficiaries are the absentee land- lords, intermediaries and faults that confront with the government agencies.

Conclusion

There are three models for rural-urban transformation which are described by Lewis, Scissors model and Public Policies. Although industry-led growth is very much possible through SEZs and EPZs but shifting of land from agriculture sector to industrial sector may be judiciously done. The shifting must take care of the interest of landowners, poor labourers, displaced villagers and a mechanism be developed for involving them as a shareholder in SEZs. There is hardly any reason to shift the ownership of land, in many such cases. This may also reduce legal battle and bring faster development of private industries.

To recapitulate, as a suggestion it may be also advocated that for industrial development through SEZ definitely there would be shifting of land from agriculture/rural sector to semi urban/urban sector for industrial base but the issue of concern is transfer of ownership of land from farmers to capitalists. This practice can be discouraged by making the landholders and shareholders or stakeholders in the forthcoming industry according to land proportion. This will also stop compensation based land transfer. However, landless labourers may be accommodated in SEZ for employment. For rehabilitation a systematic package may be evolved in order to having a pleasant rural-urban divide. We share the opinion of Bhaduri and Patkar (2009) that it is essential to strengthen and expand these rights, especially for the poor; instead they are being violated continuously, most visibly through land acquisition by the State without their consent. The role of Gram Sabhas is not recognized, nor is the legal

State-wise Distribution of SEZs in India

State	*Formal approvals*	*In-principle approvals*	*Notified SEZs*
Andhra Pradesh	101	3	67
Chandigarh	2		2
Chhattisgarh	1	2	
Delhi	1		
Dadra & Nagar Haveli	4		
Goa	7		3
Gujarat	50	11	29
Haryana	46	17	29
Himachal Pradesh		3	
Jharkhand	1		1
Karnataka	50	9	27
Kerala	21	1	9
Madhya Pradesh	14	6	5
Maharashtra	109	35	51
Nagaland	2		
Orissa	10	3	5
Pondicherry	1	1	
Punjab	10	7	2
Rajasthan	s	11	7
Tamil Nadu	69	17	49
Uttar Pradesh	34	5	16
Uttarakhand	3	-	2
West Bengal	24	13	11
Grand Total	**568**	**144**	**315**

Source: www.sezindia.nic.in

process fully and fairly followed. It is not just land but habitat after habitat, even generation's old, common property resources, such as water bodies as also tree and forest cover, that is snatched away, resulting in the poor being deprived of their livelihoods and uprooted from their socio-cultural milieu. Compensation of all this loss with acceptable alternative livelihoods and a share in the benefit, rarely come true for decades, even generations. People resist the resultant trauma and fight for survival with right to life and livelihood within our constitutional framework.

We share the second opinion also to support these resistances against land acquisition without people's consent, we ask for a referendum of the people involved, proper rehabilitation and resettlement to correct the wrong headed policies of successive governments irrespective of the colour of the government that indulges in it. The effect of taking the people's view on land acquisition would directly influence the pattern of industrialization, making it non-displacing or least displacing and truly employment generating, i.e., benefiting the local communities who would be the investors of land and all natural resources as against the others who invest non-productive monetary resources. Moreover, this would also strengthen the democratic rights and participatory role of the people in planning development and community management.

Notes:

1. *Business Today*, Special Annual Issue, 2007 from fighting for industrial licences to testing the fruits of liberalization, India Inc. has come a long way, BK Birla tells.
2. Taken from the introduction to *Special Economic Zones in India*. http://www.sezindia.nic.in/ html/about html last viewed on June 2009.
3. *Times of India*, Farmers tabs RIL to Court over SEZ land acquisition, 11 November 2006, p. 15;
4. S.G. Vombatkere, Special Economic Zones—Neo-Zamindari Zones ? In: *Mainstream*, 9th December, 2006; 9. In the same issue, there is an appeal with a demand for 'a national moratorium on all acquisition and displacement till a national consensus is arrived at'. The appeal continues to demand 'a national policy for over housing the land acquisition, SEZ and related Acts and for providing an effective blueprint to protect the interests and concerns of all the affected persons', it is *inter alia* signed by a former well-known Supreme Court Judge, Justice V.R. Krishna Iyer and many professors of eminence such as Rani Kathari and other public persons (p. 5).

5. Other sites such as Kolinganagar (Orissa), Kakinada (Andhra Pradesh) and Nandagudi in Karnataka also witnessed protests. It was Nandigram that brought the issue of land acquisition to national attention.
6. In principle approval for SEZ are accorded by the Department of Commerce for new and viable projects that have not secured the land. "Formal approvals" are however, accorded after the applicant is in possession of the land required for SEZ. In the last stage, SEZ are notified after receipt of land details and verification reports from the Development Commissioners of the SEZs.
7. By the term "Global Capital" we refer to capital that has crossed a certain threshold, in terms of size, to acquire the passport to global mobility. The significance of this categorical separation will become obvious as we go along. This type of capital is not geocentric in either source or area of investment. It has, therefore, little or no national allegiance.
8. The Government of West Bengal has used this Act to acquire land that will be handed over to the Tatas for construction of a small car factory. This has been interpreted as a public purpose because it will provide employment to the people of the state. Even if one does not contest the veracity of this highly improbable claim, one can still ask how the employment of workers by a profitable enterprise in order to enhance its profits can be termed as a deed with a public or social purpose.
9. It will be impossible to prevent land to be handed over to capital for industrial ventures from being transformed into real States if it is more profitable. According to the projections of Merrill Lynch, the Indian realty sector will grow from $ 12 billion in 2005 to $ 90 billion in 2015. ("Land Grab and Development Fraud in India", *Analytical Monthly Review*, editorial, September 2006.)
10. Second generation reform is such term sometimes used to denote in general, all the reform items leftover from the first decade or decade and a half of reform. More especially, it can take on one of three meanings:
    (a) The politically difficult reforms that have been sidestepped (labour reform, through fiscal reform, privatization).
    (b) Reforms that will be more inclusive, reducing the disparities that have given reform an anti-poor image; or
    (c) Reforms to institutions of governance to take the process of continuous policy change more transparent, predictable and efficient. See Rob Jenkins and Sunil Khilnani (eds.), *The Politics of India's Next Generation of Economic Reforms*, Special Issue on India Review (Washington DC), Vol. 3, No. 2, November 2004.
11. The four original SEZs in China were Shenzoben, Shantou, Zhuhai and Xiamen. For accessible overviews of the Chinese experience with SEZs, see George J, Crane, *The Political Economy of China's Special Economic Zones* (Armonk NY: ME Sharpe, 1990) and YC Jao and CK Leung (eds.),

China's Special Economic Zones: Policies, Problems and Prospects (Hong Kong: Oxford University Press, 1986).

The third way in which India's SEZs vary from the Chinese model has been in terms of size. The SEZ Act, 2005 specifies extremely low minimum size requirement in order to establish an SEZ. The minimum area requirement for 'multiproduct' (i.e. non-sector specific) SEZs is 1000 hectares. Sector specific SEZs have a minimum area requirement of 100 hectares, with the exception of those devoted to Information Technology and IT enhanced services, which are permitted to be as small as 10 hectares [SEZ authority, Ministry of Commerce & Industry, Government of India, Available at *sezindia.nic.in*]

12. The Indian Cabinet is a group of influential ministers who make important decision for the country headed by the Prime Minister.

References

Aggarwal, Aradhana (2006). "Special Economic Zones: Revisit the Policy Debate", *Economic and Political Weekly,* November 4.

AMR (2006). "Land Grab and Development Fraud in India", *Analytical Monthly Review,* September, Kharagpur.

Bajaj, Rahul (2007). SEZ are Turning into Land Scam, *The Times of India,* 4 May.

Balagopal (2007). "Ceiling Surplus and Public Lands, Land Unrest in Andhra Pradesh-1", *Economic and Political Weekly,* Vol. XLII, No. 38, September 22.

Basu, Pranab and K. (2007). "Political Economy of Land Grab", *Economic and Political Weekly,* Vol. XLII, No. 14, page 7, April 7.

Benrgee, Guha and Swapna (2008). "Space Relations of Capital and Significance of New Economic Enclaves: SEZs in India"; *Economic and Political Weekly,* Vol. 7, page 7, 22 November.

Bhaduri, Amit and Medha Patkar (2009). "Industrialisation for the people, by the people, of the people", *Economic and Political Weekly,* Vol. XLV, No. 1, January 3.

Bidwai, Praful (2006). "The Great Land Grab", *Frontline,* Vol. 23, Issue 18.

Carr-Harris (2005). "Struggle-Dialogue—Tools for Land Movements in India", Ekta Prasad, New Delhi.

Confederation of Indian Industry (2007). *Exim News,* Vol. II, No. 3, March.

Dev, S., and Mahendra (2003). "Agriculture, Employment and Social Sector Neglected", *Economic and Political Weekly,* Vol. 38, No. 14, p. 1355.

Ekta Prasad (2002). "A Perspective on Land and Forests in Madhya Pradesh", in Praveen K. Jha (ed.) *Land Reforms in India, Vol. 7. Issues of Equity in Rural Madhya Pradesh,* Sage Publications, New Delhi.

Government of India (2006). "Implementation of the Provisions of the SEZ Act, 2005 and SEZ Rules, Ministry of Commerce and Industry, Department of Commerce (SEZ section).

Government of India (2007). http://sezindia.nic.in/html.s/fact sheet-on-sez.s.pdf, New Delhi.

Indiresan, P.V. (2007). "Agricultural Land for Industrial Projects: Distributive Development is the key", *Business Line,* July, 23, Monday.

Knight, John and Song, Lina (1997). *The Rural Urban Divide, Economic Disparities and Interactions in China.*

Krishnamurty, J. (2008). "Indian Antecedents of Disguised Unemployment and Surplus Labour", *Indian Journal of Labour Economics,* Vol. 51, No.1.

Marx (1954). *Capital,* Vol. III, Progress Publishers, Mascow (reprint 1974).

Mazumdar, J. (2007). "Kolkata Korner: This Land is Our Land", *Outlook.*

Mondal, Sudipto (2007). "Fertile Farmland being acquired for Mangalore SEZ: *The Hindu from the South,* 12 November.

Mukherji, Rahul (2007). "Special Economic Zones in India: Recent Developments and Future Prospects." The Institute of Asian Studies, National University of Singapore, 30 December.

NRPR (2007). *The National Rehabilitation Policy Report,* New Delhi.

Sharma, EAS (2007). "Help The Rich, Hurt The Poor, Case of Special Economic Zone", *Economic and Political Weekly,* 26 May.

The Economic Times (2008). "SEZ survey soon to check real impact on farmers", 7 March.

Tyagi, Manoj (2007). *"Azadi Bachao",* Andolan Publication, Allahabad.

Weng Kwan Yuv and David Chu (1984). "Export Processing Zones and Special Economic Zones as Generators of Economic Development: The Asian Experience", *Human Geography,* Vol. 66, No. 1.

27
Rural Urban Fringe in Uttar Pradesh: Issues of Development Induced Displacement

B.K. Bajpai

Introduction

The paper analyses the problems of development projects related displacement of rural population owing to increasing urban fringes in rural areas. Displacement of rural population, falling in the catchment area of six development projects, located in four geo-economic regions of Uttar Pradesh and one in Uttaranchal (earlier Hill region of UP), shows a widespread mismanagement of the resettlement and rehabilitation programme. The impact of the development projects on displaced population has been assessed taking into consideration the existing rehabilitation policies of the government. The impact of displacement on affected families has been assessed through the study of: (i) changes in the economic profile; (ii) the process of displacement; (iii) process of land takeover and compensation; (iv) resettlement and rehabilitation plan of the project; (v) impact of displacement and resettlement on infrastructural amenities and employment; (vi) changes in the health and the environment; (vii) social and cultural impact; and (viii) performance evaluation of the rehabilitation officials. In the light of these problems, paper further makes an attempt to evaluate the existing rehabilitation policies and the compliance of Government orders in this connection.

Methodology and Sample Design

The present paper is based on the results of a broader study conducted by the author in the institute. Primary data for the study have been collected from 969 households of 29 villages in the catchment areas of different development projects located in six districts of Uttar Pradesh (including Dehradun). The secondary information has also been used to locate the location and identification of the project affected village sites. The list of affected villages coming under the catchment area of respective development project has been procured from relevant offices at the district headquarters level.

Displacement and Impact

The analysis indicates that the development projects may be a boon for some but they are a curse for the rest. The psyche of the affected population is to be understood properly. The government agencies involved in the rehabilitation programmes are hardly capable of such understanding.

The value assessment of the land and houses is done in a very old and traditional manner in order to see that the displaced are given a minimum amount as compensation. The maximum satisfaction of the oustees has seldom been an aim of the project officials.

Corruption has become a general practice in the disbursement of cash compensation in almost all the cases of development projects. The timely disbursement of the compensation money has been a rare practice. The unconcerned attitudes of the project authorities is reflected by the fact that in many development projects much more land is often acquired and it remains waste for years before the eyes of the displaced population. In case of the Lakhwar Vyasi project in Dehradun, the project work is standstill for the last so many years. The farmers are hardly allowed to cultivate on the acquired land, which is lying unused.

In case of the housing projects the government agencies involved in the process are making huge profits through the resale of the acquired land. No additional reward is paid to the original owner of the land. In the event of a loss of job in course of the displacement, it becomes the duty of the project management to provide alternative employment and impart timely training to the displaced persons for a successful future in a new job. Such efforts are seldom made by the project authorities.

Considering the mass illiteracy among the project affected population, the role of the people's representatives become very important in helping the project affected population for attainment of their claims. But many times they fail to fulfil these promises and prefer to join the administration to impose exploitative terms on the displaced population.

In the process of displacement, landowners are rewarded even if they are not present during the process of the land takeover. But tillers are not adequately compensated under this process.

In most of the cases the displaced population preferred land for land than other types of compensations. But, in the absence of the land area, none of the displaced families could be given land for land at least for agricultural purposes. The adamant attitude of the land oustees in this regard is seen because they do not want to enter new ventures. Neither they have a liking for such ventures nor they are trained enough to do so.

Most of the projects were found to be situated in remote areas inhabited by indigenous peoples. These peoples were dependent for their day to day existence on the forest and other natural resources. With the cutting of the forests, their very base of existence was uprooted. They were not having the required exposer to reorient themselves for alternative sources of livelihood. In these circumstances, they are left alone to face the adversaries of the displacement.

Displacements under most of the development projects not only uprooted the people from their homes but also from their culture and tradition. After displacement the affected population lost their temples and ancestral land, which have been a part of their life for generations and cannot be replaced at any cost. This led to a loss of the rich culture and tradition, which have been followed by them for generations. The displaced persons underwent the entire process of relocation and adjustment to an unfamiliar environment. As a consequence thereof they suffered both physical and psychological stress.

In the case of almost all the six development projects, whatever cash compensation was provided to the displaced families, a major part was spent for unproductive purposes. Most of the households ate, drank and became merry but only for a few days. Afterwards, they were paupers and a complete picture of misery. This called for a provision of 'land for land' in the project areas. But none of the development projects under this study had the provision to do the same.

In the absence of a proper resettlement and rehabilitation plan for the displaced households under the development projects, there were following negative impacts on the lives and livelihood of these affected households.

As a result of unleashing a faulty rehabilitation and resettlement system in the project area, there has been a multiplication in individual and social empowerment, including homelessness and the growth of new slums; physical, psychological and emotional trauma; insecurity for the future; medical hardships and the onset of diseases, substantially higher transportation costs, loss of livelihood and traditional lands, the removal of children from schools, arrest of those opposing an eviction, loss of faith by victims in the legal and political system, loss of culturally significant sites, confiscation of personal goods and property, substantially higher housing costs, absence of a choice of an alternative accommodation, increased social isolation, and tension with dwellers (host population) already at resettlement sites.

Rehabilitation Policy

India does not have a rehabilitation policy. In the past, R & R programmes have been found unsatisfactory. Only few states have their own R & R policy. These have not been monitored by the independent agencies.

The Ministry of the Rural Areas and Employment, Government of India is finalizing two legal measures on development induced displacement. The National Policy for Resettlement and Rehabilitation of Displaced Persons (NPRR, 1988) has many positive aspects as well as shortcomings. But the Land Acquisition Bill (LAB, 1998) ignores the Draft Policy. It enunciates the following principles:

1. Displacement should be minimized. So people displacing projects should be the last option after studying non-displacing and least displacing alternatives.
2. It recognizes that displacement results in "state-induced impoverishment" and that "non developmental project can be justified if a section of the society is pauperised by it."
3. Informed consent of those to be affected by it should be mandatory. The project is to be explained to them. They may question every aspect including its public purpose and environmental impact.
4. The definition of the DPs/PAPs goes beyond landowners to include those who depend for sustenance on land owned by others or on the Common Property Resources (CPRs). As such compensation should be given for the CPRs. and other livelihood cost.
5. The welfare of DPs/PAPs is a pre-condition of the project. Rehabilitation is mandatory and should go on side by side with

the project and should be prior to dislocation. The DPs should be resettled as communities and should have a better lifestyle after displacement than before it because they pay the price of development. They should be the first beneficiaries of jobs and other project benefits.

6. Often moneylenders and other outsiders usurp land in the area to be acquired after news spreads about the possibility of a project. When the project is notified, they get most benefits meant for the DPs/PAPs. As a protection against it, NPRR, 1998 includes among the DPs/PAPs only those who were residents of the area three years before the notification under section 4.1 of the Land Acquisition Act, 1894 (LAA, 1894).
7. Land for land is recommended as compensation or rehabilitation to all the DPs/PAPs as is mandatory for tribals.

It also has some shortcomings. The 'public purpose' for which the land is acquired under LAA has not been defined even more than a century after its enactment. In the absence of a definition, courts have generally accepted as 'public purpose' whatever the Government so declared, including transfer of land to the private sector. Abuses are intrinsic to this stand. In project after project, more land than required is acquired and then sold for profit. The social activist DP/PAP combined has been demanding a restrictive definition to include only schemes of genuine welfare of the biggest possible number, such as educational and health institutions and housing for the poor. NPRR, 1998 says that the project should be according to the public purpose, but does not define it or state that it should be defined in a restrictive manner.

Besides, it does not give adequate importance to the cultural aspects except in the rehabilitation of the tribals. Nomads are mentioned only in passing. The gender issue does not receive the importance it deserves. Though made mandatory, rehabilitation is not mentioned as a fundamental right. Thus, it remains a welfare measure. Past DPs/PAPs are alluded to but their rehabilitation is not mentioned. According to estimates at least 213 lakhs were deprived of their livelihood between 1951 and 1990. More than 40 per cent of them are tribals. Less than a third of them have been resettled even partially. Today their number must be 300 lakhs. But being voiceless they are displaced without their consent and ignored.

Besides, a policy is not legally binding. It requires a law but NPRR, 1988 makes no provision for it.

Package for Rehabilitation

On the issue of diagnosing policy package of rehabilitation for displaced population from development projects, the experts are found to have holding two extreme views. The experts belonging to social volunteers group intend to uproot the existing administrative set-up to facilitate displaced population through rehabilitation package. The experts, belonging to state administrative group, try to remain more particular towards abiding state laws while recommending rehabilitation package. This makes rehabilitation package anti-displaced population. For all practical purposes in such policy issues, a midway should be adopted. Following are some policy measures to evolve a package for rehabilitation:

1. The displacement should be avoided wherever possible and minimised when not avoidable.
2. When displacement is unavoidable, a relocation/ resettlement plan should be prepared and implemented which allocates sufficient resources to ensure that those affected are fairly compensated and rehabilitated. They should be benefited from the development process on a sustainable basis. At minimum they should be no worse-off than before displacement.
3. There should be full participation in the planning and management process by the main parties involved, in particular the communities affected.
4. The parties benefiting from the development causing the displacement should pay the full cost of the displacement and relocation process including the socio-economic rehabilitation of those affected to at least their formal level.
5. Compensation should be paid in terms of land. In case land compensation is not possible then the benefit should be in terms of employment in or outside the project. In self-employment schemes and training for skilled or semi-skilled jobs, women should also be given equal opportunity and benefits.
6. The new land source could be the degraded forestl land. Tree farming, including horticulture, should be encouraged with assured markets.
7. Only irrigated land should be reclaimed. Land without water should not be deemed fit for oustees.

8. Demonstration farming (including tree farming) should be done and land should be given only when the income becomes at least double of the original holdings of the oustees.
9. The 'tiller' should receive compensation as rightfully as owner of land receives compensation.
10. Market value should be given much before the land acquisition.
11. The minimum land should be acquired.
12. Rehabilitation should be a part of any development project. The cost should be borne by the project implementers. It should also take into account whether there are any alternative than to displace people. If displacement is unavoidable, the project-affected people should be rehabilitated as a unit not in fragments.
13. The resettlement site should be as close as to the original site and contain all the facilities, which were available earlier. Proper care should be taken to protect culture and tradition of the rehabilitated unit.
14. There should be a periodical evaluation of the government agency involved in the resettlement process and the rehabilitation programmes of the project. The evaluation should be conducted by an autonomous body.
15. While preparing the resettlement and rehabilitation programme for the project affected site, the project affected people should be involved in meetings and discussions. Transparency about R & R and other information should be maintained at all levels.
16. Loss of natural habitat should be compensated by a realistic programme and should involve the local community.
17. Integrated social groups should be resettled together.
18. The process of land take-over for development project should route through Panchayat level. No land acquisition should be allowed without prior permission from Panchayat level. All the resettlement and rehabilitation works should be undertaken under the supervision of Village Panchayat of the concerned area.
19. There should be a compulsory provision of equal compensation rate for equal quality of land in two independent development projects located at nearby places of adjoining places.

Project Employment—Compliance of National Draft Policy

After many more efforts in the past, in 1993, it was finally decided to formulate a national policy for rehabilitation of displaced persons. The document has come to be known as the Draft Policy. It proceeds from a basic assumption that displacement involves a trauma, which cannot be fully compensated but can be mitigated to a large extent in physical and economic terms. The draft policy addresses itself primarily to the needs of disadvantaged communities. Among other things, it involves a commitment to ensure that displaced persons are better-off after than before displacement, and visualizes displacement as an instrument of a positive change.

The experience of providing project related employment to displaced persons has been dismal in the past. Project employment has often gone to undeserving or unrelated persons for various reasons. The Draft Policy seeks to transfer the appropriate decision-making power to the Project Implementation Committee (PIC) in which the Project Affected Population (PAPs) and the NGOs play a significant role. According to the Draft Policy, the PIC will take a decision regarding the number of jobs to be provided, the terming of employment, etc. it is expected that the job and other benefits flowing from the project will be channelled to the deserving PAPs.

In the past, PAP has been denied skilled and semi-skilled jobs due to their lack of the requisite technical abilities and training. The policy provides for the undertaking of a survey as soon as a project is conceived and the forming of a Project Implementation Committee. This Committee would have a major say in selecting candidates from amongst the PAPs and providing them with technical training so that they are in a position to apply for the jobs by the time displacement occurs.

For providing employment opportunities to PAP, the Draft Policy cuts across the dependency syndrome. In the past, the burden of direct employment of the displaced has often fallen heavily on projects, resulting in a permanent efficiency cost. The Draft Policy makes another departure from the past by seeking to remove this dependency syndrome. The Draft Policy provides for employment of the displaced in project construction and related jobs. Sufficient economic activities are usually generated during the construction phase to sustain a large section of the PAPs even during the pre-displacement stage.

Projects generate forward linkages including those in the ancillary sector as large industries provide stimuli for growth in other sectors by the creation of both demand and supply. The Draft Policy envisages training for PAPs in entrepreneurship and the provision of capital assets so that they may meet such demands.

The Draft Plan provides that PAPs should be integrated into the project by being allowed access to these benefits. It also spells out how this may be achieved. Much is also dependent on the development of the infrastructure for enhancing human capital in the locality.

Success and Failure of Draft Policy

The Draft Policy suffers from a number of deficiencies. It has little to say on gender sensitization and female empowerment. It ignores millions of PAPs who are currently waiting for rehabilitation. Nevertheless, the Draft Policy provides a helpful framework for a national debate on these and other issues, and the possible basis of a consensus on the rehabilitation policy. The nation has yet to decide whether it is fully prepared to shoulder the burden of rehabilitation of millions of people who have been pushed below the poverty line for bringing prosperity to some sections through the development projects,

Compliance of Rehabilitation Related Government Orders in Uttar Pradesh

The Government of Uttar Pradesh have been alive with project related displacement problems and through the Government orders, issued from time to time, have impressed upon the agencies concerned to look into the matter regarding resettlement and rehabilitation of the displaced persons. The study conducted by the Giri Institute of Development Studies, Lucknow, has taken the stock of development-induced displacement and compliance of the Government Orders issued from time to time. The research findings arrived manifestly indicate that in certain cases, the Government Orders were observed in breach rather than in compliance.

After a result of faulty rehabilitation and resettlement system in the project area, there has been a multiplication in individual and social impoverishments including homelessness, and the growth of new slums and physical, psychological and emotional trauma.

Ideally, the process of displacement and resettlement should take place, simultaneously planning development project with sensitivity establishing strong linkages with process and institutions, which identify and address the disequilibrium created by the projects. The Government of Uttar Pradesh through Government orders dated 28th December, 1973 instructed the authorities concerned that appropriate provisions should be made for rehabilitation of displaced persons with no delay and employment to one member from each family should be provided. The requirement of land for the project should be kept at a minimum, as far as it is possible and the diversion of the prime agricultural land should be avoided, user and barren land should be utilized for the development project as far as it is feasible. In the process, number of Government Orders were issued and a comprehensive Government Order was issued on 29th February, 1996 in which it was underlined, that the provisions made in the Government Orders were not complied in the spirit of words, with the result that the rehabilitation/resettlement of displaced persons could not take a healthy shape. As expressed Government Orders through this Government Order, it was made compulsory to employ members from displaced families in the projects. The Government Order further expressed that the displaced persons should not be kept in a helpless situation because they have sacrificed their land, for the sake of development. It is the pious duty of the Government to look into the rehabilitation problem in toto and the project authorities should ensure that the Government Orders are well honoured. This may result into least litigation and more happiness and prosperity. The District Magistrate and Collector have been made responsible for looking into resettlement problem so that no dereliction is there. The Divisional Commissioners have been made responsible to monitor the rehabilitation problems in the respective division. The study leaves the problem with the optimistic view that such a burning problem will receive due attention and will not end with abortive efforts.

References

Bajpai, B.K. (2004). *"Development-Induced Displacement: A Package for Rehabilitation in Uttar Pradesh,* New Royal Book Co., Lucknow.

Fernandes, Walter (1994). "Development-Induced Displacement in the Tribal Areas of Eastern India". New Delhi, *Indian Social Institute (Mimeo).*

Government of India (1985). *Report of the Committee on Rehabilitation of Displaced Tribals due to Development Project,* New Delhi, Ministry of Home Affairs.

"Rehabilitation Policy and Law in India: A Right to Livelihood", 1996, Published by *ECONET, Indian Social Institute.*

28

Who Owns the Land: A Development Debate in Spatial Planning of Urban Fringe

Sunit Singh and *Rewa Singh*

Introduction

The land acquisitions by the governments for industrial or infrastructure development have been witnessing protests at many places in recent past compelling governments and political parties to open dialogue with the affected people for negotiations to resolve the problem. Although the governments still continue with conservative hegemonic approaches but organized and sustained pressure by the people at some places have made the governments realize that time is changing fast and the State cannot impose conditions arbitrarily in the name of development. The protests against projects like, Narmada Dam, Singur, Nandigram, Dadri, Singrauli, Ganga Express Way are few examples in this regard. The issues of development induced displacement along with Rehabilitation and Resettlement (R & R) provisions are gaining importance in the contemporary development planning discourse with the balance slowly tilting in favour of concerns for people and their livelihoods. The bulldozing approach of State sponsored development is at the same time being strongly criticized by the proponents of sustainable development by raising issues of ecological security and climate change.

A major ongoing displacement, across the country, is the displacement due to urban expansion. Influenced by both push and pull factors, the urban fringe is the single most important factor causing significant changes in the land use patterns. In most of the cases, it involves conversion of more fertile agricultural land to non-agricultural purposes. In the case of urban fringes, the land is generally sold by the owners rather than being acquired. In this sense such displacements are generally termed as 'voluntary' rather than forced (Shah and Kumar, 2008).

Though the scale of conversion of land is very high, there is no systematic estimate about how much land is being converted from agricultural to non-agricultural purposes every year in the fringe areas of the country. Secondly efforts have seldom been made to understand how the people who have lost their land have eventually been co-opted into the new economic order and how many remained victims of 'development', remains unknown (Sharma, 2003). This is mainly due to the fact that (a) adjustment or co-option to the new economic order is a long-drawn process; very few studies have gone into examining the process over a period of, say 15 to 20 years; and (b) although urbanization-induced loss of agricultural land is relatively larger, it remains unnoticed as much of the land is sold 'voluntarily' under the 'right to choose' use of the land by the owners (Shah & Kumar, 2008)

Generally, it is believed that urban expansions provide opportunities to villagers for getting competitive price of their land either from government or private developers which help them starting new occupations or businesses with possibilities of rise in the income levels. It is argued that they are able to get access to facilities of planned urban system in the form of electricity, roads, street lights, drinking water, recreation centre, transport and communication, schools and hospitals, and other facilities which help them improving their quality of life. The newspapers and popular magazines have regularly been publishing columns about the stories from places like Noida, Faridabad, Lucknow, Mumbai, Bangalore, Hyderabad, Allahabad or any other growing city highlighting the overnight changes in the lifestyles with conspicuous presence of costly cars, mobile phones, televisions, and other consumer durables in the homes of erstwhile struggling-hard farmers. Many farmers become contractors, building material suppliers and land market players. Suddenly, the sleepy traditional villages with scattered hamlets get transformed into fast moving, active and modern cities. The developers claim that those farmers would have never been able to earn that much of income from their land if it was not sold for urban expansion. Thus, as soon as the notification is published for expansion of urban limits the land market becomes bullish. Farmers start looking eagerly for bargain and getting their lives transformed for which they had aspired for generations. In this sense, the phenomenon is being looked at as voluntary displacement (Sharma, 2003). To a large extent, it might be true for the villages where land had been less fertile with poor irrigation facilities and the agriculture being at subsistence level. However, without analyzing the long-term impact on the lives of affected households it would be grossly unfair to draw a hasty conclusion that the 'so-called' voluntary displacements are always 'from bad to good'.

It has been pointed out that more often than not, the result has been devastating on the communities, especially the landless labourers, small entrepreneurs and local artisans (D'Rozario, 2005). In most of the cases as the demand for labourers increases with the growth of construction related activities in urban fringes the landless agricultural labourers are transformed into unskilled or semi-skilled construction labourer to meet the growing labour demand of the expanding informal construction industry. Many people consider that it is the mobility towards a better life. However, the NCEUS report revealed that the informal construction workers get less than statutory minimum wages (NCEUS, 2008). The processes unleash a situation where more and more people are being displaced from their communities and traditional ways of life (Sharma, 2003). It is a matter of fact that the private developers are mostly interested in quick profits from real estate business and are completely detached from concerns for the needs and rights of the affected rural communities. The local communities remain voiceless spectator to the alienation from their own traditional subsistence resources under the overwhelming hegemony of bureaucratic top-down interventions.

The urban fringe represents a unique set of villages with dual characteristics of rural and urban simultaneously. These villages face peculiar type of problem relating to management and planning of natural resources due to overlapping territories of local bodies and the urban development authorities. In the name of comprehensive development plans to meet the requirements of growing city population, the development authorities encroach upon the autonomy of Village Panchayats overlooking the national commitment of decentralized planning and participatory management. The development plans imposed by development authorities in urban fringe villages are contrary to the spirits of 73rd Constitutional Amendments. It is against the Constitutional intentions to bring about people's participation in governance at grass roots and negates the right to development of local people.

The continued duality in governance in fringe villages is adversely affecting the effectiveness of various development schemes intended to be implemented through Village Panchayats. As soon as the notification for inclusion of certain villages in the city limits is published, the development agencies start ignoring the authority of Village Panchayats and de-facto they are made to be vanished away. It has been pointed out that after the 73rd Constitutional Amendment, the Village Panchayat units are democratically elected statutory corporate bodies with tenure of five years (The Constitution of India Part IX). These Panchayats are entrusted to prepare economic plans for the territory they govern. They are answerable to the members of the Gram Sabha (UP Panchayati Raj Act, Ch. III Sec. 11-3 b). The Village Panchayats also function as the Land Management Committees responsible for upkeep, protection and supervision of the land within their territorial limits (UP Panchayati Raj Act, Ch. IV Sec. 28A). Now, suddenly a government notification comes out and the very existence of the Village Panchayat is put to the question. Not only Village Panchayats but several intermediate panchayats and district level panchayats also get affected without taking them into confidence.

Thus, the procedure of land acquisition for urban expansion is a reflection of hegemonic approach of the State. At no place people are consulted regarding the motives of acquisition. The planning exercises never involved people or community based organizations. It is assumed that the professionals sitting at the helm of affairs were most competent and efficient and they alone can prepare the best plans for the development. It reflects the arrogance of the policy makers and the planners and their attitude to look at the people with utter neglect. The participatory planning, decentralized governance and democratization all become mere rhetoric. There has never been any participatory process initiated in either planning or implementation. While this process obviously brings forth the critical questions regarding citizenship and democracy, it also highlights the abject neglect of these communities and their fundamental rights (D'Rozario, 2005).

Research Questions

The above discussion raises certain questions that need to be addressed for better understanding about its impacts on different sections of the affected households of the 'so-called' voluntary displacements in urban fringe areas over a period of time. These questions can be classified into three broad categories:

(i) The Land, People and Livelihoods: The conversion of land from agriculture to non-agriculture purposes in fringe areas affect different sections of village community differently according to their relationship with the land and their tenure rights. The genuine title holders are the directly affected persons while persons depending on the commons as well as on the landowners for wage employment are the indirectly affected persons. The livelihoods choices for both the sections would obviously be affected differently.

The directly affected persons might be gainers and losers both depending upon the quality and location of their land. With poor quality land farmers might gain but superior quality landowners would definitely be the losers. The latter would react aggressively. Therefore, the questions needed to be addressed are:

1. Had the farmers been taken into confidence while initiating the proposal for acquisition of their land?
2. Had they been told about the compensation measures and procedures involved in it?
3. Had there been any dialogue with the farmers regarding alternative livelihood opportunities after their land is acquired?
4. Had there been any discussion on the coping problems of farmers in the future urbanized economic model?
5. Had there been any dialogue regarding the forms of urban planning and expansion and on the ongoing urban oriented development model?

The people who are indirectly affected are the landless, village level retail traders and local artisans who might not be the title holders but their livelihoods are certainly affected after their village is transformed into a city. These are the people who are dependent on common property resources for their livelihoods in multiple ways. They do not have any right on those resources in a formal sense. Perceived as a safety net by those households the extinction of Common Property Resources (CPR) certainly increases their vulnerability and are forced to move further back to remote villages and start their lives afresh. They are forced to pay the price of the progress.

The questions needed to be addressed thus are:

(a) Have the concerns of such households been taken into consideration while acquiring the CPR?
(b) Is there any scope for such households to be considered as affected persons in the form of entitlements on the CPR?
(c) Is there any mechanism thought of for securing futures of such households?

(ii) The Institutions: The land is acquired in the name of 'public purpose' by the sovereign which cannot be challenged in any court. However, in a democratic country like India people are governed by the Union, State and Local Governments. It is a continuum of governance. If any institution in this sequence is bypassed it is undemocratic and unconstitutional. It is extremely unfortunate that the democratically elected Village Panchayats are bypassed by higher authorities in taking decisions on the issues that are vested in the Panchayats. In the present form of land acquisition for urban expansion the Village Panchayats are doomed to be sacrificed for establishing the supremacy of the higher authorities.

The questions needed to be addressed are:

(a) Being the smallest unit of governance whether the Village Panchayats are recognized as an integral part of governance?
(b) Is there any mechanism in existence ensuring participation of Village Panchayats in decision making ?

(iii) The Processes: The processes involved in land acquisition have long term implications for the democratic decentralization and inclusive growth in India.

The questions involved in this realm are:

(a) Is there any process for bringing into consideration the indigenous model of development in the planning of fringe area?
(b) Are there any provisions for integrating the existing development plans initiated by the Panchayats with the proposed model?
(c) Have the sustainability issues of the proposed development model been discussed with the people so that it does not lead to impoverishment?

The Context

The present chapter is an attempt to address the above questions involving different participatory communication methods at micro level. The recent notification by the Governor of Uttar Pradesh for expansion of Allahabad *Mahanagar* has been considered as the basis for isolating the urban fringe.

The total population of Allahabad was around 493.61 million (2001 census) out of which 372.90 million were rural residents and 120.68 million were urban dwellers. The total geographical area is about 548.2 thousand hectares of which 97.3 per cent belong to rural areas (536.5 hectare) and merely 2.7 per cent (11.7 hectares) are covered by urban areas. Administratively, the rural area of Allahabad is divided into six sub-divisions, 20 CD Blocks and 1425 Village Panchayats representing 3054 revenue villages, 2802 inhabitants and 262 uninhabited (Statistical Journal, Allahabad 2007).

On November 30, 2006, the Governor of Uttar Pradesh, through a notification declared that 442 revenue villages belonging to four sub-divisions shall be the part of Allahabad *Mahanagar* (Metropolitan city) area along with the entire area covered under Nagar Nigam, Allahabad Development Authority and the Town Area, Jhusi. The notification was published in pursuance of the powers mentioned in the section 2-45 A of U.P. Nagar Nigam Act, 1959 read along with the provisions of 243 *ta* of the Constitution of India.

Thus, 14.5 per cent villages are to be covered under the urban limits. These villages are spread in three sub-divisions and five CD blocks. The details of area to be acquired are given in Table 28.1:

In all 168 (about 12%) Village Panchayats are affected by this notification. The geographical area of these panchayats is about 287.26 hundred hectares constituting about 5.33 per cent land of the rural area. Out of which 202.59 hundred hectares land is under cultivation and nearly 75 per cent of this is of very good quality affecting livelihoods of 6.23 lakh persons (4.77% of the rural population). Among the affected people 1.85 lakh (29.7%) belong to BPL category.

Methods of Enquiry

The processes involved in the land acquisition by the government as well as private players for urban expansion produce a mix of reaction among

Table 28.1: Land and Population in Affected Villages under Urban Expansion in Allahabad

Block	*No. of GP*	*Total Area ('00 ha)*	*Area under cultivation ('00 ha)*	*Area under CPR ('00 ha)*	*Total Population ('000)*	*BPL Population ('000)*
Kaurihar	38	67.24	49.02	11.42	171.57	47.60
Soraon	40	72.78	52.27	20.52	142.55	42.52
Bahariya	11	20.00	14.56	5.43	35.74	13.62
Bahadurpur	38	75.14	55.55	19.59	139.71	42.43
Chaka	41	52.10	31.20	20.90	134.40	38.46
Total	168	287.26	202.60	77.86	623.97	184.63

Source: Governor's Notification dated Nov. 30, 2006 & District Perspective Plan for NREGA in Allahabad.

local population. The affected persons could be categorized into two categories: (i) directly affected persons whose land was likely to be acquired and (ii) indirectly affected persons generally landless who might not be losing land in the process but their livelihoods would certainly be affected after their village is transformed into a city. In order to get the complete picture it is essential to analyze the views of persons belonging to both the categories. To elicit the views and opinions about the likely impacts on the lives and livelihoods of affected persons was a challenge as the issues have strong emotional bearings. Secondly, most of the affected persons were lacking information about the government notification on the inclusion of their village into the city limits so individual interviews with conventional structured questionnaire would not be helpful. Thirdly, the perception about the likely impacts could better be understood only by applying a long-term impact analysis and for that the persons affected previously need to be included into the study. And, lastly the socio-political environmental factors are also to be taken care of for understanding the dynamic competing processes of institutions at different levels. Keeping in view the exploratory nature of the study, the qualitative methods were preferred for collecting the primary data. Following methods were applied:

Focus Group Discussions (FGDs): Three FGDs were conducted. Two with the group of farmers belonging to the villages notified for inclusion into the city. Both the villages—(i) Sarangapur (Chaka block) and (ii) Kuandeeh (Bahadurpur block) were beyond five kilometers from the Nagar Nigam limits. The third FGD was conducted with the labourers selected from the Labour Chauraha operative in a fringe locality—Jhusi. The group was comprised of labourers of young and aged; and unskilled and semi-skilled both. The labourers were selected from such locations that had been witnessing the urbanization process since last 15-20 years. It was assumed that it would help to understand the impact of urbanization on the indirectly or less affected persons.

In-depth Interviews with Key Informants: For supplementing the information collected through FGDs in-depth interviews were conducted with village pradhans, teachers, labourers, farmers, women from slums.

Findings from the Field

A. The Land, People and Livelihoods

A-1: The Farmers

The farmers, likely to be affected by the proposed acquisition were unnerved when told about the notification. They were unable to understand how any government could acquire their ancestral property without their consent. During the FGDs the farmers expressed that land is key asset for them, it is their identity, determines their social status, they could not even think that they could survive without land. Their life moves around the land. Agriculture is not simply their bread and butter; it is their life. If the land is detached, farmers would be vanished away. They expressed that government is conspiring with the real estate business houses and township developers to eliminate the farmers.

The fear was explicitly expressed by the farmers that they would never be able to cope with the lifestyles of new economic order as most of them were either illiterate or less educated. They would certainly fail to find any employment and their livelihoods would be at stake. It has rightly been observed that once displaced, the affected persons are pushed into an open-market situation as individuals competing for their survival in a hostile new environment. A majority of them proved to be losers in this new race of development (Sharma, 2003). The only way out would be to purchase land in distant villages and that would be traumatic enough as their community life would also be destroyed.

The group also narrated that the land owned by the farmers is not the basis of livelihoods for their families alone; it has linkages with off-farm activities, non-farm occupations as well as wage employment opportunities for agricultural labourers. The loss of land to the farmers would cause more hardships to the landless agricultural labourers, local artisans and village retail traders.

The issue of Common Property Resources (CPR) was also raised during the discussion. Apprehensions were raised that in the new order it would be very difficult to manage space against heavy payments for marriages and other social ceremonies whereas in the villages they could get common land for such purposes without any payment. They can keep their livestock without any problem of space which would not be possible in urban settlements.

A-2: The Agricultural Labourers, Artisans and Rural Retailers

Nearly one-third of the rural population belonged to this category of indirectly affected persons. The views and opinions that were revealed during the FGD with labourers provided a glimpse of hardships being faced by the displaced labourers and their woe of not being heard anywhere. It helped to understand the miserable conditions of those labourers who fail to cope with the urban labour market requirements. Generally, it is believed that the labourers gain in terms of better opportunities of work, higher and timely payment of wages in the urban economic order. The labourers were in agreement with the observation to some extent but simultaneously revealed that as compared to rural areas the working conditions in urban informal labour markets are worse, they are required to work for longer hours, and at certain time risk to life is also involved (NCEUS, 2008). The transformation of villages into cities destroys their traditional social networks and in the absence of any alternative social security system they become victims of what Michael Cernea calls spiral of impoverishments (quoted in Kothari, 1996).

The labourers were of the view that in rural areas they have the right to make claims for allotment of agricultural land on Gram Sabha land through Village Panchayats on preferential terms which provides some sort of food security. It has been observed that for poorer households homegrown grains constitute nearly thirty per cent of their food requirements. The labourers told that they can produce foodgrains that could provide food security for about six months. In cities there would be no such provisions hence contributing towards the process of vulnerability.

The landless labourers were aware that they were entitled to get residential sites and subsequently construct houses under Indira Awas Yojana (IAY) schemes which would not be in the case of urban areas. They were residing either on community land, railways land, embankments of village ponds or on private land of cultivators. Homelessness is one of the major causes of vulnerability for such members. It was in this backdrop the allotment of housing sites have special significance in rural areas. Further, the FGD participants expressed their helplessness in protecting their residential and agricultural land in case their neighbours or family members have sold their pieces of land or building to someone who is an influential person. They informed that in such cases they are coerced and threatened in many ways to sell out their piece of land or building and ultimately they are left with no option except to dispose of their land despite their unwillingness. Can this be called as the voluntary displacement?

B. The Institutions

The village pradhans participating in the FGDs informed that they are not clear what would be the fate of their panchayats after the inclusion of their villages in the city limits. The notification mentions that the villages mentioned in it would become the part of the Allahabad *Mahanagar*. Obvious conclusion is that the panchayats would get dissolved. The UP Panchayati Raj Act, 1947 Section II A (8) states "if the whole of the area of Gram Panchayat is included in a city, municipality, cantonment, notified area, the Gram Panchayat shall cease, and its assets and liabilities shall be disposed of in the manner prescribed. If a part of such area so included, its jurisdiction shall be reduced by that part". Then the section 34 says that subject to any special reservation made by the State Government all public property situated within the jurisdiction of a Gram Panchayat shall vest in and belong to the Gram Panchayat and shall, with all other property which may become vested in the Gram Panchayat be under its direction, management and control. At the same time, the preamble of the Act says that Act is for to establish and develop Local Self Government in the rural area of the Uttar Pradesh and to make better provisions for village administration and development. It has been mentioned that subject to such conditions as may be prescribed by the State Government from time to time, a Gram Panchayat shall perform the functions classified into twenty nine categories, which include promotion and development of agriculture and horticulture, development of wastelands and grazing lands and preventing their unauthorized alienation and use, land development, land reform implementation, assisting the Government and other agencies in land consolidation and soil conservation, implementation of rural housing programmes, distribution of house sites, preparation of plan for economic development of the area of the Gram Panchayat, preservation and maintenance of community assets. Further, section 15 A of the Act states that a Gram Panchayat shall prepare every year an economic development plan for the Panchayat area and submit it to the Kshetra Panchayat concerned before such date and in such manner as may be prescribed.

It is true that legally all the assets vested in panchayats are subject to the conditions prescribed by the State Government and can be acquired in the manner prescribed under the law. But the above arrangements seem to be contrary to the spirit of the Constitution after 73rd Amendment which is specifically in favour of decentralization and democratic participation in governance for transferring the power to the people. The participants expressed their concerns about the approach and attitudes of the State and para-statal agencies towards Village Panchayats ignoring the smallest unit of governance in taking decisions on the issues that are vested in them. They opined that such initiatives harm the institutional environment at grass roots level that has been evolved over a period of about two decades. The participants were saying that in the name of comprehensive development plans to meet the requirements of growing city population the development authorities are encroaching upon the autonomy of Village Panchayats overlooking the national commitment of decentralized planning and participatory management. They were emphasizing that it is against the Constitutional intentions to bring about people's participation in governance at the grass roots level and negates the right to development of local people. It seems that the governments at higher levels lack faith in the Village Panchayats that is why they are probably shy in sitting with panchayats for negotiating the issues related to the area

C. The Processes

The participants of FGD expressed that the fringe areas are neither city nor village, worse of both places co-exist nor they turn out to be unplanned, unhygienic and unhealthy habitations with illusionary development benefits of urbanization. These views were quite close to the observation of researchers regarding peri-urban environment or *rurban* development (Allen, 2003). Many times the area remains incomplete or unattractive to potential beneficiaries due to the absence of adequate infrastructure or, such acquired lands remain unused or are encroached. It has been observed that the lands transferred by farmers to city dwellers lead to haphazard growth on the urban periphery and prove a challenge to planners in terms of providing basic amenities in such areas. For example, the unchecked growths of metropolitan cities like Bangalore, Pune or Kanpur (Sharma, 2003). The villagers observed that the areas that were included in urban limits 20 years back are still struggling to get urban facilities as were painted at that time. They have not gain anything but are paying numerous taxes to different civic bodies—like house tax, water tax, higher electricity charges without any improvement in the services. People have lost faith in the system of payment of compensation because eight years back when their land was acquired for NTPC plant no compensation was paid to farmers. The affected farmers organized protests, they were *lathi-charged* and coerced by the state machinery in the name of development.

The participants of FGD were of the view that the entire process is with the sole objective to generate resources for para-statal bodies like development authorities and basic service agencies. They expressed that there exists a nexus between vested interests representing real estate businesses, private colonizers, the bureaucrats and persons sitting in the government. Instances were aired that the government first acquired land, transferred it to the development authority and was then handed over to a private construction company for township development. The villagers were raising allegations of conspiracy in the whole process. Some of them were blaming the government to be in hand and gloves with the World Bank and other multinationals.

There was a very serious apprehension among the participants that as soon as the notification for inclusion of villages gets published the provisions of urban ceiling are imposed upon them automatically and the land of many farmers is transferred in favour of the Nagar Nigam. They were narrating such instances where the names of farmers were struck off from the official records without serving any notices to them. Farmers agitated and expressed that their ancestral property was taken away without even consulting with them. It is an arbitrary act and cannot be termed anything but sheer grabbing of their land by the State.

Need for a Paradigm Shift

The 73rd Constitutional Amendment and subsequently concomitant changes in State Panchayati Raj Acts has raised expectations at grass roots level that the Village Panchayats have the status to negotiate on behalf of villagers and protect their interests. During last fifteen years the panchayats have completed two full terms and third is passing through the last year. Thus, the panchayats are gradually maturing as democratic institutions at grass roots level. The villagers are also progressively learning how to control and manage their panchayats and prepare plans for their economic development through it. The introduction of NREGA throughout the country has strengthened this process. People are getting educated with social audit, RTI, public accountability and transparency tools. Many NGOs are engaged in providing training to panchayat representatives for asserting their rights as institutions of governance. SHGs and other Community Based Organisations (CBOs) are being formed and capacities are being built through trainings for people's participation in the decision making that affects their lives. Public and legal advocacy campaigns by social activists and development organizations against the hegemonic attitudes of State Governments towards Village Panchayats are gaining strength day by day. The state sponsored model of development is being challenged in different parts of the country by various groups and alternative paradigms are being discussed as people oriented sustainable development models. India along with many other developing countries is intensively engaged in the contemporary debate on alternative development model; whether development preserving the lives and livelihoods or the development alienating people from their traditional sources of sustenance. In this sense, as many researchers are emphasizing that the questions of 'public purpose' and 'national interests' and 'sovereign domain' need to be redefined.

Notes

Growing social activisim against such sovereign domain of government is not only in response to untold hardships and miseries caused to the affected people but also a protest against the very model of development that alienates people from their traditional sources of sustenance (Sharma, 2003).

1. U.P. Panchayati Raj Act, 1947 Section 28 A the Gram Panchayat shall also be the Bhoomi Prabandhak Samiti (Land Management Committee) and as such discharge the duties of upkeep, protection and supervision of all property belonging to or vested in or held by the Gram Panchayat under Section 117 of the UPZALR, 1950 or under any other provision of that Act. The Gram Pradhan and Up-pradhan shall respectively be the Chairman and Vice-Chairman of the Committee and the Lekhpal of the area shall be the Secretary. The LMC for and on behalf of the Gram Panchayat be charged with the general management and control of all property referred to in Section 28 A including: the settling and management of land, the preservation, maintenance and development of forests and trees, the maintenance and development of *abadi* sites and village communications; the management and development of *haats*, bazaars and *melas*; the maintenance and development of fisheries and tanks.
2. In an overwhelming number of cases, there is an almost arrogant assumption that the project that has been drawn up for implementation is socially and economically the most appropriate and that the development intervention cannot be challenged because it has been conceived by experts and is in the 'public' and 'national' interest (Kothari 1996).
3. Quoted in Shah and Kumar: An important implication of this has been a more activated land market where many more farmers may want to sell-off at least a part of their land in order to make an entry into the urban economy for exploring alternative occupations for the subsequent generations. Thus, the fringe lands are generally more fertile and have been put to agricultural use. With increasing population pressure such lands are also bound to feel the pressure (Burton and Matson, 1996). The situation is further complicated by an aggregation of use by a variety of stakeholders. Even the farmers living in the area might find non-agricultural income sources to be more profitable and may resort to land speculations (Renaud, 1979).

4. Article 31(2) of the Land Acquisition Act, 1894 (now amended 1984) categorically states that a land can be acquired by the State only for Public Purpose. Broadly speaking, public purpose would include a purpose, in which the general interest of the community, as opposed to a particular interest of the individual, in generally and vitally concerned. Anything which is useful to the public, in the sense that it confers some public benefit, or conduces to some public advantage, is a public purpose. Section 3 (f) of The Land Acquisition Act defines public purpose includes: provision of land of village sites for planned development or improvement of existing village sites, provision of land for town or rural planning, provision of land for planned development of land from public funds in pursuance of any scheme or policy of government and subsequent disposal thereof in whole or in part by lease, assignment or outright sale with the object of securing further development as planned, the provisioı. of land for a corporation owned or controlled by the State, the provision of land for residential purposes to the poor or landless or to persons residing in areas affected by natural calamities, or to persons displaced or affected by reason of the implementation of any scheme undertaken by Government, any local authority or a corporation owned or controlled by the State; the provision of land for carrying out any educational, housing, health or slum clearance scheme sponsored by Government or by any authority established by Government for carrying out any such scheme, or with the prior approval of the appropriate Government, by a local authority, or a society registered under Society Registration Act, 1860, or a cooperative society; the provision of land for any other scheme of development sponsored by Government or with the prior approval of the appropriate Government, by a local authority; the provision of any premises or building for locating a public office, but does not include acquisition of land for companies.
5. Quoted in Kothari 1996: In 1994, the Supreme Court observed that the power to acquire private property for public use is an attribute of sovereignty and is essential to the existence of government. The power of eminent domain was recognized on the principle that the sovereign state can always acquire the property of a citizen for public good, without the owner's consent... The right to acquire an interest in land compulsorily has assumed increasing importance as s result of requirement of such land more and more everyday, for different public purposes and *to implement the promises made by the framers of the Constitution to the People of India* (emphasis added) (Kothari).
6. Unaccustomed to new ways of life, the affected people face a hostile situation where they have to compete as individuals, different from their community-based setting. Many lose out in this race for development (Sharma 2003).
7. In a village setting, the productive land is a collective source of livelihood not only to its owners but also to the indirectly affected families like the agricultural labourers, village servants (carpenter, blacksmith, cobbler, and

so on). The directly affected, as per the law, are entitled to compensation and other benefits as a part of resettlement and rehabilitation. However, the indirectly affected—depending on the owner's land—are left without any protection. Some of them get contractual jobs when the project is under the construction stage but no long-term rehabilitation measures are available to them. (Sharma 2003)

8. The common property resources (grazing lands, fuel sources, ponds, wells, 'sacred groves', worshipping places, playgrounds) deplete or are lost if the village structures are to be demolished. In the urban context PAPs lose their place of work (like hawking/vending, self-employment) if some infrastructural project results in their shifting to locations were such opportunities do not exist or take time to develop. (Sharma)
9. In the admission of persons to land as (*bhumidhar* with non-transferable rights) or *asami* under Section 195 or Section 197 (hereinafter in this section referred to as allotment of land) the LMC shall, subject to any order made by a court under Section 178 observe the following order of preference:
   - landless widow, sons, unmarried daughters or parents residing in the circle of a person who has lost his life by enemy action while in active service in the Armed Forces of the Union;
   - a person residing in the circle, who has become wholly disabled by enemy action while in active service in the Armed Forces of the Union;
   - a landless agricultural labourer residing in the circle and belonging to a Scheduled Caste or Scheduled Tribe;
   - any other landless agricultural labourer residing in the circle;
   - a *bhumidhar* or *asami* residing in the circle and holding land less than 1.26 hectares (3.125 acres);
   - a landless person residing in the circle, who is retired, released or discharged from service other than service as an officer in the Armed Forces of the Union;
   - a landless freedom fighter residing in the circle who has not been granted political pension;
   - any other landless agricultural labourer belonging to a Scheduled Caste or Scheduled Tribe not residing in the circle but residing in the Nyaya Panchayat Circle.
   - "Landless" refers to a person who or whose spouse or minor children hold no land as *bhumidhar* or *asami* and who had no land as such within two years immediately preceding the date of allotment while "agricultural labourer" means whose main source of livelihood is agricultural labour.
10. The provisions of the UPZALR Act empower the LMC to allot house sites to landless households belonging to the Scheduled Castes and the Scheduled Tribes and agricultural labourers and village artisans from the land vested in the Gram Sabha or the land earmarked for *abadi* and reserved as *abadi* sites for Harijans under the U.P. Consolidation of Holdings Act, 1953 (Section 122 (c) of UPZALR Act, 1951).

11. In the outreach projects it has been observed that the ownership of a piece of land is not merely a material gain to a landless person instead it significantly contributes in altering the attitude and behaviour of the person. The agricultural land is the key asset in rural areas for sustainable livelihood security. It has been found that the award of title not only helps in creating self-confidence among beneficiaries but they start thinking similar to the general population regarding the pay-offs of individuals' effort and hard work on this asset. And it is only then that interventions relating to poverty alleviation start appealing them.

References

D'Rozario C. (2005). www.altlawpforum.ort/globalisation/research../urban%20sprawl./file

Government of Indi⌒ (2008). *Report on Conditions of Work and Promotion of Livelihoods in the Unorganised Sector.*

Government of UP (2007). *Statistical Journal, Allahabad.*

Kothari, Smitu (1996). "Whose Nation? The displaced as victims of development" in *Economic and Political Weekly*, Special issue Vol. 31, No 24, June 15.

Ramanathan, Usha (1996). "Displacement and the law", in *Economic and Political Weekly,* special issue Vol. 31, No. 24, June 15.

Shah Amita and Kumar Animesh (2008). "Displacement of land and displacement in India". In Mahendra Dev and K.S. Babu (ed), *India's Development: Social and Economic Disparities*, Manohar, New Delhi.

Sharma, R.N. (2003). "Involuntary Displacement: A few Encounters", in *Economic and Political Weekly,* Vol. 38, No. 9, pp. 907-12.

The Land Acquisition Act, 1894 (amended in 1994).

The Uttar Pradesh Panchayati Raj Act, 1947 (amended, 2003).

The Uttar Pradesh Urban Planning and Development Act, 1973.

The Uttar Pradesh Zamindari Abolition and Land Reforms Act, 1950.

Part VI
Civic Amenities and Quality of Life

29
Social Impacts of Rural-Urban Fringe

M.S. Khan and *Gaurav Bisaria*

Introduction

The rural-urban fringe is also known as the **outskirts** or **urban hinterland**. It is the area between an urban area and a rural area. The urban population in large cities is growing naturally and rapidly and migration of peoples from rural areas to urban areas has shown settlement at the surroundings of the city boundaries. The **United Nation's Population Fund (UNFPA)** released their "State of the World Population 2007" report in June 2007 which mentioned the fact that humanity is nearing the date when for the first time more humans will be living in cities than in rural areas. The vast majority of these new urban dwellers will live in developing countries, and they will be poor. This will present major challenges for the nations least prepared to meet the inevitable strains of urban growth.

Land factor in urban growth and development has received attention for the urban planners. This leads to drastic changes in the land use pattern of urban area. The origin of parks and commercial complexes at city borders also bring changes in the land use pattern of rural areas.

Most often, the cities and towns which are close to the agricultural land develops at a much faster pace and therefore, the physical expansion of urban areas invariably makes inroads on the country's agricultural produce. With increasing population and needs for modern living, housing space, industrial space and so on, the demand for urban land is bound to increase and bring out transformation of the social, demographic and cultural structure of the fringe villages.

Theme

Urbanism

Urbanism is a way of life. It reflects an organization of society in terms of a complex division of labour, high levels of technology, high mobility, interdependence of its members in fulfilling economic functions and impersonality in social relations.

Louis Wirth has given following *four* characteristics of urbanism:

- *Transiency*: An urban inhabitant's relation with others last only for a short time; he tends to forget his old acquaintances and develop relations with new people. Since he is not much attached to his neighbours member of the social groups, he does not mind leaving them.
- *Superficiality*: An urban person has the limited number of persons with whom he interacts and his relations with them are impersonal and formal. People meet each other in highly segmental roles. They are dependent on more people for the satisfaction of their life needs.
- *Anonymity*: Urbanities do not know each other intimately. Personal mutual acquaintance between the inhabitants which ordinarily is found in a neighborhood is lacking.
- *Individualism*: People give more importance to their own vested interests.

City

Cities become possible when an agricultural surplus develops together with improved means of transportation and tend to be located at breaks in transportation. The most significant current developments in city structure are the metropolitan area. The city pulls people from various corners towards its nucleus. The rural people faced with various economic problems are attracted by the city and start moving towards the cities. The city provides ample opportunities for personal advancement. It is the centre of brisk economic, commercial, artistic, literary, political, educational, technological, scientific and other activities. Cities are not only the controlling centres of their societies but also the source of innovation and change. They act as the source of new ideas for production, the pace-setters for consumption, guardians of culture and conservers of order in society. Consensus and continuity in a society are maintained from the city centres. Urban culture has become the legitimation for control. The basic assumption was that a given rural area supports an urban centre which in turn serves the surrounding countryside.

Research Methodology

This study basically focuses on the process of urban expansion in Lucknow with special reference to the process and patterns of land acquisition for urban expansion.

Objectives: (a) To identify the rural-urban fringe of Lucknow and study the process of urban expansion; (b) To critically evaluate Lucknow's large scale land acquisition, development; (c) To examine the pattern of investment and expenditure of compensation money received after acquisition of land in the households of sample villages; (d) To observe the changes in occupational structure of the households which are uprooted as a consequence of acquisition of the agricultural land; and (e) To study the impact of planned development on urban and rural land prices in Lucknow.

Study Area: Lucknow, the capital of U.P.

Major Findings: (a) Spatial distribution of land acquired has been unequal for different settlements. (b) Distribution of compensation of land acquired has also been unequal both over time and space. Market value of land per *bigha* reveals that lands were rated very low. (c) Compensation money was used for consumption purposes, in most cases, for house construction, car purchase, marriage etc. Households having educated members invested in productive activities. Some of them purchased agricultural land and a significant amount of proceeds was also saved by landowners. Households in the higher categories of compensation invested in business, and real estate. (d) Dairying as an economic activity declined due to land shortage. Unemployment resulting from dismemberment of agriculture, tough competition in secondary and tertiary sectors, wastage of compensation money on unproductive items, failure in new ventures etc. made rent an important source of regular income for the farmers. (e) There has been drastic increase in urban and rural land prices because of construction of roads, attachment of street lights and proper water and electricity supply.

Features of Urban Society

- The urban society is heterogeneous known for its diversity and complexity.

- It is dominated by secondary relations.
- Formal means of social control such as law, legislation, police, and court are needed in addition to the informal means for regulating the behaviour of the people.
- The urban society is mobile and open. It provides more chances for social mobility. The status is achieved than ascribed.
- Occupations are more specialized. There is widespread division of labour and specialization opportunities for pursuing occupations are numerous.
- Family is said to be unstable. More than the family individual is given importance. Joint families are comparatively less in number.
- People are more class-conscious and progressive. They welcome changes. They are exposed to the modern developments in the fields of science and technology.
- Urban community is a complex multi-group society.
- The urban community replaced consensus by dissensus. The social organization is atomistic and ill-defined. It is characterized by disorganization, mental illness and anomie.
- Mass education is widespread in the city increasing democratization of the organizations and institutions demand formal education.

Advantages and Disadvantages of Urbanization

Rapid increase in urban population as a proportion of total population is resulting in rapid urbanization of the world. By the end of 2015, a majority of the world's population will be living in the cities. This paradigm shift in the dynamics of human population is attracting attention of sociologists, demographers, scientists, and politicians. Urbanization brings with it a unique set of advantages and disadvantages.

Advantages

Education

Children from low-income families know about 3,000 words by age 6, while those from high-income backgrounds know 20,000. Children from privileged families hear millions more words by age 3 than those from less affluent backgrounds. As a general rule, farm employers would prefer not to have young children around the field.

In our rapidly changing world, literacy should be seen as an important evolutionary variable in every society. For the further a society progresses, the more it needs to adjust and adapt to new demands and pressures, so that literacy is lifelong necessity for all. Literacy, in the broad sense, is the foundation for life skills, ranging from basic oral and written communication to the ability to solve scientific and social probelms. Education is a powerful motive for moving to the city. Rural education has often been neglected in favour of urban but it is also an essential urban function. Cities have always provided intellectual stimulus and educational leadership. In developing countries there is often substantially higher proportion of educated people in the cities. Urban environments often encourage improvement in women's status. It is predicted that by 2015, 22 of the 27 mega cities would be in developing countries.

Cities offer the Lure of Better Employment

With the liberalization in full swing and its impact on all sections of economy we are witness to the inexorable urbanization of the country. The unemployed people and the seasonal workers who have no work all through the years move to big cities in search of employment. It is because cities provide economic opportunities with the available infrastructure. Large manufacturing units are situated in or close to the cities considering the available infrastructure like power, roads, rail and ports. In every state there are about half a dozen big towns with two or three big cities. The industries cluster around these places with larger units nearer to metros. The jobs are not seasonal as in farming but all through the year. Ancillary industries grow and service industries also thrive side by side. Both skilled and unskilled labourers find ready jobs.

There is wide area and large number of industries and companies running successfully which require good employees. The requirement can be for the managerial post, i.e. a person who is having management knowledge and can also be for skilled workers as well as labourers. There is widespread division of labour and specialization opportunities for pursuing occupations which are numerous. If this trend is not reversed quickly the rural income would become a small fraction of urban income. The urban population will grow beyond manageable levels with most living in slums.

Health Care

In rural areas the women are giving births to children in open fields and in trucks and DHAI MA is there for operations which is not very good and hygienic while in urban areas everything is done with utmost care and proper check-ups are done with the guidance.

Environmental conditions of rural areas influence certain health risks. The environment exposes children to a high risk of diarrhoeal diseases and parasitic diseases. The people of rural areas suffer from malaria which has become an urgent problem in villages. Data that are available indicate a range of rural health hazards and associated health risks are substandard housing, insufficient or contaminated drinking water, inadequate sanitation and solid waste disposal services, increased motor vehicle traffic, stress associated with poverty and unemployment, among others. Now nearly half the world's population lives in urban settlements.

Transportation

India is a large country with a large population. For the economy to prosper, people and goods have to be efficiently moved fast over large distances. India is approximately ten times as densely populated as the US. It, therefore, cannot afford the solution that works for the US for transporting people, namely, air travel. **What India needs is a land-based system and more specifically a rail-based transportation system for both goods and people.** The technology exists for super-efficient, super-fast rail systems. India has to seriously invest in that and replace the century-old current railway system. Further, within cities, India needs to have efficient public transit system and not rely on automobiles. These are not available with the rural areas. The rural areas are not able to match its pace with the development of Transport System in the urban areas. Above all, Time is not the hindrance for the availability of public transport system in urban areas as compared to rural areas.

Better Quality of Life

Urbanization can have a positive impact on development issues such as poverty, inequality and environmental degradation, so long as the appropriate policies are in place to manage the problems and challenges. It also offers opportunities for economic growth. The South African city of Cape Town has been rapidly urbanizing for the past three or four decades. The modern cities succeed to the extent that they link their populations with the nation's economy and the nation's economy with the global economy. The city tries to get their right to improve life for the very poor and to enable all to have opportunities in the city. There are compact, well-designed and well-managed cities which can generate a "fantastic" quality of life at a relatively low level of greenhouse gas emissions.

Disadvantages

Health Risk

Health risks that urbanization has brought to developing countries are urban dwellers, particularly children, women, and elderly people, are vulnerable to health threats associated with overcrowding, pollution, and a host of familiar urban problems that include mental and physical diseases, homelessness, drug abuse, and sexually transmitted diseases as well as violence and social alienation. The evidence available indicates that poor populations have higher rates of maternal mortality and infant mortality and morbidity. Data that are available indicate a range of urban health hazards and associated health risks: substandard housing, crowding, air pollution, insufficient or contaminated drinking water, inadequate sanitation and solid waste disposal services, vector-borne diseases, industrial waste, increased motor vehicle traffic, stress associated with poverty and unemployment, among others. The impact of these problems on the health of urban dwellers requires an assessment of environmental health services and a revitalized role of public health in solving them. The WHO continues to play a role in the development of the concept of adopting a holistic and integrated approach to improving the health status of the population. However, rapid and often unplanned urban growth is often associated with poverty, environmental degradation and population demands that outstrip service capacity.

Mental Health

Urbanization is affecting the entire gamut of population especially the vulnerable sections of society—elderly, children and adolescents, and women. Rapid urbanization has also led to creation of "fringe population" mostly living from hand to mouth which further adds to poverty. Poverty and mental health have a complex and multidimensional relationship. Urban population is heavily influenced by changing cultural dynamics leading to particular psychiatric problems like depression, alcoholism, and delinquency. Judicious use of resources, balanced approach to development, and sound government policies are advocated for appropriate growth of advancing economies of South-Asian region. The multiculturalism of today's cities contributes to increased tolerance, better quality of life, and socio-cultural stimulation; at the same time, it often contributes to heightened social tensions, interethnic striving, and cultural conflicts—all of which undoubtedly carry mental health ramifications.

Multiculturalism

The multiculturalism of today's cities contributes to increased tolerance, better quality of life, and socio-cultural stimulation; at the same time, it often contributes to heightened social tensions, interethnic striving, and cultural conflicts—all of which undoubtedly carry mental health ramifications. The range of disorders and deviancies associated with urbanization is enormous and includes psychoses, depression, sociopathy, substance abuse, alcoholism, crime, delinquency, vandalism, family disintegration, and alienation. Such negative impact often results in unreasonable means which may result in communal violence. Negative impact is also experienced by behaviour constraints practiced or imposed upon the urban people. If behaviour is unduly suppressive, it may result in learned helplessness leading to stress-related disorders. Migration to cities has increased dramatically over the past few decades. Most migrants come from rural areas, bringing values, beliefs, and expectations about mental health that are often very different from the ones they encounter in their new location. In many instances, people coming from rural areas have endured years of isolation, lack of technologic connection, poor health, poverty, unemployment, and inadequate housing. They need to acculturate and adapt not only to a new challenging urban environment, but also to alternative systems of symbols, meanings, and traditions. The multiculturalism of today's cities can only be developed if one has **increased tolerance.**

Old Age

Urbanization alters the dynamics of society at large and family in particular. Rapid urbanization has created a huge population of older men and women left to fend for themselves in the rural areas while the young make their living in the cities. This also means less availability of caregivers when older people fall ill.

Women

Women are particularly vulnerable and they often disproportionately bear the burden of changes associated with urbanization. In the rural set-up, they would work mostly at homes but the predominantly nuclear set-up of the cities and sheer economics is forcing women to venture out. Domestic violence is also highly prevalent in urban areas. In both developed and developing countries, women living in urban settings are at greatest risk to be assaulted by intimates. Women had significantly higher prevalence rates for neuroses, affective disorders, and organic psychoses than men. A survey carried out in Nepal demonstrated that women had a higher psychiatric morbidity than men. In deprived countries, women bear the burden of responsibilities of being wives, mothers, educator, and careers; at the same time a part of labour force. In 25-33 per cent households, they are the prime source of income. Significant gender discrimination, malnutrition, overwork, domestic, and sexual violence add up to the problems. Social support and the presence of close relationships (more commonly observed in rural society) appear to be protective against violence. The women although have a greater role to play in the urban set-up, but the rise in hierarchy in society that should rightfully accompany this increased demand on them is still missing. The rate of mental distress has been reported to be high also in working which has lead to the development of topic for discussion i.e.

Urbanization and Psychiatry

Children

By 2025, 6 of 10 children will live in cities. As a result of rural-urban migration and high fertility rates, it is estimated that about 50 per cent of the urban population in developing countries is younger than 25 years. In addition, there are approximately 30 million street children worldwide, and most of them are involved in illegal activities in urban areas. Children and adolescents in socio-economically deprived urban areas are often drawn to anti-social behaviour. Although not exclusively an urban phenomenon, it thrives in inner cities where degradation, poverty, drug use, and unemployment result in an explosive blend favouring violent solutions.

Economy

Rapid urbanization has also led to creation of "fringe population" mostly living from hand to mouth which further adds to poverty. Poverty and mental health have a complex and multidimensional relationship.

Hospitals

Migration to cities has increased dramatically over the past few decades. Most migrants come from rural areas, bringing values, beliefs, and expectations about mental health that are often very different from the ones they encounter in their new location. These countries tend to have a higher burden of diseases and have an already compromised primary health care delivery system. They are also plagued by lack of awareness of the constituting population, stigma associated with mental illness, poverty, and illiteracy.

Rapid urbanization puts immense pressure on both physician and patient. Sound doctor-patient relationship becomes almost impossible in busy clinics. In view of large number of patients, time constraints and wide range of diseases, making accurate diagnosis and proper follow-up are almost impracticable. This leads to a high rate of clinical errors and superfluous diagnostic tests.

Thus, it is a heterogenous mix of problems and categorizing them to one particular subtype seems daunting and undesirable.

Conclusion

Rapid and extensive urbanization is one of the most significant features of life in Uttar Pradesh. The city life will become more of influences and responses. There is really a requirement of study in terms of social, cultural and demographic impacts on cities life. There are changes due to urbanization but in my view the essence of rural environment should be maintained. Though the peoples are moving to cities but still the real and the majority of INDIA lives in the villages having their own importance and the lifestyle. The companies should either protect them by performing social responsibilities rather capture them.

References

Anas, M. and Siddique, M. (1979). 'Land Use Control in Old Delhi'. *Geographer*, Vol. 24, No. 1 (January 1979), pp. 17-21.

Bansal, S.P. (1995). 'Contributions of DDA to Planning and Development of the National Capital City: An Appraisal'. *Spatio-Economic Development Record,* Vol. 2, No. 5, pp. 43.

Baviskar, Amita (2002). 'Politics of the City'. *Seminar,* no. 516 (August 2002), pp. 40-42.

Benjamin, Solomon J. (1991). "Jobs, Land, and Urban Development: The Economic Success of Small Manufacturers in East Delhi, India". Cambridge, Masschussetts: *Lincoln Institute of Land Policy*

Bentinck, J.V., Skornsek, J. and Vries, de A.C. (1999). "The Degradation of Rural Land in the Rural-Urban Fringe of Delhi: *Integration of GIS and Remote Sensing* [Geographic Information Systems]". In Chapman, Graham P., Dutt, Ashok K.

Bhan, Chander and Singh, Shivinder (1988). 'Land Acquisition and Social Imbalances in Rural Delhi'. In Lamba, P.S. and Solanki, S.S., eds. *Science, Technology and Rural Development.* Delhi: Anmol Publications, pp. 46-48.

Bradnock, Robert W., eds. *Urban Growth and Development in Asia.* Vol. 2: *Living in the Cities.* Aldershot, England; Brookfield, USA: Ashgate Publishing Company, pp. 451-465.

Brush, John (1968). 'Spatial Patterns of Population In Indian Cities'. *Geographical Review,* Vol. 58, No. 3 (July 1968), pp. 362-391.

Buch, M.N. (1981). 'Delhi 2001—Land Policy Implications'. *India International Centre Quarterly,* Vol. 8, No. 2 (June 1981), pp. 159-168.

Divakar Ashok, Urban Expansion and Rural Land Acquisition in the Fringe Villages: A Case Study of the Union Territory of Delhi, xviii, 538 p.: *col illus,* 1991.

Dupont, V. and Houssay-Holzschuch, M. (2001). 'Fragmentation and Access to the City: Cape Town and Delhi in a Comparative Perspective: Paper presented to the *International Symposium on Space, Territories and Identities in South Africa and India.* A Comparative Perspective. University of Paris X Naterre.

Dutt, Ashok K. and Parai, Anindita (1999). 'Defining Urban Corridors: Case Studies of four Mega Cities of India [Mumbai (Bombay), Chennai (Madras), Kolkota (Calcutta), Delhi]'. In Chapman, Graham P. Dutt, Ashok K. and Bradnock, Robert W., eds. *Urban Growth and Development in Asia. Vol. 2: Living in the Cities.* Aldershot, England; Brookfield, USA: Ashgate Publishing Company, pp. 93-107.

Jain, A.K. (1989). 'Delhi: Planning and Growth'. *International Journal of Environmental Studies,* Section A, Vol. 34, Nos. 1-2, pp. 65-77.

Ritu Priya (1993). 'Town Planning, Public Health and Urban poor: Some Explorations from Delhi'. *Economic and Political Weekly,* Vol. 28, No. 17 (April 24, 1993), pp. 824-83.

Sharma A.K. *et al.* (2000). 'Rejuvenating City Centres by Activity and Transport Systems Management: Lessons from Chandni Chowk, Delhi experiment'. *Spatio-Economic Development Record,* Vol. 7, No. 3 (May-June), pp. 5-20.

30

Health Care Facilities in Fringe Areas of Aligarh City: A Case Study

Nadia Anis and *Hifzur Rahman*

Introduction

India is passing through a phase of rapid urbanization brought with the process of general development; industrialization and migration of population from rural to urban areas within the country in search of better opportunities for earning livelihood.

During pre-independence period population living in cities in India was 13.9 per cent in 1941, which increased to 17.3 per cent in 1951. Before independence nearly 15 per cent people were living in towns, and presently their share has doubled. The reasons for this change in the urban population may be many, but mainly it is attributed to migration of rural people to urban areas.

The growth of population in urban areas is related with a shift of population from villages to urban areas in search of better livelihood. During 1961-71 about 24 million people migrated from rural to urban areas in the country. Each year on an average basis about 4 million people migrate to cities like Mumbai, Delhi and Kolkata. These cities and towns are, however, not prepared to absorb this phenomenal increased incoming inhabitant which leads to haphazard and unorderly growth of population. This floating population adds new problems in these cities to municipal bodies that with limited financial resources are incapable of serving such an ever increasing population.

This gap between accessibility and requirement for urban infrastructural facilities has widened a gap over the years which severely affect the problems of space, environment and keep intact the quality of life in urban areas. Several studies have indicated that a large segment of urbanites do not have access to basic services like drinking water, sanitation, basic health and educational facilities.

Over the last fifty years since independence, the country has developed extensive public delivery systems provisions for health care. The Bhore Commission in 1946 recommended that basic health services should be provided to all through Primary Health Centres (PHCs). On the basis of recommendations, PHCs were set-up throughout the country, each serving about 30,000 inhabitants in their vicinity. The health services, provision for all in India has also largely been envisaged with in the public delivery system even though this sector has a significant presence of private providers. Since independence, the government has launched a number of schemes and programmers for increasing health care awareness among all the sections of the society. Recently, there has been a growing demand for privatization and growth in number of private institutions. This phenomenon is more strongly visible in the urban areas where a greater proportion of literate populations live.

The Food Insecurity Atlas of Urban India (MSSRF, 2002) suggests approximately 38 per cent of children below the age of three years in urban areas are underweight and more than 35 per cent short for their age. Further, a high proportion of urban poor are not able to meet the nutrition norms laid down by the Indian Council of Medical Research (ICMR).

Both large survey-based case studies have repeatedly shown that health services in the country are characterized by inadequate and inferior infrastructure, poor public service delivery, lack of quality choices for consumers and lack of access especially for the people living in fringe areas due to a high dependence on relatively expensive private facilities.

Review of Literature

Kent and Sandova (1984) in their work have given an account of shortcomings in provision of health care facilities in 114 districts of Peru and the related informations were obtained through the postal survey, and suggested that hospitals and dispensaries should be equipped with needed machinery and they further suggested for better improvements.

Singh and Rehman (1998) analysed the problems of housing and health in low income households of the Aligarh city with the help of extensive surveys. They found that the city is lacking in health facilities and suggested a number of measures improvement.

Field (2000), accounted for measures and needs of primary health care taking the study of some districts of California. According to him, local conditions like housing, primary health care and education are the major indicators for maintaining and planning of the quality of life in urban areas. He emphasized, that proper health care facilities should be extended to all sections of the society.

Stephens (2000) analysed the inequalities and variations in the provision of health care facilities in some selected cities of the world. He observed that health care is an important parameter in marinating and planning of the quality of life, but these facilities are inadequate in the cities which he considered. He further emphasized that, these amenities are very much inaccessible to the people belonging to low income groups.

Bhakar and Bhargava (2003) attempted to find out inter-district disparities in infrastructural development in Rajasthan on the basis of health care facilities. They considered all blocks of district and in each district the least developed blocks were identified by applying Z score statistical technique.

By considering health care expenditure in some Asian countries Emran (2005) confirmed that health and health care treatments are expensive in almost all the big cities of the continent, therefore many of the poors found themselves unable to reach to the medical care centres.

Bhandari (2006) attempted to find out the problems in provisions of health care and education. He stressed that, health care facilities are inaccessible to the poors in India, and suggested that primary health care centres should be set-up at appropriate locations in urban and rural areas by the government for the poors for free treatment.

Objectives

The present study has the following objectives:

1. To examine the distribution of the present social infrastructural facilities, like health care facilities in selected wards located in the fringe of Aligarh city.
2. To examine the conditions of the medical facilities available in selected wards.
3. To examine whether these facilities are easily available and accessible to people living in the fringe areas.

The Study Area

Aligarh is a medium sized city which spreads over an area of 36.70 sq km to form a part of the state of U.P. with a population of more than 0.7 million. It is located in between 27.53′N latitude and 78.04′ longitude, and lies at about 130 km south-east of New Delhi. (Fig. 30.1)

Like other cities of the state, Aligarh also has a distinct demarcation between the old and the new parts. Delhi-Kolkata Railway Line separates the old and the new parts. The old part of the city comprises of 48 wards and the new part 22 wards. The old city presents the picture of decadence having narrow roads, old and congested houses with improper educational and health facilities, and no open spaces. The new part of the city is much clean than old part, which comprises spacious of Aligarh Muslim University, which spreads over thousands of hectares of land. But new residential colonies and innumerable shopping centers have sprung up making this part congested. Gradually, the outskirts of the city are expanding and encroaching upon rural lands and therefore slums have emerged and are seen roadsides radiating from the city centre.

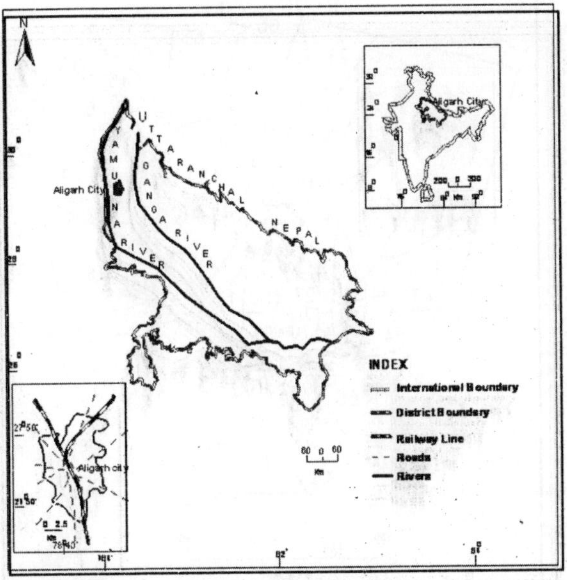

Fig. 30.1: Location of Aligarh City in Uttar Pardesh.

Data Base

This study is based mainly on the data collected from primary sources, but some information was also obtained from the secondary sources. Primary data were collected through extensive city and households surveys, and interviews conducted with the residents in each ward.

Five wards, namely **Jamalpur, Nagla Jamalpur, Badam Nagar, Hamdard Nagar** and **Maulana Azad Nagar** (Fig. 30.2) were selected which are located in the northern part of the city for conducting households surveys. Detailed information pertaining to health care facilities were collected with the help of a questionnaire, by contacting the residents of the respective wards.

The surveys were undertaken during the months of January and February 2009. On the basis of stratified random sampling 30 to 35

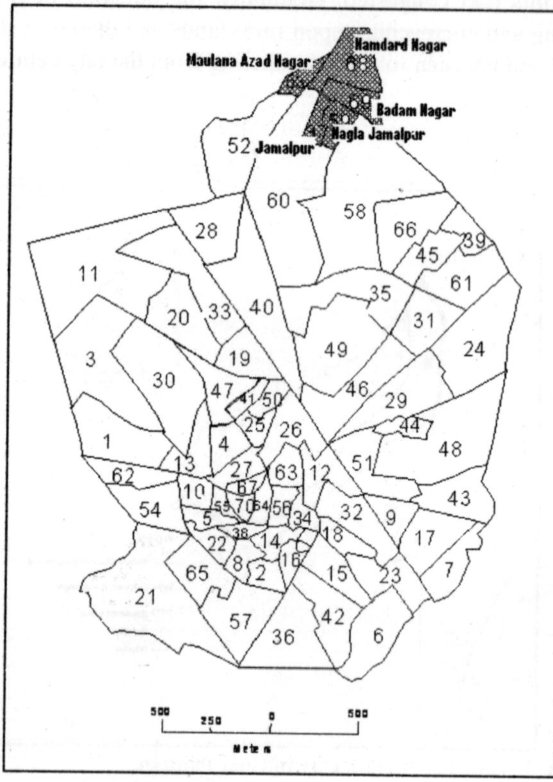

Fig. 30.2: Aligrah City Study Area.

households were contacted for survey purpose. Some other information was obtained from the offices of Municipal Board of Aligarh city (Seva Bhawan) and Chief Medical Officer (CMO) Aligarh city.

Monthly Income of the Sampled Households

Five income categories were considered for this study. In some of the households respondents were reluctant to respond their correct monthly income. Therefore, their income was estimated on the bases of the assets they were in possession.

Table 30.1 shows that about 91 per cent households in Maulana Azad Nagar come under the low income group, majority of these households are labourers and rickshaw pullers who earn even less than Rs. 100 to Rs. 200 per day.

Hamdard Nagar is the only ward having high income households i.e 20 per cent. They are mainly engaged in high class jobs, so they can easily afford the expensive treatment in private clinics. In almost all the wards the percentage of low income households are very high. From this we can figure out that more than half of the households in these wards are poor and have hand to mouth income so they are unable to spend money on treatment in private clinics.

Health Care Facilities

Health facilities in Aligarh city are of medium standard. There are three important hospitals, namely Jawahar Lal Nehru Medical College Hospital (JNMCH), Malkhan Singh Hospital and Gandhi Eye Hospital. Besides these, there are number of private clinics and nursing homes located quite apart in different wards. (Table 30.2)

Table 30.1: Monthly Income of Sampled Households in Aligarh City, 2007

(Income in Rs./households in percentage)

Name of Ward	*1500–5000*	*5000–10000*	*10000–15000*	*15000–20000*	*>20000*
Jamalpur	48	20	32	—	—
Maulana Azad Nagar	91	9	—	—	—
Nagla Jamalpur	65	30	5	—	—
Hamdard Nagar	21	32	19	8	20
Badam Nagar	35	48	17	—	—

Source: Based on Author's Field Survey, 2007.

Table 30.2: Health Care Facilities in Aligarh City, 1971–2001

Year	No. of doctors	No. of hospitals	No. of private clinics	No. of maternity homes	Total	Decennial growth	
						Year	Per cent Growth
1971	49	3	9	—	—	—	—
1981	85	5	18	3	61	1971–81	81.96
1991	109	7	35	5	111	1981–91	40.54
2001	255	12	75	12	156	1991–01	126.92
		Grand Total			354	1971–01	480.33

Source: Office of the Chief Medical Officer, Aligarh, 2001.

Table 30.3 shows inadequacy of health care facilities in the wards, as compared to the facilities in the whole city. Table also shows the absence of government hospital in these wards. People residing in these areas mainly belong to low income group, hence they face financial problem to avail medical care in private clinics.

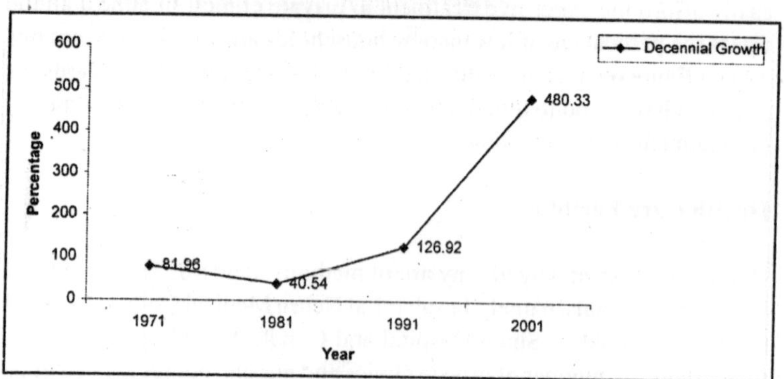

Fig. 30.3: Health Care Facilities in Aligarh City, 1971-2001.

Table 30.3: Distribution of Health Care Facilities in Aligarh City, 2007

Name of ward	No. of Govt. hospitals	No. of private clinics	Nursing homes	Hospitals
Jamalpur	–	30	5	–
Maulana Azad Nagar	–	4	–	–
Nagla Jamalpur	–	10	–	–
Hamdard Nagar	–	33	–	–
Badam Nagar	–	12	–	–

Source: Based on Author's Field Survey, 2007.

It is evident from Table 30.3, that the highest numbers of private clinics are in Hamdard Nagar, but there is no nursing home or hospitals here (Fig. 30.3). In Maulana Azad Nagar, there are 4 private clinics which is a lowest figure. In selected wards, Jamalpur ward has 10 private clinics ensuring medical care.

Table 30.3 further shows that wards like Jamalpur and Hamdard Nagar have more private clinic whereas, Badam Nagar and Maulana Azad Nagar wards lack in number of private clinics and nursing homes. (Fig. 30.4)

It is evident from Table 30.4 that, about 85 and 82 per cent households in Jamalpur and Hamdard Nagar respectively have easy access to medical facilities, whereas 10 and 11 per cent residents of both wards have to travel for a distance of 2 kms. to avail these facilities. This is all due to the presence of quite good number of private clinics in wards.

Wards like Maulana Azad Nagar and Badam Nagar (Fig. 30.4) have few private clinics, 41 and 35 per cent households respectively have to travel to a distance around 3 km to avail medical facilities.

Table 30.4: Accessibility of the Sampled Households to the Medical Facilities Centres; in terms of Distance in Wards of Aligarh City, 2007

Name of ward	*1 km*	*2 kms*	*3 kms*
Jamalpur	85	10	5
Maulana Azad Nagar	3	56	41
Nagla Jamalpur	48	37	15
Hamdard Nagar	82	11	7
Badam Nagar	24	41	35

Source: Based on Author's Field Survey, 2007.

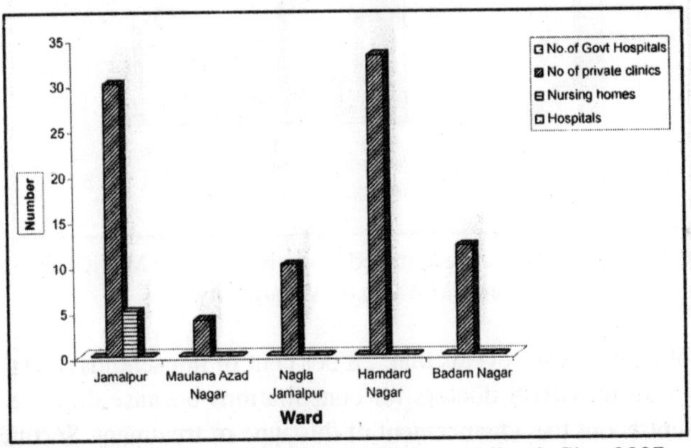

Fig. 30.4: Distribution of Health Care Facilities in Aligarh City, 2007.

Table 30.5 shows that around 50 to 70 per cent of households in almost all the residents of the wards visit to BUMS doctors for treatment. The reason for such a high percentage of visitors is that BUMS doctor's clinics are easily accessible and charges less for treatment as compared to other MBBS doctors. Therefore, the percentage of households consulting and attending MBBS doctor's clinics is low.

Many of the people have shifted towards the homoeopathic treatment, and there is a significant rise in number of the members of households going for homoeopathic clinics. Whereas, the percentage of households going for Ayurvedic treatment is very low (Fig. 30.5), because of ignorance and unawareness about this type of patients medical treatment.

Table 30.5: Preference of Households for Taking treatment from Profession-wise Medical Practitioners in Wards of Aligarh City, 2007

Name of ward	*MBBS*	*BUMS*	*Ayurvedic*	*Homeopathic*
Jamalpur	13	70	1	16
Maulana Azad Nagar	2	65	3	30
Nagla Jamalpur	10	60	4	26
Hamdard Nagar	28	50	8	14
Badam Nagar	9	65	1	25

Source: Based on Author's Field Survey, 2007.

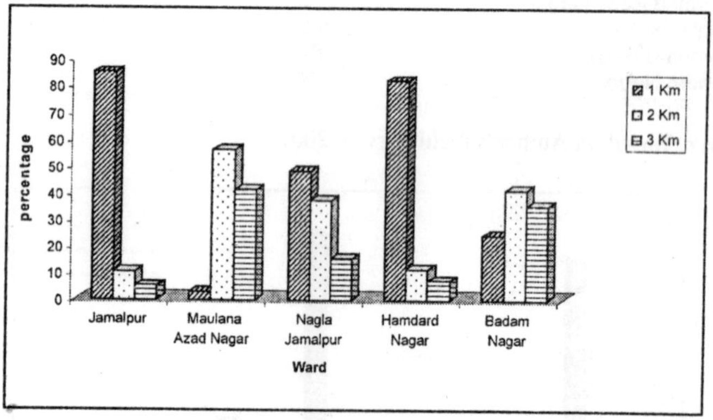

Fig. 30.5: Accessibility of the Sampled Households to the Medical Facilities in terms of Distance in Wards of Aligarh City.

Table 30.5 also reveals that, 28 per cent of households in Hamdard Nagar visit to MBBS doctors for consultations because they are much confident about the advancement of this type of treatment. Secondly, as most of these residents belong to high income group, so they can easily afford this way of treatment. Whereas, households in wards of Maulana Azad Nagar, Nagla Jamalpur and Badam Nagar mostly visit to BUMS doctors as most of them belong to low income group.

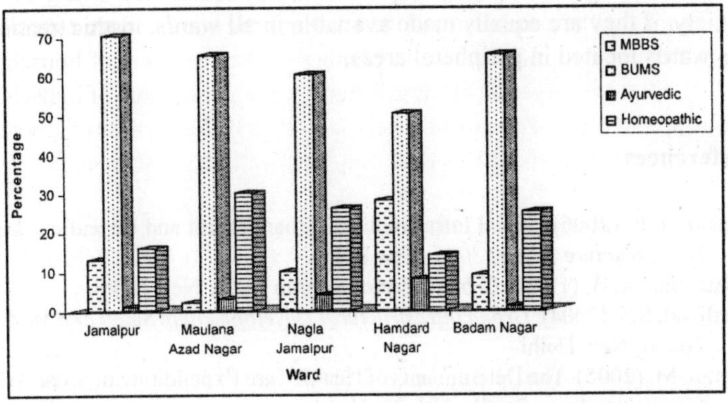

Fig. 30.6: Perference of Households for Taking Treatment from Profession-wise Medical Practitioners in Wards of Aligarh City, 2007.

Conclusion

Healthy people build a healthy nation with a healthy growth. Still health care facilities in the cities do not receive the importance specially in fringe areas. The present study shows paucity of health care facilities in wards located in fringe areas and it also explains that whatever the facilities are inaccessible to the residents.

It is the prime duty of the concerned departments and should made the efforts not only to provide proper health care facilities but the facilities accessible be to the people living in fringe areas, by opening government dispensaries at proper distances so the residents can avail them in each ward.

Proper transport and the arrangement of low cost medical buses to and fro for the fringe wards so that people can easily avail good health amenities which are present in core areas of the city. Besides this, the availability of mobile medical vans and ambulances will be of great help.

Conditions of medical institutes and hospitals should be improved by increasing number of beds and doctors, and by facilitating them with advanced appliances. Free treatment dispensaries with qualified doctors and proper facilities should be opened for poors. There is also a need to create awareness among people regarding their health with the help of urban health programmes we can do this.

From the above discussion, it can be concluded that health and health care can bring a substantial improvement in social well-being of the society, if they are equally made available in all wards, more especially the wards located in peripheral areas.

References

Bhandari, L. (2006). Social Infrastructure: Urban Health and Education, *India Infrastructure Report 2006,* New Delhi.

Bhattacharya, B. (1979). *Urban Development in India,* New Delhi.

Dhaliwal, S.S. (2004). *Urban Infrastructural Development in Small and Medium Towns,* New Delhi.

Emran, M. (2005). The Determinants of Health Care Expenditure in Some Asian Countries, *Asian Profile,* Vol. 33, No. 4.

Field, K. (2000). Measuring the Need for the Primary Health Care: an index of relative disadvantage, *Applied Geography,* Vol. 20, No. 4, pp. 305-333.

Kent, R.B and Sandoval Ricci, L. (1984). The Evolution and Provision of District Public Services in the Central Sierra of Peru, *Revista Geografica,* Vol. 99, pp. 35-55.

Kopardekar, H.D. (1986). *Social Aspects of Urban Development,* Mumbai.

Majumdar, R. (2003). Infrastructural Facilities in India, *Indian Journal of Regional Science,* Vol. 34, No. 1, pp. 1-23.

Mc Gee, T.G. (1972). The Urbanization Process in the Third World, London.

Mohanty, L.N.P. (1999). *Management of Urban Development in India,* New Delhi.

Praston, S.H. (1979). Urban Growth in Developing Countries: A demographic reappraisal, *Population and Development Review,* Vol. 5, No. 2, pp. 195-215

Pugh, C. (2005). *Sustainable Cities in Developing Countries,* London.

Singh, A.L. and Rehman, A. (1998). Housing and Health in Low Income Households of Aligarh City, *Indian Journal of Regional Science*, Vol. 30, No. 2.

Stephens, C. (1996). Healthy Cities or Unhealthy Island: the health and social implications of urban inequality, *Environment and Urbanization,* Vol. 8, No. 2, pp. 9-11.

Thiagarajon, D. (1982). Need for a National Policy on Urbanization, *Social Welfare*, Vol. 29, No. 3, June.

31

Educational Facilities in Fringe Areas of Azamgarh District: A Case Study

Sana

Introduction

Education has been considered as an important factor in achieving rapid development through technological progress and in creating a social order with social justice and equal opportunities. Earlier education was considered as an investment in human capital contributing to higher productivity and income. The successful national planning and development policies for ensuring balanced development is possible only when socio-cultural aspect like education is looked into proper perspective. Education proves an instrument for social change, development and equity. The first important pre-condition is that adequate opportunities for education are available and different groups in societies have access to them. The education sustains the human values which contribute to individual and collective well-being. It forms the basis for lifelong learning and inspires confidence to face challenges. The researches have shown that the life expectancy rises as much as two years for every 1 per cent increase in literacy.

As education is the means for bringing socio-economic transformation in a society, various measures are being taken to enhance the access of education to the marginalized sections of the society. One such measure is the introduction of the reservation system in the institutes of higher education. Under the present law, 7.5 per cent seats in the higher educational institutes are reserved for the Scheduled Tribes, 15 per cent for Scheduled Castes and 27 per cent for the non-creamy layers of the Other Backward Classes (OBCs). Under the Indian Constitution, various minority groups can also set-up their own educational institutes. Efforts are also being taken to improve the access to higher education among the women of India by setting up various educational institutes exclusively for them or reserving seats in the already existing institutes. The growing acceptance of distance learning courses and expansion of the Open University system is also contributing a lot in the democratization of higher education in India. The quality of human resource of nation is easily judged by the number of literate population living in it. This is to say that education is must if a nation aspires to achieve growth and development and more importantly sustain it. This may explain the fact that the rich and developed nations of the world have very high literacy rate and productive human resource. In fact these nations have started imparting selective training and education programme so as to meet the new technical and business demands of the 2st century.

Importance of education can not be neglected by any nation and in today's world, the role of education has become even more vital. It is an absolute necessity for economic and social development of any nation.

Schools in India: India has the second largest education system in the world between 1950-2002, the number of primary schools increased nearly three-fold in India, from 209674 to 651382 respectvily. 84 per cent of the rural habitation in India now have primary schools located within a distance of 1 km. Of the 651382 schools in 2002 the government or local bodies managed about 90 per cent. As of 2002 about 123 million students were enrolled in class 1-5 and about 47 million students in class 6-8. The number of teachers during the same period was about 191 million and 158 million. Besides these schools, there are a quarter of million non-formal education centres. (Table 31.1)

A comparison of the number of primary schools between the Sixth All India Education Survey (1993) and the Seventh All India Education Survey (2002) conducted by the NCERT suggest an increase of about 25 per cent in the number of primary schools in the country. Drop-out rate also declined somewhat from 39.09 per cent to 34.89 per cent during this period.

The high growth in number of students and schools has however been predominantly in the private sector. Through the 1990s and till early 2000 annual growth has varied between 7 to 10 per cent in the number of unaided private schools. However, the private schools aided by the government and the public schools have grown at much more stable 2 per cent. (table 31.2)

Table 31.1: Growth of primary schools in India (1993–2002)

Primary schools	*All India*
1993	570455
2002	651382
Per cent change	14.19

Source: NCERT (2002).

Table 31.2: Annual percentage growth in number of schools by management

Type of institution	*2002*	*1997–02*
Public	1.8	2.4
Private aided	1.9	2.1
Private unaided	10.4	7.5

Source: GoI (2003).

Objectives

The objectives of the study are as follows:

1. To assess the educational facilities in fringe area and core areas of Azamgarh district.
2. To find the regional disparity of education up to higher secondary level.
3. To examine the inequalities among centre and fringe area of the district.

Study area

Azamgarh district occupies 4234 sq km. of Uttar Pradesh. It is located between 25°38″ and 26°27″ north of latitude and the meridians of 82°40″ and 83°52″ east of longitude. It is bounded by Mau on the east, Gorakhpur on the north, Ghazipur on the south-east, Jaunpur on the south-west, Sultanpur on the west, and Ambedkar Nagar on the north-west. The district Azamgarh is a level plain without any hills or natural eminence. The variation in the surface been caused by the banks of the small streams that drain it. Except the proximity of the Ghaghra, the land slopes very gently towards the south-east. The district has an immense reservoir of fresh water, stored in the more porous, coarse strata, beneath the level of saturation, which is easily accessible by means of ordinary borings in the form of wells. The few deep boring that have been made, have given proof of the prevalence of artesian condition in some parts of the district and in a few cases artesian borings have been made with successful results. A considerable amount of success has been attained in tube wells boring experiments in the district at many places. The climate of the district is moist and relaxing except in winter and hot season. The vast potential of human resources needs to be assessed and harnessed in the context of economic and social planning. Therefore, the study of population characteristics is important not only in the context of overall development of the district but also for the reason that the manpower constitutes a major input in the agricultural activity.

Azamgarh is the highest populated district in the eastern Uttar Pradesh. According to 2001 census, the district had a population of 3.94 million persons with 1.95 million males and 1.99 million females. Among the districts of Uttar Pradesh Azamgarh is the second largest populated district only after the Kanpur Nagar (4.13 million). But in terms of area Azamgarh stands sixth position among the district of eastern U.P. and occupies about 5 per cent of Eastern U.P.'s total area, while Sonbhadra stand first with 8 per cent and is followed by Allahabad (6.17 per cent), Bahraich (5.52 per cent), Mirzapur (5.32 per cent) and Sultanpur (5.22 per cent). The literacy rate for the district during 2001 census was 45.44 per cent. Palhani block with 48.31 per cent, records the highest literacy rate followed by Azmatgarh 47.83 per cent, Rani-ki-Sarai 47.76 per cent, Mirzapur 47.50 per cent, Lalganj 47.37 per cent, Tarwa 47.12 per cent, Atraulia 47.07 per cent and Mohammadpur 47.01 per cent. The lowest literacy rate of 39.76 per cent is found in Maharajganj block.

Data Base and Methodology

For the present study the data are obtained from the secondary sources, i.e. statistical hand book and village directory of Azamgarh district. The methodology adopted here with the help of certain indicators of educational development considering the literacy rates, the number of institutions, and the number of enrolment. This is again supplemented by simple pooling all the sum total rank orders of individual variables and giving the final rank order. Presenting the data on the four variable of educational development ranks are then summed up for each variable. Thus, pooling together all the rank orders of the individual variable and arriving at the composite rank order has been made in Table 31.5. Based

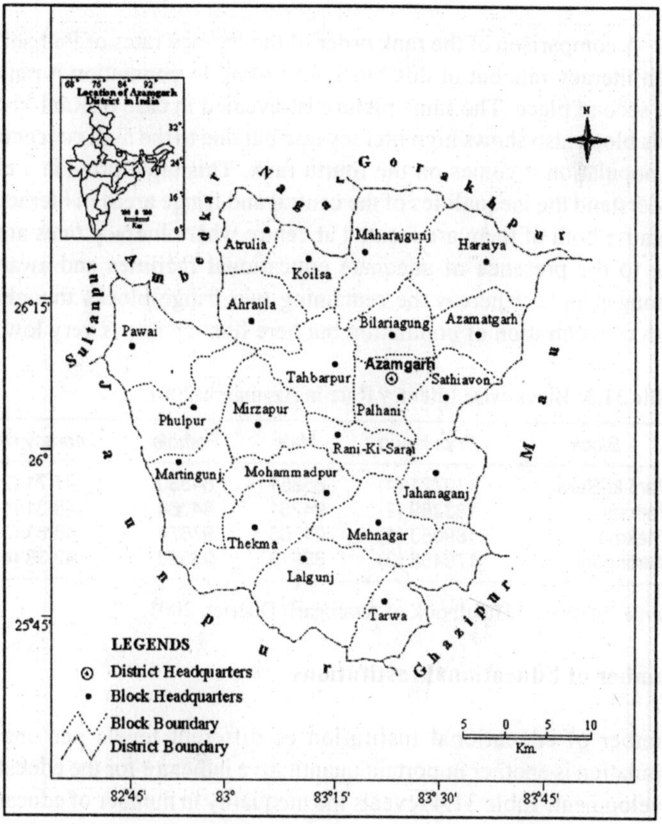

Fig. 31.1: Azamgarh District Addministatiove Divisions, 2004.

on this table the inequalities among the central block and fringe block in educational facilities are shown. Thus, as per the result of Table 31.5, Rani-ki-sarai has much better educational facilities whereas in *Martinganj* there is lack of educational facilities.

Literacy Rate in Azamgarh District

The fringe area and central area inequalities in literacy would be evident from the analyses of the data presented in Table 31.3. In Table 31.3, the block-wise total population, male and female literacy rates for the year 2001 have been presented.

A comparison of the rank order of the literacy rates of Palhani show high literacy rate but in this block according to population it ranked in the second place. The same picture is revealed in case of Rani-ki-Sarai. This block also shows high literacy rate but due to the high concentration of population it comes on the fourth rank. This table provide a clue to understand the inequalities of the central and fringe areas in literacy rate, because both of them are located at centre where literacy rates are high due to the presence of adequate educational facilities and awareness among people, whereas the remaining two fringe blocks though have high concentration of population but here literacy rate is very low.

Table 31.3: Block-wise Literacy Rate in Azamgarh-2001

Block	*Population*	*Male*	*Female*	*Literacy rates*
Rani-ki-Sarai	170721 (4)	85851	84880	47.71 (2)
Palhani	183289 (2)	94251	84064	48.31 (1)
Thekma	189053 (1)	91363	97674	43.81 (3)
Martinganj	179458 (3)	85913	93523	42.38 (4)

Source: Statistical Handbook of Azamgarh District, 2001.

Number of Educational Institutions

Number of educational institution of different levels per one lakh population is another important quantitative indicator for the educational development. Table 31.4 reveals the inequality in number of educational institutions in the block.

Block Rani-ki-Sarai and Palhani show high educational institutions both of them ranked first and second but the fringe block Thekma and Martinganj are again ranked third and fourth.

Number of Enrolment Ratio

Enrolment at different levels of education as a percentage of the population of the school going age group is one of the important variable of educational development.

Table 31.5 reveals the block-wise enrolment ratio of all levels of education for the year 2001. It has been shown that enrolment ratio is high in Rani-ki-Sarai and Palhani block which are known for better facilities of education because both of the blocks are situated in the central part of the district where better facilities are provided. Whereas Thekma

Table 31.4: Block Wise Number of Educational Institutions per Lakh Population in Azamgarh District, 2001

Block	*Primary schools*	*Senior primary schools*	*Higher secondary schools*	*Rank order score*
Rani-ki-Sarai	90.66 (1)	24.29 (1)	5.68	3.5 (1)
Palhani	67.87 (4)	18.87 (2)	6.30	2 (2)
Thekma	76.52 (4)	10.64 (4)	5.68 (1.5)	7.5 (3)
Martinganj	72.79 (3)	11,75 (3)	4.71 (3)	9 (4)

Source: Statistical Handbook of Azamgarh District, 2001.

Table 31.5: Block-wise enrolment ratio in Azamgarh district, 2001.

Block	*Primary School*		*Senior primary school*		*Higher secondary school*		*Sum of the rank*
	Boys	Girls	Boys	Girls	Boys	Girls	
Rani-ki-sarai	4. 37 (1)	4.47 (1)	3.73 (1)	4.05 (1)	0.41 (1)	2.40 (4)	9
Palhani	3.76 (3)	3.97 (2)	3.66 (2)	3.17 (2)	0.33 (2)	2.51 (3)	14
Thekma	3.13 (4)	3.41 (4)	3.55 (3)	2.68 (3)	0.27 (3)	4.95 (1)	18
Martinganj	3.97 (2)	3.90 (3)	2.68 (4)	1.70 (4)	0.15 (4)	4.08 (2)	19

Source: Statistical Handbook of Azamgarh District, 2001.

and Martinganj are situated in the fringe area of the district. Enrolment ratio shows lack of better educational facilities.

Teacher Ratio in Educational Institutions

In Table 31.6 it has been shown that there exists variation in the teacher ratio. Moreover, the ratio has not remain constant for all the levels of education in particular block.

Presenting the data on the four variables of educational development, Ranks are then summed up for each variable. Thus pooling together all the rank orders of the individual variable and arriving at the composite rank order has been made in Table 31.7. Based on this table the inequalities among the central block and fringe block in educational facilities are shown. Thus as per the result of Table 31.7, Rani-ki-Sarai has the much

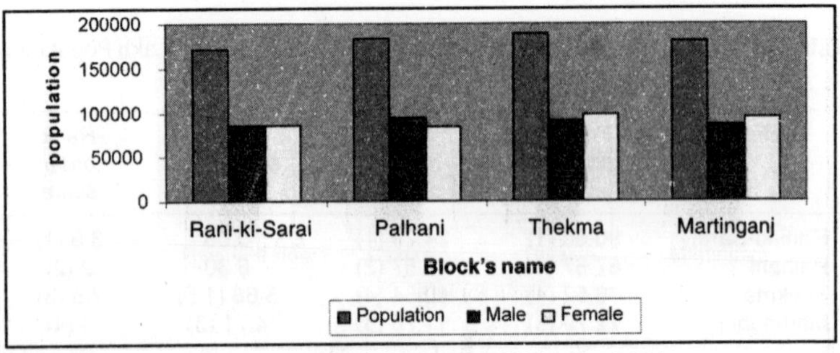

Fig. 31.2: Block-wise population in Azamgarh District, 2001.

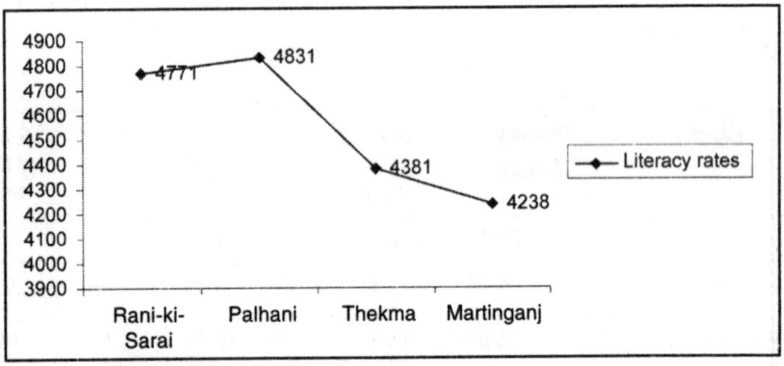

Fig. 31.3: Literacy rates.

better educational facilities whereas in Martinganj there is lack of educational facilities.

Conclusion and Suggestion

The empirical evidence of the present paper indicates that there exist central and fringe areas inequalities in educational development. Education is highly concentrated in urban location and at places with better connection.

In order to remove the regional inequalities, considering the socio-economic and geographical features of the region appropriate regional planning for education at grass roots level is required. People awareness need to be developed through motivation programmes.

Nevertheless, a planned educational policy should be taken up by the Government for upliftment of the educational attainment in the country.

Government should set-up higher level institutes in these areas, with proper facilities.

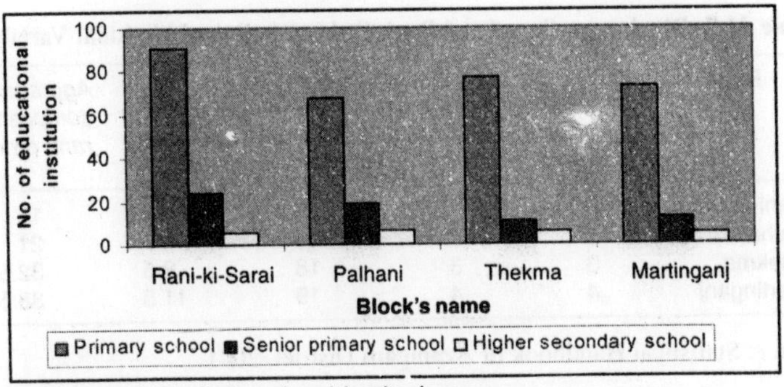

Fig. 31.4: Number of educational institutions.

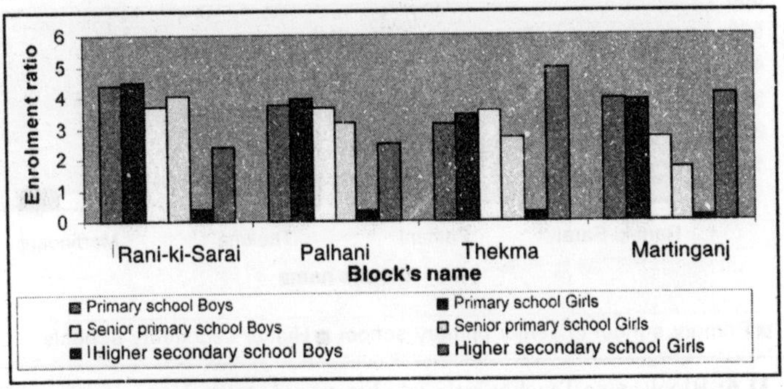

Fig. 31.5: Block-wise enrolment ratio.

Table 31.6: Block–wise Teacher Ratio in Educational Institutions in Azamgarh District, 2001

Block	*Primary school*	*Senior primary school*	*Higher secondary school*	*Sum of the rank order*
Rani-ki-Sarai	490 (1)	127 (2)	67 (3)	6
Palhani	429 (2)	131 (1)	138 (1)	4
Thekma	275 (3.5)	79 (3)	114 (2)	8.5
Martinganj	275 (3.5)	50 (4)	60 (4)	11.5

Source: Statistical Handbook of Azamgarh District, 2001.

References

Bahdur, S. and Ahmad A. Inequalities in higher education in India, *Indian Journal of Regional Science,* Vol. 13, No. 2, 1981, pp. 181-186.

Table 31.7: Block-wise Sum Total Rank Orders of all the Individual Variables

Block	Rank Order Score				Aggregate composite rank order
	Literacy rate	Institutions	Enrolment	Teacher ratio	
Rani-ki-Sarai	2	1	9	6	18
Palhani	1	2	14	4	21
Thekma	3	3	18	8.5	32.5
Martinganj	4	4	19	11.5	38.5

Source: Statistical Handbook of Azamgarh District, 2001.

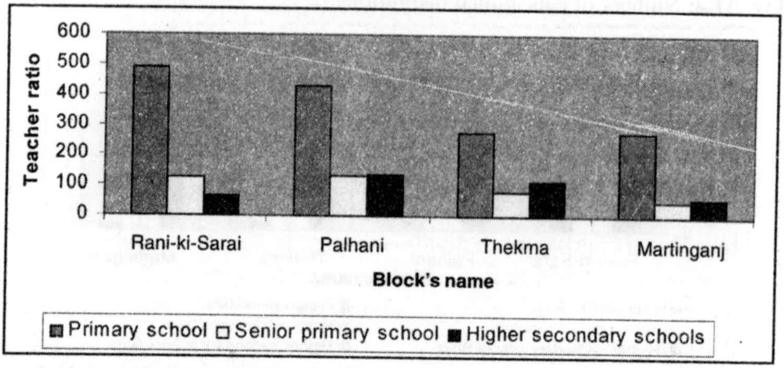

Fig. 31.6: Block-wise Teacher ratio in educational institutions.

Bhat, L.S.: *Regional Planning in India,* Statistical Publishing Society, Calcutta 1972.

Bhuiyan, R. and Banerjee S., Regional disparities of lower level educational development of Bangladesh, *Indian Journal of Regional Science,* Vol. 23, no. 1, 1991, pp. 181-186.

Dash, T.R., Regional Inequality in Educational Development in Orissa, *Indian Journal of Regional Science,* Vol. 25, no. 1, 1993, pp. 19-30.

Kanchan, R: Regional Development and Planning in Madhya Pradesh, *Indian Journal of Regional Science,* Vol. 23, No. 1, 1991, pp. 95-107.

Raza, M. and Aggarwal, Y.P.: Inequality in the levels of literacy: A regional analysis, Niepa, 1982 New Delhi, 9.

Rao, H., *Educational Development and inter taluk disparities in Karnataka Education and Regional Development,* 1986. pp. 296-315.

Reddy, G., *Planning and Regional Development,* 1995.

Zaidi, A.N.: Educational planning and regional disparities, *Education and Regional Development,* 1986, pp. 170-182..

32

Rural-Urban Fringe Land Use Transition Threatens Inland Water Bodies

Ravindra Kumar

Introduction

Cities are engines of growth. But the unplanned sprawl of cities creates the problem of urban-rural divide on many fronts. The conflicts of interest on priority of utilization of land resources and encroachment diminish land resources due to increasing urbanization and industrialization. Water reservoirs are diminishing around cities and groundwater table is dipping day by day. Therefore, potential aquifer in and around cities-rural fringe should be declared protected zone and encroachment prohibited. The State is supposed to ensure that its subjects lead a comfortable life in a dignified manner.

'It is the duty of government to make it difficult for people to do wrong, easy to do right', said W.E. Gladstone.

Discussions and Options

At present there is no penalty for a person who has converted his agricultural land into an *abadi* land. Section 143 of UPZALR Act, 1951 needs drastic changes. A provision in the law to prevent misuse of land should be made. The term "misuse" should be defined in such a way, so as to cover all aspects, which create hindrance in proper use of the land.

State Land Use Board may be provided statutory base and invested with necessary powers.

Formulation of comprehensive legislation with the various aspects of optimum use of land resources for the benefit of population as a whole is necessity of time. The proposed Act may include matters such as:

(i) Definition for classification of all types of land referred in UPZLRA, 1950 and UP Planning and Development Act, 1973 and Land Acquisition Act, 1984.

(ii) RS/GIS maps suggesting current various uses of land taken into consideration.

(iii) Cropping pattern should be decided for each area depending upon the suitability/capability of land and demand. Penal provisions required to punish the guilty on violation of land policy.

(iv) Master Plan for at least 25 years of every district should be known to everyone who matters in planning and project implementation.

(v) The land use policy should reflect aspiration of people and should fulfil the need of people of the area.

(vi) The outflow from rural to urban may be checked addressing regional imbalances in development.

(vii) Small scale cottage industry may provide both employment and income in case of failure of agriculture due to natural calamities of drought and flood and any other epidemic.

(viii) Deterioration of soil and excessive use of water should also be included as integrate part of programmes for 'maximizing land use'.

(ix) In any land use policy, the following objective should specifically be included:

   (a) Appropriate preventive measures to prevent any further deterioration in productivity of land;

   (b) Integration in formulation and implementation of:

      (i) Water resources management

      (ii) Forest management; and

      (iii) Urban planning within the overall resources allocation.

(x) We have also to consider the Industrialization as well as growing demand for *abadi*, particularly in those areas, which are nearer to cities when the land is acquired for colonization purposes. Effort should be made to acquire non-agricultural land, i.e. *banjar*, wasteland etc. for developmental work. For industrial and commercial purposes, only wasteland should be acquired, how far it may be from the main city. In case, if not possible for any reason, then the Company management should be asked to develop *banjar* land at some other places.

(xi) For successful implementation of any land use policy, computerization of *Khasra-khatauni*—which gives an idea of nature and extent of land use in the village, must give more comprehensive information.

(xii) Maximum area for residential purposes should also be fixed so that the 'have' community may not misuse land by constructing palatial buildings.

(xiii) Plantation on government land by people should be allowed to protect environment, recharge water and absorb carbon emission.

(xiv) Education should infuse Compassion, Ethics, Integrity and Courage to enable persons to stand-up for social goods and justice.

(xv) What is happening to agricultural lands, grasslands, wetlands, forests and freshwater system and even earth capacity to support nature and civilization around bulging ugly cities? How much human impact on ecosystems has altered the degree to which agricultural land have been degraded around the fringe areas of rural-urban divide by the build-up of salts and the loss of nutrients, dead zones caused by pollutants flowing into the rivers from sewer drains, many of the statistics are staggering: half the world's wetlands have been lost in the past century, 80 per cent of grasslands are suffering from soil degradation; 20 per cent of dry lands are in danger of becoming deserts; and groundwater is being depleted almost everywhere. The findings collected through satellite imaging and other forms of remote sensing, target critical areas deserving attention and pinpoint likely trouble spots in the future town planning under climate change contexts.

(xvi) Inescapable fact is economies cannot remain forever healthy in an unhealthy environment. Natural world is an economic asset that delivers irreplaceable goods and services. Ecosystems temper climate, purify and store water, recycle wastes, produce food and support all other things that humanity needs. Despite the universally acknowledged importance of these life-creating natural networks, the entire march of human progress has occurred against a backdrop of landscapes transformed from their natural state to suit the needs of agriculture and industry.

(xvii) And in this process cities diverted and despoiled their rivers and re-engineered their inland water bodies and wetlands.

Potential groundwater aquifers are encroached. Mining of their groundwater reservoirs have caused river to dry along the city stretches under population pressure increasing day by day by migration of rural population to urban and poor shifting from urban to fringe areas.

(xviii) The genius of the market economy is that it enables a city/state to buy from other places or re-create through technology some of the benefits once derived from the local habitat. The genius of the nature is that ecosystems can absorb shocks and sustain damage and still rebound.

Outstripping Capacity

(xix) One reason governments have been slow to respond to these concerns is that land is still churning out plenty of goods-enough fibre, grain and water to support 16.6 crore population of which 3.45 crore are urban (20%). Many are malnourished, of course malnutrition is more evident in surrounding villages, but that's primary a matter of bad distribution.

(xx) Algal booms, fed by pollution and agricultural run-off, are increasing and lakes are becoming stratified and depleted of oxygen. All these changes have taken place just in 20 years. We claim increase in food basket and livestock production, but the trade-offs have been depleted, polluted water supplies, exhausted soils and destroyed habitats.

Legislative/Policy Framework in the State

(a) Land

- U.P. (Urban) Zamindari Abolition and Land Reform Act, 1976.
- U.P. Zamindari Development and Land Management Act, 1976.
- Land Acquisition Act, 1997.
- Urban Land (Ceiling and Regulation) Act, 1976.
- U.P. Soil and Water Conservation Act, 1963.
- U.P. Urban Planning Act, 1973.
- U.P. Consolidation Act, 1953.
- U.P. Ceiling on Cultivation Act, 1960.
- U.P. Industrial Area Development Act, 1976.
- Indian Easement Act, 1882.

- U.P. Revenue Act.
- U.P. Construction Work Regulation Act, 1958.
- U.P. Awash Vikash Parishad Act, 1965.
- U.P. Forest Panchayat Act.
- U.P. River Valley Project Act, 1999.

(b) Water Resources Development and Management

- Uttar Pradesh Water Resources Management and Regulatory Commission Act, 2008.
- State Participatory Irrigation Management Act, 2009.
- National Ganga River Basin Authority, MOE Notification 20th Feb., 2009.
- Uttar Pradesh State Ganga River Conservation Authority, MOE Notification, 30th Sept., 2009.

Northern India Canal and Drainage Act, 1873. This is the most significant law relating to irrigation, navigation and drainage, which has withstood test of times for more than 130 years.

(c) Water Pollution

- The Rivers Boards Act, 1956.
- The Merchant Shipping Amendment Act, 1970.
- The Water (Prevention and Control of Pollution) Act of 1974 revised in 1988.
- The Water (Prevention and Control of Pollution) Rule 1975
- The Water (Prevention and Control of Pollution) Cess Act of 1977: Revised in 1997 & 2003.
- The Water (Prevention and Control of Pollution) Cess Rule of 1978.
- U.P. Water (Commercial Effluent and Sewage Disposal Rule, 1981).

(d) Air Pollution

- Indian Boilers Act, 1923, Motor Vehicle Act, 1939 (Revised in 1988).
- The Factory Act, 1948 (Revised in 1987).
- The Industries (Development and Regulation) Act, 1951.

- The Mines and Minerals (Regulation and Development) Act, 1947 (Revised in 1986).
- The Air (Prevention and Control of Pollution) Act, 1981 (Revised in 1987).
- The Air (Prevention and Control of Pollution) Rule, 1982.
- National Ambient Air Quality Standard Notification, 1994.

(e) Forestry and Bio-diversity

- The Wildlife (Protection) Act, 1972.
- The Indian Fisheries Act, 1897.
- Indian Forest Policy, 1927.
- Bio-diversity Cruelty Abatement Act, 1960.
- Bio-diversity Cruelty Abatement Rule, 2001.
- Zoo Establishment Rule, 1992.
- State /UT Small Forest Produce Act, 2005.
- Guidelines for Change in Forest Landuse for Other Purposes, 1994.
- U.P. (Tree Conservation in Rural and Hill Areas) Act, 1976.
- U.P. Building Wood and Other Produce Transport Rule, 1978.
- The Forest (Conservation) Act, 1980 revised in 1988.
- The Forest (Conservation) Rule, 2003.
- Bio-diversity Act, 2003.
- Bio-diversity Act, 2002.
- Wildlife (Protection) Rule, 1995.
- Panchayat Notified Area Extension Act, 1996.
- Bio-diversity Rule, 2004.

(f) Radiation

- The Atomic Energy Act, 1962.
- Radiation Protection Rule, 1971.

(g) Pesticides

- The Poison Act, 1919.
- The Prevention of Food Adulteration Act, 1954.
- The Factory Act, 1948 (revised in 1987).
- U.P. Agricultural Diseases and Pest Control Act, 1954.
- The Insecticides Act, 1968.

(h) Environment in General

The Environment Protection Act, 1986; Patent Act, 1970, Hazardous Chemical Manufacturing, Storage and Import Rule, 1989 (revised in 2000), Environment (Protection) Rule, 1986, The Noise (Pollution Control and Regulation) Rule, 2000 (revised in 2002), Hazardous Effluents (Management and Handling) Rule, 1989 (revised in 2003), Hazardous Microbial, Hereditary Effected Micro-organism or Cell Manufacturing Experiment, Import and Storage Construction Rule, 1989, Public Insurance Act, 1991 (revised in 1992, in 1993), Environmental Impact Assessment Notification, 1994 (revised 2005), National Environmental Judicature Act, 1995, National Environment Appellate Authority Act, 1997, Recycle Plastic Manufacturing and Use Rule, 1995 (revised in 2003), Environment (Establishment of Industrial Project) Rule, 1999, Batteries (Management and Handling) Rule, 2001, Bio-Medical Waste (Management and Handling) Rule, 2001, Urban Solid Waste (Management and Handling) Rule, 2000, Central Groundwater Board Authority, 1997 (revised in 2000), Fly Ash Filter and Expense Notification, 1999 (revised in 2003), Eco Mark Notification, 1991, Cosmetic Substance Eco-friendly Labelling Notification, 1992, Chemical Accident (Emergency Planning and Preparedness) Rule, 1996, Ozone Non-Degradation Substance (Regulation and Control) Rule, 2000.

Environmental Policy

Policy: State Environmental Policy, 2009, National Forest Policy, 1988, National Water Policy, 2002, Tourism Development Policy, 1990, National Population Policy, 2000, Abetment of Pollution Related Policy Statement, 1992, National Conservation Policy and Environment and Development Policy Statement, 1992, National Environment Policy, 2006, U.P. State Forest Policy, 1998, U.P. State Minerals Policy, 1998, U.P. State Tourism Policy, 1999, U.P. Agriculture Policy, 1999 and U.P. Water Policy, 1999.

Conclusion

Despite armed with many legal and policy framework, in absence of enabling authority invested to state land use boards, all efforts appear to fail in the past. Let us provide teeth to SLUB. In order to meet challenges before the country to support and meet the increasing demand of population and better standard of living, the necessity for a National Land Use Policy was felt. Accordingly, National Land Use Policy Outline and Action Points was prepared and placed before the National Land Use and Wasteland Development Council under the Chairmanship of Prime Minister. The Council agreed to the adaptation of policy.

Framing of suitable legislation and its sincere enforcement is the key of success by imposing penalties, on violations thereof. Thus, the problem of land management of rural-urban fringe is the issue of governance and requires support of all in its implementation.

Part VII
Planning for Rural-Urban Fringe

33

Spatial Planning for Rural-Urban Fringe Areas

J.B. Kshirsagar and *Pawan Kumar*

Example: Magarpatta City, Pune—A Rural-Urban Township

Magarpatta city is a modern township on the outskirts of Pune which was conceived and implemented by a group of farmers on their own land. The concept of Magarpatta city took root in the early 1990s when real estate developers and Pune city administrators wanted to convert the village to an urban zone. The farmers pooled their lands to form a co-operative where each family got shares equal to the size of land each family owned. The city consists of essential elements of modern Indian urban life. At present, it has dwellings for 12,000 families and 4 million square feet in work space for 40,000 people. The project of the farmer-turned-promoter consists of all amenities and services as per required standards. At present, it is only an example to allow agriculture land to be pooled together in fringe areas for construction of residential and commercial townships.

Planning and urban development are state subjects and hence laws pertaining to rural-urban fringe are mainly enacted by the State Legislature. The development of rural-urban areas is governed by Village Panchayats, Nagar Panchayats, District Administration, District Planning Committees (DPCs), Metropolitan Planning Committees (MPCs), Development Authorities, etc. The functions of various agencies are also overlapping and uncoordinated. There is need of Controlled Area Development Plan to control haphazard growth of such areas. It is advisable to prepare Perspective Plan of rural-urban fringe for a horizon year of 20 years along with Development Plan, with development controls to ensure orderly growth and development of both urban and rural areas.

Rural-urban fringes are an integral component of District Plan Area, Regional Plan Area, etc. and hence for proper implementation and enforcement mechanism for the area, Special Authority under the DPC should be set-up which will be responsible for regulating, planning, development and management of only rural-urban areas.

Introduction

Rural-Urban Fringe Areas are either transitional areas or interactive areas where urban and rural activities are juxtaposed and natural features are subject to rapid modifications. These areas are characterized by various unacceptable land uses; transformed hydrological, ecological, geo-morphological and environmental systems; deteriorated built environment; variable socio-economic profile; etc. and are generally neglected by both rural and urban local bodies. In terms of spatial planning, rural-urban fringe areas are disorganized city expansions that involve high cost of service management, infrastructure maintenance, environmental protection, etc. due to large concentration of population and economic activities.

The growth of rural-urban fringe areas is dynamic, interactive and transformative because it is directly related to land use, socio-cultural transformation, demographic characteristics and propagation of urban attitudes. However, these areas are also affected by the process of migration, poverty, provision of basic human needs, infrastructure, transport, disposal of wastes, atmospheric contamination of ecosystems, pollution of surface and groundwater, etc. Hence, spatial planning approach is required to ensure healthy spatial growth of peri-urban areas as well as reduce vulnerability of stakeholders such as farmers, landless labour, etc. to prevent slumming.

1. Characteristics of Rural-Urban Fringe Areas

The development of rural-urban fringe area occurs not only on periphery but may often penetrate along hilltops, water fronts, river valley and well into inside urban areas. The impact of economic growth and physical expansion of the urban area are not confined to urban boundaries but they reach into much wider areas surrounding urban centres creating "rurban areas", "urban fringe areas" or "peri-urban areas". The peri-urban area retains the characteristics of the rural area subject to major modifications and changes which take place with respect to physical configuration, economic activities, social relationships, etc. However, the extent of peri-urban area depends upon the size of the city and its surrounding countryside.

Urbanization is a continuous process of concentration and intensification of human life and activities in the physical environment. 'Proximity to the city' is not the only criteria to define peri-urban area but rural-urban continuum, uncontrolled urbanization, prevailing socio-cultural and political environment, etc. have direct impact on the formation of such areas.

However, rural-urban fringe areas are transformative and reciprocal in nature and directly linked by economic activities, spatial distribution, social fabric of individual and family, flow of migrants and their networks.

2. Problems of Rural-Urban Fringe Areas

Generally, rural-urban fringe areas are not statutorily declared areas except in certain cases like Chandigarh where they are defined as a belt of 16 kms. around the city. The problems of peri-urban areas are due to general changes in land uses to meet urban requirements as well as local needs. Similarly, activities in such areas have a strong interface with the city and complement its needs. The areas may be divided in two parts:

- **Urban Fringe:** Area which is adjacent and touching the municipal boundary having direct impact of urbanization and experiencing rapid pace of transformation.
- **Area Beyond Urban Fringe:** It is the rest of peri-urban areas. In these areas, setting up of new townships to maximize profit out of periphery by converting the area from agriculture to non-agricultural area is the main concern.

Rural-urban fringe areas are characterized by both authorized and unauthorized developments including informal settlements having inadequate provision of services and infrastructure. The quality of life is also poor. There are major conflicts pertaining to the change of landuse from agriculture to non-agriculture (urban development). The shifts from traditional food crops to high value cash crops are quite common due to high demand from the mother city and agro-based industries. The agricultural loss of productivity due to constantly increasing presence of buildings in rural-urban fringe areas, also affects rural economy.

The swelling of the number of urban poor and conversion of good agricultural land for urban uses, rehabilitation of displaced farmers, conversion and development of land for malls, SEZs, etc. are other challenges for planners. The increase of the economic value of real estate due to transformation puts further pressure to violate any Periphery Control Act.

In the large urban agglomerations, rural-urban fringe areas have a tendency to grow along the various corridors such as:

- Transport Corridor,
- Nearby Religious Spots,
- Heritage and Archeological Sites,
- Scenic and Natural Beauty Sites, etc. at a much faster rate.

The transformation of such areas is generally unplanned and haphazard. In the urban context, rural-urban fringe areas are considered incentives for setting up industries and are often declared as Free Enterprise Zone. Similarly, liberal grant of permission to change land use as well as construction is also one of the reasons for haphazard development in the periphery. There is always a gap between demand and supply of housing stock in the city with the population explosion which puts pressure on the rural-urban fringe areas and compels the Governments to grant permission which are generally not permitted in these areas. There is need to adopt spatial planning approach to regulate and control such developments.

As per 2001 census, 35 million plus cities constituted more than one-third (37.85%) of the total urban population. During the last decade (1991-2001), the number of million plus cities increased from 23 to 35 and is likely to increase to 50 by 2011. There is close relation between growth of core city (main city) and periphery of metropolitan city.

Table 33.1 states that the growth tendency of six mega cities is not uniform. All mega cities except Bangalore have recorded higher growth in their peripheries than in the core city. Huge population, lack of infrastructure and amenities, cost of living, and stringent land laws, may have decelerated the holding capacity of the core areas of these cities to absorb the marginal increase of population, which, as a matter of fact, find a place in and around the core city, indicating a faster growth of Urban Agglomerations (UAs).

3. Rural-Urban Fringe Areas: Legal Framework

The growth of rural-urban fringe areas is parallel to the growth of any town/city. Due to rapid growth and expansion of the city, commercial

Table 33.1: Growth Differentials of Core and Periphery of Mega Cities in India

Sl. No.	*Mega Cities*	*1981–91*		*1991–2001*	
		Core	Periphery	Core	Periphery
(i)	Greater Mumbai	1.86	4.22	1.82	2.62
(ii)	Kolkata	0.64	1.72	0.4	1.82
(iii)	Delhi	3.59	3.8	3.09	4.18
(iv)	Chennai	1.59	2.23	0.93	1.7
(v)	Bangalore	0.71	3.36	4.79	3.2
(vi)	Hyderabad	3.31	5.2	1.58	2.42

Source: Census of India 1981, 1991, Paper 2, Rural-Urban Distribution, Census of India 2001. *The Handbook of Urbanization in India*, by Sri K.C. Shivaramakrishnan, Amitabh Kundu, B.N.Singh, pp. 43.

interest of rural-urban fringe areas also increases. The prominent features of rural-urban fringe areas also contribute to sustainable growth of the city and public policies may be directed to retain the same for overall development.

(i) Punjab New Capital (Periphery) Control Act, 1952

The Punjab New Capital Periphery Control Act was enacted in 1952 by the Punjab Government to control and regulate the use of land around acquired boundary of capital city and provide permanent green belt around the city with the sole idea of regulating development within 8 kms. radius beyond city to protect the surroundings from degeneration. The limit was extended to 16 kms. (10 miles) by subsequent amendment in 1962. In 1999, the proposal for Chandigarh Inter State Metroplitan Region Plan was authored by Prof. E.F.N. Riberio for the region taking into account radius of 50 kms. including the radius of 16 kms. for the periphery as well. The region extends over 2400 sq. kms. and involves Himachal Pradesh as the third state.

(ii) Master Plan for Delhi, 2021

As per 2001 Census, NCT of Delhi (1484 sq. kms.) had a total population of 138 lakh which was projected to 182 lakh and 230 lakh by the year 2011 and 2021 respectively. In 2001, about 702 sq. km. of area was estimated to have been built up, accommodating about 138 lakh population. To accommodate the projected population of 230 lakh by the year 2021, the following strategy has been adopted:

- To encourage deflection of population to NCR towns,
- To increase population holding capacity of the area within the existing urban limit through redevelopment, and
- Extension of the present urban limits.

Due to land constraints in NCTD, the areas earmarked as rural/agricultural in the previous Master Plans have always been under pressure for utilization for various urban activities. In future, urbanization has to be in areas along the major transport corridors and fringes of already urbanized areas. It is envisaged that major rural areas would be absorbed as urban extensions over a period of time.

The Plan stipulates that the land up to the depth of one peripheral village revenue boundary along the border of NCTD, wherever available, would be Green Belt. However, new motels shall not be permitted in green belt and Government of NCTD shall be responsible for ensuring utilization of land in Green belt in accordance with permissible use.

(iii) Magarpatta City, Pune: An Example of Rural-Urban Fringe Township

Magarpatta city is a modern township on the outskirts of Pune which was conceived and implemented by a group of farmers on their own land. The concept of Magarpatta city took root in the early 1990s when real estate developers and Pune city administrators wanted to convert village to an urban zone. The farmers pooled their lands to form a co-operative like structure where each family got shares equal to the size of land each family owned. The city consists of essential element of modern Indian urban life. When the city will be completed in 2008, it will have dwellings for 12,000 families and 4 million square feet in work space for 40,000 people. The project of the farmer-turned-promoter consists of all amenities and services as per required standards. At present, it is only an example to allow agriculture land to be pooled together in peri-urban areas for construction of residential and commercial townships.

4. Management of Rural-Urban Fringe Areas: Way Ahead

(i) Planning Legislation

Planning and urban development are state subjects and hence law pertaining to such subjects are mainly enacted by the State Legislature.

However, planning legislation related to rural-urban fringe area development is almost missing except the Punjab New Capital (Periphery) Control Act, 1952 which was enacted to control and regulate the use of land within 16 kms. belt around acquired boundary of capital city. Such problem is in each and every city and state and hence there is need to formulate such legislation to promote healthy development in periphery areas.

(ii) Controlled Area Development Plan

The development of peri-urban areas is governed by Village Panchayats, Nagar Panchayats, District Administration, District Planning Committees (DPCs), Metropolitan Planning Committees (MPCs), Development Authorities, etc. Due to poor resource and less expertise, rural local bodies are unable to control the development in such areas. There is lack of legislation to control such areas through Town and Country Planning Acts. The functions of various agencies are also overlapping and uncoordinated. There is also need of Controlled Area Development Plan to control haphazard growth of such areas.

(iii) Perspective Plan of Rural-Urban Fringe Areas

Master Plan is a coordinated set of proposals for physical development of town as a whole rather than parts taking into account not only the present needs but also the future requirements. In fact, Master Plan consists of legal planning tools which can guide development of such areas which extend beyond the municipal limit. There is need to re-examine such provisions and restrictions in Master Plan in the present context to regulate and plan the development as per requirements and needs.

It is advisable to prepare Perspective Plan of Peri-urban Area for a horizon year of 25 years along with Development Plan, with appropriate development controls to ensure orderly growth and development of both urban and peri-urban areas.

5. Concluding Remarks

Those towns which are near rural-urban fringe areas may be developed as satellite towns/counter magnets so that they may attract population and activities to reduce pressure on the rural-urban fringe areas. Recently, the concept of development of satellite towns of million plus Cities is being taken up by the Government of India. The self-contained new townships may be located at a reasonable distance (say 40-50 kms.) from the mother city and may be developed with fast track and efficient public transport, which could provide solutions to problems of housing and infrastructure.

The development of satellite cities/townships has shown good results in countries like USA, France and UK in sixties and seventies. The development of satellite cities around million plus cities/big cities will be helpful in achieving greater efficiency to control and regulate human settlements both inside and periphery of urban areas.

Rural, urban fringe areas are an integral component of District Plan Area, Regional Plan Area, etc. and hence for proper implementation and enforcement mechanism for the area, Special Urban Planning and Development Authority should be set-up under DPC which will be responsible for regulating, planning, development and management of only rural-urban fringe areas. Such authority will be solely responsible for carrying out any development, demolition, renewal and expansion with the consultation with the State Government.

34

Rapid Urbanization in India and the Governance Challenges

J.S. Simlai

Introduction

Urbanization is not a side effect of economic growth but an integral part of the process. The urban regions of the north make major contributions to the country's economy. Although less than one-third of India's population live in cities, the urban centres generate over two-third of the country's GDP and account for 90 per cent of the government revenues, according to a World Bank report.

India's urban space have expanded rapidly as increasing number of people migrate to the cities in search of better livelihood. Slums now account for ¼ of all urban housing. In Mumbai, more than half of the population lives in slums and many of which are situated close to the heart of the city. Meeting the needs of India's soaring urban population is

Table 34.1: Urbanization

State	*UA*	*Town*	*Cities*
Chandigarh	0	1	1
Chhattisgarh	12	97	32
Delhi	1	62	32
Haryana	1	57	28
H. Pradesh	7	75	1
J & K	11	152	4
M.P.	15	378	35
Punjab	25	222	20
Rajasthan	0	9	26
U.P.	8	86	64
Uttaranchal	11	106	5

Source: Census 2001.

Table 34.2: Trends in urbanization in million-plus cities (% growth)

	Population (Million)	*1981–91*	*1991–2001*
Delhi	12.79	43.2	36.2
Kanpur	2.69	25.8	35
Jaipur	2.32	49.2	59.4
Lucknow	2.27	70.8	36.3
Indore	1.64	31.6	46.3
Bhopal	1.45	58.3	34.9
Ludhiana	1.4	71.7	33.7
Agra	1.32	28.5	29.2
Varanasi	1.21	29.6	18.4
Meerut	1.17	67.9	42.5
Jabalpur	1.12	20.8	22
Faridabad	1.05	86.7	70.8
Allahabad	1.05	86.7	70.8
Amritsar	1.01	19.2	27.3

Source: Census 2001.

and will continue to be a policy matter of great importance and this prescription of the World Bank rings true for the north Indian states such as Delhi, Punjab and Haryana as well. Critical issues that need to be addressed in these states are poor local governance, weak finances, inappropriate planning that leads to high costs of housing. Critical infrastructure shortages which include erratic supply of water and power, and woefully inadequate public transport.

According to the World Bank report, many Urban Governments lack a modern planning framework. The multiplicity of local bodies obstructs efficient planning and land use. Rigid master plans and restrictive zoning regulations limit the land availability for building and other commercial constriction activities. Building regulations that limit urban density—such as floor space indexes—reduce the number of houses available, thereby pushing up property prices. Outdated rent control regulations also reduce the number of houses available on rent—a critical option for the poor and new immigrants: Such planning and regulation deficiencies lead to the proliferation of slums. Weak finances of urban local bodies and service providers leave them unable to expand the trunk infrastructure that housing developers need while developing new sites. Hence, the service providers are unable to recover the operations and maintenance costs, and heavily depend on the governments for finance, says the World Bank report.

Most urban bodies do not generate the revenues needed to renew infrastructure, nor do they have the creditworthiness to access capital

Table 34.3: Status of Urban Water Supply and Sanitation (% of Population with Access) as of March, 2004

State	*Water supply*	*Sewerage and sanitation*
Chhattisgarh	90	80
Chandigarh	100	100
Delhi	100	51
Haryana	82	58
H. Pradesh	100	83
J & K	94	47
M.P.	90	80
Punjab	77	92
Rajasthan	100	79
U.P.	99	55
Uttarakhand	100	48

Source: Working Paper to XI Plan.

markets for funds. Urban Transport planning needs more holistic approach. According to an-indepth analysis by D.P. Tiwari, former Town and Country Planning Chairman of Bhopal, the existing municipal laws are totally inadequate to enable the Urban Local Bodies (ULBs) to discharge new responsibilities delegated to them under the 74th Constitutional Amendment. Although the State Governments have amended the municipal Acts, as a follow-up of the 74th Amendment, the amended Acts do not specifically assign functions to the local bodies, especially in the area of urban planning. The following measures have to be undertaken to enable the ULBs to serve as agencies for plan preparation, enforcement and implementation:

- Clear division of functional responsibilities and linkage among different levels of government to ensure upward and downward accountability, and to enable the SPCs in their constitutional task of devolution of funds to ULBs.
- Division of municipal functions into essential functions, agency functions, and joint functions with the State and Central Governments, avoiding the traditional distinction between 'obligatory' and 'discretionary' functions since such classification results in uncertainties and non-transparent system of municipal accountability.
- Essential functions of municipalities to include urban planning, including town planning regulation of land use and construction of buildings, and planning for economic and social development.

According to Mr. Tiwari, for a more dynamic urban planning exercise, the following modifications in the planning approach are needed. Primarily, plans must have flexibility, to provide for ever-growing and ever-expanding city boundaries. The plan should be flexible to respond not only to the present needs but also to the changing conditions in the foreseeable future.

Secondly, people's participation in preparation of policies, perspective plan, development plan and annual plans should be ensured through elected representatives in the municipal councils corporations and ward committees. Thirdly, a well-maintained information system could make possible the fine-tuning of the plan proposals at the various stages of implementation, the development potential may be assessed for the areas located in the periphery of the developed areas. A profile of the development potential and the possibility of optimizing the existing infrastructure should determine the prioritization of development in these areas.

Given the paucity of resources, it would be more feasible and desirable to promote strategic development initiatives in the selected secondary cities, growth centres and their hinterlands. In the growth centres, the location of infrastructural and environmental services could form the 'core' of the development plan.

More importantly, the zoning regulations need to be simplified. The land use package should not be altered by any authority except as part of the review of the development plan at the city/town level.

Land development and infrastructure investment need to be coordinated through integration of physical-financial and investment planning. There is a need to link spatial development plan with the resource mobilization plan, focusing on credit enhancement mechanisms. The plan must provide for and cater to the needs of the informal sector so as to make them as an integral part of the city development process.

Finally, as opposed to the process of compulsory land acquisition and the related issue of low compensation rates, the urban bodies should adopt collaborative approaches within the existing legal framework. Plan implementation would call for a legal framework so as to make it enforceable and mandatory. The legal framework has to be supported by an effective and efficient machinery which would see that no distortion of master plan proposals take place at the ground level. Plot sizes, layout and social overheads need to be designed to reduce costs aligned to the affordability of different income groups. Also, sale prices for lower income groups can be reduced by differential pricing. Building bye-laws and zoning regulations for the city/town should match the local needs. However, the existing bye-laws need to be simplified and transparent.

The planning exercise needs continuous data collection, analysis, interpretation and updation. A computer-generated data-base and information system in GIS environment should be developed at various levels which would provide support to the planners. The preparation of development plans should be completed, within a period of 12 months and should be finally approved within 3 months after that. The approval authority of development plans should be the ULB in consultation with the director of town planning department.

"If the government embraces technology and innovation, it can make substantial change to peoples' lives. With networking sites becoming a platform for people to voice their opinion, the government can use this medium to understand public opinion and act accordingly", said Yogesh Bansal founder and CEO of Apna Circle. Com.

Hence, the Town Planning Acts need to be modified to enable the formulation of interrelated plans by specifying the definition, scope and contents of different plans.

Cities are social artifacts. They originated as a result of the emergence of the ruling classes; they are reflections of the historico-political-administrative processes. They are also economic entities that have a parasitic existence as they seek support from their hinterlands. Urbanization is also a geographical process as there is growth and migration particularly rural to urban. The occurrence of the rural-urban "Rurban" fringe is a recent phenomenon around the Indian cities. It is asserted that this was non-existent even around the largest cities before 1950. The physical expansion of the city inevitably brings in concomitant changes in the social aspect of its fringe villages. There are changes in industry, commerce, administration, institutions health etc. which affect the market forces and produce significant changes in rural land uses causing the inhabitants around a city to adopt a quasi-urban way of life. The fringe thus enters a transitional phase between rural and urban societies and becomes an area "in a state of flux".

Planned development is required in the urban areas and even more so in the Rural-Urban Fringe as the city of the future lies therein also for urban corridors, satellites and suburbs, green belts, new towns and urban counter magnets. Governance must take into account occupational changes, urban land-use growth, development of infrastructure law and order. There is, therefore, an urgent need to evolve policy guidelines that are equitable to the urban areas, the fringes and the rural areas.

A meaningful and pragmatic urbanization policy should recognize the significance of the spontaneous and voluntary urbanization processes at work in the country. Unfortunately, the policy makers appear to be negative in their approach towards urban areas. The opposition towards urbanization surfaces in the negative attitude towards growth of big cities, the rising urban land values, the general inflation, the need to strengthen municipal administration which is actually crumbling, the emphasis on slum clearance and the reluctance to provide land for the poor within the urban area—all of these indicate an attitude bent on increasing the urban problems rather than looking for solutions.

Most of the urban policies in India have a utopian ring. It is necessary to set aside impractical approaches if we genuinely seek a treatment for the urban malaise. A positive, honest and practical approach will go a long way to identify the basic components and perspectives of the urban policy framework. A framework that is supported by sound governance evolved at the state level based on the assumption that urbanization is a spontaneous and desirable process.

Broadly speaking, an urbanization policy statement at the state level should cover three major aspects:

(a) City size and spacing,
(b) rural-urban migration policy, and
(c) rural-urban fringe policy.

With respect to the first there are inequalities in size and spacing of urban settlements not only between states but also within states. Strengthening of infrastructure, education, hospitals, *mandis*, green belts, water supply, drainage, sewage etc. should receive high priority. In the case of Rural-Urban migration—provision of education, recreation and amenities and an enhancement of a symbiotic relationship between rural and urban areas needs to be reinforced. The third is the Rural-Urban Fringe where problems encompass four major areas:

(a) the growth of urban land-use
(b) the lack of urban amenities
(c) the problems relating to administration and governance, and
(d) fair and just compensation for land acquired for urban uses.

One of the major challenges of the rural-urban fringe is the haphazard location of major urban land-uses. The fringe zone is mainly used as the peripheral dumping ground, both literally and in a symbolic sense. Most unpleasant land-uses in the city are shifted or located in the fringe zone.

A fresh look at the administrative framework for city and city region planning in the Indian context is necessary both for the urban areas and the rural urban areas as well as the rural areas to tide over the excruciating problems that confront planners, administrators politicians and the population at large.

References

Comm J.R.C., Irwin P.G. (1981). *Space, People, Place Economic and Settlement Geography, 1981*, Longman Cheshire Pvt. Ltd., pp. 464-489.

Edwin, Tina, Cities of the Northern Region: Wilting under Flow of Migrants. *The Economic Times,* Feb. 19, 2009, p. 3.

Guha, Rajat, The Governance Pangs. *The Economic Times,* Feb. 19, 2009, p. 8.

Hartshorn T.A. and Alexander J.W. (1988). *Economic Geography,* Prentice Hall International Inc., pp. 325-350.

Knox Paul (1984). *Urban Social Geography.* Longman Group Limited, pp. 34-41, 192-209.

Northham Ray M. (1975). *Urban Geography.* John Wiley & Sons Inc., pp. 389-403.

R. Ramachandran (1992). *Urbanization and Urban Systems*, Oxford, pp. 120-150, 322-340.

Sridhar S. Kala—Technology for Cities, *The Economic Times,* Feb. 25, 2009, p. 8.

35

Post Reform Restructuring of Employment in Urban Peripheries: A Case Study of National Capital Region of India

Rupinder Kaur

I. Introduction

Metropolisation can be defined as an urban phenomenon based on two movements: the concentration of population and wealth in the biggest agglomerations and expansion of these agglomerations that overwhelmed the classical opposition between rural and urban areas. A metropolitan area usually combines an agglomeration with peripheral zones not themselves necessarily urban in character but closely bound to the centre by employment or commerce, these zones are also known as commuter belt. After the market oriented reforms in early 1990's, following the East Asian model, foreign investment is seen as key to economic growth and metropolises are seen as likely foreign investment destinations, so the state takes action to reconfigure the metropolis to accommodate new growth. With this view, advocacy of decentralization stem from the perception that the existing metropolitan central business districts are very congested and therefore unmanageable and inefficient, so the growth has to be accommodated elsewhere within the metropolitan area. In this connection, it is expected that these structural changes would alter the pattern of urbanization as well as employment structure in metropolitan areas during reform period, i.e. 1991 to 2000.

Delhi has been one of the fastest growing metropolises over the past few decades in India covering 33,578 sq. km. spanning 14 districts in Haryana, Rajasthan, and Uttar Pradesh and NCT of Delhi. It is in this context that present chapter attempts to analyse the changes in the structure of employment and its spatial distribution in National Capital Region of India. Section II details the data source and concepts used. Section III looks at the pattern of urbanisation. Section IV considers the size and composition of workforce. Section V analyses the industrial distribution of workers. Section VI looks at the share of male and female workers in major industries. Section VII analyses distribution of main and marginal workers in different industries. Section VIII deals with industrial distribution of migrant workers. Section IX is about sectoral and spatial concentration of employment and Section X i.e. final section is concluding note.

II. Data Source and Concepts

Since the chapter aims to examine the changes in workforce structure in Naticnal Capital Region (NCR), a district level data has been used provided by census of India in its 'b series'. Since, the classification of employment categories changed between two years, the comparable figures were obtained using National Industrial Classification 1987.

The analysis has been done for males and female separately in both rural and urban areas, for National Capital Territory Delhi and ten adjoining districts comprising NCR according to 1991 census as three new districts namely Jhajjar, Bhagpat and Gautam Budh Nagar were carved out between two censuses. Census classify workers into two categories: a person who has worked for six months or more during the last one year is termed as 'Main Worker' otherwise he/she is a 'Marginal Worker'. To show the distribution of migrant workers in various industrial groups, migrant workers whose last residence was outside the district are taken into consideration. Pattern of urbanization has been shown using census typology of urban places based on population size.

III. Pattern of Urbanization

Urbanization may have different connotation for different people, for instance it's a concentration of population at a particular place, and process of social change, and modernization but for our concern urbanization is best seen as shift from agriculture to manufacturing and tertiary sector or movement of capital from primary to secondary and tertiary circuit.

Table 35.1 shows the distribution of different size class towns in 1991 and 2001 indicating heterogeneous pattern of urbanization and disproportionate growth of towns where number of towns in lower size

Table 35.1: Distribution of Towns in NCR

Sl. No.	State/ District	I		II		III		IV		V		VI		Level of Urbanization	
		1991	2001	1991	2001	1991	2001	1991	2001	1991	2001	1991	2001	1991	2001
1.	Delhi	10	17	5	11	12	20	15	13	18	8	13	4	89.93	93.01
2.	Panipat	1	1	–	–	–	3	2	1	–	1	–	–	27.16	40.51
3.	Sonipat	1	1	–	–	1	2	1	1	–	–	–	–	23.58	25.13
4.	Rohtak	1	2	1	1	2	1	3	3	1	2	–	–	21.31	31.76
5.	Rewari	–	1	1	–	–	–	1	2	1		–	1	15.27	17.82
6.	Gurgaon	1	1	–	–	–	1	6	9	4	1	–	–	20.30	22.28
7.	Faridabad	1	2	1	–	1	1	–	1	2	2	–	–	15.27	55.63
8.	Alwar	1	1	—	–	2	4	4	3	1	1	–	–	13.95	14.53
9.	Meerut	1	1	3	3	3	5	14	12	2	2	–	1	37.02	40.49
10.	Ghaziabad	4	4	1	3	6	3	7	4	5	3	1	–	46.16	50.31
11.	Bulandshahr	1	1	2	3	6	7	7	4	6	1	–		20.80	23.05
	NCR	22	32	14	21	33	47	60	53	40	21	14	6	33.10	37.68

class has declined and large towns have increased during this period. With the highest level of urbanization at both the points of time Delhi has shown little increase in its urbanization as it is near to its saturation level. Districts like Faridabad, Panipat and Rohtak have recorded a significant increase in their level of urbanization, while other districts have shown marginal increase in their urban proportion. Thus, National Capital Region is characterized by a heterogeneous urban pattern. Such regions are called Desakota, the term used by Terry McGee to refer Asia's sprawling urban settlements, combining the word desa (village) and kota (city) to highlight the mixed rural-urban character of such agglomerations. Basically, it is an impact of extended metropolis in the outskirts or hinterland of rural areas which gets transformed when urbanization spillover.

IV. Size and Composition of Workforce

Tables 35.2 and 35.3 present total, male and female Workforce Participation Rates (WPR), for both rural and urban areas during 1991 and 2001 for all constituent district and NCR as a whole and Table 35.2 shows the growth rate of WPR and level of urbanization as well as their correlation. In NCR, the total WPR has increased by 6 per cent points, i.e. mainly due to huge increase in female WPR as male WPR has remained stagnant during the same period.

Rural areas have recorded 7 per cent increase in WPR compared to 1 per cent in urban areas. Male WPR in rural areas has shown only a marginal increase of 1 per cent whereas it has declined by 2 per cent points in urban areas. On the other hand, female WPR has significantly increased in both rural and urban areas especially in rural areas indicating the feminisation of employment. Among the districts, Alwar is the least urbanised district of NCR and recorded highest WPR at both points of time especially in case of female workers and rural areas. There is only marginal increase in male WPR but female WPR has increased significantly in most of the districts except Delhi, Ghaziabad and Meerut which are more urbanized districts of NCR because female WPR has increased much sharply in rural areas as higher female WPR is primarily associated with agriculture distress and poverty which is mainly concentrated in rural areas. The relationship between the growth rate of level of urbanization and WPR during this period is found to be negative indicating that higher level of urbanisation leads to lower WPR whereas higher WPR in rural areas is a consequence of distress agriculture.

Table 35.2: Work Participation Rates in National Capital Region – 1991

Sl. No.	*State/district*	*Total*			*Rural*			*Urban*		
		Total	Male	Female	Total	Male	Female	Total	Male	Female
1.	Delhi	31.64	51.72	7.36	29.12	48.23	5.46	31.92	52.11	7.57
2.	Panipat	30.25	49.56	7.65	30.36	48.87	8.53	29.97	51.43	5.32
3.	Sonipat	30.65	47.89	10.15	31.65	48.29	11.62	27.42	46.54	5.52
4.	Rohtak	31.42	46.80	13.35	32.55	46.87	15.56	27.24	46.51	5.36
5.	Rewari	27.79	42.72	11.67	27.75	41.72	12.88	27.99	48.04	4.65
6.	Gurgaon	32.06	46.52	15.46	33.08	46.35	17.78	28.05	47.18	6.47
7.	Faridabad	30.34	48.07	8.91	30.68	45.78	12.74	29.97	50.46	4.79
8.	Alwar	40.37	47.76	31.97	42.20	47.74	35.95	29.09	47.89	6.47
9.	Meerut	30.51	49.69	8.00	32.24	50.74	10.19	27.58	47.86	4.37
10.	Ghaziabad	30.23	48.24	8.58	30.98	48.13	10.38	29.36	48.38	6.48
11.	Bulandshahr	28.97	47.41	7.42	29.64	47.74	8.33	26.44	46.16	4.03
12.	NCR	31.59	49.24	10.69	32.62	47.86	14.72	30.57	50.60	6.68

Source: Census of India, 1991.

Table 35.3: Work Participation Rates. in National Capital Region – 2001

Sl. No.	State/district	Total			Rural			Urban		
		Total	Male	Female	Total	Male	Female	Total	Male	Female
1.	Delhi	33.06	52.45	9.43	31.79	49.49	9.84	33.16	52.67	9.40
2.	Panipat	40.02	51.41	26.30	42.66	50.25	33.60	36.15	53.10	15.46
3.	Sonipat	40.76	49.41	30.47	44.38	50.51	37.06	29.99	46.10	10.97
4.	Rohtak	41.06	49.34	31.30	45.32	50.45	39.26	30.50	46.57	11.54
5.	Rewari	42.86	48.98	36.05	45.68	49.31	41.71	29.83	47.53	9.03
6.	Gurgaon	38.40	47.53	27.96	40.04	46.77	32.36	32.70	50.14	12.50
7.	Faridabad	35.62	47.97	20.90	41.23	46.02	35.65	31.14	49.49	8.87
8.	Alwar	48.79	53.05	43.99	51.63	53.79	49.23	32.09	48.87	12.06
9.	Meerut	30.23	46.27	11.68	32.77	47.18	16.02	26.49	44.92	5.36
10.	Ghaziabad	28.93	45.95	9.03	29.71	45.18	11.66	28.15	46.72	6.43
11.	Bulandshahr	40.16	50.92	27.94	40.16	50.92	27.94	40.16	50.92	27.94
12.	NCR	38.17	49.39	25.00	40.49	49.08	30.39	31.85	48.82	11.78

Source: Census of India, 2001.

V. Industrial Distribution of Workforce

Table 35.4 presents the distribution of total workers among broad industrial groups. In terms of sectoral distribution of workforce NCR has experienced shift from agriculture to secondary sector. In 1991, primary sector was the largest sector in NCR employing 40 per cent of workforce, followed by service sector (39%) and secondary sector (21%). Whereas in 2001, service sector was major sector with 38.5 per cent of workforce which was followed by agriculture (36.4 %) and secondary sector (25.1 %). During 1991 to 2001 primary sector has declined from 40 per cent to 36.4 per cent in terms of its share in total workforce whereas secondary sector has grown by 4 percentage points while service sector remained stagnant with its 39 per cent share in total workforce. Taking rural urban areas separately, rural areas have dominance of primary sector at both points of time followed by service sector and secondary sector, while in urban areas service sector is largest sector followed by secondary sector and primary sector.

Delhi which is the core urban centre of this region has huge portion of its workforce in service sector at both points of time, i.e. 65 per cent in 1991 and 64 per cent in 2001. Its service sector accounts for 32.4 per cent workforce in 1991 and 34.1 per cent in 2001 while primary sector with its smallest share has declined from 3 per cent in 1991 to 2.3 per cent in 2001. Thus, no sector has shown a significant change in Delhi. Among the other districts Alwar with lowest level of urbanization is mainly characterized by primary sector with its 79 per cent share in 1991 and 76.8 per cent in 2001. But within primary sector, it has shown some diversification by increased share of workers in livestock, forestry and allied activities.

All the districts except Sonipat have observed decline in share of cultivators in workforce but it has shown a considerable increase in livestock, forestry, fishing, hunting plantation, orchards and allied activities moving towards non-farm diversification. A huge increase in share of Allied activities is a consequence of surplus labour in declining agriculture sector which has not been absorbed by secondary and service sector because this part of labour force is largely illiterate and unskilled. Share of workers in manufacturing sector is common in all districts. In case of non-household manufacturing industry only Faridabad and Ghaziabad have declining share of workers as their service sector particularly trade and commerce and transport storage and communication are absorbing more workforce, while Gurgaon has improved its share in

Table 35.4: Industrial Distribution of Total Workers (1991)

Sl. No.	State/District	(I)	(II)	(III)	(IV)	(Va)	(Vb)	(VI)	(VII)	(VIII)	IX)
1.	Delhi	1.16	0.93	0.64	0.24	1.43	23.18	7.80	23.86	8.28	32.48
2.	Panipat	33.93	22.05	0.40	0.00	2.61	14.38	1.85	9.40	2.51	12.87
3.	Sonipat	32.99	18.82	0.52	0.00	1.43	11.64	2.11	7.79	4.76	19.93
4.	Rohtak	44.77	16.32	0.81	0.01	0.94	6.14	2.26	7.16	3.50	18.00
5.	Rewari	46.38	13.52	0.92	0.29	2.19	8.24	2.82	7.18	3.56	14.88
6.	Gurgaon	43.23	16.48	0.86	0.30	1.31	7.19	2.56	7.51	3.74	16.83
7.	Faridabad	28.49	12.64	0.58	0.65	0.87	24.81	3.65	9.56	3.18	15.56
8.	Alwar	68.35	9.63	0.86	0.41	1.50	4.39	1.30	4.07	1.64	7.85
9.	Meerut	34.29	22.13	1.25	0.01	3.01	11.52	2.00	9.02	3.04	13.72
10.	Ghaziabad	26.85	13.72	0.77	0.03	1.40	17.12	3.40	10.12	4.13	22.45
11.	Bulandshahr	45.56	21.93	0.63	0.01	1.72	6.24	1.52	6.90	2.00	13.48
12.	NCR	27.86	11.29	0.76	0.19	1.64	14.98	4.15	13.29	4.82	21.04
Industrial Distribution of Total Workers (2001)											
1.	Delhi	0.82	0.35	0.82	0.35	3.03	23.40	7.71	23.17	8.63	31.71
2.	Panipat	23.12	14.22	5.65	0.15	4.53	25.15	4.03	10.05	2.95	10.15
3.	Sonipat	36.38	16.76	5.85	0.13	2.34	11.81	3.75	7.23	3.37	12.38
4.	Rohtak	42.74	12.03	4.04	0.07	2.26	11.57	4.10	7.20	3.46	12.53
5.	Rewari	45.23	13.56	6.46	0.26	2.38	8.76	4.09	6.46	2.48	10.32
6.	Gurgaon	30.75	9.10	11.41	1.71	2.50	11.07	6.46	8.51	4.41	14.08
7.	Faridabad	23.86	10.52	5.47	0.57	2.93	18.68	6.15	11.72	4.24	15.86
8.	Alwar	62.03	8.80	5.62	0.34	2.17	5.40	2.82	4.80	2.30	5.70
9.	Meerut	29.26	14.35	4.97	0.05	4.77	11.87	5.85	11.27	3.81	13.80
10.	Ghaziabad	19.56	8.03	4.01	0.20	4.48	16.31	7.16	13.68	5.48	21.10
11.	Bulandshahr	35.77	16.68	11.98	0.04	5.69	6.89	3.26	8.31	2.53	8.85
12.	NCR	23.69	7.92	4.52	0.32	3.41	15.80	5.82	14.00	5.32	19.20

Note: NIC I Digit Classification: (I) Cultivators, (II) Agricultural Labourers, (III) Livestock, Forestry, Fishing, Hunting & Plantations, Orchards & Allied Activities, (IV) Mining & Quarrying, (Va) Manufacturing, Processing, Servicing & repairs in HHI, (Vb) Manufacturing, Processing, Servicing & repairs in other than HHI, (VI) Constructions, (VII) Trade & Commerce, (VIII) Transport, Storage & Communications and (IX) Other services.

manufacturing and construction industry. Distribution of rural workers in broad industrial groups shows a decline in share of agricultural labourers in total workforce for all districts, same is the case of cultivators' category except for Sonipat where its share has increased between 1991 and 2001. There is considerable increase in share of workers in livestock, forestry, fishing, hunting and plantations, orchards and allied activities for all districts. This increase along with the decline in agricultural labourers is a positive sign for agriculture sector. Added to this, there is increase in the share of workers in manufacturing sector and construction and trade and commerce industry which have positive implications for rural development as well as urbanization. In case of urban workers, there is considerable decline in their share in agriculture sector, while household manufacturing industry and construction have grown in terms of their share in workforce for all districts. Growing construction industry in the adjoining districts of Delhi is employing a significant portion of unskilled and semi-skilled workers. It is also creating a built environment in these districts which is necessary for the expansion of service sector especially more sophisticated economic activities. According to David Harvey, this is the most important phase for the development of a region. There is a decline in share of non-household industry in districts of Faridabad, Sonipat, Rewari, Alwar and Ghaziabad. All the districts have shown decline in their share of workers in other services category. In rural workforce structure, it is observed that there is a shift of employment from agriculture to non-farm activities with declining share of agricultural labourers within the agriculture sector along with increasing share of workers in manufacturing construction and trade and commerce industry which leads to the spread of growth in rural areas as well. On the other hand, in the urban workforce structure there are not such major shifts besides increasing share of household industry, construction industry along with the decline in non-household industry and growth of trade and commerce in some selective districts.

VI. Industrial Distribution of Male-Female Workers

Tables 35.5a and 35.5b present distribution of male and female workers in major industrial groups. During 1991, a large proportion of both males (24.69%) and females (45.10%) were cultivators. The second major industrial group employing both the genders was other services while in 2001 major industry other than cultivators was agriculture labourers for males and allied activities for females. During this period, some industries like manufacturing in other than HHI, transport storage and communication and other services have experienced decline in their share for both the genders whereas proportion of agricultural labourers, allied activities and manufacturing in HH industry has increased for males and females both. Two industries namely cultivators, construction and trade and commerce have also shown increase in their share in case of male workers.

It is observed that share of female workers in total workforce has increased in case of both rural and urban areas during 1991 and 2001in NCR. In 1991, females constituted 15.5 per cent of workforce which increased by 8 per cent, reaching 24 per cent in 2001.

This increase in share of female workers was marginal in Delhi while it is mush significant in districts of Haryana. Further the share of female workers in rural areas has shown a significant increase compared to their urban counterpart. In rural areas females constituted 21 per cent of workforce compared to 10 per cent in urban areas, while in 2001 they accounted 35 per cent of rural workforce and 13 per cent of urban workforce. In terms of proportion of male-female workers in different industries one common expected fact is that all industrial groups are dominated by males at both points of time except for one category, i.e. livestock, forestry, fishing, hunting and plantations, orchards and allied activities, showing a reversed trend. During 1991, share of female workers in this category was 15 per cent in NCR ranging from 7 to 27 per cent while in 2001 it was 69 per cent. Besides construction industry where share of female workers has declined and other industries have recorded an increase in share of female workers.

During 1991-2001 proportion of female workers in total workforce has increased from 16 per cent to 24 per cent.

A large part of female workforce has been concentrated in agriculture sector but there was a shift within agriculture sector from cultivators and agricultural labourers to allied activities, along with marked increase in share of allied activities and manufacturing in HH industry.

VII. Share of Main and Marginal Workers among Broad Industries

During 1991 to 2001, share of marginal workers in total workforce has increased from 7 per cent in 1991 to 19 per cent in 2001. Compared to other districts, Delhi has smallest share of its marginal workers at both points of time, i.e. 0.4 per cent in 1991 and 5 per cent in 2001 while other districts have shown a significant increase in their proportion of marginal

Table 35.5a: Industrial Distribution of Male-Female Workers (1991)

Sl. No.	State/ District	(I)	(II)	(III)	(IV)	(Va)	(Vb)	(VI)	(VII)	(VIII)	(IX)
						Male					
1.	Delhi	1.17	0.86	0.67	0.22	1.40	24.68	8.00	25.20	8.89	28.91
2.	Panipat	33.66	20.21	0.41	0.00	2.70	14.92	2.08	10.48	2.83	12.71
3.	Sonipat	30.94	16.58	0.56	0.00	1.55	12.82	2.37	8.90	5.53	20.73
4.	Rohtak	40.40	15.05	0.92	0.01	1.04	6.99	2.67	8.74	4.41	19.78
5.	Rewari	41.48	11.49	0.94	0.35	2.09	10.01	3.45	8.87	4.43	16.89
6.	Gurgaon	39.22	12.59	1.00	0.35	1.40	8.81	3.18	9.39	4.77	19.28
7.	Faridabad	25.47	10.76	0.63	0.64	0.93	27.78	4.05	10.72	3.64	15.39
8.	Alwar	60.36	7.27	1.20	0.61	1.82	6.61	2.00	6.35	2.60	11.19
9.	Meerut	33.11	20.87	1.10	0.01	2.86	12.26	2.26	10.05	3.44	14.05
10.	Ghaziabad	26.51	13.25	0.66	0.03	1.39	18.86	3.73	11.35	4.70	19.52
11.	Bulandshahr	46.23	21.40	0.52	0.01	1.63	6.79	1.71	7.71	2.26	11.75
12.	NCR	24.69	10.25	0.77	0.19	1.65	16.85	4.60	15.07	5.55	20.38
						Female					
1.	Delhi	1.08	1.48	0.42	0.49	1.66	10.52	6.07	12.45	3.07	62.76
2.	Panipat	35.95	35.99	0.30	0.00	1.93	10.26	0.11	1.27	0.13	14.05
3.	Sonipat	44.49	31.37	0.29	0.00	0.75	5.01	0.63	1.58	0.44	15.44
4.	Rohtak	62.74	21.59	0.38	0.01	0.53	2.64	0.60	0.66	0.17	10.68
5.	Rewari	65.73	21.57	0.83	0.05	2.61	1.27	0.34	0.50	0.13	6.96
6.	Gurgaon	57.10	29.89	0.36	0.11	0.99	1.58	0.43	1.00	0.18	8.36
7.	Faridabad	48.15	24.89	0.28	0.70	0.54	5.48	1.08	2.01	0.23	16.65
8.	Alwar	81.91	13.65	0.28	0.06	0.95	0.63	0.11	0.22	0.02	2.17
9.	Meerut	42.88	31.25	2.29	0.01	4.14	6.20	0.14	1.57	0.16	11.35
10.	Ghaziabad	29.21	16.90	1.51	0.03	1.48	5.38	1.18	1.81	0.28	42.21
11.	Bulandshahr	40.61	25.92	1.45	0.02	2.40	2.15	0.11	0.86	0.06	26.42
12.	NCR	45.10	16.93	0.71	0.18	1.58	4.74	1.72	3.62	0.82	24.62

Note: NIC I Digit Classification–(I): Cultivators, (II): Agricultural Labourers, (III) Livestock, Forestry, Fishing, Hunting & Plantations, Orchards & Allied Activities, (IV): Mining & Quarrying, (Va): Manufacturing, Processing, Servicing & repairs in HHI, (Vb): Manufacturing, Processing, Servicing & repairs in other than HHI, (VI): Constructions, (VII): Trade & Commerce, (VIII): Transport, Storage & Communications, (IX): Other services

Table 35.5b: Industrial Distribution of Male-Female Workers (2001)

Sl. No.	State/ District	(I)	(II)	(III)	(IV)	(Va)	(Vb)	(VI)	(VII)	(VIII)	(IX)
						Male					
1.	Delhi	0.68	0.28	0.66	0.38	2.81	25.02	8.22	25.20	9.46	27.29
2.	Panipat	19.57	5.90	1.82	0.39	2.99	18.77	7.13	17.27	6.74	19.42
3.	Sonipat	21.51	10.77	1.63	0.21	3.89	28.47	5.34	13.40	4.14	10.64
4.	Rohtak	32.46	13.36	1.99	0.20	2.19	14.58	5.10	10.16	5.04	14.92
5.	Rewari	36.37	9.68	1.64	0.11	2.18	13.90	5.59	10.30	5.25	14.97
6.	Gurgaon	38.84	8.93	1.56	0.43	2.60	13.22	6.20	10.11	4.02	14.08
7.	Faridabad	27.72	5.85	3.10	2.31	2.10	14.52	8.82	12.09	6.55	16.93
8.	Alwar	19.14	6.52	2.11	0.73	2.74	23.71	7.70	14.94	5.67	16.73
9.	Meerut	55.88	6.16	2.44	0.54	2.26	8.26	4.50	7.79	3.94	8.24
10.	Ghaziabad	28.71	12.42	2.72	0.06	3.95	13.34	6.94	13.16	4.58	14.11
11.	Bulandshahr	19.32	6.92	2.47	0.22	3.65	17.68	8.07	15.22	6.24	20.21
12.	NCR	38.73	15.49	4.25	0.06	3.80	8.71	4.69	10.65	3.71	9.92
						Female					
1.	Delhi	1.81	0.78	1.91	0.17	4.49	12.48	4.21	9.43	3.01	61.73
2.	Panipat	36.98	14.45	13.20	0.10	4.74	6.24	1.61	3.44	0.74	18.50
3.	Sonipat	26.90	22.34	15.12	0.03	6.04	17.33	0.93	2.16	0.14	9.01
4.	Rohtak	43.96	23.34	13.30	0.01	2.61	6.45	1.14	1.55	0.15	7.48
5.	Rewari	54.57	16.41	8.49	0.00	2.41	7.22	1.33	1.43	0.14	7.99
6.	Gurgaon	54.86	20.54	13.86	0.01	2.05	2.04	0.90	0.94	0.15	4.66
7.	Faridabad	36.66	15.41	27.57	0.53	3.27	4.36	1.85	1.55	0.25	8.55
8.	Alwar	36.77	21.45	14.65	0.14	3.45	4.92	1.91	2.89	0.33	13.48
9.	Meerut	70.39	12.40	9.96	0.07	2.05	1.52	0.55	0.74	0.06	2.26
10.	Ghaziabad	31.78	23.18	15.31	0.00	8.50	5.13	0.82	2.63	0.29	12.35
11.	Bulandshahr	21.01	14.63	13.20	0.06	9.41	8.18	1.75	4.48	0.92	26.36
12.	NCR	29.65	19.15	27.96	0.00	9.61	3.12	0.31	3.46	0.09	6.65

Note: NIC I Digit Classification–(I) Cultivators, (II) Agricultural Labourers, (III) Livestock, Forestry, Fishing, Hunting & Plantations, Orchards & Allied Activities, (IV) Mining & Quarrying, (Va) Manufacturing, Processing, Servicing & repairs in HHI, (Vb) Manufacturing, Processing, Servicing & Repairs in other than HHI, (VI) Constructions, (VII) Trade & Commerce, (VIII) Transport, Storage & Communications, (IX) Other services.

workers. Industries in primary and secondary sector have higher proportion of marginal workers at both points of time compared to service sector. In 1991, marginal workers in service sector industries generally accounted less than 1 per cent of total workers in all districts whereas in 2001, there is marked increase in share of marginal workers in all industrial groups especially in manufacturing, construction and service sector in all districts. Increase in the share of marginal workers in these industries is linked with the growth of informal sector in NCR which absorbs a large number of unskilled and semi-skilled labour in low paid jobs. Construction is another major industry emerging in NCR creating a built environment in adjoining districts of Delhi as a consequence of suburbanization and decentralized planning in this region. During 1991 to 2001, share of main workers in total workers has declined in rural and urban both the areas but it is much sharper in rural areas. Marginal workers have larger proportion in agriculture sector in 1991. Their share in cultivators was 16 per cent and 15 per cent in agricultural labourer followed by livestock, forestry, hunting, fishing and allied activities, manufacturing and cultivators. In urban areas between 1991 and 2001, there was significant increase in share of marginal workers in agricultural labourers, livestock, forestry, hunting, fishing and allied activities and manufacturing.

Among main workers share of female workers has increased from 10 per cent in 1991 to 16 per cent in 2001 in NCR but it is mainly concentrated in agriculture sector while among marginal workers share of female workers has declined from 91 per cent to 58 per cent during the same period. The large increase in the share of marginal workers during the reference period may be attributed to the large scale movement of surplus labour from distress agriculture to non-farm activities like allied activities, construction and manufacturing in HH industries growing in this region and also comprise a major portion of their workforce as casual labourer.

VIII. Industrial Distribution of Migrant Workers

Table 35.6 shows the distribution of migrant workers (whose last residence was out of district) in major industrial groups. Between 1991 and 2001 number of migrant workers coming to NCR has shown a sharp increase, i.e. 20,42,887 in 1991 and 46,24,072 in 2001. In 1991, Delhi accounted for 73 per cent of total migrant workers coming to NCR, while in 2001 it declined to 56 per cent. During 1991, large proportion of migrant workers

Table 35.6: Industrial Distribution of Migrant Workers (1991)

Sl. No.	State/ District	(I)	(II)	(III)	(IV)	(Va)	(Vb)	(VI)	(VII)	(VIII)	(IX)
1.	Delhi	0.30	0.69	0.74	0.28	1.20	21.70	10.26	21.45	8.34	35.04
2.	Panipat	9.00	14.45	0.52	0.00	3.35	35.76	3.14	9.71	3.61	20.46
3.	Sonepat	15.71	15.29	0.89	0.01	1.53	31.58	2.76	8.36	3.43	20.44
4.	Rohtak	31.67	15.41	0.86	0.00	1.00	19.56	3.04	6.73	2.68	19.04
5.	Rewari	27.19	11.45	0.73	0.32	2.50	24.73	2.05	7.32	4.23	19.48
6.	Gurgaon	22.25	12.71	1.39	0.10	1.43	19.11	4.43	10.19	3.91	24.50
7.	Faridabad	4.10	3.72	0.41	1.09	0.72	48.48	5.81	11.68	4.18	19.81
8.	Alwar	49.77	7.29	1.01	0.62	1.62	17.31	1.19	6.16	2.06	12.98
9.	Meerut	7.27	7.50	2.50	0.01	3.36	28.41	2.62	12.11	5.47	30.74
10.	Ghaziabad	2.52	3.52	0.77	0.02	1.29	32.21	5.73	13.74	7.63	32.57
11.	Bulandshehr	22.44	16.07	1.76	0.01	2.52	12.70	1.80	9.56	2.47	30.67
Industrial Distribution of Migrant Workers (2001)											
1.	Delhi	0.37	0.29	0.88	0.41	2.49	26.24	10.03	20.86	9.11	29.33
2.	Panipat	13.72	12.28	8.05	0.29	4.36	38.63	4.21	6.58	2.22	9.66
3.	Sonepat	29.13	16.88	9.40	0.27	2.41	22.00	4.22	4.41	1.86	9.43
4.	Rohtak	36.89	12.11	6.06	0.13	2.10	21.21	4.23	4.08	1.68	11.51
5.	Rewari	41.34	16.16	11.47	0.20	2.19	12.51	3.75	3.58	1.16	7.64
6.	Gurgaon	20.40	8.70	15.86	1.31	2.80	18.97	6.95	6.60	2.57	15.82
7.	Faridabad	9.54	7.70	4.92	0.83	2.74	29.58	7.84	12.64	4.64	19.59
8.	Alwar	57.10	11.40	9.66	0.13	2.12	9.95	1.94	2.51	0.82	4.37
9.	Meerut	22.76	15.31	10.30	0.08	5.71	11.91	3.35	7.91	3.48	19.18
10.	Ghaziabad	6.13	3.90	4.10	0.32	4.33	21.52	7.87	13.99	7.00	30.85
11.	Bulandshehr	28.03	19.45	22.65	0.03	7.20	5.18	0.87	4.51	1.15	10.92
12.	NCR	24.13	11.29	9.40	0.36	3.50	19.79	5.02	7.97	3.24	15.30

Note: NIC I Digit Classification–(I) Cultivatours, (II) Agricultural Laborers, (III) Livestock, Forestry, Fishing, Hunting & Plantations, Orchards & Allied Activities, (IV) Mining & Quarrying, (Va) Manufacturing, Processing, Servicing & repairs in HHI, (Vb) Manufacturing, Processing, Servicing & repairs in other than HHI, (VI) Constructions, (VII) Trade & Commerce, (VIII) Transport, Storage & Communications and (IX) Other services.

was concentrated in few urban districts in close proximity to Delhi. These districts are Faridabad with 7 per cent of total migrant workers and Ghaziabad (4%). While in 2001, the spatial pattern of migrant workers was dispersed, where Delhi has only 56 per cent share of migrant workers in NCR, followed by Faridabad (7%), Ghaziabad (9%), Rohtak (5%) and Gurgaon (4%). It suggests that towns in these adjoining districts are acting as counter magnets for attracting migration as well as industries which are creating employment opportunities in the hinterland of Delhi and search for employment has driven the newest in migrants far beyond the saturated labour market of Delhi to remote parts of NCR.

During 1991, larger proportion of workers in NCR was engaged in manufacturing, processing, servicing and repairs in other than household industry (26.5%), followed by other services, cultivators, trade and commerce and agricultural labourers, while in 2001 largest proportion of workers was concentrated in cultivators, followed by manufacturing, processing, servicing and repairs in other than household industry, other services and agricultural labourers.

Between 1991, and 2001 there was increase in proportion of migrant workers in manufacturing, processing, servicing and repairs in household industry whereas it declined in manufacturing, processing, servicing and repairs in other than household industry. There was increase in proportion of migrant workers in agriculture sector, but their proportion has declined in service sector. In 1991, large proportion of rural migrant workers were cultivators or engaged in other services, agriculture labourers and manufacturing in non-HH industries while in 2001, besides cultivators, manufacturing in HH industry was major sectors employing rural migrant workers followed by agricultural labourers and other services. In case of urban migrant workers, their larger share is employed in other services, manufacturing in non-HH industries and trade and commerce. Here it is important to be noted that rural migrants are mainly employed in low productive industries requiring unskilled and semi-skilled labour, on the other hand, urban migrants having certain level of education and skill manage to find job in relatively productive sectors which require skilled labour. During this period, three industries—allied activities, cultivators and manufacturing in HH industry have reported increase in case of rural and urban migrants both, while construction industry has shown rise in its share of rural migrant workers only since this is an expanding industry in this region and constitute large part of informal employment.

IX. Sectoral and Spatial Concentration of Employment

As shown in Table 35.7, this section shows the sectoral and spatial concentration of employment in NCR region using Herfindhal-Hirschman index (HH index) for major industrial groups. The HH index is defined as the sum of the squares (in %) of employment shares in each state. HH index has maximum value of 10000 when only one sector has all the employment (100%) and has a lower bound of 1111 that is all the sectors have an equal share. Lower the estimated HH index more equal the sector shares and more diversified is the economy.

The HH index in 2001 showed a decline in its value showing negative change in index during 1991 to 2001 which implies diversification of employment in all constituent districts of NCR. But what important here is to be noted that rural districts have shown more diversification of employment compared to urban districts, as the core urban centre of NCR Delhi has reported minimum diversification while the rural districts of Bulandshahr, Gurgaon, Faridabad and Panipat have shown much high diversification. The HH index of spatial concentration shows decentralization of employment in all industrial groups except agriculture and allied activities which have shown concentration of employment but it is more prominent in case of allied activities.

These industrial categories are primarily concentrated in rural districts like Alwar, Rewari and Sonipat. On the other hand, maximum decentralization of employment in construction and manufacturing in HH industry which are expanding industries in this region. This expansion of these industries can be attributed to the planning policies which emphasise on decentralization, large scale infrastructure projects.

X. Conclusion

The new economic policy adopted in early 1990s has a significant impact on industrial structure of economy, specifically in large metropolitan areas as they act as growth engines of economy characterised by concentration of industries and scale of economies as well as cumulative effects of growth. The industrial restructuring in metropolitan areas is closely associated with changing structure of employment in these areas. Present chapter attempts to analyse the changes in employment structure in NCR between 1991 and 2001. It is observed that there is emergence of a new polycentric spatial structure of employment and urbanization in this region during same period. In this process Delhi has become core of an expanding

Table 35.7: Sectoral Concentration of Employment

Sl. No.	*State/district*	*HH index*		*Change in HH index*
		1991	*2001*	
1.	DELHI 07	2295.69	2235.34	–2.63
2.	Panipat	2114.66	1650.42	–21.95
3.	Sonipat	2065.37	2014.96	–2.44
4.	Rohtak	2703.18	2364.07	–12.54
5.	Rewari	2701.49	2524.67	–6.55
6.	Gurgaon	2554.87	1622.39	–36.50
7.	Faridabad	1945.54	1512.50	–22.26
8.	Alwar	4869.64	4059.58	–16.63
9.	Meerut	2091.68	1616.37	–22.72
10.	Ghaziabad	1840.03	1462.73	–20.51
11.	Bulandshahr	2835.06	1945.52	–31.38
12.	NCR	1790.53	1532.42	–14.42

Spatial Concentration of Employment

Sr. No.	*Indusrial group*	*HH index*		*Change in HH index*
		1991	*2001*	
1.	Cultivators(I)	1404.22	1503.31	7.06
2.	Agricultural Labourers (II)	1249.52	1298.57	3.93
3.	Allied Activities (III)	98.78	1091.20	1004.63
4.	Mining & Quarying (IV)	791.77	628.28	–20.65
5.	Manufacturing HHI (Va)	145.33	100.26	–31.01
6.	Manufacturing non HHI (Vb)	488.15	373.33	–23.52
7.	Constructions (VI)	1066.74	185.55	–82.61
8.	Trade & Commerce (VII)	865.85	604.69	–30.16
9.	Transport, Storage & Com (VIII)	726.94	546.00	–24.89
10.	Other Services (IX)	432.39	614.23	42.05

Source: Ramaswamy, K.V. (2007). Regional Dimension of Growth and Employment, EPN.

urban region. Added to this, between 1991 and 2001, increase in work participation rate has been marginal in Delhi while it is much significant in other districts of NCR like Panipat, Sonipat, Ghaziabad and Bulandshahr, as these districts have emerged as new industrial districts in NCR. In terms of share of workers in different industrial groups, Delhi has declined in agriculture sector, while other industrial groups have either shown decline or stagnating. Whereas manufacturing in household and non-household industry and construction industry has shown a significant growth in other districts in terms of their share of employment. This shift of employment from core city to its hinterland is also observed in case of spatial distribution of migrant workers coming to NCR. There is sharp decline in proportion of migrant workers in Delhi, whereas Ghaziabad,

Faridabad, Rohtak and Gurgaon have become new destinations for migrant workers in NCR.

The change in the structure of employment in NCR is closely associated with planning process which emphasises on decentralised planning in Delhi metropolitan area. For instance National Capital Region Planning Board (NCRPB) was established under NCR Planning Board Act, 1985 by the Ministry of Urban Development to systematically develop India's National Capital Region. The NCRPB emphasises building water supply and sanitation infrastructure and has plans to scale up support for urban infrastructure development. The NCRPB has provided financial assistance to participating state governments, Urban Local Bodies (ULBs), housing boards and development authorities for infrastructure development projects in the NCR and identified counter-magnet area towns over the last 20 years. To date the NCRPB has financed 171 infrastructure projects. Regional development plans like master plan of Delhi has played an important role by improving connectivity between Delhi and adjoining districts by means of national highways, express highways and flyovers which helped in process of decentralization of economic activities as well as employment. Besides, this decade has also experienced a shift of certain industrial units like hazardous industries out of Delhi. The emergence of these industrial districts is also linked with the decline of core metropolitan district and rise of some bordering districts in terms of investment. Chakravarty (2000) pointed out that after the structural adjustment in India, suburban districts have become more important investment destinations than core urban districts. Advance regions have been favoured by new investment but within the advance region, the old most favoured districts no longer enjoy that primacy, but different districts, usually within same cluster have forged ahead (Chakravarty, 2000).

Thus, evolution of NCR from monocentric to polycentric metropolis suggests a restructuring of employment as well as reordering of urban space which is manifested on space as concentrated decentralization.

References

Brian J. Godfrey (1995). 'Restructuring and Decentralization in a World City', *Geographical Review*, Vol. 85, No. 4, Thematic Issue: American Urban Geography.

Chakravorty, S. (2000). 'How Does Structural Reform Affect Regional Development? Resolving Contradictory Theory with Evidence from India', *Economic Geography,* Vol. 76, No. 4, pp. 367-394

Coffey, W.J., and Shearmur, R.G. (2002). 'Agglomeration and Dispersion of High-order Service Employment in the Montreal Metropolitan Region, 1981-96', *Urban Studies,* Vol. 39, No. 3, pp. 359-378.

Guillain, R., Gallo, J.L., and Orain, C.B. (2006). 'Changes in Spatial and Sectoral Patterns of Employment in Ile-de-France, 1978-97', *Urban Studies,* Vol. 43, No. 11, pp. 2075-2098.

Himanshu (2003), 'Changes in Workforce Structure among Social Groups in Rural India', *Indian Journal of Labour Economics,* Vol. 46, No. 4.

Hinderink, H., and Titus, M., 'Small Towns and Regional Development: Major Findings and Policy Implications from Comparative Research', *Urban Studies*, Vol. 39, No. 3, pp. 379-391.

Pollard and Storper, M. (1996). 'A Tale of Twelve Cities: Metropolitan Employment Change in Dynamic Industries in the 1980s', *Economic Geography*, Vol. 72, No. 1, pp. 1-22

Ramaswamy, K.V., (2007). 'Regional Dimension of Growth and Employment' *Economic and Political Weekly*, special article, December 8, pp. 47-56

Seminar Recommendations

The main suggestions which were thrown up in the seminar for proper management and planning of the rural-urban fringe are given below:

1. For high economic growth and poverty reduction urbanization is necessary. Expansion of urban area will encroach on urban-rural fringe. Although urban expansion cannot be restricted, but with proper management and planning we can restrict and direct this expansion in desired and sustainable way, with protecting the fertile crop lands.
2. Due to high demand of land low lying areas are also being filled up for various development purposes without considering any environmental impact. There is, therefore, need to protect farm land from the point of view of production, soil-conservation, bio-diversity, watershed protection, etc.
3. There is need to have a desirable land use pattern through a sectoral approach, formulation of economically viable projects for each sector and generate a strong political and administrative will to enforce strict laws for land use conservation.
4. Urban fringe of major cities of the state should be properly identified and delimited with the help of high resolution satellite data.
5. Large tracts of wastelands around major cities should be identified for setting up industries, malls, housing and other facilities as far as possible.
6. There should be strict regional urban planning policy so that urbanization should take place in a balanced manner in every region. A comprehensive planning policy should be adopted to promote urban growth so that each and every small and medium urban centre can serve its population and those living in surrounding rural areas.

7. Towns which are near rural-urban fringe areas may be developed as satellite towns/counter magnets so that they may attract population and activities to reduce pressure on the rural-urban fringe areas. Proper infrastructural facilities must be provided in these towns. These towns should be linked to major city centres through rapid transport system.
8. Perspective Plan of Rural Urban fringe area around the major cities should be adopted taking a long-term perspective of 30-40 years as has been done in case of cities like Chandigarh. Suitable legislation should be passed for that and an Authority for regulating land use in Rural Urban Fringe should be established. This authority should be responsible for looking after major issues and planning and management process in the urban-rural fringe.
9. Land use control and regulations are important tools to regulate growth and associated sprawl.
10. Proper management of Common Property Land Resources which are rapidly disappearing is the need of the hour.
11. Purchase and sale of land in the urban fringe should be regulated by law to prevent land speculation by land sharks leading to dispossession of land from the agriculturists.
12. Land acquisition for urban growth should take stock of the interest of landowners, poor labourers and displaced villagers. There should be a transparent policy to acquire land and on what price the land be acquired should be well defined. Proper compensation at market rates should be paid to persons from whom land is acquired. Prompt payment of compensation amount should be ensured.
13. A proper policy for relief and rehabilitation of displaced rural population should be put in place. Development authorities/ industries acquiring land should be made responsible for this.
14. Proper development of facilities in the rural areas as planned under the PURA project will help in reducing migration of population to urban areas and reduce pressure on large cities.
15. Agro-based industries should be established in rural-urban fringe areas. It will increase the price of commodities and provide job for the people of surrounding areas directly and indirectly to promote the production for raw material. The agro-processing centres can contribute for preserving the local agricultural systems while promoting economic development and sustainable

environment in the rural-urban fringe areas. The town and village enterprises for rural industrialization based on the Chinese model would be suitable for India.

16. Livestock activities and high value agricultural crops should be promoted in rural-urban fringe, for which necessary inputs and facilities should be provided. Farm produce exploitation by the middlemen should be minimized. The small producers should be organized into SHGs or cooperatives for marketing their produce so that they get due share in the price paid by the consumer. Suitable market places should be developed on the outskirts of cities where these producers can bring their products for sale directly to the consumers.

17. Proper health care can bring substantial improvement in social well-being if they are evenly distributed, especially in the wards located in peripheral areas. Proper medical and health facilities should be provided to the people living in the fringe areas, which should be accessible as well. Mobile medical vans and ambulances, together with low cost transport facilities should be made available to the fringe localities so that people can avail good health amenities present in core areas of city. Condition and infrastructures of medical institutions and government hospitals should be improved. Health awareness among poor people must be created.

18. Educational facilities should be developed in the fringe areas including technical education so as to improve their employment opportunities.

19. On fringes of the metropolitan cities the green belts and the ponds and lakes should not be touched rather they should be well maintained, for healthy environment.

20. There is an urgent need for policy initiatives and management techniques to tackle the most urgent problem of conserving water resources in the fringe areas. The existing water bodies need to be protected and developed.

Index